SAP® BusinessObjects™ Web Intelligence

**PRESS**

SAP PRESS is a joint initiative of SAP and Galileo Press. The know-how offered by SAP specialists combined with the expertise of the Galileo Press publishing house offers the reader expert books in the field. SAP PRESS features first-hand information and expert advice, and provides useful skills for professional decision-making.

SAP PRESS offers a variety of books on technical and business related topics for the SAP user. For further information, please visit our website: *www.sap-press.com*.

Greg Myers and Eric Vallo
SAP BusinessObjects System Administration
2012, 530 pp., hardcover
ISBN 978-1-59229-404-6

Christian Ah-Soon and David Gonzalez
SAP BusinessObjects Security
2013, 525 pp., hardcover
ISBN 978-1-59229-437-4

Ingo Hilgefort
Reporting and Analysis with SAP BusinessObjects (2nd Edition)
2012, 501 pp., hardcover
ISBN 978-1-59229-387-2

Heilig, Kessler, Knötzele, John, and Thaler-Mieslinger
SAP NetWeaver BW and SAP BusinessObjects
2012, 795 pp., hardcover
ISBN 978-1-59229-384-1

Jim Brogden, Heather Callebaut Sinkwitz, Mac Holden,
Dallas Marks, and Gabriel Orthous

SAP® BusinessObjects™ Web Intelligence

The Comprehensive Guide

Bonn • Boston

Galileo Press is named after the Italian physicist, mathematician, and philosopher Galileo Galilei (1564—1642). He is known as one of the founders of modern science and an advocate of our contemporary, heliocentric worldview. His words *Eppur si muove* (And yet it moves) have become legendary. The Galileo Press logo depicts Jupiter orbited by the four Galilean moons, which were discovered by Galileo in 1610.

Editor Emily Nicholls
Acquisitions Editor Kelly Grace Harris
Copyeditor Pamela Siska
Cover Design Graham Geary
Photo Credit iStockphoto.com/logoboom
Layout Design Vera Brauner
Production Graham Geary
Typesetting SatzPro, Krefeld (Germany)
Printed and bound in the United States of America, on paper from sustainable sources

ISBN 978-1-59229-430-5

© 2012 by Galileo Press Inc., Boston (MA)
2nd edition 2012

Library of Congress Cataloging-in-Publication Data
SAP BusinessObjects Web intelligence : the comprehensive guide /
Jim Brogden... [et al.]. -- 2nd ed.
p. cm.
ISBN 978-1-59229-430-5 -- ISBN 1-59229-430-8 1. BusinessObjects.
2. Business intelligence--Data processing. 3. Management information
systems. I. Brogden, Jim, 1972-
HD38.7.S265 2012
658.4'038028553--dc23
2012026609

Contents at a Glance

Dear Reader,

The task of assembling a comprehensive compendium about a dynamic business topic can be overwhelming. Add to the agenda an ambitious editorial schedule, important updates to reflect version changes, and a busy team of co-authors, and the project can quickly move from overwhelming to Herculean in nature.

But Jim Brogden proved to be the informed industry expert and nimble project manager that a manuscript with so many moving pieces needed. He masterfully handled the writing schedule and production concerns of a second edition, and successfully pooled the expertise of Web Intelligence experts Heather Callebaut Sinkwitz, Mac Holden, Dallas Marks, and Gabriel Orthous. The result is an unrivaled resource full of valuable insight into the Web Intelligence world and the features and tools that govern it.

I feel confident you'll benefit from the hard work that this Web Intelligence team invested in this project, and we welcome your feedback. Your comments and suggestions are the most useful tools to help us improve our books for you, the reader. We encourage you to visit our website at *www.sap-press.com* and share your feedback about the second edition of *SAP BusinessObjects Web Intelligence*.

Thank you for purchasing a book from SAP PRESS!

Emily Nicholls
Editor, SAP PRESS

Galileo Press
Boston, MA

emily.nicholls@galileo-press.com
www.sap-press.com

Contents

24 Feature Pack 3 (Service Pack 4) Enhancements 537

Appendices 553

Online appendix

The SDK and Web Intelligence 4.0 (*www.sap-press.com*)

Foreword

All around the world companies are using analytics to tap into their corporate data and revolutionize the way they make decisions. Informed enterprises that can optimize their decision-making lifecycles gain significant advantage over their competitors and foster long-term organizational success.

The first key to achieving this optimized lifecycle is to offer the right users the right tools to access the right information. In order to be impactful, that information needs to be aligned with corporate goals and objectives so that all levels of the organization are implementing a common strategy. When an enterprise can react to changes in a way that is secure and in compliance with regulatory restrictions, it can adapt to a constantly evolving economy and marketplace and survive—or even thrive—in today's business world. The ability to inform, align, and adapt is driving a decision-making revolution—one that is pushing companies to truly transform the way they do business. This revolution also delivers a real impact to the bottom line, making it a movement that many companies can't afford to miss.

Like other adaptive organizations, SAP is responding to the changing needs of its customers. Consumers, not IT departments, now dictate the trends of technology, and at a faster pace. Users equipped with a variety of mobile devices expect to access the information they need within seconds, regardless of where they are. These users then expect to connect with others and collaborate around information and shared experiences.

While predefined reports designed by IT are a powerful resource, these users also need the flexibility to ask questions and perform ad hoc analysis. SAP Business-Objects Web Intelligence serves both of these scenarios, and provides trusted data and security measures through SAP BusinessObjects Business Intelligence (BI). As a result, SAP BusinessObjects Web Intelligence continues to be one of the most broadly used BI tools in the market, informing users all across the enterprise.

With the latest release of SAP BusinessObjects Web Intelligence, SAP continues to invest in its ongoing leadership of the BI market. SAP BusinessObjects Web Intelligence 4.0 will help you to drive your business forward. SAP has enhanced its powerful ad hoc reporting capabilities with features to support the contemporary user; on top of the SAP HANA platform, SAP BusinessObjects Web Intelligence 4.0 provides fast, real-time data analysis, enabling employees to react to the present, not linger in the past. The SAP BusinessObjects Mobile solution enables users to access their SAP BusinessObjects Web Intelligence reports from any location at each critical moment of decision.

In our experience with SAP BusinessObjects Web Intelligence at Softchoice Corporation, the solution delivers a business performance transformation that is increasing customer satisfaction and making a tangible impact on the bottom line. Its business requirement of combining data from multiple sources to create reports once required manual data extraction, cleansing, and eventually aggregation into spreadsheets. We found that the introduction of SAP BusinessObjects Web Intelligence into the Softchoice workflow eliminated much of this labor and enabled the IT department to redeploy six IT employees from manual data translation activities to higher value data modeling and business analyst activities. In addition, sales people that used to spend a substantial amount of time processing data now create reports 30% to 50% faster, leaving more time for customer-facing activities.

More and more, companies are seeing business intelligence as a foundation for driving their business. While there is a vibrant array of specialized and niche tools available in the market, SAP BusinessObjects Web Intelligence continues to address a wide range of BI needs, from sophisticated dashboard reports to ad hoc data discovery.

But with a tool that offers so much power and flexibility comes complexity. The detailed content in this book will be equally valuable to new SAP BusinessObjects Web Intelligence users who are ready to learn the basics, as it will be to experienced users tapping into its advanced functionality. This book can help you to push your enterprise BI agenda forward and drive improved business performance through better utilization of information within your organization.

Are you ready to transform your business? Join the decision-making revolution. Arm your users with intelligence at their fingertips and take up the battle cry. Inform, align, adapt!

John Schweitzer
Senior Vice President and General Manager of Analytics at SAP

Acknowledgments

I'd like to begin by thanking the publishing team at Galileo Press, including Kelly Harris and Emily Nicholls, for all their assistance and direction throughout the writing and development process. A special thanks goes to Emily Nicholls for her hard work and dedication to the project. Her attention to detail and positive attitude made a tremendous difference. I'd also like to express sincere appreciation to Olivier Duvelleroy and Gregory Botticchio from SAP for their technical assistance and guidance. Special thanks to Eric Vallo for his technical guidance.

I would like to extend my appreciation to the leadership at Daugherty Business Solutions for providing encouragement and support, and also for cultivating a company culture that embraces innovation, technology, and a rich work/life balance.

Last, I would like to express many thanks to my wife, Christi, for her constant support and patience while enduring several months and countless evening hours of me being glued to the laptop while working on this edition. Special thanks go to my sons, Jamie and Hunter, for providing me the motivation to work hard every day.

Jim Brogden

I have had the pleasure of working with so many inspiring, innovative people during my career whose passion and energy continuously motivate me as I work through new challenges in this industry. The colleagues, friends, and family who provide my foundation, my support, my inspiration, and my passion are too many to mention, but their incredible roles and the amount of gratitude I hold for them are not diminished at all—so thank you! I want to make a special mention of my Rural/Metro Corporation family and fabulous team members, whose spirit and support is overwhelming.

Finally, I want to thank my family and friends—especially my beautiful boys, Zen and Max—for their kind words, support, and understanding while I worked on this book.

Heather Callebaut Sinkwitz

I would like to thank the SAP staff members from various offices around the world for the help, examples, and even program code they provided when we were putting together these chapters. Of course, the online SAP developer library at *http://scn.sap.com/docs/DOC-27465* also offers a wealth of advice and examples.

Mac Holden

First I would like to thank my mom and dad for everything. Special thanks are due to Jerry Bedilion, my tenth grade English teacher, who endured a lot of bad grammar and patiently taught me to enjoy writing. Thanks to Jim Brogden for inviting me to participate in this book-writing adventure.

I am grateful to Jeff Bartel and Tom Somerville, who gave me my start with SAP BusinessObjects and totally changed the trajectory of my professional career. I am also grateful to Bob Dissinger and Sharon Peters for the years we organized the Southern Ohio/Northern Kentucky BusinessObjects User Group. I would also like to thank Penny Brewer, Deanna Glinka, Eileen King, Gary Kuertzel, and Alan Mayer for helping me become a better instructor and presenter.

Thanks to Diversified Semantic Layer hosts Greg Myers, Jamie Oswald, and Eric Vallo. I value your friendships as much as your professional advice.

Last, I'd like to thank my wife, Kristin, and my children, Emily, Catherine, and Benjamin, for their patient love and support during the development of this book.

Dallas Marks

I would like to extend my greatest gratitude to the people who have supported me throughout my career as a Business Intelligence professional. First, I'd like to thank my wife, Adriana, and our kids for always believing in me and allowing my "side projects."

Additionally, I would like to thank my mother and father, Martha and Juan, for building an environment where I could shine. With their undivided support, I was able to overcome the odds and learn the value of education and hard work. In the words of Juanito, *"Para atrás ni para echar impulso."*

Last, I would like to thank my mentor and colleague, Louise Kulczewski. She has helped me understand and focus on important aspects of my BI career. For example, six years ago she taught me the "NYC Rule" for report creation, which states: "Create a report and leave it lying in the middle of New York City. If someone picks it up, would they know what it is? Or how to use it?" With Louise's encouragement, I've been able to grow as a BI professional and take on multiple challenges. She is truly a Level-5 leader, and I'm lucky to call myself her friend.

Gabriel Orthous

The long-anticipated release of SAP BusinessObjects Business Intelligence 4.0 brings with it many useful improvements to the enterprise suite and several new and noteworthy features to Web Intelligence. The hallmark of this release is the ease of connecting to SAP data sources and delivering an improved user experience through the redesigned user interface.

1   SAP BusinessObjects Web Intelligence 4.0

The industry's most powerful business intelligence ad hoc query and analysis reporting tool received a major facelift with version 4.0. The completely redesigned user interface gives business users the ability to create more persuasive and engaging analysis documents than ever before. SAP BusinessObjects Web Intelligence 4.0 (which we'll refer to as Web Intelligence) comes with a new charting engine for much-improved presentation of data, metrics, and analytics. These new visual attributes provide users with the capability to create powerful dashboard/report hybrids known as *dashports*.

Web Intelligence 4.0 delivers an ideal self-service reporting experience with the capability to query SAP InfoCubes using Business Explorer (BEx) queries, use SAP BusinessObjects Analysis workspaces for multidimensional reports, and access traditional relational databases and OLAP sources with SAP BusinessObjects universes.

Web Intelligence provides business users with the tools to make better decisions and offer deeper insight into company data. The major benefits include the ability to drill, pivot, chart, track changes, publish, schedule, and share business information online and within a single online portal. The combination of an enhanced Report Panel, seamless connectivity to an extensive list of data sources, and the capability to contain vast amounts of data makes Web Intelligence the premier tool of choice for analyzing data.

This chapter introduces you to the key features and core functionality of the Web Intelligence reporting tool. We'll also discuss the steps for setting up the report viewing properties, introduce the reporting analysis environments, and describe the basics of viewing and saving reports.

1.1   Features of Web Intelligence

Web Intelligence has been known for many years by report developers as "WebI" (pronounced "webby"). It's best known as a highly intuitive, web-based query and analysis tool that provides business users with the capability to create and modify queries without having to write a single line of SQL.

Because Web Intelligence reduces the complexity of report building, business users have unprecedented opportunities to analyze and leverage company information. Self-service business intelligence has become a reality in Web Intelligence 4.0, which boasts an enhanced Report Panel designed for more intuitive report development, and data interaction. Reporting documents are published and shared through the BI Launch Pad portal, a convenient and efficient way of distributing reports to users across the enterprise.

The architecture of SAP BusinessObjects Business Intelligence (BI) 4.0 lets Web Intelligence reports operate purely within a web browser. This delivery style significantly reduces deployment costs, making it easier for companies of all sizes to use the SAP BusinessObjects reporting suite. Web Intelligence plays a very important role in extending analysis across the enterprise and to a large audience of casual users, power users, and executives. This means that report viewers of every skill level can easily leverage Web Intelligence to interact with and analyze data on a frequent basis to solve business problems.

Key Strengths of Web Intelligence 4.0

- ▶ Improved charting engine for a standardized data visualization experience across BI 4.0 reporting tools
- ▶ Ribbon-style controls for comfortable and intuitive interaction
- ▶ Ability to build multidimensional queries and analyze hierarchical data sets sourced from SAP BEx queries, SAP BusinessObjects Analysis workspaces, and OLAP universes
- ▶ New chart types, including tag cloud chart, polar bubble and scatter charts, pie with variable slice depth, box plot chart, tree map chart, and heat map
- ▶ Ability to generate SQL without knowledge of underlying data structures
- ▶ Ability to develop and analyze reports in a zero-client online portal structure
- ▶ Self-service access to company data for business users
- ▶ Ability to merge dimensions of multiple data providers for more robust reports
- ▶ Drill-down functionality in reports

▶ Extensive set of out-of-the-box (OOB) report section functions

▶ Ease-of-use in creating analytical documents with a variety of chart types

▶ Integration with Microsoft Office via SAP BusinessObjects Live Office

▶ Easy access to SAP InfoCubes through SAP BEx queries

▶ Use of web services, text files, and Excel spreadsheets as data sources

▶ Capability to copy queries, variables, tables, and charts from one document to another

▶ Enhanced reporting styles and new charting features

▶ Ability to add hyperlinks and element links to report objects

In the following sections, we'll discuss the core product functionality of Web Intelligence, including its six primary functions (query, report, analyze, share, customize, and integrate).

1.1.1 Core Product Functionality

The primary function of Web Intelligence 4.0 is twofold: to provide the capability to query a set of data without any knowledge of the SQL language, and to interactively analyze data to further restrict, expand, and modify the way information is displayed and delivered. After data is retrieved, formatting can be easily applied to present results in a variety of customized formats.

The data retrieved with Web Intelligence 4.0 is displayed in the report section by using report element templates. The available templates include data tables, charts, and freehand cells designed to meet a wide variety of reporting requirements. After your query has been refreshed and the results are returned, you can easily visualize the data by inserting report elements and result objects into your reports.

You can quickly organize reports by inserting breaks to group the data and by applying block-level or report-level filters with just a few clicks of the mouse. Notice the extensive set of shortcut icons that assist with frequently used customizations. These icons are located at the top of the screen in the Web Intelligence design mode and are grouped into three toolbars.

When you're ready to share your work, you can easily publish your documents to the BI Launch Pad. Users across the enterprise will then have the opportunity to view and interact with your reports by logging on to the BI Launch Pad through a web browser without any installation requirements.

Extended interaction is available to users by right-clicking on a report or report element for on-the-fly modification and customization in design mode.

Let's consider the primary Web Intelligence functions:

▶ **Query**
Building queries in Web Intelligence 4.0 is much easier than in previous versions of this software. In Web Intelligence 4.0, you have the capability to connect to an SAP BEx query as a data source, Analysis View as a data source, or include multiple universes within the same document. In addition, you can quickly and graphically generate complex SQL statements within the Web Intelligence Query Panel that contain subqueries and unions (referred to as combined queries). With Web Intelligence Rich Client in version 4.0, additional data source options include Excel spreadsheets, texts files as a data source, and web services.

▶ **Report**
Over the course of this book, you'll learn to create everything from simple reports to complex analysis documents with multiple report tabs. You can unlock the full potential of Web Intelligence 4.0 by using the built-in editing and formatting features available for presenting data quickly and accurately. Reporting with Web Intelligence is also very flexible and intuitive. Never again will your reporting solution cause the bottleneck in your business intelligence solution.

▶ **Analyze**
You'll learn how to use drill filters, report filters, block filters, and built-in report functions to provide detailed, laser-targeted analyses. You'll discover the extensive list of report functions and contexts available for creating precise variables and formulas.

Web Intelligence 4.0 enables you to provide deep analysis, deliver valuable analytical reports to the user community, and become a more insightful analyst and subject matter expert (SME) with your clients' data. You can perform on-the-fly modifications to reports with an extensive set of options available when you right-click on a report in design mode.

▶ **Share**

You'll be able to publish your Web Intelligence report documents to the BI Launch Pad portal for collaborative analysis. The documents can then be scheduled to execute the generated SQL statements and distribute the reports to enterprise user inboxes or through external email.

BI Launch Pad delivers Web Intelligence reports within the default folder structure or within a folder-like structure known as categories. Reporting documents can also be delivered in the BI workspace (previously known as Dashboard Builder).

You can distribute reports to the mobile devices of your workforce with SAP BusinessObjects BI Mobile. Mobile integration is a powerful feature of SAP BusinessObjects BI 4.0.

▶ **Customize**

Have you ever wondered how to make modifications that enrich the visual and functional capabilities of Web Intelligence? You can take your SAP Business-Objects installation to the next level by editing SDKs to produce customized business intelligence reporting solutions that reflect your aesthetic and functional goals. Access the online appendix "The SDK and Web Intelligence 4.0" on the book's website at *www.sap-press.com* for more information about these solutions.

▶ **Integrate**

You'll discover the capabilities of integrating a variety of data sources such as SAP NetWeaver BW with Web Intelligence 4.0. For dashboard integration, you can generate web services for use as consumable data sources by other SAP products, such as SAP BusinessObjects Dashboards.

These six areas describe the capabilities of Web Intelligence and are the focus of this book.

1.1.2 Web Intelligence Offline

Operating remotely gives users greater flexibility and the freedom to work offline and outside the BI Launch Pad. Offline mode, also known as standalone mode, is possible with the client tool called Web Intelligence Rich Client.

This portable version of Web Intelligence provides report developers with the capability to disconnect from the Central Management Server (CMS) and work outside the BI Launch Pad. Web Intelligence Rich Client also lets you use a local data source; for example, you can import an Excel spreadsheet or text file as a local data source to create Web Intelligence documents.

Figure 1.1 shows the initial screen you see when you launch Web Intelligence Rich Client 4.0. Your options are split into two categories: NEW DOCUMENT and OPEN DOCUMENT.

In the NEW DOCUMENT box, you can choose from creating a report sourced from SAP BusinessObjects Universe, Excel, SAP BEx, Analysis View, text, or web services. The OPEN DOCUMENT box allows you to quickly reopen recent documents.

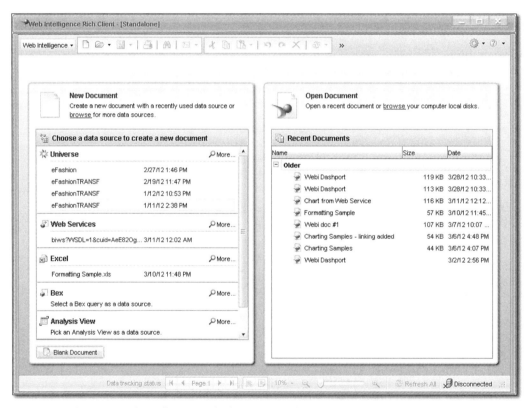

Figure 1.1 Web Intelligence Rich Client 4.0 Initial Screen

Web Intelligence Rich Client is one of nine client tools available in SAP Business-Objects BI 4.0 that can be installed on a user's computer. See Chapter 20 for a closer look at the Web Intelligence Rich Client tool.

1.1.3   SAP BusinessObjects BI 4.0 Client Tools

Figure 1.2 shows the full list of SAP BusinessObjects BI 4.0 client tools. The highlighted tool, Web Intelligence Rich Client, can be launched to connect to the SAP BusinessObjects BI 4.0 system or used in standalone mode.

Other valuable SAP BusinessObjects BI 4.0 client tools are the Business View Manager, Data Federation Administration Tool, Information Design Tool, Query as a Web Service Designer, Report Conversion Tool, Translation Management Tool, Universe Design Tool, and Widgets.

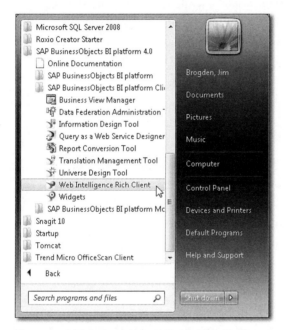

Figure 1.2 SAP BusinessObjects BI 4.0 Client Tools

If Web Intelligence Rich Client doesn't already exist on your computer, you can install it by going to the View or Modify section located in the Web Intelligence settings on the Preferences page. Click on INSTALLATION REQUIRED, which is located to the right of the desktop selection to begin the installation.

Each client tool is mutually exclusive and the tools provide completely different functionalities. Most business users will need only the tools used for accessing data, such as Web Intelligence Rich Client and Query as a Web Service Designer.

1.1.4 Web Intelligence and the Microcube

After a query has been refreshed in Web Intelligence, the data is stored in memory in an unseen microcube. A *microcube* is a data storage structure existing within each report to store the query results behind the scenes. Users can present any combination of the data with any type of data block or chart type while also providing the ability to drill down and apply report-level or block-level filters.

By storing the result data of each document for the last query that was successfully executed, the microcube allows you to analyze data using different dimensions in separate report tabs and report blocks while revealing only the data that you request. Until the data becomes visible in a report, it remains stored behind the scenes in the microcube. The style, format, and presentation of the data remain the decision of report designers to most effectively display data to solve business problems.

1.2 Reading Web Intelligence Reports

The BI Launch Pad is the centralized web portal designed to provide access to all of your business intelligence content, securely and within a single platform. The BI Launch Pad lets you create, modify, save, share, and analyze valuable company data from a single location and within a browser.

SAP BusinessObjects BI 4.0 will help you enable business users to make more-informed decisions. The built-in structures of Web Intelligence work seamlessly within the BI Launch Pad, providing the capability to analyze data with ease.

Web Intelligence allows users to conveniently create and modify reports through an Internet browser or by working locally with Web Intelligence Rich Client with standalone and disconnected capabilities.

Working in offline mode allows report developers to disconnect from the CMS and work locally with saved Web Intelligence documents rather than through a browser. This functionality facilitates the frequently requested task of saving and editing Web Intelligence documents outside of the BI Launch Pad portal.

Figure 1.3 shows a custom-formatted Web Intelligence report with drill filters being read in a browser within the BI Launch Pad.

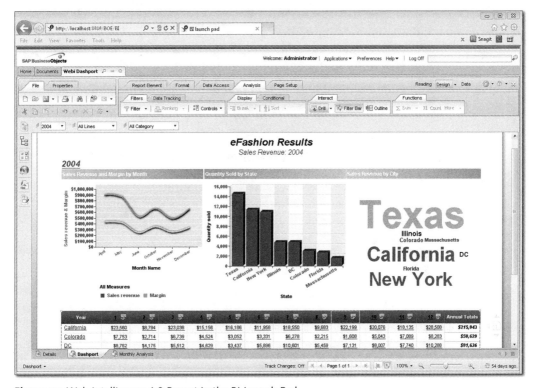

Figure 1.3 Web Intelligence 4.0 Report in the BI Launch Pad

Most report consumers will need only to read or view reports; designing reports is generally left to power users and report developers. While reading reports, users will have the opportunity to drill, filter, and export results to PDF or Microsoft Excel files.

1.3   Adjusting Web Intelligence Preferences

A number of configurable settings are available to enhance the user experience when reading and interacting with Web Intelligence reports in the BI Launch Pad.

To adjust settings for reading and designing reporting documents, begin by clicking on the PREFERENCES link located in the upper right corner of the BI Launch Pad (see Figure 1.4).

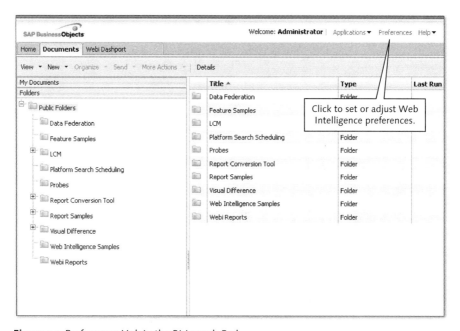

Figure 1.4 Preferences Link in the BI Launch Pad

Depending on your security permissions, the Preferences page allows you to modify several general settings and the default settings for viewing/reading and modifying/designing reporting documents.

Figure 1.5 shows the Web Intelligence preferences that you can adjust locally in a web browser. In addition to these Web Intelligence preferences, you can adjust the following seven other preference groups with settings in the BI Launch Pad:

▶ GENERAL

▶ CHANGE PASSWORD

▶ LOCALES AND TIME ZONE

- ANALYSIS EDITION FOR OLAP
- WEB INTELLIGENCE
- BI WORKSPACES
- CRYSTAL REPORTS

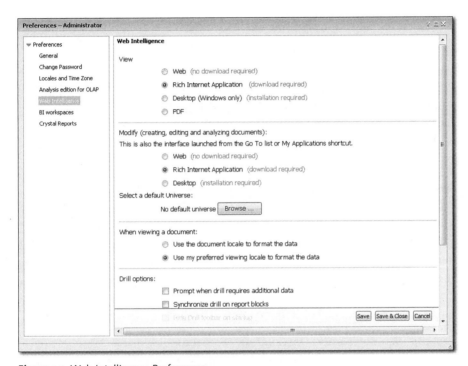

Figure 1.5 Web Intelligence Preferences

Web Intelligence settings consist of the following:

- VIEW
- MODIFY
- SELECT A DEFAULT UNIVERSE (OPTIONAL)
- WHEN VIEWING A DOCUMENT
- DRILL OPTIONS
- START DRILL SESSION
- SELECT A PRIORITY FOR SAVING TO MS EXCEL

Let's explore them further.

1.3.1 Setting the View and Modify Selection Types

Depending on whether you're a casual user who needs only to read and print reports or a report designer who requires access to the Query Panel, the selections made to view and modify reports play an important role in the features that will be available to you.

Let's examine the selection types available for both View and Modify:

▶ **Web (no download required)**
The web setting provides a fully functional HTML panel that allows users to read and design reporting documents with all of the features in the Report Panel. The biggest advantage of using the web setting to read and design documents is the ability to link to a document. This feature is covered in detail in Chapter 14. The disadvantage of using the web setting is that the Query Panel is not accessible.

▶ **Rich Internet Application (download required)**
The Rich Internet Application setting is the selection used for creating queries with Web Intelligence in the BI Launch Pad and creating advanced interactive reports with a Java plugin. This setting is generally used by power users or advanced report consumers that benefit from the features in the Query Panel.

The disadvantage to this setting is that linking to another document is not available and the full OpenDocument syntax is required to link to another published report, document, or dashboard.

▶ **Desktop (Windows only) (installation required)**
This selection is used to automatically launch Web Intelligence Rich Client when reports are viewed or modified.

The PDF option is unique to the View preference list and has very little interactive functionality. The primary feature of this viewing format is to open the Web Intelligence report in a PDF. After the document opens, you can print or save the PDF report. PDF reports can be easily shared with users across the enterprise, emailed, posted to an FTP site, or published to the SAP BusinessObjects BI 4.0.

There is one setting that is unique to the Modify list: Select a default universe. This feature is available so a specific universe can be assigned as the default universe for when new reports are created.

The next set of properties describes how to set the viewing locale and time zone for reports and the BI Launch Pad. This feature is an important descriptive value, showing accurate times for when reports were last saved and refreshed.

1.3.2   Locale When Viewing a Document

When viewing a Web Intelligence document, the data can be formatted by either the document locale or preferred viewing locale. To set the preferred viewing locale to be different from the default browser locale, follow these steps:

1. Click on the USE MY PREFERRED VIEWING LOCALE TO FORMAT THE DATA option under the Web Intelligence preferences.

2. Select the LOCALES AND TIME ZONE preferences section, which is shown in Figure 1.6.

3. Change the PRODUCT LOCALE setting to either USE BROWSER LOCALE or ENGLISH.

4. Choose the PREFERRED VIEWING LOCALE from over 130 locale options.

5. Select a CURRENT TIME ZONE or use the selection LOCAL TO WEB SERVER.

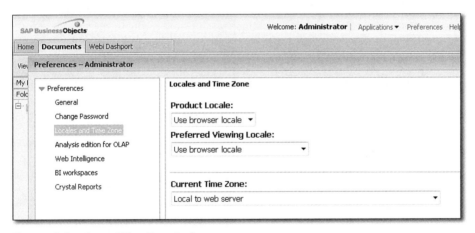

Figure 1.6 Locales and Time Zone Preferences

1.3.3   Drill Option Preferences

In addition to providing drill filters in drill mode, many data tables and charts let you drill down with a single click. This type of drilling is available when drill mode is activated and the dimension objects have been added to a hierarchy in the universe.

As shown in Figure 1.7, three settings are available for selection under DRILL OPTIONS when setting Web Intelligence preferences:

- PROMPT WHEN DRILL REQUIRES ADDITIONAL DATA
- SYNCHRONIZE DRILL ON REPORT BLOCKS
- HIDE DRILL TOOLBAR ON STARTUP

Any combination of these settings can be selected. We recommend that you select PROMPT WHEN DRILL REQUIRES ADDITIONAL DATA and SYNCHRONIZE DRILL ON REPORT BLOCKS. You can also show or hide the drill toolbar when opening a report.

You also have the choice of defining where a drill session starts: on duplicate report or on existing report. The default selection is ON EXISTING REPORT.

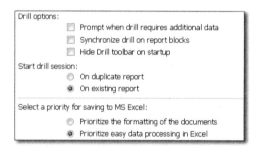

Figure 1.7 Drill Option Settings and Drill Session Start Type

1.3.4 Saving to Microsoft Excel Priority

The final setting in Web Intelligence preferences is to assign the priority for saving reports to Excel: either the formatting of the documents or easy data processing in Excel (the default setting).

> **Note**
>
> Be sure to click on the SAVE or the SAVE & CLOSE button in the lower right corner of the Preferences window to complete your changes. Refresh your browser to ensure that all preference changes are enabled and integrated into your session.

Adjusting the Web Intelligence preferences based on your needs ensures that you optimize the features for viewing, modifying and creating reports. Let's explore the reporting and analysis environments next.

1.4 Web Intelligence Reporting and Analysis Environments

Web Intelligence reporting is delivered to business users in either a zero-client or thin-client method. Reporting documents are accessed through a web browser by logging on to the BI Launch Pad or opened in the locally installed Web Intelligence Rich Client tool.

1.4.1 Zero-Client Online Analysis

You don't have to install SAP BusinessObjects BI 4.0 software to experience the benefits of Web Intelligence. With just a web browser, you can log on to the BI Launch Pad to view, create, edit, analyze, schedule, or interact with Web Intelligence reporting documents.

1.4.2 Thin-Client Development

Since the addition of the Web Intelligence Rich Client, analysis has been extended to power-users who need to analyze data when disconnected from the CMS or enterprise portal. When you are connected to the CMS, you can export or publish documents directly to the enterprise system for online analysis. Once published, reports created in Rich Client are easily shared with other enterprise users through standard group security permissions.

The next section describes display modes for viewing reports.

1.5 Report Display Modes

Web Intelligence reports can be viewed in the BI Launch Pad with two different display modes: PAGE mode and QUICK DISPLAY mode (see Figure 1.8). Page mode allows you to view the report the way it fits onto a printed page while also providing the capability of drilling into the data. Quick display mode is used primarily for reports intended for analysis but not for printing.

Each mode displays data differently and you can easily toggle back and forth between modes as necessary by following these steps:

1. Enter design mode by clicking on DESIGN in the upper right corner.

2. Select the PAGE SETUP tab from the primary REPORT PANEL tab set.

3. Select the DISPLAY tab from the third group of subordinate tabs.

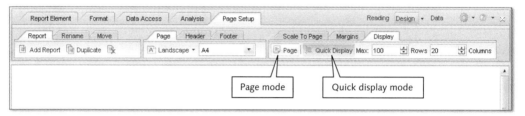

Figure 1.8 View Modes Available in Web Intelligence

Web Intelligence documents can be saved to the repository of the CMS by clicking on SAVE AS from the SAVE menu. To save the report outside of the enterprise platform, select SAVE AS after clicking on the SAVE icon and then select either DESKTOP, DOCUMENTS, or COMPUTER as the export location. When exporting the data outside the enterprise, choose one of the following file types: XLS, XLSX, or PDF.

By clicking on SAVE, you overwrite the existing version. Depending on your rights, you can update Web Intelligence documents that reside in the folder structure within the BI Launch Pad.

1.6   Summary

Web Intelligence provides an extensive set of mature features that combine complex query building with detailed analytical reporting capabilities. This best-in-class reporting tool introduced in 1997 has evolved to become the standard ad hoc analysis and reporting tool for many businesses around the world. With version 4.0, you can easily source reports from BEx queries, Analysis Views, and patented semantic layer universes.

The core functionality of Web Intelligence contains an extensive list of valuable data analysis features. Report building becomes much easier for business users because they can develop complex queries visually without knowledge of the underlying SQL. The ability to query multiple data sources within the same document and link the results by merging dimensions is an extremely valuable analytical report development feature.

Web Intelligence reports can be easily viewed and analyzed by using only a web browser connected to the BI Launch Pad. Reporting documents can be shared with selected users across the enterprise and then scheduled to be refreshed and delivered to a user inbox or external email address.

You can take analysis offline with Web Intelligence Rich Client. Report developers can now save Web Intelligence documents locally and analyze data without being connected to the CMS. With all of the functional capabilities delivered within Web Intelligence 4.0, SAP has completely replaced its predecessor reporting tool, which was known in previous versions as Desktop Intelligence with Web Intelligence. In BI 4.0, Desktop Intelligence has been retired and existing reports from a previous version need to be converted to Web Intelligence to be viewed in 4.0. See Appendix A for a checklist that describes the nine steps of report conversion.

Chapter 2 focuses on working in the Query Panel of Web Intelligence 4.0 to retrieve data for interactive reporting analysis. Accessing data is a fundamental requirement in report building, and the enhancements to the Query Panel in this version provide business users with even more functionality when querying databases.

Create queries graphically with the highly intuitive and enhanced Query Panel in Web Intelligence 4.0. Use the Result Objects pane and Query Filters pane to access the data you need from universes, SAP BEx queries, Analysis Views, web services, Excel files, and text files, and then create and share powerful analysis documents with business users.

2   Creating New Documents and Queries

The Query Panel in Web Intelligence provides business users with an intuitive interface for retrieving and filtering data. Much more than a simple tool for querying relational data sources, Web Intelligence 4.0 lets you connect directly to SAP BEx queries and Analysis Views (a user-defined subset of multidimensional OLAP data sources from Analysis workspaces).

Queries are created graphically as objects (database fields) and are inserted into the Result Objects pane on the Query Panel. This collection of objects is translated into the Select section of the generated SQL statement and the where clause gets its information from the objects included in the Query Filters pane. Query filters can be hard-coded conditions created in the universe or dimension objects inserted into the Query Filters pane with manually assigned values.

After a query has completed successfully, the retrieved data is stored within each document in an unseen *microcube*. At this point, the data is ready to be formatted and presented in a report.

This chapter takes you through every aspect of creating a Web Intelligence 4.0 document from within the BI Launch Pad portal and outlines the different query types available. With Web Intelligence Rich Client, a standalone version of the tool, users are provided with the capability to access a *local data source* by connecting to Excel files, text files, or even web services.

A common purpose for accessing local data sources is to use existing Excel files to create documents with all of the powerful filtering and visualization features available in SAP BusinessObjects Web Intelligence 4.0.

2.1   Creating a Web Intelligence 4.0 Document

The new portal interface in SAP BusinessObjects BI 4.0 provides two ways to launch the Web Intelligence query and analysis tool in the BI Launch Pad. After logging on to the BI Launch Pad and going to the HOME tab, you'll notice a column on the right-hand side of the page with six application shortcuts. These links are beneath the heading MY APPLICATIONS.

Figure 2.1 shows the shortcut icons for these six applications in the BI Launch Pad:

- BEX WEB APPLICATIONS
- MODULE
- ANALYSIS, OLAP EDITION
- CRYSTAL REPORTS FOR ENTERPRISE
- BI WORKSPACE
- WEB INTELLIGENCE APPLICATION

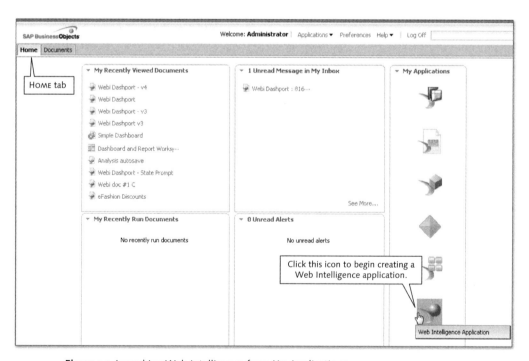

Figure 2.1 Launching Web Intelligence from My Applications

Click on the bottom icon in the list to begin creating a Web Intelligence application.

An alternate method of launching Web Intelligence from within the BI Launch Pad is by clicking on the APPLICATIONS link located in the top menu of the page. Links to the same six applications as previously described will appear, but in a different order.

Figure 2.2 shows the result of clicking on the APPLICATIONS menu link and selecting WEB INTELLIGENCE APPLICATION from the list provided.

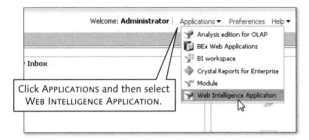

Figure 2.2 Launching Web Intelligence from the Applications Menu Link

Web Intelligence opens to a blank screen with all of the shortcut icons disabled except for two choices:

▶ Create a new document ($\boxed{\texttt{Ctrl}}$+$\boxed{\texttt{N}}$)

▶ Open (retrieve) a document from the server ($\boxed{\texttt{Ctrl}}$+$\boxed{\texttt{O}}$)

From the WEB INTELLIGENCE tab itself, you have additional options to interact with the document by clicking on one of three small icons located beside the document name. This is where you can enlarge the screen by opening the document in a new window or simply close the Web Intelligence application. There are three clickable icon options on the WEB INTELLIGENCE tab:

▶ Open in a new window

▶ Pin (or unpin) this tab

▶ Close

Figure 2.3 shows the options available after launching the Web Intelligence application and before a document is created or opened.

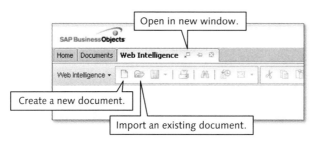

Figure 2.3 Options Available Before Creating or Opening a Document

Click on the BLANK DOCUMENT icon to create a new Web Intelligence document. You'll have three data source options (SAP BusinessObjects Universe, SAP BEx, and Analysis View) when working from within the BI Launch Pad and a fourth option for *no data source*.

The option to create Web Intelligence documents sourced directly from a BEx query or Analysis View is a new feature introduced in version 4.0. Access to these two data sources greatly expands the reach of Web Intelligence; it allows users working in an SAP Business Warehouse environment with existing hierarchical BEx queries to leverage the strengths of the Web Intelligence product and extensive Report Panel capabilities.

Figure 2.4 shows the data sources available for creating a new document.

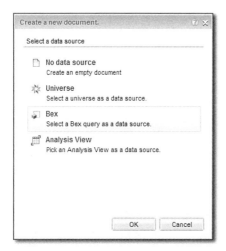

Figure 2.4 Selecting a Data Source for Creating a New Document

Let's explore each of these data sources.

2.1.1   Universe as a Data Source

The patented SAP BusinessObjects semantic layer known as the universe remains the primary method for connecting reporting documents to traditional data warehouses and relational databases. Version 4.0 introduced the Information Design Tool to allow universes to be created from multiple sources; it also changed the name of the tool previously known as Designer to the Universe Design Tool.

But little has changed from a user's perspective of connecting to a layer between the reporting document and the database. Database fields, known in the universe as objects, are used in the Query Panel to retrieve data and to restrict the results to only the information needed.

After selecting UNIVERSE as the data source for a new document, you are presented with a list of available universes that you have permission to access. Click on a universe in the list and click on SELECT to proceed. Figure 2.5 shows an example list of available universes that are available as a data source.

Figure 2.5 Available Universes

After you make your universe selection, the Web Intelligence Application tool will be launched and opened to the Query Panel. Before you can begin analyzing information and creating reports, you need to retrieve information from your data source. The Query Panel is your window for accessing that data.

Figure 2.6 shows the Query Panel and the shortcut icons for toggling four of the five primary panes within the Query Panel on and off. The Query Panel will be described further in Section 2.2.

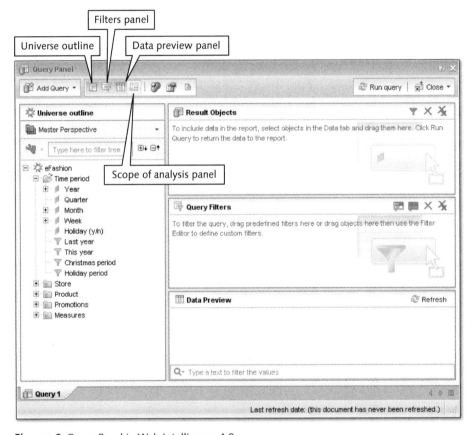

Figure 2.6 Query Panel in Web Intelligence 4.0

Another option is to use a BEx query as a data source.

2.1.2   Direct Connection to a BEx Query

One of the most exciting new enhancements to Web Intelligence in version 4.0 is the ability to connect directly to a BEx query. This new feature allows SAP BW customers to utilize Web Intelligence while also being able to view and interact with hierarchical data created by a BEx query.

To begin the process of connecting to a BEx query with Web Intelligence, you need to create a new OLAP connection that utilizes the *SAP BICS client* and then releases each BEx query to be used as a data source for Web Intelligence.

Releasing BEx Queries to be Accessed by Web Intelligence

To make your BEx queries accessible to Web Intelligence, you need to release each query for external access in the BEx Query Designer. In the Properties section, locate RELEASE FOR OLE DB AND OLAP and then check the box beneath it labeled ALLOW EXTERNAL ACCESS TO THIS QUERY. This setting certifies a BEx query for external use and allows it to be consumed by the Web Intelligence Application in SAP BusinessObjects BI 4.0.

Creating an OLAP Connection

To create a connection that allows Web Intelligence to connect to a hierarchical BEx query, open the Universe Design Tool and create a new OLAP connection. This method of connectivity lets you access BEx queries directly without going through the universe layer.

After logging on to the Universe Design Tool, select FILE • NEW • OLAP CONNECTION, as shown in Figure 2.7.

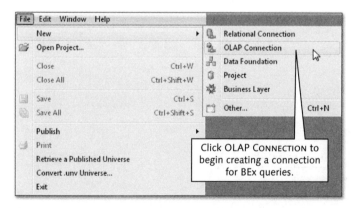

Figure 2.7 Creating an OLAP Connection in the Universe Design Tool

You should give your new OLAP connection an identifiable resource name to be selected in reporting documents when connecting directly to a BEx query. We also recommend that you add a description of the resource; this can be very helpful in environments with multiple resources.

Figure 2.8 shows the screen for creating a resource name and description.

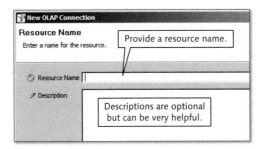

Figure 2.8 Creating a Resource Name and Description for a New OLAP Connection

After entering a resource name, click on NEXT to proceed and then select the SAP BICS CLIENT network layer listed under SAP NETWEAVER BI 7.x.

Figure 2.9 shows the OLAP Middleware Driver Selection window displayed when you choose your OLAP driver. Depending on the databases and drivers available to you, it's important to note that OLAP connections can be made to other multi-dimensional database vendors such as Microsoft and Oracle.

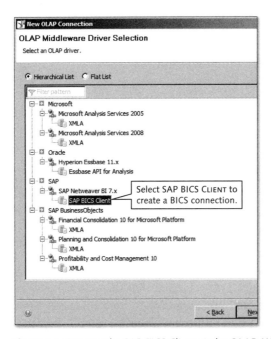

Figure 2.9 Creating the SAP BICS Client as the OLAP Middleware Driver Selection

Figure 2.10 shows the list of parameters needed to make a successful connection to the SAP BICS Client and SAP NetWeaver BI 7.x. In addition to a username and password, you need to know the following properties to log on:

▶ CLIENT NUMBER

▶ SYSTEM ID

▶ APPLICATION SERVER NAME and SYSTEM NUMBER or MESSAGE SERVER NAME and GROUP NAME

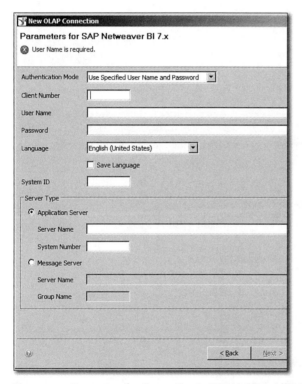

Figure 2.10 Parameters for Connecting to SAP NetWeaver BI 7.x

The final step is to select a cube from the list of available choices in the INFOAREA or FAVORITES folder. You can also create connections to several multidimensional data vendors.

After making your cube selection, click on NEXT to define the repository where the connection will be published. Figure 2.11 shows the Cube Selection window used when creating a new OLAP connection.

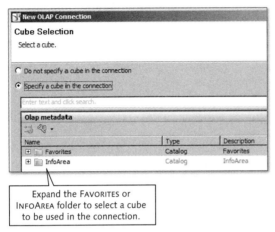

Figure 2.11 Cube Selection Window for Creating a New OLAP Connection

To display the expandable FAVORITES and INFOAREA folders for selecting specific cubes, select the option to SPECIFY A CUBE IN THE CONNECTION.

Click on FINISH to publish the new connection to your repository. Figure 2.12 shows the message that appears after successfully publishing a new connection.

Figure 2.12 OLAP Connection Published Successfully

Next we'll examine using Analysis Views as a data source.

2.1.3 Analysis Views as a Data Source

Analysis Views are created to give users access to a subset of data derived from an *Analysis workspace* and multidimensional dataset. This new capability provides a means of accessing a specific arrangement of cube data within the Web Intelligence application and outside of the Analysis workspace.

Using Analysis Workspaces to Create Analysis Views

Many hierarchical dimensions and measures can be included in an Analysis workspace to solve complex business problems and provide very detailed information. But many users see the vast amounts of data in a cube as overwhelming and difficult to use.

The addition of Analysis Views solves this issue by allowing a specified set of dimensions and measures to be viewed and analyzed in Web Intelligence. This new data source lets users leverage the benefits of working in Web Intelligence while also getting the value of interacting with data that originated from a multidimensional cube.

To begin creating Analysis Views, connect to a multidimensional data source in Analysis, OLAP edition, as shown in Figure 2.13.

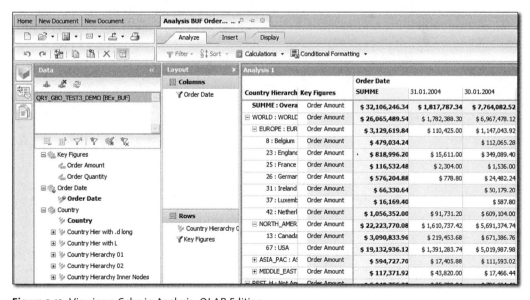

Figure 2.13 Viewing a Cube in Analysis, OLAP Edition

Creating an Analysis View

You can add columns and rows to the workspace to create an arrangement of dimensions and measures to share with other business users within Web Intelligence 4.0 or Crystal Reports for Enterprise. Recall that the three primary data sources available for creating reporting documents with version 4.0 are universes, BEx queries, and Analysis Views.

Figure 2.14 shows a multidimensional workspace in Analysis, OLAP edition, with the EXPORT icon selected.

To save the grouping of column and row objects in a view to be accessed by Web Intelligence 4.0 or Crystal Reports for Enterprise, with EXPORT selected, click on ANALYSIS VIEW from the list of choices.

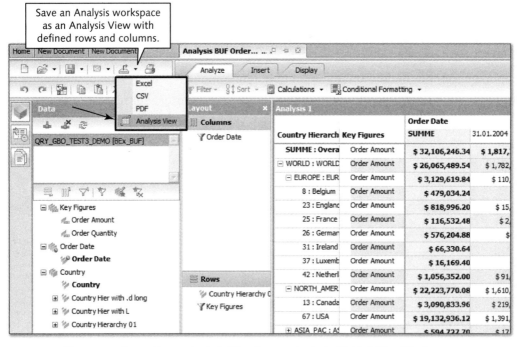

Figure 2.14 Generating an Analysis View from an Analysis, OLAP Edition Workspace

When publishing an Analysis View to the SAP BusinessObjects BI 4.0 repository, you should select a folder with the appropriate group and user permissions. Secure distribution is an important consideration when publishing content because information should be made accessible only to the intended group of users.

Typical reasons for creating and publishing Analysis Views generally relate to the requirement of providing users with appropriate and relevant information in a format that is easy to use in Web Intelligence or Crystal Reports for Enterprise.

Figure 2.15 shows the window provided when saving an Analysis View to the repository. Select an appropriate folder to save the object to, provide a name for the new Analysis View, and then click on SAVE to publish.

After an Analysis View has been published, users can open it with Web Intelligence to quickly analyze and interact with the data and utilize the extensive functional capabilities in the Report Panel such as charting, drilling, and filtering.

Figure 2.15 Saving an Analysis View to the Folder Structure in the Repository

> **Note**
>
> Analysis Views can also be created by saving a workspace in SAP BusinessObjects Advanced Analysis 1.1, Microsoft edition (or higher), which is built from an OLAP connection created in the Information Design Tool of Web Intelligence 4.0 and saved to the BI 4.0 repository.

More users can take advantage of the rich feature set in Web Intelligence 4.0 with the option to create reports sourced from Analysis Views. The next section introduces the Query Panel and describes the panes used for retrieving data.

2.2 The Query Panel in Web Intelligence 4.0

The Query Panel in Web Intelligence 4.0 provides an intuitive interface for selecting objects and retrieving results from universes, BEx queries, Analysis Views, web services, Microsoft Excel files, and text files.

Figure 2.16 shows a glimpse of the full Query Panel at the beginning of the query building process after you have selected a universe as the data source.

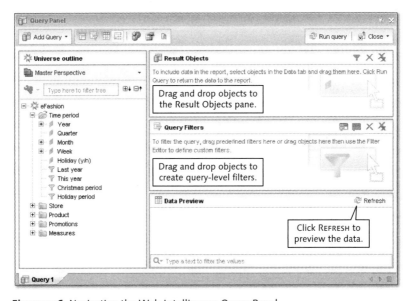

Figure 2.16 Navigating the Web Intelligence Query Panel

The Query Panel consists of five major sections:

► Universe outline: Contains the objects available in the universe or BEx query in the connected data source

► Result Objects: Retrieves data from the database when you drag and drop objects from the Universe outline pane to this pane to begin creating a query

► Query Filters: Restricts the results returned from the data source

- SCOPE OF ANALYSIS: Shows the hierarchy and drill path of the objects in the universe

- DATA PREVIEW: Displays a preview of the result set based on the objects included in the Result Objects pane

> **Note**
>
> The SCOPE OF ANALYSIS and DATA PREVIEW panes cannot be displayed at the same time. Toggle between these sections by using the shortcut icons in the upper left corner of the Query Panel.

2.2.1 Universe Outline Pane

The *Universe outline pane* is located on the left side of the document and shows you the database fields or objects that can be retrieved or used to filter the query.

This pane allows objects to be displayed in two different groupings. You can switch between these two perspectives to see objects categorized by class or sorted by navigation paths. Figure 2.17 shows the two perspective selections for viewing objects in the universe outline.

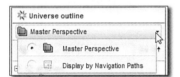

Figure 2.17 Perspectives for Viewing Objects in the Universe Outline

The purpose of the Universe outline is to provide the list of objects available in the connected data source to be used as result objects or filters in the query. This pane contains the classes and objects that were previously set up in the universe or BEx query used as the source. The terminology used for object aliasing in universe design begins to play an important role in the Query Panel when deciding which objects to include in the query.

> **Tip**
>
> The objects in your universes should be consistently named with business terms to provide users with the simplest and most intuitive approach to retrieving the data they need.

2.2.2 Query Properties

Query properties are used to set properties for eight different categories in the current query. You can access the properties by clicking on the QUERY PROPERTIES icon located at the top of the Query Panel.

The first property to be updated is the query name. This setting becomes very useful when multiple queries are added to a single Web Intelligence document. Let's examine the eight query properties shown in Figure 2.18.

▶ NAME: This property allows you to revise the name of any query in the document or Query Panel.

▶ UNIVERSE: This property is read-only and displays the name of the current universe.

▶ LIMITS: You can apply the MAX ROWS RETRIEVED and MAX RETRIEVAL TIME(S) settings to restrict the result size and retrieval duration of the query by clicking on the checkbox beside the desired setting and then revising the associated number to your preference.

▶ SAMPLE: Sampling enables you to retrieve a fixed or random sample of the data when querying databases that support it. Random sampling is applied by default unless FIXED is selected. Sampling is disabled if your database doesn't support sampling.

▶ DATA: This property provides the option to retrieve duplicate rows or unique rows when refreshing. Both settings are unchecked by default.

▶ SECURITY: This section provides the option to allow other users to edit all queries and is checked by default. If unchecked, only the report developer can make revisions to the current document.

▶ PROMPT ORDER: This section allows you to change the order of the prompts if multiple prompted filter objects exist in the Query Filters pane.

▶ CONTEXT: This setting provides the option to reset contexts upon refreshing (unchecked by default). A checkbox is provided to clear contexts before the next refresh.

Tip

Choosing to display the objects by hierarchies gives you an opportunity to see the relationship of the dimension objects in the universe. This is useful when setting up drillable report filters with cascading values.

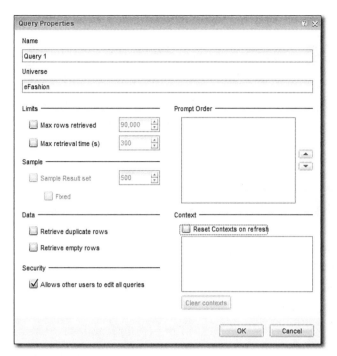

Figure 2.18 Query Properties

Understanding the properties available in the Query Panel is important for effectively producing queries with a desired outcome, such as limiting the number of rows retrieved by a query or defining the order of prompted filters. The next section describes how you can add new queries and edit existing queries.

2.3 Adding and Editing Queries

Queries are easily created in SAP BusinessObjects Web Intelligence 4.0 and can be done by performing the first or both of the following actions:

▶ Adding data objects to the Result Objects pane

▶ Adding custom or predefined filters to the Query Filters pane to restrict the data being returned (optional)

Objects can be moved to these panes by dragging them from the Universe outline and dropping them into the desired panel. The same result can be accomplished by double-clicking on objects in the Universe outline.

> **Tip**
>
> When double-clicking on an object predefined as a condition, the object will be inserted into the Query Filters pane only.

The combination of result objects and query filters produces an SQL statement used to access data from universes. The next section describes how this SQL script can be viewed and edited.

2.3.1 Evaluating Generated SQL Script

After a query has been created, you have the opportunity to review and edit the query script generated by the Query Panel. You can view the SQL script generated from the query by clicking on the VIEW SCRIPT shortcut icon at the top of the Query Panel. Two options are available in the Query Script viewer to either view or edit the query script:

- ▶ Use the query script generated by your query
- ▶ Use custom query script

The script becomes editable when you select the USE CUSTOM QUERY SCRIPT option. The Query Script window now includes numbered rows to assist in reading and editing the syntax of the query.

> **Tip**
>
> The Report Panel is displayed after a query has been refreshed. To return to editing the query, switch to design mode, click on the DATA ACCESS tab, select the DATA PROVIDERS tab, and then click on EDIT QUERY.

Figure 2.19 shows the options available when viewing the script of the query. The default selection is the USE THE QUERY SCRIPT GENERATED BY YOUR QUERY RADIO BUTTON.

Click on the USE CUSTOM QUERY SCRIPT radio button to make changes to the generated script.

Figure 2.19 View Query Script Generated by the Query Panel

A Word of Caution

Modifying the generated script should be attempted only if you understand SQL syntax, understand the underlying database table relationships, and have a legitimate business reason for manually overriding the generated SQL statement.

When the Select section of the generated SQL statement is modified, the number of objects, data types of result objects, and the order of the data types must match the items in the Result Objects section.

When the Use custom query script option is selected, the grayed-out script becomes modifiable. Editing the script will enable the Undo button located at the bottom of the Query Script viewer. You can also copy the script for use outside of the document. This is helpful if you need to paste the SQL statement into another window to edit it or email it to a colleague.

A Validate button is also present when modifying the original script. This is a very handy feature that protects you from submitting a custom SQL statement to the database that contains errors.

Restricting the Modification of Generated SQL

From an administrative perspective, the rights to view SQL and edit the query script can be denied in the Central Management Console (CMC). This is accomplished by modifying the included rights of an access level.

Locate the application collection and the Web Intelligence type for a full list of specific modifiable rights in the CMC. The name of the right is listed as QUERY SCRIPT–ENABLE VIEWING (SQL, MDX...).

Every Web Intelligence document can contain data sourced from multiple queries with varying source types. The following section explains how new queries are added and how the results can be used within the reporting document.

2.3.2   Adding Queries and New Data Providers

New queries can be added to documents that are made up of result objects that have absolutely nothing in common with the result objects in the existing query. This is common if reporting requirements present elements from both unrelated data sets on the same report or within the same document.

There are two ways to add new queries and new data providers to an existing document. The option NEW DATA PROVIDER is available on the DATA ACCESS tab in the Report Panel while in design mode (see Figure 2.20).

Figure 2.20 Adding a New Data Provider from the Report Panel

The option ADD QUERY is available in the upper left corner of the Query Panel, as shown in Figure 2.21.

Figure 2.20 shows the data sources that are available while adding a NEW DATA PROVIDER from the Report Panel of a Web Intelligence document while working within the BI Launch Pad. The same data sources are available when the ADD QUERY button is clicked from the Query Panel.

Figure 2.21 Adding a New Query from the Query Panel

Including New Result Data

After a new query has been added to a Web Intelligence 4.0 document and the query is refreshed for the first time, you are prompted to choose how the new results are to be displayed. Figure 2.22 shows the three available choices described here:

▶ INSERT A TABLE IN A NEW REPORT: This selection adds the results from the new query to a new REPORT tab (default selection).

▶ INSERT A TABLE IN THE CURRENT REPORT: A data table containing the results from the new query will be added to the previously existing report.

▶ INCLUDE THE RESULT OBJECTS IN THE DOCUMENT WITHOUT GENERATING A TABLE: This selection includes the data in the microcube but doesn't add it to a report.

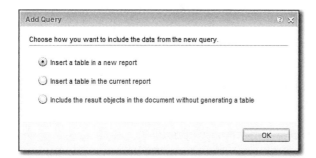

Figure 2.22 Choosing How Data from the New Query Is Displayed

Data Synchronization Properties

Web Intelligence can merge your dimensions automatically if the AUTO-MERGE DIMENSIONS checkbox is checked in the document properties accessed through the PROPERTIES tab in the Report Panel. Click on the DOCUMENT link to launch the Document Summary window displayed in Figure 2.23.

Document Summary Options

The Document Summary window contains a couple of very important property settings to enhance the effectiveness of particular reports. The most commonly used options include REFRESH ON OPEN for prompted reports, AUTO-MERGE DIMENSIONS for queries with multiple data sources, and ENABLE QUERY STRIPPING to improve performance when connecting to BEx queries or OLAP universes. Figure 2.23 shows the Document Summary options accessed through the PROPERTIES tab in the Report Panel.

Figure 2.23 Document Summary Options

Let's examine each of these Document Summary options:

- ENHANCED VIEWING: This option applies the page definition with page margins set by the system administrator or report developer.

- REFRESH ON OPEN: This option forces the query to be refreshed when the report is opened. This feature is useful in prompted reports and when the data is restricted to the user logged on to the BI Launch Pad.

- PERMANENT REGIONAL FORMATTING: This option permanently sets the locale or regional formatting of the document.

- USE QUERY DRILL: This option modifies the underlying query when drilling down or drilling up in a report. Dimensions are added or removed to the Result Objects section of the query, and query filters are added dynamically based on the drill selection. The scope of analysis is also modified dynamically. The query drill feature is most commonly used when reports contain aggregate measures calculated at the database level.

- ENABLE QUERY STRIPPING: This feature allows BEx queries to be generated with only the objects used in the Report Panel.

- HIDE WARNING ICONS IN CHARTS: This feature hides general warnings that could potentially appear in the upper left corner of a chart.

- AUTO-MERGE DIMENSIONS: This option automatically merges dimensions when more than one query is added to the document that contains objects with the same name, same data type, and from the same universe.

- EXTEND MERGED DIMENSION VALUES: This selection shows all of the data in a report that contains synchronized or merged dimension objects, not just the values relating to the merged objects.

2.3.3 Setting Up a Combined Query

The idea behind combined queries is to return a single set of data that would otherwise be impossible to retrieve with a single query. Combined queries are created in the Query Panel and merged at the database level to compare the rows in one query to the rows retrieved by an additional query.

The returned values can be displayed in one of three different relationship types:

- Union: Includes the rows from both queries
- Intersection: Includes the rows common to both queries
- Minus: Includes the rows from the first query minus the rows from the second query

> **Combined Query Requirements**
>
> These are the primary rules for creating a combined query:
>
> - Result objects in each query must contain the same number of objects or the query won't refresh.
> - The order of the objects in both queries must have matching data types. If the data types don't match, then the query won't refresh.

Unions

Unions are most commonly used when you are attempting to build a result set with incompatible objects that can't be included in the same block in a report because of database or universe configurations.

In many cases, all of the result objects will be exactly the same in both queries (except for minor differences in result objects or query filters). The results from both queries are pushed to the database to complete the merging, and a single set of results is returned.

The first query in a union is created like any other query. To add a union query, you need to click on the ADD A COMBINED QUERY shortcut icon located in the Query Panel in design mode (see Figure 2.24).

Figure 2.24 Adding a Combined Query to Create a Query Union

After a combined query has been added, Query 1 changes names to become COMBINED QUERY 1, and a COMBINED QUERY 2 is inserted. You can toggle back and forth from these two queries by clicking on the buttons that include the new query names located in the lower half of the universe outline.

> **Tip**
>
> The default combined query type is union. To change from union to intersection or minus, double-click on UNION in the Query Manager pane located to the left of the combined query names (as shown in Figure 2.25).

Figure 2.25 shows the universe outline after a combined query is inserted.

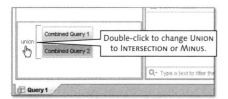

Figure 2.25 Combined Query Added to the Universe Outline

Intersection

You can add intersections when you want to produce a combined query that returns only the values that appear in both queries. The purpose of this type of query is to cut away any nonintersecting data.

Minus

You can use the minus combined query to remove everything in the results of the first query from the results of the second query. The purpose of this type of combined query is to find the results in the first query that aren't in the results of the second.

Remove a Combined Query

To remove a combined query, drag the unneeded COMBINED QUERY button to the Universe outline section that includes the classes and objects.

Now that we've discussed the basics of adding and editing queries, the next section describes the how to create queries sourced from BEx queries.

2.4   Creating BEx Queries

Direct access to BEx queries is one of the key enhancements to Web Intelligence in version 4.0. This new capability allows SAP NetWeaver Business Warehouse (BW) customers to leverage their existing BEx queries as a data source for building Web Intelligence documents.

Setting up connectivity to BEx queries was discussed in Section 2.1.2; this section focuses on creating a Web Intelligence document based on a BEx query used as data source. When a BEx query is used as the source, objects placed in the Result Objects pane will have new hierarchical capabilities in the Query Panel.

To get started using BEx as a data source, create a new query or document in Web Intelligence and select BEx as the data source, as shown in Figure 2.26.

After selecting BEx as your new data source, you are prompted to choose the BW BEx query from a list of certified queries displayed within your preconfigured connections. Expand the connection to display available queries, as shown in Figure 2.27.

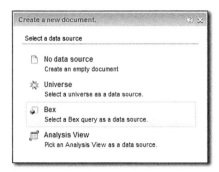

Figure 2.26 Selecting BEx as the Data Source for a New Document

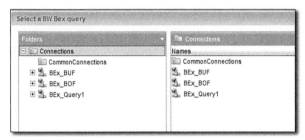

Figure 2.27 Available Connections When Selecting a BW BEx Query

After you expand the connection containing the required query, select the query from the right side of the panel and click on OK to proceed. Figure 2.28 shows examples of two BEx queries that can be selected as the data source.

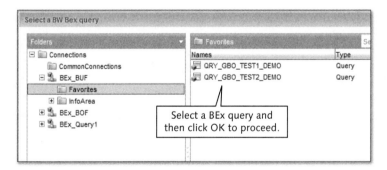

Figure 2.28 Selecting a BW BEx Query

When a BEx query is selected as the data source for a Web Intelligence 4.0 document, the Query Panel contains very different functionality than when sourced from a universe. The Result Objects pane takes on a whole new set of capabilities and allows users to drill into hierarchical member data within the BEx query. Figure 2.29 shows a query sourced from a BEx query with a single object added to the Result Objects pane.

To interact with hierarchical objects, select the icon located immediately to the right of the object name once it's been added to the Result Objects pane. This will launch the Member Selector pane, allowing you to expand, collapse, and check any of the member values to retrieve exactly the information you need.

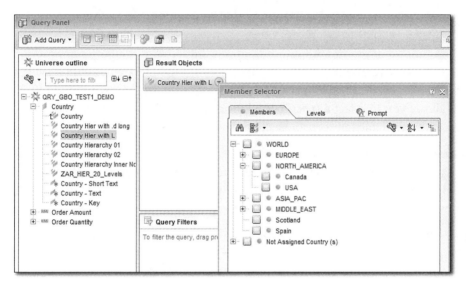

Figure 2.29 Viewing the Member Selector Pane of a BEx Result Object

You can also right-click on a specific member to launch additional capabilities. The following options are displayed in Figure 2.30:

- SELF: Selects only the member
- CHILDREN: Selects only the child members of the selected member
- DESCENDANTS: Selects all descendants of the selected member
- DESCENDANTS UNTIL NAMED LEVEL: Returns all descendants through a specified level
- DESCENDANTS UNTIL: Returns all descendants until reaching a chosen value

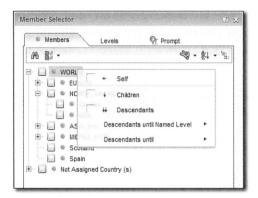

Figure 2.30 Right-Click Options Available within the Member Selector

The MEMBER SELECTOR lets you to navigate through the hierarchies with a LEVELS tab, which displays the number of levels within the selected hierarchical object and allows you to select a specific level for analysis. All levels—or any combination of the available levels—can be chosen.

Hierarchical data will be returned to the Report Panel for intuitive and logical navigation of the multitiered data structures. Expandable and collapsible data blocks are available in the Report Panel specifically designed for hierarchical interaction for reports originating from BEx query data sources.

The Member Selector window allows you to perform in-place filtering rather than requiring additional steps and the Query Filters pane. However, query filters can still be used as long they contain objects not in the Result Objects pane. Figure 2.31 shows the LEVELS tab selected and how to enable levels.

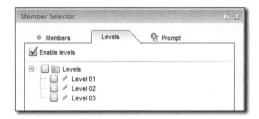

Figure 2.31 Levels of a Selected Member in Result Objects

BEx member prompting is also available to provide a form of guided analysis. Use the PROMPT tab shown in Figure 2.32 to enable prompting and ask users for input when reading reports. Users can be prompted to select specific members or levels in a hierarchical structure for selective analysis. This setting saves time and helps users get directly to the information they need and at the right level of detail.

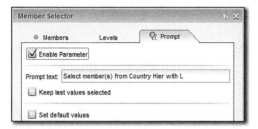

Figure 2.32 Prompt Tab of a Selected Member

The capability to create reporting documents directly connected to BEx queries gives SAP Business Warehouse customers the same reporting features as customers accessing relational databases connected with universes.

The next sections discuss the features available for restricting the amount of data returned in a query by using filters.

2.5 Query Filters

Query filters are used to generate the Where clause for the SQL script that is submitted to the data source. These objects work very closely with the Result Objects pane to provide a simple and intuitive interface for retrieving and restricting data from the data source.

Query filters allow you to minimize the amount of data returned from the query by restricting the results to specific criteria. For example, you can add the Month dimension to the Query Filters pane and set it to July, and then add the Year dimension and set it to 2009. Doing this will retrieve all the values for the objects included in the Result Objects pane for July 2009. Query filters offer you the following benefits:

▶ Ability to return only the data you need to fulfill reporting requirements

▶ Ability to restrict confidential data from being displayed in reports or being returned to the microcube

▶ Ability to retrieve manageable result sets that can be exported to Excel, exported as a PDF, or printed

Filters are identified by two major categories: predefined filters (or conditions) and custom filters.

2.5.1 Predefined Filters

Predefined filters are created by a developer or administrator and saved in the universe as *conditions*. These predefined conditions are easily recognizable in the Query Panel because a yellow filter icon appears to the left of the condition name.

An example of a very simple predefined filter is the `This Year` condition predefined in the demo eFashion universe. The following line of code was added to the `Where` section in the properties of the condition to create the filter:

```
Calendar_year_lookup.Yr = '2006'
```

A more accurate and user-friendly name for this object would be `Year 2006` rather than `This Year` to minimize any potential confusion in the future.

Predefined filters are created in the universe and can contain a variety of complex SQL formulas. By creating predefined filters, users can easily and intuitively constrain their queries to return specific data sets without having to create their own filters.

Condition Segments

Universe developers can create conditions containing any of the following segments:

- Case statements: Provide `If/Else/Then` logic to a condition or object.
- And/or logic: Multiple filters can be applied within a single condition.
- In list: Allows a condition to be created for many items in a list.

2.5.2 Custom Filters

Custom filters are conditions created by report developers. These types of filters are created when dimension objects are dragged and dropped into the Query Filters pane, an operator is chosen, and a value is entered or selected.

After a dimension object has been added to the Query Filters pane, you can choose how to set up the filter. This includes modifying the operator, assignment type, and configuring the filter properties.

A dimension object can be set up as a filter with one of the following five types:

▶ Constant: Manually enters a custom value

▶ Value(s) from list: Provides a list of values for one or more selections

▶ Prompt: Prompts the user to enter or select a value when the query is refreshed

▶ Object from this query: Provides the capability to select a predefined object or variable as the dimension value (although you can't use the In List or Not In List operators)

▶ Result from another query: Allows filters to be created using a result object retrieved by a different query within the same document

The default operator when a dimension is added to the Query Filters pane is In List, and the default assignment type is Constant.

The operators available when creating a condition are as follows:

▶ In List: Retrieves the data for one or more selected or entered values

Example: City IN ('Austin','Boston','Chicago','Dallas')

▶ Not in List: Restricts the query from returning data for one or more selected or entered values

Example: City NOT IN ('Austin','Boston','Chicago','Dallas')

▶ Equal To: Obtains data equal to a selected or entered value

Example: Lines = Sweaters

▶ Not Equal To: Obtains data not equal to a selected or entered value

Example: Lines <> Jackets

▶ Greater Than: Retrieves only the data greater than an entered value

Example: Sales revenue > 1500

▶ Greater Than or Equal To: Retrieves only the data greater than or equal to a selected or entered value

Example: Sales revenue >= 1500

▶ Less Than: Retrieves only the data less than a selected or entered value

Example: Sales revenue < 1500

▶ Less Than or Equal To: Retrieves only the data less than or equal to a selected or entered value

Example: Sales revenue <= 1500

▶ Between: Retrieves only the data between two values

Example: `Sales revenue BETWEEN 1500 and 2000`

▶ Not Between: Retrieves only the data not between two values

Example: `Sales revenue NOT BETWEEN 1500 and 2000`

▶ Is Null: Retrieves only the values that don't have data (that is, have a null value)

Example: `Lines IS NULL`

▶ Is Not Null: Retrieves only the values that have data

Example: `Lines IS NOT NULL`

▶ Matches Pattern: Retrieves the data that matches the pattern of a selected or entered value. This operator is translated as Like when the SQL script is generated. In the example, rows for all objects where the lines begin with S will be returned:

Example: `Lines Matches pattern 'S%'`

> **Note**
>
> The wildcard character (%) is used to represent an indefinite number of characters. The underscore symbol (_) is used to represent a single character. An example of using three underscore wildcard characters is a formula written as `City = 'Bos___'` used with the `Matches pattern` operator. The result returns Boston.

▶ Different from pattern: Retrieves the data that doesn't match the pattern of a selected or entered value. This operator is translated as `Not Like` when the SQL script is generated. The following example returns all the rows where the value in the lines object does not begin with S:

Example: `Lines Different from pattern 'S%'`

▶ Both: Retrieves data that corresponds to two values; if the `Both` filter is used with a dimension object, an intersection is generated

▶ Except: Retrieves the data for other values in the dimension while restricting a selected or entered value; a minus query is generated when this operator is used

2.5.3 Quick Filters

Quick filters are created when you select a dimensional object from the Result Objects pane and click on the FILTER icon located in the upper right corner of the pane. This procedure opens the Add Quick Filter dialog box, where you can quickly define the new condition or filter.

Figure 2.33 shows the Add Quick Filter dialog box that opens when a quick filter is added for the *lines* object. The operator is set to `Equal To` if a single value is selected, but if multiple values are selected from the displayed values, the operator will be set to `In List`. You can modify the operator of the object after the new filter has been created and added to the Query Filters pane.

Figure 2.33 Adding a Quick Filter to a Result Object

2.5.4   Subqueries

Subqueries are used in Web Intelligence to produce a query within a query. This type of document is used when the primary query needs to be filtered by the inner query or subquery. When a query containing a subquery is refreshed, the subquery runs first and then returns the values to be filtered in the main query.

This type of query is used when the main query needs to be filtered by a value that isn't known at the time of refresh.

Figure 2.34 shows how you can add a subquery to an existing filter by simply clicking on the ADD SUBQUERY button in the upper right corner of the Query Filters pane.

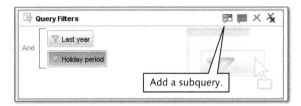

Figure 2.34 Inserting a Subquery into the Query Filters Pane

After adding subquery to your document, you need to drag predefined filters or custom-defined object filters into the new Subquery Filter window to create the "query within a query" effect.

An example scenario for using a subquery is the requirement to return all cities within two selected states. This is accomplished with the following steps:

1. Create a query from the eFashion universe, and then add the City and State objects to the Result Objects pane.

2. Select the City object in the Result Objects pane.

3. Click on the ADD A SUBQUERY button in the Query Panel to create a subquery for the City object.

4. Drag the State object into the Subquery pane of the City object.

5. Set the State operator to In List.

6. Select Value(s) from List for the State filter and then move California and Texas to the Selected Value(s) frame.

7. Run the query.

The results returned will include only cities within California and Texas. Figure 2.35 shows the City and State subquery used in the example.

Figure 2.35 Subquery Example for City and State

2.5.5   Nested Conditions

Query filter conditions can be grouped by using AND and OR to perform extended business logic with conditions.

Figure 2.36 shows a Query Filters pane with four predefined and grouped conditions. These conditions are grouped to provide a more customized filtering technique. Rather than just dragging all four conditions into the pane, they are added as condition pairs or groups.

You can group filters by following these steps:

1. Drop an object or predefined condition to the very bottom of the condition that you want to group it with.

2. By default, the objects will appear in an AND group.

3. If OR is required, double-click on the new AND group operator and the group operator will become OR.

The example in Figure 2.36 will return only the values associated with Last year's Christmas period **OR** the Holiday period for This year.

Figure 2.36 Nested Predefined Query Filter Conditions

Query filters minimize or completely eliminate returning unnecessary information. You can apply a combination of custom and predefined filters that accurately restricts information. You can also add prompted filters to documents that require user input when opening or refreshing reports.

2.6   Prompted Queries

Prompted queries require report consumers to make selections before a Web Intelligence document is opened. This is achieved by following two steps:

1. Create prompted query filters.

2. Set the document to REFRESH ON OPEN.

2.6.1   Saving a Report to Refresh on Open

To save a report so that it refreshes on open, follow these steps:

1. Edit the report in design mode in the Report Panel.

2. Select the PROPERTIES tab located in the upper left corner of the Report Panel, then select the DOCUMENT link.

3. Check the REFRESH ON OPEN selection under OPTION as described in Section 2.3.2. Click on OK to accept.

Alternately, you can set a document to be refreshed on open while saving a Web Intelligence document by following these steps:

1. Click on SAVE AS while either reading or designing a report.

2. When the Publish a Document to the Server window appears, click on the ADVANCED button beside the report name.

3. Check the REFRESH ON OPEN box, select a folder to save the document to, and then click on SAVE.

Figure 2.37 shows how to force a document to be refreshed when it's opened.

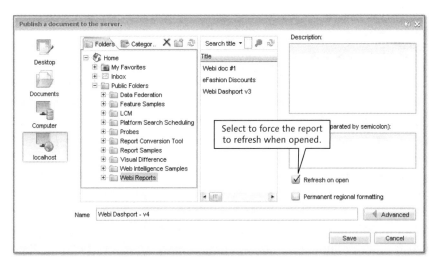

Figure 2.37 Forcing a Document to Refresh when Opened

2.6.2 Creating a Prompted Filter

To create a prompted filter, follow these steps:

1. Click on the PROPERTIES button located to the right of the filter object to reveal five filter condition types.

2. Select PROMPT as the condition type.

3. Click on the PROMPT PROPERTIES button located immediately to the left to set up the properties for the prompted condition.

2.6.3 Setting Prompt Properties

Let's look at modifiable prompt properties. The available parameter properties for a prompted filter are shown in Figure 2.38:

▶ PROMPT TEXT: This text box lets report developers create customized and appropriate messages for business users when they are prompted to enter or select values. This property is important because it can be used when creating hyperlinks.

▶ PROMPT WITH LIST OF VALUES: This property provides the user with a distinct list of values for the prompted dimension.

▶ KEEP LAST VALUES SELECTED: This property lets the user maintain the values of the previous refresh. This setting shouldn't be selected when the data being queried is of a sensitive nature.

▶ SELECT ONLY FROM LIST: This property prohibits users from entering values and requires that they select only from the list of values.

▶ OPTIONAL PROMPT: This property is used to set the prompt to be optional.

▶ SET DEFAULT VALUES: This property lets the user enter one or more default values.

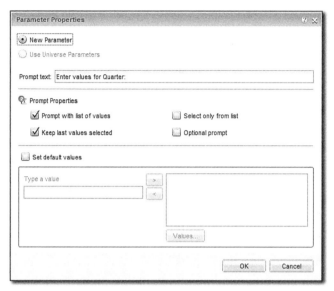

Figure 2.38 Prompt Filter Properties

2.7 Summary

You can use the highly intuitive Query Panel in Web Intelligence for self-service access to company data from just about any type of data source. Ad hoc report building is painless with the extensive set of query features available for business users in the zero-client web-based version of SAP BusinessObjects Web Intelligence 4.0.

The Web Intelligence Query Panel offers users the following strengths:

- Offers intuitive self-service access to company data
- Graphically generates SQL scripts from universe objects
- Interacts with dimension members sourced from BEx queries
- Accesses data sourced from Analysis workspaces with Analysis Views
- Provides easy-to-learn drag-and-drop web-based interface
- Retrieves data from multiple data sources into a single document
- Merges dimensions to combine results from different sources

- Makes more than 15 different condition types available when filtering objects
- Produces combined queries: union, intersection, minus
- Creates a query-within-a-query results with subqueries
- Uses custom SQL by modifying generated SQL statements
- Applies condition groupings with AND and OR
- Limits the query retrieval time and row counts with query properties
- Prompts users for input when reports are refreshed when opened
- Adds quick filters for speed and accuracy
- Sources documents from web services, Excel files, and text files

Using the drag-and-drop interface of the Query Panel, you can create queries to graphically transform prebuilt universe objects into analytical reports. The objects added to the Result Objects pane and Query Filter pane generate script to access data sources without users having to write a single line of code.

Report developers of all experience levels benefit from the ease-of-use of Web Intelligence. You can also take your queries even deeper by retrieving data from multiple data sources. Once only available in Desktop Intelligence, dimensions from different data sources can now be merged within the same document to provide a robust set of data for analytical report building.

Also, with just a few clicks of the mouse, you can create complex documents with combined queries and subqueries by modifying generated SQL statements. Precise results are returned by constraining values at the database level with a rich set of operators for query filtering. You can group your conditions in nested pairings with the AND and OR operators for more complex filtering.

You can learn to control your row counts by limiting the maximum number of rows retrieved by a query. Your DBAs will appreciate the reduced stress on the database when you set a maximum retrieval time on your queries.

Several features make Web Intelligence 4.0 the best-in-class query and analysis solution for any data warehouse, data mart, or business intelligence reporting environment: the combination of an extensive set of query features, an intuitive web-based report development interface, access to cube data through Analysis Views, and the capability to connect directly to BEx queries.

Now that we've discussed creating queries and retrieving data from universes, BEx queries, and Analysis Views, Chapter 3 discusses how information is displayed in the Report Panel in Web Intelligence 4.0.

Web Intelligence 4.0 reports are used to analyze, present, and interact with highly formatted data, which enables accurate and more informed decisions. You can use drill filters, input controls, charts, Available Objects tables, block filters, and a lengthy set of report functions to produce highly customized reports. Additionally, with a new and improved charting engine, users of Web Intelligence 4.0 are able to consume rich graphical and visualization reports.

3 Creating a Report in Web Intelligence 4.0

Using SAP BusinessObjects Web Intelligence 4.0 reports, you can view, analyze, and share company data in a secure, customized, and drillable web-based delivery format. Reports are saved to the file repository server and delivered to the end user using the BI Launch Pad (the SAP BusinessObjects Business Intelligence 4.0 reporting portal).

Web Intelligence enables you to present company data in your reports by adding data blocks and charts to the Report Panel via several provided report templates. You can group data by adding multiple sections and breaks to produce analytical documents by including sorts and drill filters.

After creating a Web Intelligence reporting document, users can quickly share their findings with other users across the enterprise by saving reports in the file repository and folder structure storage area accessed with BI Launch Pad. Depending on permissions, users are either granted or denied access to view, schedule, or even edit documents while working within the BI Launch Pad.

The application also enables users to identify significant values by including *conditional formatting* in your reports. Conditional formatting can be applied to many columns in a report, assigned to every column or row in an Available Objects table, or applied to single columns and headers of Available Objects table reporting elements. You can easily identify and track data changes by activating *data tracking*.

Web Intelligence also allows users to create precisely designed reports with the aid of a *report grid* and *snap to grid* functionality. In addition, you can maintain defined formatting and object placement relationships by assigning *relative position* attributes to report elements.

Due in part to the broad set of features available in the Web Intelligence Report Panel, report developers can produce highly customized free-form presentations for better insight into company data.

Let's begin our discussion of report creation in Web Intelligence 4.0 by describing the different report panels available to report developers, introducing the various sections in the Java Report Panel, and then taking you through the process of presenting data in a report.

The Web Intelligence Report Panel is available in four different formatting tool types for view mode (web, Rich Internet Application, desktop, and PDF) and three tool types for modify mode (web, Rich Internet Application, and desktop). These options are shown in Figure 3.1. You can select the tools to use by clicking on PREFERENCES in the BI Launch Pad and then choosing a Web Intelligence view tool or modify tool.

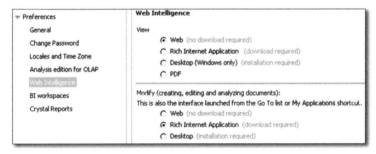

Figure 3.1 Web Intelligence Preferences

> **Note**
>
> We recommend that all report designers users use the Rich Internet Application for editing Web Intelligence reports. This will provide the most functionality, thus increasing performance and enhancing user experience.

3.1   Adding Data to Report Elements

Data is added to reports by adding result objects or variables to any of the report elements such as a table, chart, or cell.

Follow these steps to add a report element to the document pane of a Web Intelligence report after your query has been refreshed:

1. Click on DESIGN.
2. Select REPORT ELEMENT from the ribbon toolbar.
3. Select the TABLE tab and select the downward arrow beside the data table to be added.
4. Drag DEFINE CROSS TABLE to the canvas. (As shown in Figure 3.2, you can also use shortcut keys Ctrl + Shift + X .)
5. In the Insert Report Element window, select VERTICAL TABLE and click on OK.
6. Select DESIGN and WITH DATA. (As shown in Figure 3.3, you can also use shortcut keys Ctrl + 3 .)

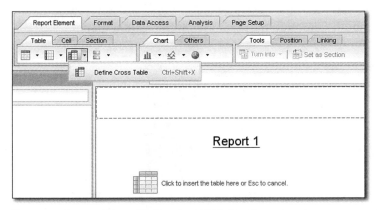

Figure 3.2 Drag and Drop "Define Cross Table" to Canvas

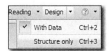

Figure 3.3 Design Button with Data Option

3.1.1 Populate a Cross Table

Table objects are the basic elements in reports; the following steps guide you through adding a cross table (crosstab) to a report. Start by dragging a result object from the AVAILABLE OBJECTS tab in the left pane, and then drop it into the appropriate section in the cross table. Figure 3.4 shows where to drop dimension and measure objects in a cross table.

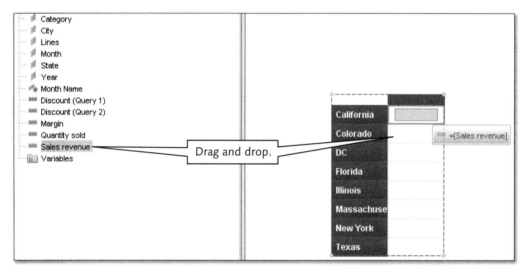

Figure 3.4 Drag and Drop "Sales Revenue Measure" to Crosstab

The Structure view is an easy way to see what elements and objects have been defined in a report. You can access the Structure view by clicking on STRUCTURE ONLY. Figure 3.5 shows a cross table and a horizontal bar chart in Structure view.

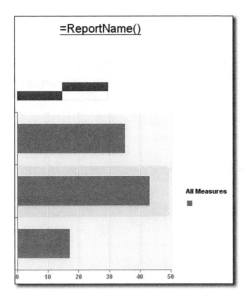

Figure 3.5 Crosstab and Horizontal Bar Chart in Structure View

3.1.2 Populate a Chart

To populate a chart, click on DESIGN/STRUCTURE ONLY to display the areas in the chart to drop the dimension objects and measure objects from the AVAILABLE OBJECTS tab in the left pane. You can review the results once you drag and drop your result objects onto the correct location on the chart. Click on DESIGN/VIEW WITH DATA to return to the report and see the data populated in the charts and tables.

> **Note**
>
> A chart must include at least one dimension object and one measure object.

The next section discusses how you can use sections and breaks to enhance the readability and functionality of a report.

3.2 Sections and Breaks

Grouping data in Web Intelligence is accomplished by setting sections for dimension objects or applying breaks to columns displayed in tables. *Sections* are used to group data into visually separated segments. *Breaks* provide the capability to quickly insert subtotals into Available Objects tables.

You can add multiple sections to a single report; subsequently added sections display data in subsections. One restriction of a section is that it can't be a measure object.

3.2.1 Setting as Section

Figure 3.6 shows the City object in a vertical table being set as a section.

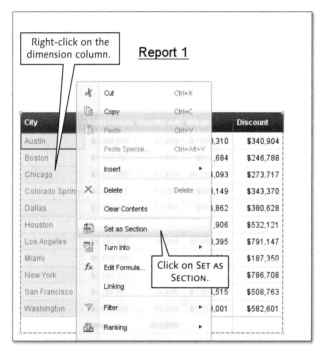

Figure 3.6 City Object Set as a Section

To add a section to a report, follow these steps:

1. Use an existing data table containing result objects. After you have inserted a table into your report and populated it with result objects, identify an object to set as the section.

2. Right-click on the object, and select SET AS SECTION. This will split the rows into groups based on the values of the dimension defined as the section.

After you have set an object as a section, it will be removed from the table and added as a table header. The remaining values in the table will be separated by the values of the dimension section.

Figure 3.7 shows the outcome of setting the existing result object re-sort column to a section. The re-sort object has been added as a block header and the object is no longer a column in the table.

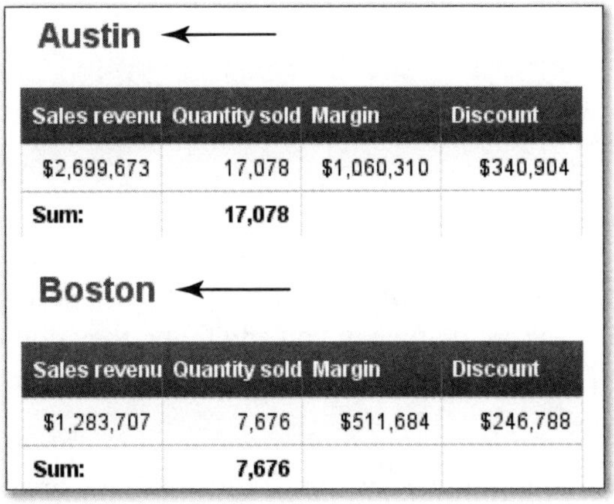

Austin ←————

Sales revenu	Quantity sold	Margin	Discount
$2,699,673	17,078	$1,060,310	$340,904
Sum:	**17,078**		

Boston ←————

Sales revenu	Quantity sold	Margin	Discount
$1,283,707	7,676	$511,684	$246,788
Sum:	**7,676**		

Figure 3.7 City Dimension Object Set as a Section

After you've added the section, you can also add additional report elements to that section. The values in any additional elements are grouped by the same values in the section heading.

To view the size of a section(s) and structure of a report, click on the DESIGN arrow and select STRUCTURE ONLY (also accessible using shortcut keys Ctrl + 3). View the report structure to resize the height of the section.

Figure 3.8 shows the Structure view of the report that contains the section you added in the previous step.

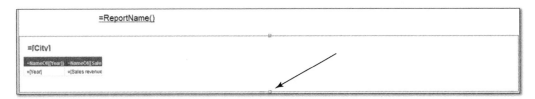

Figure 3.8 Structure Only View of a Report

If you're in drill mode, then you can take advantage of another functionality new to BI 4.0: the ability to right-click on a section header and choose whether to expand or collapse the children. Figure 3.9 shows the menu options available when you right-click on a section.

Figure 3.9 Menu Options—Expand or Collapse

3.2.2 Grouping Data with Breaks

Another way of grouping table data in a Web Intelligence report is by using breaks. Breaks are similar to sections, except that when you add them, they don't include block headings. When you add a break, a new set of break properties becomes available for customization.

To edit the properties of a break, right-click on the column that includes the break and then locate the Manage Breaks under Breaks.

Figure 3.10 shows the break properties available when designing a report.

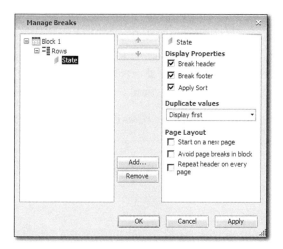

Figure 3.10 Managing Break Properties

Once a section or break has been created on a table, a new functionality can be applied to the table for interactivity.

3.3 Show/Hide Outline and Navigation

The outline feature adds collapsing and expanding "sections" on the left side of the Report Panel. Figure 3.11 shows a collapsed outline in a table with defined sections.

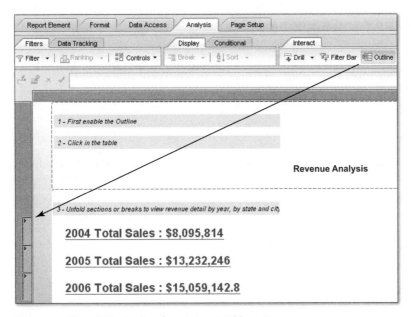

Figure 3.11 Show/Hide Outline from Interact Ribbon Menu

The outline adds a layer of interactivity to your Web Intelligence BI 4.0 reports because users have a choice of whether to show or not to show detailed information. This allows for increased "real estate" on the canvas because all reports can start in the summarized view and choose whether or not to expand to see the details.

Page navigation has also been improved in this release. Now all reports have a navigation icon that lets the user know whether additional pages exist in each direction. Figure 3.12 shows the PAGE NAVIGATION icon placed on the right lower side of each Web Intelligence report. When additional pages are present in a report, the icon will highlight in blue the direction arrow the user should click on to continue to next page.

Figure 3.12 Page Navigation

The following section describes how to insert sorting and ranking into a report.

3.4 Sorting and Ranking

Sorting and ranking data is a simple technique that increases report readability and displays the most significant information to report consumers in the shortest amount of time. Let's first examine sorting.

3.4.1 Sorting

Sorting can be applied to tables or charts in a report and to either dimension objects or measures. Sorting is always applied within breaks and sections. Figure 3.13 shows the Sort menu options available in the toolbar menu under the ANA-LYSIS/DISPLAY tab.

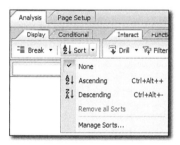

Figure 3.13 Sort from the Toolbar Menu under Analysis/Display

Four sort types are available to you while viewing a report in BI Launch Pad or when editing a Web Intelligence document:

▶ NONE: Natural sorting occurs based on the type of data in the columns.

▶ ASCENDING: Sorting begins with the smallest value at the top (for example, A, B, C, or 2, 4, 6).

▶ DESCENDING: Sorting ends with the smallest value at the top (for example, C, B, A, or 6, 4, 2).

▶ CUSTOM: Sorting is defined by the user; often applies to character names but doesn't apply to measures. It is accessible via MANAGE SORTS in the menu options.

Sorting data in charts or tables allows users to quickly access data points in alphabetical or numerical order.

Applying Sorting

To apply sorting within a table, follow these steps:

1. Select the column or result object to be sorted.

2. Select the SORT option in the ANALYSIS/DISPLAY tab.

3. Select the sort type.

4. Select NONE to remove applied sorting and return to default.

Figure 3.14 shows a measure column sorted in descending order in a table.

To apply sorting within a chart, follow these steps:

1. Click on DESIGN/STRUCTURE ONLY located on the main toolbar to switch from Data view to Structure only view.

2. Click on the object in the chart to be sorted.

3. Select the SORT option on the ANALYSIS/DISPLAY tab.

4. Select the sort type.

5. Click on DESIGN/WITH DATA to return to see the sort selected.

6. Return to the Structure view, and add, remove, or edit an existing sort.

7. Click on the SORT icon again to remove the sort.

Custom Sorting

Custom sorting is available only for dimension objects and while editing a document in the Report Panel.

When you select custom sorting, the dimension values of the object will be displayed in natural or descending order. You can re-sort the item values by selecting values individually and clicking on the up or down arrows until the values are in the order that you prefer.

An example of this sorting is when a month name object sorts alphabetically rather than chronologically. For months to appear in chronological order, you need to create a custom sort to reorder the values. If you have data only through June, then July through December values won't appear in the list.

This is when you need to include *temporary values*. Enter the month names from July to December, add them to the existing list, and then order them chronologically rather than alphabetically. This will keep the month data sorted correctly for all future refreshes.

Figure 3.14 shows Available Objects table with the month abbreviation field. The only way to sort the months correctly is to apply a custom sort.

	California	Colorado	DC	Florida	Illinois	Massachuse	New York	Texas
April	$666,321	$191,846	$275,751	$158,363	$278,195	$96,106	$617,851	$901,465
August	$339,651	$86,830	$119,664	$84,942	$114,890	$54,601	$288,166	$475,473
December	$616,205	$171,163	$234,192	$174,343	$230,092	$235,835	$592,567	$835,928
February	$410,620	$126,135	$177,509	$104,562	$174,747	$88,596	$400,589	$619,780
January	$692,714	$193,912	$278,756	$215,327	$375,172	$122,435	$836,078	$1,125,918
July	$515,407	$144,586	$201,581	$129,514	$180,673	$83,311	$652,721	$667,380
June	$420,305	$128,635	$177,787	$136,504	$209,522	$79,876	$591,598	$634,289
March	$796,347	$205,635	$310,557	$195,799	$296,490	$101,866	$750,448	$1,129,872
May	$673,522	$179,595	$252,909	$195,131	$362,877	$115,449	$818,641	$963,523
November	$504,464	$143,069	$221,179	$131,686	$207,226	$98,344	$566,677	$736,391
October	$768,555	$209,508	$341,052	$179,634	$277,572	$95,671	$735,190	$1,024,197
September	$1,075,459	$279,361	$371,014	$173,354	$315,203	$111,618	$731,694	$1,003,450

Figure 3.14 Default or Natural Sorting Applied to the Month Abbreviation

Custom Sort Dialog Box

Figure 3.15 shows the Custom Sort dialog box used to sort the month name abbreviations. Click on the values in the provided list box, and then use the arrows to the right to move them up or down the list.

The left side of the Custom Sort screen allows you to add temporary values for items that don't currently appear within the list of values.

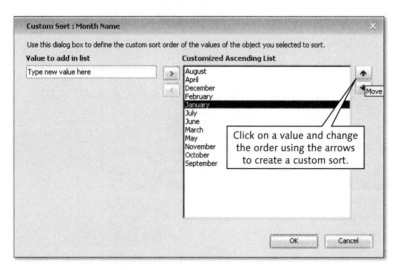

Figure 3.15 Custom Sorting

Remove Custom Sort Value

If a custom sort has been added but needs to be removed, click on the temporary value in the list of values to enable the DELETE CUSTOM SORT button. Click on the button to permanently remove the custom value from the list.

Figure 3.16 shows sorting being set on a measure within a data table and within a section.

> **Note**
>
> Notice that custom sorting isn't an option when sorting on a measure object. Custom sorting is only available for dimension objects.

Like sorting, ranking also helps the report consumer access the most significant information.

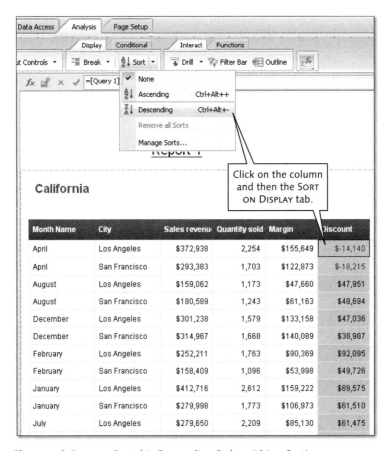

Figure 3.16 Revenue Sorted in Descending Order within a Section

3.4.2 Ranking

Ranking is used to display the top or bottom number of objects within a block. Values are ranked by dimensions and are based on measures of several different types and calculation modes.

▶ Top or bottom number of values: Select TOP, BOTTOM, or both, and then use the up and down arrows or text box to set the values.

▶ BASED ON [measure]: Select a measure to use for ranking.

▶ RANKED BY (optional): This selected dimension object is used by the ranking to create the top or bottom values.

► CALCULATION MODE:

  ► Count: This mode returns the top or bottom n records of the BASED ON selection.

  ► Percentage: This mode returns the top or bottom n% of records of the total number of records and the BASED ON selection.

  ► Cumulative sum: This mode returns the top or bottom records for the cumulative sum of the measure selected and (optionally) the BASED ON selection; doesn't exceed n.

  ► Cumulative percentage: This mode returns the top or bottom records for the cumulative sum of the measure selected and (optionally) the BASED ON selection; doesn't exceed n%.

Ranking takes precedence over any sorts previously set up in a report block.

> **Note**
>
> Web Intelligence includes *tied rankings*, which means that if you want to display the top 10 values, and 3 records have the same value, 13 records will appear in the top 10 list.

To add a ranking, follow these steps:

1. Modify or edit your Web Intelligence document. (Ranking can be applied only in edit mode.)
2. Select a table or chart to be ranked.
3. Click on the APPLY/REMOVE RANKING button located on the reporting toolbar.
4. Select the RANKING PROPERTIES in the Ranking dialog box.

Add the ranking option from the ANALYSIS/FILTERS tab on the ribbon toolbar. Two options—EDIT RANKING and REMOVE RANKING—will be available if a ranking has already been added to a report element because only one ranking can be added to a report element.

Figure 3.17 shows the Ranking dialog box opened when ADD RANKING or EDIT RANKING is selected. This dialog box allows you to configure the ranking properties by checking the TOP, BOTTOM, or both ranking property types followed by selecting the BASED ON, RANKED BY, or CALCULATION MODE to create or edit a ranking.

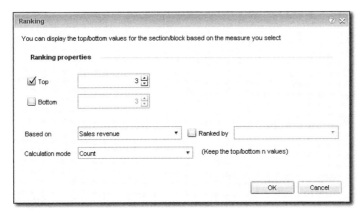

Figure 3.17 Ranking Dialog Box for a Vertical Table

The next section discusses conditional formatting rules and how they can be used to alert report consumers about important conditional elements in Web Intelligence reports.

3.5 Conditional Formatting

Web Intelligence reports use conditional formatting rules (previously known as alerters) to highlight values that meet a specified set of criteria. When a set of criteria has been met, values can be displayed with customized formatting. This includes the capability to modify the following areas:

- Text: Font, type, size, color, underline, strikethrough
- Background: Color, skin, image from URL, image from file
- Border: One or more sides, border size, color

Figure 3.18 shows the NEW RULE icon for conditional formatting on the ribbon toolbar. The following are some of the major limitations of applying conditional formatting in a report:

- Up to 30 conditional formatting rules can be applied to a single Web Intelligence reporting document.
- Conditional formatting can be applied to a maximum of 20 different rows or columns in a table report element.

- Up to 10 different alerts can be applied to a single column.
- A single conditional formatting can contain up to 6 conditions.

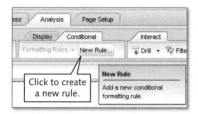

Figure 3.18 New Rule Icon on the Ribbon Toolbar

Click in the Formatting Rule Editor window, which is shown in Figure 3.19. From this window, revise the following items to create the criteria for the conditional formatting:

- NAME: Be sure to give the conditional rule a descriptive and unique name; this is important in case you have many rules. The default value in this field is "conditional format."
- DESCRIPTION: Be sure to type a clear description of what this conditional rule will perform.
- FILTERED OBJECT OR CELL: Select the field or result object to be evaluated.
- OPERATOR: Select the operator to be used (for example, Equal To, Greater Than, and so on).
- OPERANDS: Type in a value for the conditional formatting.

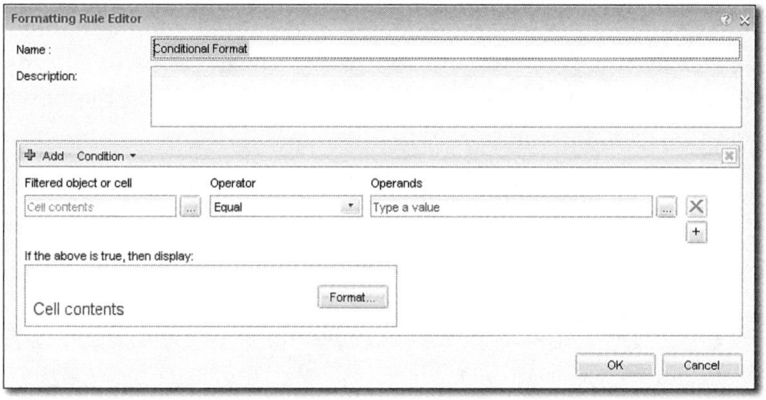

Figure 3.19 Formatting Rules Editor

After configuring these five settings, click on the FORMAT button to launch the Formatting Rules Editor window. Figure 3.20 shows the Formatting Rules Display window that is launched.

Figure 3.20 Formatting Rules Display

From this window, revise the following items to create the criteria for the Conditional Display:

▸ TEXT: Change the default font size and font color. Default color is already selected to red, but you can choose another color by pressing on the down arrow and selecting from the color palette.

▸ BACKGROUND: Choose colors, patterns, or images to apply to the cell background.

▸ BORDER: Choose any style for the cell border to accentuate the cell.

> **Note**
>
> Use the Preview area to visually design your conditional rule. Figure 3.21 shows how a rule would show if text, background, and borders were accentuated in different colors.

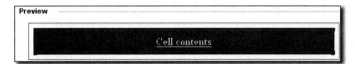

Figure 3.21 Preview of a Conditional Rule in Formatting Rules Display Window

After you've created a conditional formatting rule, select a column or table heading, and then click on the FORMATTING RULES icon on the ribbon toolbar under the ANALYSIS/CONDITIONAL tabs. All available conditional formatting will have an open checkbox located to the left of the conditional formatting name.

Check the rule that you want to apply to the selected column, and click on OK. Figure 3.22 shows a conditional formatting rule being applied with these three steps:

1. Select the column to apply the conditional formatting to.

2. Click on the FORMATTING RULES icon.

3. Check the conditional format(s) to be applied to the selected column(s).

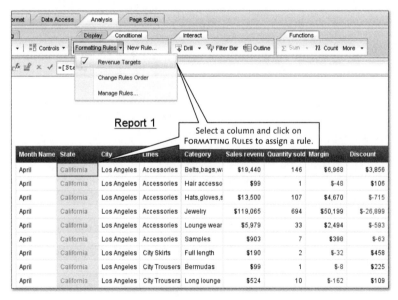

Figure 3.22 Conditional Formatting Rules Applied to Columns in a Table

The next section explains how to modify report headers and footers and describes the method for including background images in reports.

3.6   Headers, Footers, and Background Images

The header and footer sections in a Web Intelligence document can be hidden or displayed depending on your preference or business requirements.

In design mode, click on the SHOW button under PAGE SETUP • HEADER or FOOTER tabs on the ribbon toolbar. Figure 3.23 shows the HEADER SHOW button selected with a header height of 0.55 inches.

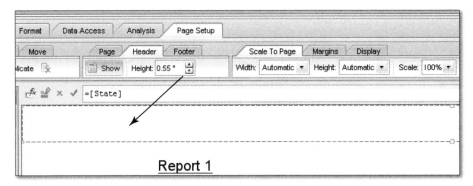

Figure 3.23 Header Visible in a Report

If the page header and footer have both been removed from a report and you need to add them back in, follow these steps:

1. Click on the PAGE SETUP • HEADER tab on the ribbon toolbar.
2. Click on the SHOW button to turn the header on. You can also set the height of the header in this step.
3. Click on the PAGE SETUP • FOOTER tab on the ribbon toolbar.
4. Click on the SHOW button to turn the footer on. You can also set the height of the footer in this step.

Quite often, report developers need to include background images or company logos in Web Intelligence reporting documents. You can easily do this by following just a few steps:

1. Go to the REPORT ELEMENTS • CELL tab on the ribbon toolbar. Drag the BLANK icon onto the canvas.
2. After the blank cell has been added, right-click on the cell, select FORMAT CELL and choose APPEARANCE in the Format Cell window. You can also click on the

APPEARANCE icon under FORMAT/STYLE on the ribbon toolbar. Figure 3.24 shows the properties available for the blank cell under APPEARANCE.

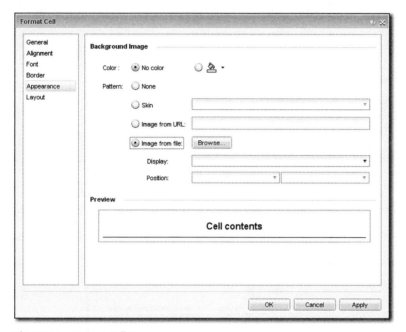

Figure 3.24 Format Cell Appearance

The Background Image dialog box opens to provide four options under PATTERN:

▶ NONE: Default selection

▶ SKIN: Shows five predefined photos

▶ IMAGE FROM URL: Opens a dialog box for manual URL entry

▶ IMAGE FROM FILE: Enables browsing to locate and select a local image

These options are shown in Figure 3.25.

You can create background images with the following file types: PNG, BMP, GIF, JPG, or JPEG.

Images are presented with five different display types:

▶ NORMAL

▶ STRETCH (NOT SUPPORTED IN HTML)

▶ TILE

► HORIZONTAL TILE

► VERTICAL TILE

The position of the images can be displayed in any of these combinations:

► Top, Center, Bottom

► Left, Center, Right

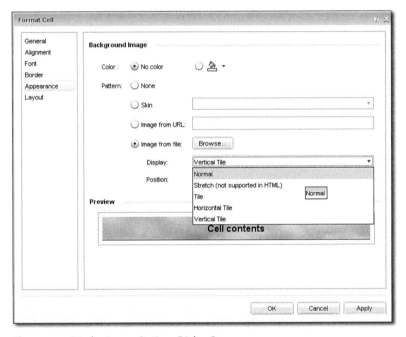

Figure 3.25 Display Image Options Dialog Box

Headers, footers, and background images can be used to add context to Web Intelligence reports. Report headers and footers can contain document names, company logos, or page numbers. Images can be useful to illustrate concepts. Choosing the right placement for images and creating a consistent look-and-feel is imperative in achieving strong usability for report consumers.

3.7   Summary

Reports in SAP BusinessObjects Web Intelligence BI 4.0 are created for viewing, analyzing, and sharing company data in a secure, customized, and drillable web-based delivery format. You can create them by using the result objects and report elements, and by setting properties in the tabs provided by the left pane. Reports are physically presented in the document pane and easily enhanced with the extensive list of shortcut icons in five provided toolbars.

Web Intelligence allows you to present multiple reports within a single reporting document that contain a variety of data visualization component types. You also have the ability to create drillable and highly formatted reports that include sections, breaks, sorting, ranking, and report filters to produce effective analytical documents.

Changes in report data can be easily identified when data tracking is enabled and when detailed conditional formatting has been created.

SAP BusinessObjects Business Intelligence 4.0 provides a full spectrum of reporting components for displaying data. These include Available Objects tables, freehand cells, and more than 25 different types of charts.

The Report Panel provides a highly intuitive development canvas that allows business users to create, edit, and share reports with ease.

Chapter 4 describes how to navigate the Web Intelligence reporting interface and explains the newly revised ribbon-based toolbar. This is important because the SAP BusinessObjects Web Intelligence 4.0 interface has changed from previous releases of the SAP BusinessObjects product. A bit of familiarization is necessary to get used to all the icons and their placements; however, you will find that the grouping of icons is much more intuitive because it is based on their functional areas.

The new streamlined interface in Web Intelligence 4.0 is easy to use for both report developers and consumers. A new ribbon toolbar has been introduced, which gives you faster and more intuitive access to icons based on various functional areas.

4 The Web Intelligence 4.0 Report Panel

This chapter begins by exploring the Web Intelligence 4.0 Report Panel, a robust reporting interface that allows report designers to create dynamic data presentations and visualizations. The new reporting interface in Web Intelligence 4.0 positions all icons on a new and enhanced toolbar in tabs grouped by functional areas for logical and effective development. The updated left pane replaces the Report Manager from previous versions and allows for easy access to useful areas such as Available Objects, Document Summary, Report Map, and Input Controls. The newly designed reporting interface also positions a robust status bar at the bottom of the report page, which allows you to easily refresh reports, enable tracking, and navigate pages.

4.1 The Web Intelligence 4.0 Reporting Interface

The Rich Internet Application Report Panel, shown in Figure 4.1, contains several areas that can be modified when creating or editing Web Intelligence reports.

The new reporting interface in Web Intelligence BI 4.0 has two main view options—reading and design—to accommodate different types of user interaction within a report. The reading mode has been exclusively designed for report consumers who only need to view and filter a report rather than edit it. The design mode gives report developers the full spectrum of editing capabilities.

In the top right corner of the screen, you can access different viewing options such as READING, DESIGN, and DATA. Figure 4.2 shows the READING dropdown menu, which presents two options:

▶ HTML: This mode displays only the report elements (charts, tables, freestanding cells) and is primarily used for analysis.

▶ PDF: This mode launches the report data in PDF within the BI Launch Pad panel.

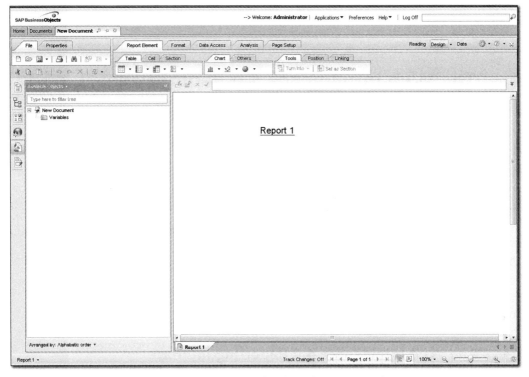

Figure 4.1 Web Intelligence Report Edited in the Rich Internet Application

Figure 4.2 Reading Dropdown Choices

An important option in the reporting toolbar is the STRUCTURE ONLY selection found in the DESIGN menu and shown in Figure 4.3. The DESIGN • STRUCTURE ONLY button allows you to access the document structure of a report, a step used for editing the size of sections.

Figure 4.3 Design Button Allows Access to Structure Only Mode

For easy access to all of these view options, right-click on the top bar and select the APPLICATION MODE menu shown in Figure 4.4.

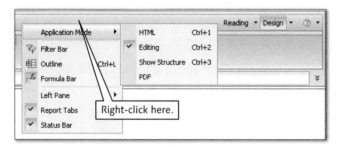

Figure 4.4 Application Mode Menu

Now that you are familiar with the new view modes, the next section describes the new ribbon-style toolbar.

4.2   Reporting Toolbars

The new formatting toolbar is similar to the Microsoft Office® ribbon-style tool-bars that you're probably already familiar with. This new method of displaying properties allows for easier access to report formatting icons. The toolbar becomes very useful when editing report elements, configuring formatting, mod-ifying data access, and page setup properties. Figure 4.5 shows the formatting toolbar in design mode. Whether you are updating a horizontal table, vertical table, cross table, form, or freestanding cell, the ribbon toolbar allows you to instantly revise the format of entire columns with only a couple clicks.

Figure 4.5 Formatting Toolbar in Design Mode

> **Note**
>
> The reading mode toolbar is different from the design mode toolbar. They were designed to execute separate functions, to be more in line with the needs of report consumers and report designers. The reading mode toolbar is much more streamlined for optimal viewing and filtering capabilities.

The ribbon toolbar in design mode contains the following primary tabs that each provides categorized functions and shortcut icons:

▶ FILE: Located on the left side of the window, this tab is used for adding new reports, opening existing documents, saving, and printing.

▶ PROPERTIES: This tab allows you to view and revise document and application properties.

▶ REPORT ELEMENT: This tab delivers report elements for displaying data.

▶ FORMAT: This tab delivers a large number of formatting properties.

▶ DATA ACCESS: With this tab, you can add new data providers, edit existing ones, or add new variables to a reporting document.

▶ ANALYSIS: You can use this tab to create filters, input controls, enable data tracking, add conditional formatting, and much more.

▶ PAGE SETUP: This tab contains all page formatting options in one location.

Let's explore the options available in each section below.

File

Figure 4.6 shows the FILE tab and its associated icons:

▶ NEW: This icon is used to create a new document.

▶ OPEN: This icon allows you to access previously saved Web Intelligence documents.

▶ SAVE: This icon is used to save reports with SAVE, SAVE AS, or SAVE TO ENTERPRISE options.

▶ PRINT: This icon provides one-click report printing.

▶ FIND: This icon allows you to search report data with the Find toolbar.

▸ HISTORY: If this report has been previously scheduled, the report instances will be available through this icon.

▸ EXPORT: With this icon, you can create a new document or save a document either locally as a PDF, XLS, CSV, or to the CMS and file repository.

▸ EMAIL: Use this icon to send this report to an email address, another user, or to an FTP server. Note that the SAP BusinessObjects administrator is required to configure plugins on the server in order to utilize this functionality.

▸ UNDO/REDO: This icon lets you undo or redo previous actions.

▸ CUT/COPY/PASTE: This icon lets you cut, copy, and paste any report element, including charts and tables.

▸ DELETE: Use this icon to delete selected components.

▸ REFRESH: This icon allows for new data to be brought into the report. Being able to refresh data is a primary function when generating reports.

Figure 4.6 File Tab

Properties

Figure 4.7 shows the View menu of the PROPERTIES tab. The following menus are associated with this tab:

▸ VIEW: Allows report developers to access the FILTER BAR, OUTLINE (also known as FOLD/UNFOLD), FORMULA BAR, and LEFT PANE. Additionally, you can toggle the REPORT TABS and STATUS BAR on and off using their respective checkboxes.

▸ DOCUMENT: Provides a summary of configurable document properties. Includes type, author, description of the document, and creation date. Figure 4.12 shows all additional options that can be set in the Document Properties window.

▸ APPLICATION: Allows developers to set units of measurements to display in centimeters or in inches.

Figure 4.7 Properties Tab

Report Element

Figure 4.8 shows the REPORT ELEMENT tab and its associated icons. This is the first primary tab used for displaying data on the report canvas.

Figure 4.8 Report Element Tab

First let's examine the tabs under the REPORT ELEMENT tab section by section.

- ▶ TABLE
  - ▶ VERTICAL TABLE: Displays header cells at the top of the table
  - ▶ HORIZONTAL TABLE: Displays header cells to the left of the table
  - ▶ CROSS TABLE or CROSSTAB: Displays dimensions across the top and along the left side of the table while displaying measures in the body of the table
  - ▶ FORM: Displays categorized dimension descriptions or mailing addresses
- ▶ CELL
  - ▶ BLANK CELLS: Used for custom headings or subheadings or to display information that should appear in an Available Objects table
  - ▶ PREDEFINED: Predefined single value containing metadata about report

- ▶ SECTION
  - ▶ INSERT SECTION: Allows report developers to insert a section using available objects
- ▶ CHART (chart types examined in Chapter 5)
  - ▶ COLUMN: Graphically presents values in vertical or horizontal charts (available column charts: stacked column, 100% stacked column, dual axis column, dual axis column and line, and 3D column)
  - ▶ LINE: Displays data graphically with connected data points (available line charts: vertical/horizontal mixed, vertical/horizontal stacked, vertical/horizontal percent, 3D line, 3D surface, dual axis line, and surface)
  - ▶ PIE: Displays data as a percentage of the whole with pie slices (available pie charts: pie with variable slice depth, doughnut, 3D pie, and 3D doughnut)
- ▶ OTHERS
  - ▶ BAR: Graphically represents horizontal bar charts (available bar charts: vertical/horizontal stacked bar, 100% stacked bar, vertical/horizontal grouped, vertical/horizontal perfect, vertical/horizontal bar and line, and 3D bar)
  - ▶ RADAR CHARTS: Include radar line, stacked area radar, polar, and scatter charts.
  - ▶ BUBBLE CHARTS
  - ▶ MORE
- ▶ TOOLS
  - ▶ TURN INTO: Transforms selected object into a different type table or chart
  - ▶ SET AS SECTION: Allows report developers to insert a section using selected object
- ▶ POSITION
  - ▶ ORDER
  - ▶ ALIGN
- ▶ LINKING
  - ▶ ADD HYPERLINK
  - ▶ LINK TO DOCUMENT
  - ▶ ADD ELEMENT LINK

- ▶ TABLE LAYOUT: Appears only when a data table on the report canvas has been selected
  - ▶ BREAK
  - ▶ INSERT
  - ▶ HEADER
  - ▶ FOOTER
- ▶ CELL BEHAVIORS
  - ▶ HIDE
  - ▶ PAGE BREAK
  - ▶ REPEAT: Allows tables, headers, or breaks to repeat on every page

Format

Figure 4.9 shows the FORMAT tab and its associated icons:

- ▶ FONT
- ▶ BORDER
- ▶ CELL
- ▶ STYLE
- ▶ NUMBERS
- ▶ ALIGNMENT
  - ▶ WRAP TEXT: Allows a word wrap style of formatting to be applied to the selected column or columns so that a carriage return takes place within the cell rather than extending the value horizontally
- ▶ SIZE
- ▶ PADDING
- ▶ TOOLS
  - ▶ FORMAT PAINTER: Applies formatting. Quickly copy the format of an existing cell or column and apply it to an additional cell or column by first selecting a cell that contains the preferred formatting, clicking on the FORMAT PAINTER icon, and then clicking on the text to which you would like to apply the formatting

- ▶ FORMATTING: Displays all formatting options for the selected report element

- ▶ CLEAR FORMAT: Resets all formatting to the default formats

Figure 4.9 Format Tab

Data Access

Figure 4.10 shows the DATA ACCESS tab and its associated icons:

- ▶ DATA PROVIDERS

  - ▶ NEW DATA PROVIDER: Adds a new query to the existing document

  - ▶ EDIT: Returns to the Query Panel to edit a query

  - ▶ PURGE: Purges report data. This is important when publishing reports to the file repository with restricted data. You can purge all data from all data providers or choose an individual data provider to purge

  - ▶ REFRESH: Submits the query to the data source to retrieve the most recent data.

- ▶ TOOLS

  - ▶ CHANGE SOURCE

  - ▶ EXPORT DATA

- ▶ DATA OBJECTS

  - ▶ NEW VARIABLE

  - ▶ MERGE

Figure 4.10 Data Access Tab

Analysis

Figure 4.11 shows the ANALYSIS tab and its associated icons:

▶ FILTERS

   ▶ FILTER

   ▶ RANKING

   ▶ CONTROLS

▶ DATA TRACKING: Prompts you to set the reference point for data tracking. A variety of data tracking options are available when tracking has been enabled. These options include font formatting for dimension insertions and deletions, detail changes, and increased/decreased values for measures

▶ DISPLAY

▶ CONDITIONAL

▶ INTERACT

   ▶ DRILL: Used to enable drill mode. It also provides a drill pane to drop result objects for simple report filtering. Drill mode allows report consumers to drill up or drill down the drill path for deeper and quicker analysis

   ▶ FILTER BAR

   ▶ OUTLINE

▶ FUNCTIONS

   ▶ SUM

   ▶ COUNT

   ▶ MORE

   ▶ FORMULA BAR

Figure 4.11 Analysis Tab

Page Setup

Figure 4.12 shows the PAGE SETUP tab and its associated icons:

- ▶ REPORT
  - ▶ ADD REPORT
  - ▶ DUPLICATE
  - ▶ DELETE
- ▶ RENAME
- ▶ MOVE
  - ▶ MOVE LEFT
  - ▶ MOVE RIGHT
- ▶ PAGE
  - ▶ PAGE ORIENTATION
  - ▶ PAGE FORMAT
- ▶ HEADER
  - ▶ SHOW BUTTON
  - ▶ PAGE HEADER HEIGHT
- ▶ FOOTER
  - ▶ SHOW BUTTON
  - ▶ PAGE FOOTER HEIGHT
- ▶ SCALE TO PAGE
  - ▶ WIDTH
  - ▶ HEIGHT
  - ▶ SCALE
- ▶ MARGINS
  - ▶ TOP MARGIN
  - ▶ BOTTOM MARGIN
  - ▶ LEFT MARGIN
  - ▶ RIGHT MARGIN

▶ DISPLAY

    ▶ PAGE MODE

    ▶ QUICK DISPLAY

    ▶ ROWS

    ▶ COLUMNS

Figure 4.12 Page Setup Tab

The updated ribbon-based toolbar in Web Intelligence 4.0 is a robust interface that allows users to quickly access all functions related to creating reports. The next section describes the usability of the left pane, which also provides main functions necessary for report maintenance and creation.

4.3 The Left Pane

The left pane contains tabs that give additional information and is required for creating Web Intelligence 4.0 reporting documents. The left pane also plays a critical role in editing existing documents. Figure 4.13 shows the first tab of the left pane, which is DOCUMENT SUMMARY.

The left pane, which can be displayed in normal or minimized mode, is different for reading mode, design mode, and data mode. Let's examine each of these now.

▶ Reading mode:

    ▶ DOCUMENT SUMMARY: This tab includes information about the report, such as author, date created description, keywords, last refreshed, last modified date, last modified by, duration of previous refresh, document options, data options, and parameters. This metadata about the report is useful for the administrator because it shows who has created and refreshed the document. Additionally, the duration of previous refresh records the number of seconds the report took to refresh on the previous refresh. (Note that if never run, then this value will be zero.)

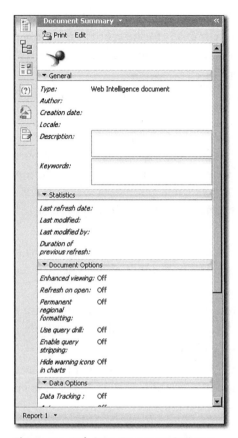

Figure 4.13 Left Pane–Document Summary

- ▶ REPORT MAP: This tab provides a linked list of the reports and section values within each report in the document.

- ▶ INPUT CONTROLS: This tab allows report users to identify whether any components have been used to filter report data using input controls. The user can select a map of all input controls already saved on the document, choose to reset the values of saved input controls, or both.

▶ Design mode:

- ▶ DOCUMENT SUMMARY: This tab includes information about the report, such as author, date created description, keywords, last refreshed, last modified date, last modified by, duration of previous refresh, document options, data options, and parameters. This metadata about the report is useful for the administrator because it shows who has created and refreshed the document. Additionally, the duration of previous refresh records the number of seconds the report took to refresh on the previous refresh. (Note that if never run, then this value will be zero.)

▸ REPORT MAP: This tab provides a linked list of the reports and section values within each report in the document.

▸ INPUT CONTROLS: This tab allows both report developers and users to include a variety of components in filtering report data. The report designer can create new input controls by clicking on the NEW button under the INPUT CONTROLS tab. The user can select a map of all input controls already saved on the document, choose to reset the values of saved input controls, or both.

▸ WEB SERVICE PUBLISHER: This tab allows the report designer to create Web services using existing components or blocks from Web Intelligence reports.

▸ AVAILABLE OBJECTS: This tab contains the fields included in the Result Objects pane in the Query Panel and locally created formulas and variables. All objects in this tab are available to be displayed in reports.

▸ DOCUMENT STRUCTURES AND FILTERS: DOCUMENT STRUCTURES provides a detailed listing of all objects existing within the document. FILTERS shows filters that exist on report elements and data blocks within the reports.

> **Note**
>
> Design mode has two options: The With Data view refers to displaying any data that has been refreshed in the report, and the Structure Only view refers to displaying only the structure or "formulas" used in the report blocks.

▸ Data mode:

▸ DATA: This tab contains the fields included in the Result Objects pane in the Query Panel and locally created formulas and variables. All objects in the AVAILABLE OBJECTS tab are available to be displayed in reports.

Figure 4.14 shows the result objects from the Query Panel in the AVAILABLE OBJECTS tab. The data for the fields displayed in the AVAILABLE OBJECTS tab has been retrieved from the database and exists within the document's microcube.

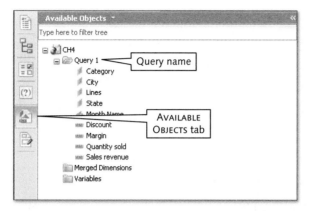

Figure 4.14 Web Intelligence Report in Data Mode using the Rich Internet Application

Click on the DOCUMENT SUMMARY tab in either reading mode or design mode. To reveal the report information, click on EDIT to update fields such as DESCRIPTION or KEYWORDS. The REFRESH ON OPEN option is used to prompt users for input each time a report is opened and also refreshed.

4.4 Report Panel

The Report Panel or report canvas is where report elements are placed when you create Web Intelligence reports. The report canvas is the primary section in the Report Panel of a Web Intelligence document and is the section of the report used for displaying data.

The report canvas or document pane consists of three sections:

- Report header (optional)
- Report body
- Report footer (optional)

Tip
When a query is refreshed for the first time, the result objects will appear in the document pane in a report titled Report 1. All result objects will also appear in the left pane. For any additional refreshes after the initial refresh, the left pane will be updated with the latest list of result objects, but the objects appearing on the document pane won't change unless revised by the report developer.

The default report names are shown in Figure 4.15.

Figure 4.15 Default Report Names in the Document Pane

You can make changes to the report tab names. To rename, insert, duplicate, or delete report tabs, use these methods:

▶ Right-click on the report name tab located in the lower left of the report.

▶ Select RENAME to change the name of the report tab.

▶ Select ADD REPORT to add a new report tab.

▶ Select DUPLICATE to make a duplicate copy of the current report.

▶ Select DELETE REPORT to remove the current report tab.

Figure 4.16 shows the actions available when you right-click on the report name tab located at the lower left of the document pane. The MOVE option is enabled only when two or more reports exist within the document.

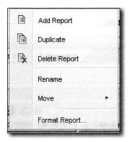

Figure 4.16 Actions Available When Right-Clicking on the Report Tab

Activating data tracking from the status bar is a recent addition to Web Intelligence and has become a valuable analysis feature. To activate data tracking in a report, click on TRACK CHANGES in the status bar located under the Report Panel. You are immediately prompted to set the reference point for data tracking.

The page navigation toolbar on the status bar (see Figure 4.17) allows you to scroll from the current page being viewed to the next page, last page, previous page, and first page.

There are two modes for displaying reports:

▶ Quick Display mode: This is the default display mode. The maximum displayed vertical and horizontal records can be defined in the PROPERTIES tab.

▶ Page mode: This mode displays reports as they would appear if printed.

Figure 4.17 shows the QUICK DISPLAY and PAGE MODE icons.

The zoom options on the status bar (see Figure 4.17) allow you to increase the zoom of the page from a minimum of 10% to a maximum of 500%. There is also an option to zoom to Page Width or Whole Page (also known as Fit to Page). The default value is 100%.

The REFRESH icon on the status bar is a new function. The ability to refresh data is the primary function when generating reports. The refresh function allows new data to be retrieved from a data source and inserted into the report. Figure 4.17 shows the REFRESH button and information as to the last time the report had been refreshed.

Figure 4.17 Page Navigation on the Status Bar

The formula bar provides quick access to the object definition. You can save time by revising object definitions in the formula bar. To access the bar, right-click on the gray part of the ribbon bar to toggle the formula bar on and off. Note that the formula bar is accessible only in design mode. Figure 4.18 shows the menu to access the formula bar.

The new formula bar can also be expanded to allow report developers to see more code on the screen. Figure 4.19 shows the formula bar expanded by using the double up arrows.

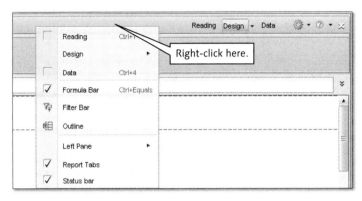

Figure 4.18 Menu to Access the Formula Bar

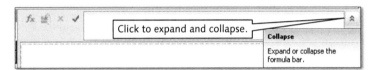

Figure 4.19 Formula Bar Expanded

4.5 Report Property Categories

There are five major report element formatting types in the Web Intelligence 4.0 ribbon-based toolbar: Report Elements, Formatting, Data Access, Analysis, and Page Setup. The functional areas make it easy for you to identify which category to select when looking for a particular icon. This section explains in detail each one of these report property categories.

4.5.1 Report Elements

The REPORT ELEMENTS tab on the ribbon toolbar offers many shortcuts to most used objects such as tables, charts, and predefined cells. When a report element is selected on the Report Panel, you will see that the REPORT ELEMENTS tab on the toolbar displays specific icons for the type of element selected. Figure 4.20 shows two additional tabs (TABLE LAYOUT and BEHAVIORS) containing icons to format a table.

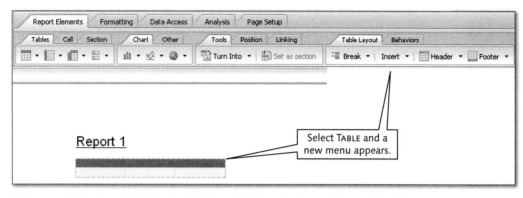

Figure 4.20 Selecting a Table Displays Additional Tabs on the Report Elements Toolbar

Report elements allow report developers to add elements to the canvas and create robust visualizations for report consumers. You can quickly convert an existing table to a chart or convert an existing dimension column into a section. Follow these steps to convert a table into a bar chart:

1. Select an existing table from the canvas.

2. Select the TOOL tab on the Reports Elements toolbar.

3. Select the TURN INTO icon and select BAR CHART.

The table has been converted to a bar chart. Note that there are two new tabs added to the REPORT ELEMENTS tab on the toolbar. If a chart is selected, then CHART STYLE and CELL BEHAVIOR appear on the toolbar.

Proper report element alignment and relative positioning will improve the overall attractiveness and effectiveness of your Web Intelligence reports. When business users view reports that contain charts and data tables aligned in unusual ways, the reports aren't usually as convincing as well designed and properly formatted reporting documents.

Use the alignment functions to format the placement of report elements and the Relative Position feature to maintain consistent spacing and alignment when one or more blocks or report elements exist on a report.

Figure 4.21 shows the alignment types available when two or more report elements are selected:

▶ ALIGN LEFT

▶ ALIGN CENTER

▶ ALIGN RIGHT

▶ ALIGN TOP

▶ ALIGN MIDDLE

▶ ALIGN BOTTOM

▶ RELATIVE POSITION

Figure 4.21 Align Types from the Position Tab under the Report Elements Tab

The Relative Position setting allows two report elements to be tied together and spaced by a selected number of pixels (inches).

To set up relative positioning, select a secondary report element, and then select Relative Position from the ALIGN icon under the POSITION tab. Figure 4.22 shows the Relative Position properties of a table in a report.

To position an object within a report, follow these steps:

1. Select LEFT EDGE, RIGHT EDGE, or NONE from the first box at the top, and then select TOP SIDE OF, BOTTOM SIDE OF, or NONE from the bottom setting.

2. Select the object(s) to assign the relative distance to.

3. Choose the relative distance for both the top section and the bottom section.

Relative positioning of charts and data tables gives reports the flexibility to present data in a similar format when the amount of data being reported fluctuates.

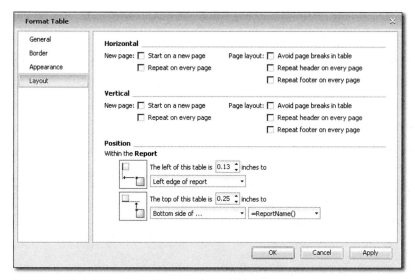

Figure 4.22 Relative Position Properties for a Table

4.5.2 Formatting

The FORMATTING tab on the ribbon toolbar offers report developers many formatting functions, such as font size, styles, borders, alignment, and much more. The TOOLS tab allows report developers to copy the format of previously produced components onto new components. Figure 4.23 shows the FONT, STYLE, ALIGNMENT, and TOOLS tab icons under the FORMATTING tab.

Figure 4.23 Formatting Toolbar

Under the TOOLS tab are three icons that help report developers tremendously when duplicating report elements:

▶ FORMAT PAINTER: Allows for duplicating formatting from one object and applying it to another object

▶ FORMATTING: Displays all formatting options for the selected report element

▶ CLEAR FORMAT: Resets all formatting to the default formats

Follow these steps to duplicate formatting from one cell to another:

1. Move the Document Name predefined cell from the REPORT ELEMENTS • CELL tab onto the canvas.

2. Select the newly added cell by clicking on it.

3. Select the FORMATTING tab and, under the STYLE tab, select ITALIC and UNDERLINE. Then change text color to red.

4. Place the Last Refreshed Date predefined cell from the REPORT ELEMENTS • CELL tab onto the canvas.

5. Select FORMAT PAINTER from FORMATTING • TOOLS tab and apply the Document Name cell format to the Last Refreshed Date cell. Figure 4.24 shows two predefined cells and how to duplicate one cell's format onto the other.

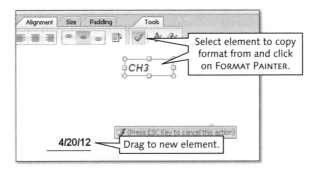

Figure 4.24 Applying Formatting from One Cell to Another

Note

You can copy and duplicate cell formats to any type of objects. You can also duplicate table and chart formats. Formatting of report elements provides a consistent appearance for ease-of-use.

4.5.3 Data Access

The DATA ACCESS tab on the ribbon toolbar offers many functions for managing data providers and dealing with data in general. Whether your data comes from a centralized universe or simply from an Excel file, it is important to understand when to refresh, purge, or redefine data providers. Please refer to Chapter 2 for more information on creating Data Providers. Figure 4.25 shows the PURGE icons under the DATA ACCESS tab.

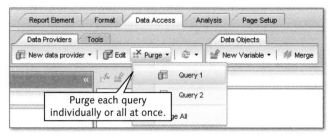

Figure 4.25 Refresh and Purge Icons under the Data Access Tab

By restricting the amount of data returned from a data source, report developers can manage performance of the report while constructing it. A good way to achieve this is by understanding how much data is needed per data provider. When multiple data providers are generated for a particular report, developers may choose to refresh or purge individual data providers to increase the performance to the report at design time.

Follow these steps to purge the results from an individual data provider:

1. Create two data providers and refresh all data.

2. Click on the PURGE dropdown arrow.

3. Select the first data provider to purge.

You will now have data from only the second data provider. Figure 4.25 shows the PURGE button options when dropdown arrow is pressed.

Reports with highly secure data should be purged before they're published to the CMS. Users with the appropriate permissions will be able to refresh the reports and retrieve the results. Users without the necessary permissions will not be able to see the data since the reports were published after the results were purged.

4.5.4   Analysis

The ANALYSIS tab on the ribbon toolbar offers many functions for interacting with the report data. Filtering, ranking, input controls, breaks, sorts, drilling, outline, and functions provide a robust way to interact with report elements. By using these analysis functions, you can customize and filter data to meet business requirements. By allowing for this level of customization, you can create a reporting solution to be consumed by many different types of users. Figure 4.26 shows the expanded MORE button under the FUNCTIONS subtab of the primary ANALYSIS tab.

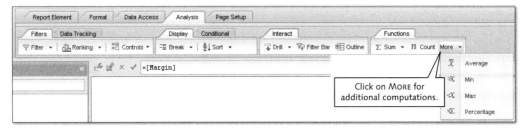

Figure 4.26 Expanded More Button under the Functions Tab

You can easily access predefined functions such as Average, Sum, Min/Max and Percentage from the FUNCTION tab.

Follow these steps to create a summed value in a data table:

1. Create a table with numeric measure object column.

2. Select the column to apply the sum to.

3. Click on SUM under the FUNCTION tab and check SUM.

A new row appears at the end of the table with the column summed up, as shown in Figure 4.27.

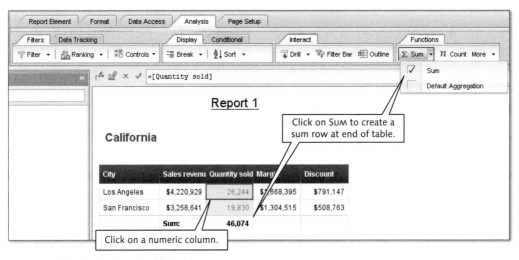

Figure 4.27 Sum Table Column

4.5.5 Page Setup and Layouts

Page margins in a Web Intelligence report can be modified to fit business requirements or standards. The default margins in a report are as follows:

▶ Top margin: 0.79 inches

▶ Bottom margin: 0.79 inches

▶ Left margin: 0.79 inches

▶ Right margin: 0.79 inches

You can adjust the margins by accessing the MARGINS subtab in the primary PAGE SETUP tab. Locate the margin properties, and then use the up or down arrows to change the size.

The changes take effect when you click off of the size adjustment arrows. Figure 4.28 shows the margins properties and highlights the top margin adjustment arrows for modifying the margin sizes.

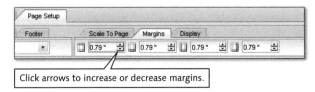

Figure 4.28 Adjusting Page Margins

Report property categories are functional groupings for formatting icons based on their functional area. These groupings in tab format make it easier for the report designer to access these icons.

4.6 Summary

Web Intelligence 4.0 provides a full spectrum of reporting components as well as a full line of icons to format every element for a customizable look-and-feel. New navigation functionality has been introduced with more streamlined "ribbon-based" toolbars and the left pane. Users and report developers can now access several different formatting tools and from multiple ways. This includes toolbars, right-click menus, and the status bar. An example of the multiple ways of performing a function is the REFRESH button. This feature can be found in three different locations: the status bar, the DATA ACCESS/DATA PROVIDERS subtab on the ribbon toolbar, or the reading mode toolbar.

Chapter 5 describes how to display data in tables in a Web Intelligence report. Tables are powerful reporting elements and the primary method of delivering data in a Web Intelligence report. They can be quickly and precisely formatted by using the icons located on the new ribbon-based toolbar.

The features in SAP BusinessObjects Web Intelligence BI 4.0 display data and transform business information into analytical and data-rich reports. You can strategically group, break, and position data tables and freehand cells in the Report Panel to convey information to the user in the most meaningful way.

5   Displaying Data with Tables

You can display data in Web Intelligence BI 4.0 by inserting result objects into four different data table types and 25 different chart types. These are known in Web Intelligence as report elements.

This chapter focuses on presenting data using the four report element tables and the blank cells located on the ribbon toolbar. We'll discuss charts in detail in Chapters 6 and 7.

Figure 5.1 shows the tables available in the Report Panel used by Web Intelligence to display data. The four table types are HORIZONTAL TABLE, VERTICAL TABLE, CROSS TABLE (or crosstab), and FORM. Each table contains an extensive set of properties that can be modified to allow for detailed reporting customizations.

After you refresh a query for the first time in a new document, the full list of result objects is displayed in a vertical table in the Report Panel by default. Any subsequent refreshes that include additions to the Result Objects pane in the Query Panel won't automatically include the additional fields in the report, but the result objects will appear in the AVAILABLE OBJECTS tab on the left side panel in the report. These objects can be easily added to new or existing report elements by dragging them from the Available Objects pane and then dropping them onto charts or cells in a data table.

> **Tip**
>
> The AVAILABLE OBJECTS tab is used to maintain the list of result objects and variables available to be added to report element tables and charts. These objects can be sorted alphabetically or by query.

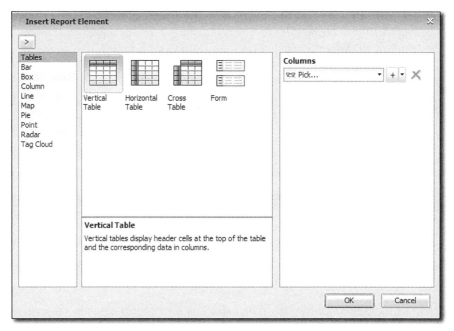

Figure 5.1 Tables Available for Displaying Data

Figure 5.2 shows the default appearance of data as it appears in the Report Panel when five result objects are added to the Query Panel in the initial refresh of a document.

A report title will be added by default in a text cell, given the title "Report 1," and underlined, making it easy to locate.

You can add formulas and result objects to the report title of a report to provide a dynamic title based on user interactions. An example of a dynamic report title can be created by using one of the following formulas:

▶ `=DrillFilters(" / ")`

▶ `=If(Count([City])=1;[City];"All "+Count([City])+" Cities")`

> **Note**
>
> Both example formulas require objects to be added to the report filter toolbar. The second formula requires the City object to be added to the report filter.

Report 1			
Year	**State**	**City**	**Sales revenue**
2004	California	Los Angeles	$982,637
2004	California	San Francisc	$721,574
2004	Colorado	Colorado Spr	$448,302
2004	DC	Washington	$693,211
2004	Florida	Miami	$405,985
2004	Illinois	Chicago	$737,914
2004	Massachuset	Boston	$238,819
2004	New York	New York	$1,667,696
2004	Texas	Austin	$561,123
2004	Texas	Dallas	$427,245
2004	Texas	Houston	$1,211,309
2005	California	Los Angeles	$1,581,616
2005	California	San Francisc	$1,201,064
2005	Colorado	Colorado Spr	$768,390
2005	DC	Washington	$1,215,158

Figure 5.2 Default Display in the Report Panel

Chapter 11 will focus on writing formulas and variables to solve business problems. This chapter offers many examples and syntax explanations to give you the tools to create your own set of valuable and creative calculations.

So let's first examine how to effectively use tables to convey data to the reader.

5.1 Using Tables

Tables are the Web Intelligence BI 4.0 reporting components used to present data to business users. Tables provide many customizable properties to help you quickly format and design useful reports and display the data in a style that best fits your requirements. Figure 5.3 shows options available in the TABLE LAYOUT subtab when you click on an existing table. This subtab is found in the primary REPORT ELEMENTS tab.

Figure 5.3 Table Layout Subtab Under the Report Elements Tab

These properties are available in two primary categories, which are represented as tabs:

▶ TABLE LAYOUT

  ▶ BREAK: Allows for the adding and removal of breaks

  ▶ INSERT: Allows for inserting rows above, below, left, or right of the position of the cursor on an active table

  ▶ HEADER: Toggles the table header on and off

  ▶ FOOTER: Toggles the table footer on and off

▶ BEHAVIORS:

  ▶ HIDE: Hides the selected dimension or the entire table

  ▶ PAGE BREAK: Inserts a page break to avoid a page break

  ▶ REPEAT: Allows repeating table on every page and for repeating of selected columns or rows

5.1.1 Add Report Elements While Designing Reports

To add a report element to a report, simply drag an element from the TABLE or CHART subtabs under the REPORT ELEMENTS tab and drop it onto the Report Panel. The option to add data tables or charts while viewing reports is very useful to ad hoc report consumers and developers but it must be done in design mode.

Figure 5.4 shows the shortcut icons used to access the different types of data tables that can be included in the main Report Panel.

> **Note**
>
> While designing a report, you can right-click anywhere on the Report Panel or report canvas and click on INSERT from the menu to add a specific data table type or chart from the list of choices.

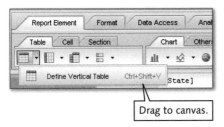

Figure 5.4 Shortcut Icons to Add Report Elements

Figure 5.5 shows the table types that you can add to a Web Intelligence report while designing it.

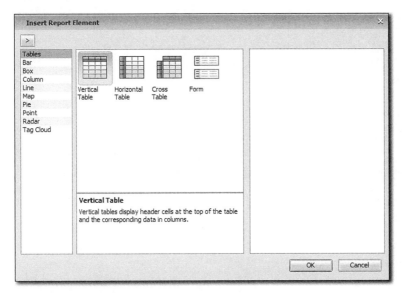

Figure 5.5 Table Types

After dropping a report element into the Report Panel of your document, you can begin adding result objects to your report and populating the new table by clicking on the AVAILABLE OBJECTS tab on the left panel and then dragging available objects and dropping them onto the table element recently added. Another method of adding objects to a report element is to right-click on the object and select ASSIGN DATA.

Figure 5.6 shows the City result object being added to an empty cross table while designing a report.

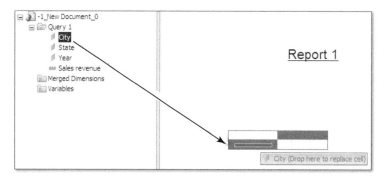

Figure 5.6 Available Object Added to a Cross Table–Viewing a Report

---

Note

With BI 4.0, you must be in design mode to add objects to tables and charts. Reading mode is view-only.

5.1.2 Manage Table Properties

Every table has an extensive list of properties to allow for modification and customization. Figure 5.7 shows the properties associated with a vertical table. In addition to table properties, specific elements within tables can be modified.

To access table properties, right-click on the table element, then select FORMAT TABLE.

General Property

The General property pane contains a Name setting that allows you to rename the selected block. Figure 5.7 shows the name as "Vertical Table." Click on the name to replace the default name with a new name of your choice.

Tip

If Relative Positioning will be included in your reports, it's a best practice to rename your table and chart blocks with a descriptive or meaningful name. Because Web Intelligence provides a default name for all objects, setting up Relative Positioning can become confusing without descriptive or meaningful name assigned to each object or block.

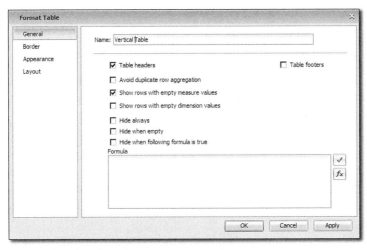

Figure 5.7 General Properties of a Vertical Table

Border Property

The Border property pane allows you to modify many border aspects of a table. You can add a border using the STYLE subtab within the primary FORMAT tab or by right-clicking to select the Border grouping in the Format Table window. You can specify a border style, thickness, and color for the table border. Figure 5.8 shows the properties that can be specified for table borders.

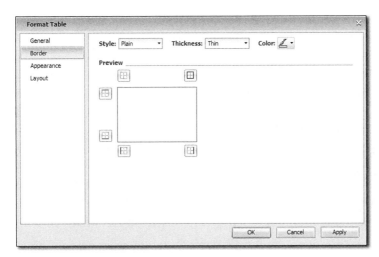

Figure 5.8 Border Properties of a Vertical Table

Appearance Property

The Appearance property pane allows you to modify many visual aspects of a table. Figure 5.9 shows the properties that can be adjusted for table appearances.

- BACKGROUND COLOR: Changes the background color of headers, rows, columns, or cell spacing if the spacing is set to 1 pixel or greater
- BACKGROUND PATTERN: Applies one of these four background images to a selected table section:
  - NONE
  - SKIN: Curve, SAP BusinessObjects, Dots, Draft, Final Copy
  - IMAGE FROM URL: Prompts you to choose display and position of image after entering URL
  - IMAGE FROM FILE: Prompts you to browse for a local or network image
- SPACING: Changes the space format of the cells by modifying the following settings:
  - HORIZONTAL: Modifies the cell spacing of a table (default spacing value set at 0 inches)
  - VERTICAL: Modifies the cell spacing of a table (default spacing value set at 0 inches)
- ALTERNATE COLOR: Adjusts the frequency and color of the alternate row or column coloring

Layout Property

The Layout property pane allows you to assign a variety of positioning settings to report elements in a report. Figure 5.10 shows the properties that can be specified for table layouts. Below is a complete list of page layout properties for both horizontal and vertical table layout:

- START ON A NEW PAGE: Sets the block to start on a new page
- REPEAT ON EVERY NEW PAGE: Sets the cell to repeat on every new page
- AVOID PAGE BREAK IN TABLE: Fits the table onto one page where possible
- REPEAT HEADER ON EVERY PAGE: Repeats the table header on every page
- REPEAT FOOTER ON EVERY PAGE: Repeats the table footer on every page

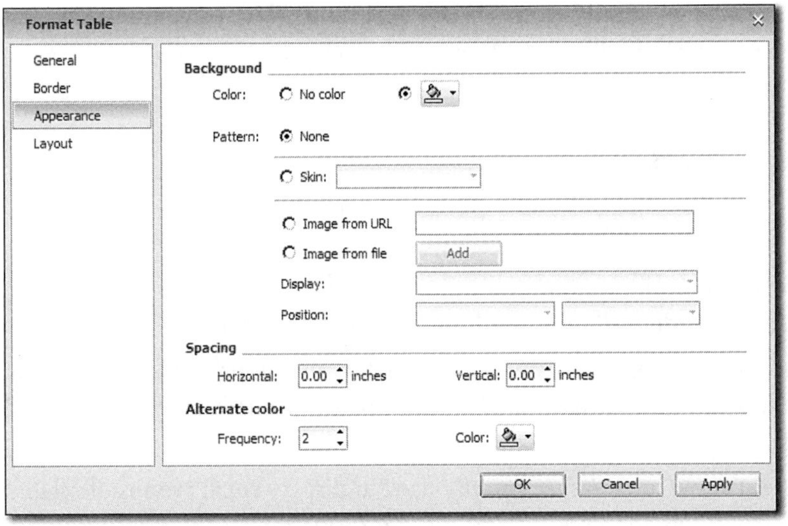

Figure 5.9 Appearance Properties of a Vertical Table

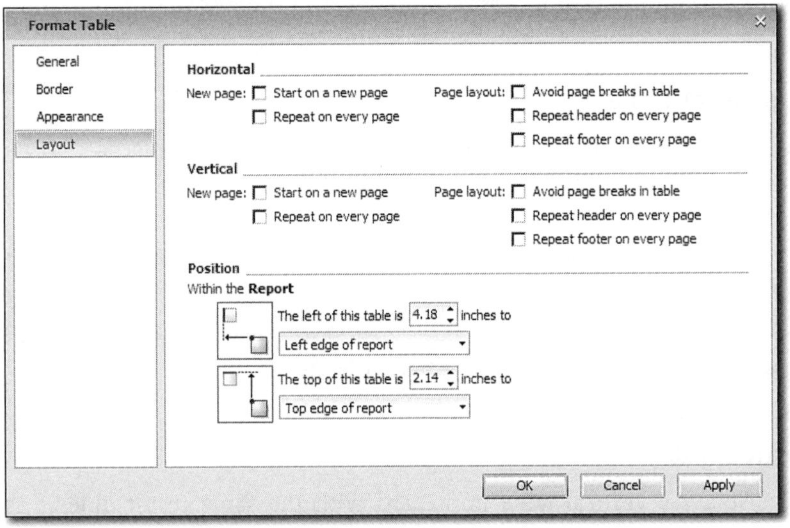

Figure 5.10 Layout Properties of a Vertical Table

You can assign the upper-left corner of a table, chart, or cell to another block by choosing two settings in the Position section of the Layout screen: the left edge and the top edge.

The next section discusses the types of data tables available for you to use in the Report Panel of a Web Intelligence reporting document.

5.2 Table Types

Four table types are available in Web Intelligence BI 4.0:

▶ Horizontal table: Header cells are listed on the left of the table.

▶ Vertical table: Header cells are listed on the top of the table.

▶ Cross table: Dimensions are listed across the top and along the left side of the table. Measures are displayed in the body as a cross-section of the charted dimensions. These are also known as crosstabs.

▶ Form table: These tables are commonly used to display small groups of related information such as addresses or employee information.

The vertical and the cross table are the most commonly used tables. Let's take a look at each table type.

5.2.1 Horizontal Table

Figure 5.11 shows a horizontal table populated with three result objects: [city], [state], and [sales revenue].

City	Austin	Boston	Chicago	Colorado Spr	Dallas	Houston	Los Angeles	Miami	New York	San Francisc	Washington
State	Texas	Massachuse	Illinois	Colorado	Texas	Texas	California	Florida	New York	California	DC
Sales revenu	$2,699,673	$1,283,707	$3,022,658	$2,060,275	$1,970,034	$5,447,957	$4,220,929	$1,879,159	$7,582,221	$3,258,641	$2,961,950

Figure 5.11 Horizontal Table Populated with Three Result Objects

5.2.2 Vertical Table

Figure 5.12 displays a vertical table populated with the same result objects as Figure 5.11.

> **Note**
>
> You can easily add vertical tables to a report by selecting multiple result objects in the AVAILABLE OBJECTS tab and then dragging and dropping them onto the Report Panel.

City	State	Sales revenue
Austin	Texas	$2,699,673
Boston	Massachuset	$1,283,707
Chicago	Illinois	$3,022,658
Colorado Spr	Colorado	$2,060,275
Dallas	Texas	$1,970,034
Houston	Texas	$5,447,957
Los Angeles	California	$4,220,929
Miami	Florida	$1,879,159
New York	New York	$7,582,221
San Francisc	California	$3,258,641
Washington	DC	$2,961,950

Figure 5.12 Vertical Table Populated with Three Result Objects

5.2.3 Cross Table

Figure 5.13 shows a cross table with two dimension objects and a measure.

	2004	2005	2006
Austin	$561,123	$1,003,071	$1,135,479
Boston	$238,819	$157,719	$887,169
Chicago	$737,914	$1,150,659	$1,134,085
Colorado Springs	$448,302	$768,390	$843,584
Dallas	$427,245	$739,369	$803,421
Houston	$1,211,309	$1,990,449	$2,246,198
Los Angeles	$982,637	$1,581,616	$1,656,676
Miami	$405,985	$661,250	$811,924
New York	$1,667,696	$2,763,503	$3,151,022
San Francisco	$721,574	$1,201,064	$1,336,003
Washington	$693,211	$1,215,158	$1,053,581

Figure 5.13 Cross Table with Three Result Objects

Figure 5.14 displays a cross table that contains the same fields as in Figure 5.13, but the dimension objects across the top and along the left side of the table have switched positions to provide the user a different perspective when analyzing the data.

Cross tables are often referred to as *pivot tables* because of their ability to pivot or switch the dimension objects from the top and left sides of the table.

	Austin	Boston	Chicago	Colorado Spr	Dallas	Houston	Los Angeles	Miami	New York	San Francisc	Washington
2004	$561,127	$238,819	$737,914	$448,302	$427,245	$1,211,309	$982,637	$405,985	$1,667,696	$721,574	$693,211
2005	$1,005,071	$157,719	$1,150,659	$768,390	$739,369	$1,990,449	$1,581,616	$661,250	$2,763,503	$1,201,064	$1,215,158
2006	$1,135,479	$887,169	$1,134,085	$843,584	$803,421	$2,246,198	$1,656,676	$811,924	$3,151,022	$1,336,003	$1,053,581

Figure 5.14 Cross Table Displayed with Three Result Objects

5.2.4 Form Table

A form table is most commonly used to display information relating to customers, employees, or other sets of closely related fields and objects.

It is recommended that you add a dimension object at the top of the form table with detail objects added beneath the related dimension item.

Figure 5.15 shows where to drop an object in a form table so it appears as the second dimension in the table.

Year	2004
Sales revenue	$8,095,814

Year	2005
Sales revenue	$13,232,246

Year	2006
Sales revenue	$15,059,143

=[State]

Figure 5.15 Dimension Added to an Existing Form Table

Figure 5.16 shows the finished result of the action displayed in Figure 5.15.

Year	2004
Sales revenue	$1,704,211
State	California

Year	2004
Sales revenue	$448,302
State	Colorado

Figure 5.16 Form Table Displayed with Two Result Objects

The next section discusses the process of converting or turning existing report elements into different display types. You can turn charts into cross tables or vice versa in just a few clicks.

5.3   Converting Table Formats and Types

Tables can be quickly converted to other table types or report element types by right-clicking on a table and selecting TURN INTO. Figure 5.17 shows a selected vertical table with the right-click menu displayed.

Figure 5.17 Right-Click Menu with a Table Selected

> **Note**
>
> To copy and paste a report element, right-click on the table or chart, and click on COPY. Then right-click in the Report Panel, and click on PASTE.
>
> The commonly used procedure of `Ctrl` + `C` followed by `Ctrl` + `V` can also be used to copy and paste report elements in the Report Panel.

When a report is in design mode and TURN INTO is selected by right-clicking on a table or chart, a MORE TRANSFORMATIONS option will be displayed to provide users with more report element choices outside of the six types listed. This option allows you to change the data table to any table or chart with one more click.

Figure 5.18 shows the TURN INTO that is used to convert the current report element to a different element or component type. The current report element type is labeled in the window, and a visual representation of the element type appears, as in Figure 5.18.

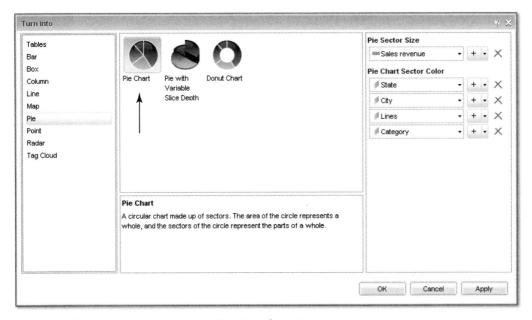

Figure 5.18 Turn Into Options–More Transformations

The next section discusses the use of single blank cells in a report.

5.4 Blank and Predefined Cells

Blank and predefined cells are flexible report elements that can be used for a variety of purposes. These cells can be placed anywhere in the report canvas and can be used for many functional reasons such as displaying informational text, last refreshed dates, and listing drill filter selections and values.

5.4.1 Blank Cells

Blank cells, shown in Figure 5.19, can be used to enhance reports by providing many different descriptive pieces of information. Examples of common uses for blank cells include adding them to display headings, subheadings, instructions, contact information, refresh dates, text labels, single values, formulas, or calculations.

Figure 5.19 Blank Cells Available in the Report Elements Tab

Insert the blank cell report element to strategically place text labels, headings, or other custom values in a report to provide a better context for report consumers. With the blank cell element, you also have the capability to create hyperlinks to other reporting documents, link to a Dashboards flash object, or link to a website. Chapter 14 will go into more detail about hyperlinking in reports.

5.4.2   Predefined Cells

The following nine predefined cells are available in the CELL subtab under the primary REPORT ELEMENTS tab. You can use these cells to insert a specific element of information into a report by inserting the object into the report canvas.

▶ DOCUMENT NAME: Displays the name of the Web Intelligence document. The `DocumentName()` formula is used in this object.

▶ LAST REFRESH DATE: Object used to display the last refresh date of the query in a Web Intelligence document. If two or more queries exist in the document, a Data Provider window will prompt you to select the query to identify the last refresh. The `LastExecutionDate()` formula is used in this object.

▶ DRILL FILTER: A single cell object containing the `DrillFilters()` function. This function becomes useful when dynamic headings or subheadings are required to display the dimensional selections made by users when objects are added to the report filter toolbar.

▶ QUERY SUMMARY: Provides many details relating to the query or queries in the document, including query name, universe name, last refresh date, execution duration, number of rows retrieved, and result objects returned. The `Query Summary()` function is used in this object.

▶ PROMPT SUMMARY: Displays the details of prompted filters. The `Prompt-Summary()` function is used in this object.

▶ REPORT FILTER SUMMARY: Provides details on the filters used in the Report Panel of a document. The function `ReportFilterSummary()` is used in this object.

▶ PAGE NUMBER: Uses the function `Page()` to display the page number.

▶ PAGE NUMBER/TOTAL PAGES: This cell uses the following functions concatenated together to display the current page number followed by the total number of pages in the document: `Page()+"/"+NumberOfPages()`. The end result will be displayed as 1/16 for page 1 of 15. This formula can be modified to display Page 1 of 16 rather than 1/16 by using the following formula: `="Page "+Page()+" of "+NumberOfPages()`.

▶ TOTAL NUMBER OF PAGES: Displays the total number of pages in a report. The function `NumberOfPages ()` is used in this object.

Figure 5.20 shows all available predefined cells that you can drag and drop onto the report canvas.

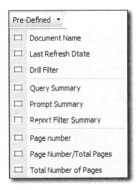

Figure 5.20 Predefined Cells in the Ribbon Toolbar Under Report Elements

5.5   Summary

Tables are the components used by Web Intelligence to visually deliver data in a reporting document. Remember that you can use four different types of tables to present table data, and you can adjust properties settings to modify every aspect of a table report element.

Tables offer the convenience of quickly adding result objects and variables to a report to view data returned from your queries. Table data can be grouped into sections or include breaks to create visually separate groups—all with a single table report element. Enable users to quickly convert table objects into charts with as few as two clicks and use blank or predefined cells to enhance reports to display single value calculations, dynamic headings, hyperlinks, and page numbers.

Chapter 6 will provide an in-depth discussion of displaying data with charts and describe all of the features in the new charting engine introduced in version 4.0.

You can graphically display business data in Web Intelligence reports by using 25 different chart types from 9 different categories. You can add charts to report sections to display data in multiple chart instances by using only a single object.

6   Displaying Data with Charts

Web Intelligence received a major upgrade in version 4.0 with a new charting engine that provides enhanced visual and functional capabilities. Each chart type includes an extensive set of adjustable properties for designing reports that meet any business requirement and display standard.

You can quickly make a visual impact with reports by using one or more of the 25 chart elements to present information. Charts complement data in reports by allowing users to discover data trends graphically, identify issues, and pinpoint outliers at a glance. By using the most appropriate chart for each unique business scenario, you can build powerful reporting applications. Figure 6.1 shows the different report element categories in the left-hand panel, along with the seven column chart types available.

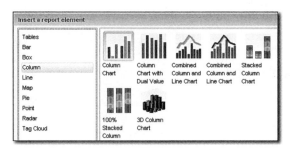

Figure 6.1 Categories of Chart Type Report Elements

In addition to displaying data, charts can function as clickable and interactive objects with the new *element linking* feature or when *drill* is enabled. The drill feature provides the capability for charts or data tables to dynamically navigate up or down a dimensional hierarchy and reveal details at different levels.

Let's first examine how to add chart elements to a report.

6.1   Adding Charts to a Report

You can use two basic methods to add charts to a report, both of which are only available while working in design mode or while you are editing a report.

The first method is accessed by clicking on the REPORT ELEMENT tab in the Report Panel then choosing either the CHART or OTHERS subtab, depending on the chart category required. Figure 6.2 shows these tabs with the CHART tab selected.

Figure 6.2 Adding Common Chart Components from the Report Element Tab

The three most commonly used chart categories are available from within the CHART tab. From this tab, you can add up to 13 different types of column, line, and pie charts to your reports.

Select the OTHERS tab to add bar charts, point charts, or one of the five non-categorized chart types to your report canvas. Figure 6.3 indicates how to access these chart types with the OTHERS tab selected.

Figure 6.3 Adding Chart Components from the Others Tab

Click on the small down arrow located immediately to the right of each chart category to display several specific chart types within the selected category. The following section describes each of these chart types.

Another way to add charts to a report is by right-clicking on a report canvas. From the right-click menu, mouse over INSERT to view several report elements that can be easily added. This option provides a quick way of inserting a new section, data table, chart, or other type of report element into a report.

Figure 6.4 shows the right-click menu and the choices available after hovering over INSERT. Once you make your selection from the list of available choices, you are guided to pick an area on the report canvas to place the element. Click on INSERT A REPORT ELEMENT to view a menu containing every type of report element.

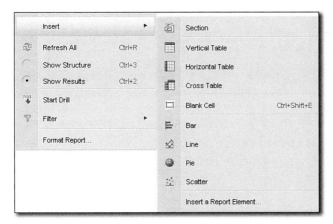

Figure 6.4 Right-Clicking on a Report Canvas Then Hovering Over Insert

Figure 6.5 shows the window with easy access to every chart type or data table separated into functional report element groupings. Select a report element category from the menu to display the available chart types associated with the selection.

Notice that the tools used for assigning data values to the selected report element are listed on the right side of the window. These tools deliver three basic functions:

▶ **Select an object**
Select from any of the available objects in the document. This includes objects retrieved by a query or variables created locally.

▶ **Add an additional object**
Click on the plus (+) symbol or downward arrow symbol to insert, hide, edit, or select a number format of a numerical object.

▶ **Remove an object**
Click on the X symbol to remove any optional object.

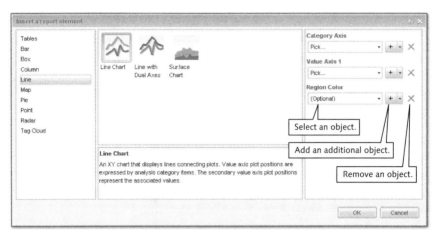

Figure 6.5 Inserting a Report Element

Now that we've covered how to add a chart to a report, let's shift our attention to differentiating between the various types of charts that are available to you.

6.2 Chart Types

A single Web Intelligence report can contain any combination of report elements, and several different charts can appear on the same report. The variety of chart types available provides report designers with the tools needed to create highly customized reporting documents that target the unique needs of displaying complex data while also meeting user requirements. This could mean creating reports with well over 100,000 rows of data or building interactive and visual reports that function similarly to dashboards.

Figure 6.6 shows a report that provides a visual alternative to data tables by displaying data in four different types of charts. The extensive set of editable properties for each chart type makes it possible for designers to customize reports to fit any color scheme or style requirements.

Each chart type provides several different modifiable properties for adjusting the area display, data values, palette and style, background, border, and layout.

Additionally, you can make several modifications to the category axis, value axis, plot area, legend, title, and global features of a bar, column, or line chart. These properties are described in Section 6.3.

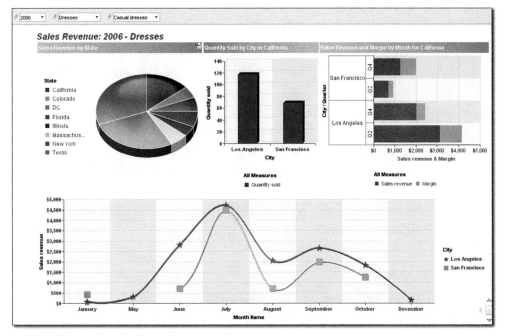

Figure 6.6 Four Charts Types in a Single Report

Sections and Charts

When sections are added to a report, charts containing the section object will break by the section and appear as multiple charts.

6.2.1 Column Charts

Column charts display data vertically and are available in seven different types, including dual axis value, combined, stacked, 3D, and basic columnar style.

The following is the complete list of column chart types as they're described in the Web Intelligence XI 4.0 Report Panel.

▸ Column chart: A chart constructed of vertically oriented rectangular bars. The height of the rectangles is proportional to the values associated with different category items.

▸ Column chart with dual value axes: A column chart with two value axes. It allows one part of a data series to be plotted against one axis and another part of the data series to be plotted against the other axis.

157

▶ Combined column and line chart: A chart displaying a combination of a column chart and a line chart. The chart types share the same value axis.

▶ Combined column and line chart with dual value axes: A chart displaying a combination of a column chart and a line chart. The chart types have their own value axes.

▶ Stacked column chart: A chart constructed of vertically-oriented stacked colored rectangular bars. Rectangles are colored according to the legend entries.

▶ 100% stacked column: A 100% stacked column chart with data displayed as parts of a whole (as percentages). A whole is a column and a series is a subdivision of the column.

▶ 3D column chart: An XYZ column chart. It has a secondary axis that represents an additional analysis category item.

Column Charts

Column charts, which compare dimensional values from at least one measure and dimension object, are the most commonly used chart types for this task. With the new charting engine introduced in Web Intelligence 4.0, these chart types include over 140 adjustable properties for customizing chart objects to fit into any visual style.

In fact, 3D column charts allow the same type of comparisons but with a different graphic effect. Although these chart types are less commonly used than column charts, they provide a useful alternative for communicating results. With a 3D chart, an optional secondary value can be included to visually compare results. Figure 6.7 shows a standard column chart and a 3D column chart with a secondary measure value on the same axis.

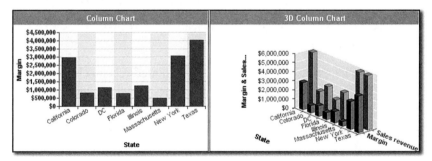

Figure 6.7 Column Chart and 3D Column Chart

Charts are populated with data after they've been added to the report canvas. Once you've added the chart, right-click on a chart and then select ASSIGN DATA from the menu of available choices. Begin assigning dimension or detail objects to the Category Axis section and measure objects to the Value Axis section.

Figure 6.8 shows the Assign Data window that connects data objects to chart elements. You can assign multiple dimensions and measures to a single chart element and you can change the column color using the REGION COLOR option.

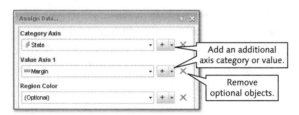

Figure 6.8 Assigning Data to Chart Elements

Dual Value Axes Column Charts

Report designers have several options for displaying multiple measure objects within a single chart. Multiple measures can be displayed in charts on the same axis, but if they have a significantly different factor, they should be displayed on a different axis for readability. Dual value axes chart types are available to handle this requirement.

Figure 6.9 shows a *column chart with dual value axes* and a *combined column and line chart with dual value axes*. Though both charts display the [Margin] and [Sales Revenue] object data, only the version on the right includes a line chart to differentiate the values.

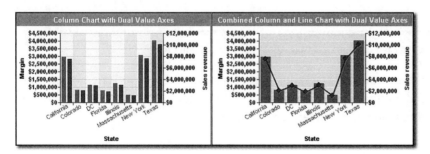

Figure 6.9 Displaying Data in Dual Value Axes Charts

Stacked Column Charts

Stacked column charts are also used to display values from two or more measure objects simultaneously. These chart types should include measure objects representing individual parts of a whole. 100% stacked column charts also display values as part of a whole but with a 100% scale. Each column in a 100% stacked column chart represents the total value, while the stacked items are the individual parts. Figure 6.10 shows a stacked column chart and a 100% stacked column chart that both contain the [Margin] and [Sales revenue] objects charted by [State]. You can mouse over each charted data element to view the dimensional description and value of the item. This feature exists for every chart type and is a beneficial to users when analyzing data subsets. When drill is enabled, the charted columns and category axis values can be used to navigate up and down the hierarchy of dimensional objects as preconfigured in the universe.

> **Note**
>
> When drill is enabled, mouse-over information for charted measures is displayed. This information is replaced with a statement indicating what will occur if the column is clicked. The message displayed on mouse-over with drill enabled will generally read *drill up to <dimension object name>* or *drill down to <dimension object name>*.
>
> You must disable drill to view the charted values on mouse-over.

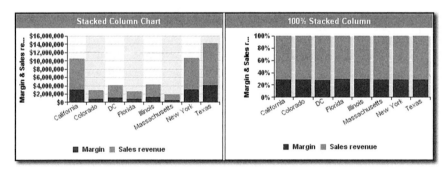

Figure 6.10 Stacked Column Chart and 100% Stacked Column Chart

One requirement of the stacked column chart is to include at least two measure objects and a dimension or detail object. Without a second measure object, the chart will function as a standard column chart.

The 100% stacked column chart requires at least two measure objects. With only a single measure object, every column would convert to 100%.

A second dimension object can also be added to a stacked column chart. Visual groupings in the category axis are created when a second dimension object is added. Figure 6.11 shows a stacked column chart with two measures and two dimensions while hovering over the charted revenue value for Los Angeles.

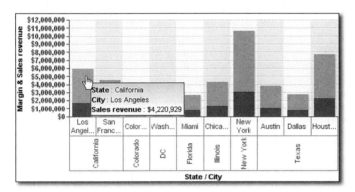

Figure 6.11 Stacked Column Chart with Two Dimensions and Two Measures

6.2.2 Line Charts

Line charts are primarily used to measure performance over a period of time. When you measure values using line charts, you can quickly identify upward and downward trends over time intervals, reoccurring patterns, and spikes of proportionally high and low values.

Line charts allow users to pinpoint patterns and quickly identify points in time when significant trends start, end, and peak. One method that can be used to easily identify when trends are significant is to add a variable to a line chart that calculates the average of a measure being charted. By adding this additional object, movement of data above or below the average is easily detected. This method of analysis provides an additional visual indicator for the user and helps demonstrate exactly when a measure began trending above or below an average and whether the trend is worthy of further investigation.

Line Chart Types

These are three different types of line charts, as described in Web Intelligence 4.0:

▶ Line chart: An XY chart that displays lines connecting plots. Value axis plot positions are expressed by analysis category items. The secondary value axis plot positions represent the associated values.

▶ Line with dual axes: An XY chart with two axes displaying lines connecting plots. Category axis plot positions signify analysis category items. The value axis plot positions, on both axes, represent the associated values.

▶ Surface chart: An XY chart that displays a surface made up of a connection of plots.

Let's examine each of these.

Line Chart Types

Standard line charts are the primary component used to display data trends over intervals of time. Use *line charts with dual axes* to display the correlative trend of two measures across a specified period of time. These chart types are used when the values are related but are of a significantly different factor.

In Figure 6.12, a standard line chart is presented along with a line chart with dual axes. In the dual axes example, the monthly correlation of the [Quantity sold] and [Sales revenue] measures is displayed. Because the factor of these two measures is significantly different, the dual axes chart resolves the issue.

Key Applications of Line Charts
▶ Display data across time
▶ Analyze patterns in interval data
▶ Identify data shifts in trend data
▶ Recognize seasonal cycles
▶ Pinpoint high and low spikes in the data

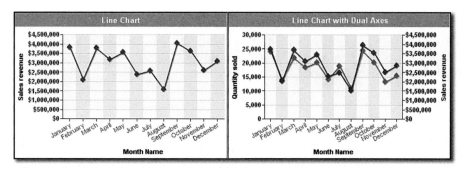

Figure 6.12 Standard Line Chart and a Line Chart with Dual Axes

Surface Charts

Surface charts—also known as area charts—are used to provide a visual representation of data made up of connection plots. These chart types are used in similar scenarios as line chart and display a series of data points connected by a line with the area filled in below the line. Surface charts and line charts are the only chart categories intended to display contiguous data.

Web Intelligence 4.0 provides a large number of adjustable properties to modify the appearance of charts. Within these properties is the capability to modify the *region type* of a chart type. You can access this setting by right-clicking on a chart and selecting FORMAT CHART. Locate the Global property group and select REGION TYPE. From this window you can change the type to bars, lines, or surfaces. Select SURFACES as the region type to convert it to an area display. Figure 6.13 shows a surface chart and a *line chart with dual axes* with the [Quantity sold] object's region type property changed to surface.

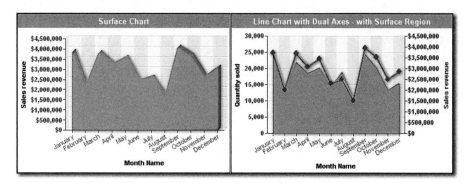

Figure 6.13 Surface Chart and Line Chart with Dual Axes with Surface Region

> **Note**
>
> Surface regions should never be used on both axes of a dual axes chart because the shaded surface area from one value axes will always cover at least a portion of the charted surface of the other axes.

6.2.3 Pie Charts

Pie charts are used to show dimensional values as a proportion of the whole dataset. The pie or donut represents the sum total of a measure, while each slice represents the individual parts that are added together to become the whole.

Only one dimension can exist in a pie chart, and values can't represent over 100% of the measure being evaluated. These are the three chart types available in Web Intelligence 4.0, followed by their descriptions as they appear in the Report Panel:

► Pie chart: A circular chart made of sectors. The area of the circle represents a whole, and the sectors of the circle represent the parts of a whole.

► Pie with variable slice depth: A circular chart made up of sectors. The area of the circle represents a whole, and the sectors of the circle represent the parts of the whole. The sectors may have some depth expressing a third value.

► Donut chart: A ring-shaped chart that is similar to a pie chart.

Let's expand on these further.

Pie and Donut Charts

Pie charts are useful when displaying values as proportions of the whole. Data values in pie charts are displayed in slices for each dimension object value and interpreted as a percentage of the whole. Properties can be configured to display several descriptive data labels including the value, label, percentage, or a combination of two labels. The data label position can be assigned to appear either inside or outside the pie, and the label layout can be positioned on the side of the pie or in a circular layout.

Other attributes can also be enabled or configured including the following: 3D look, color palette adjustments, textures, light and shadow effects, background color assignment, and border assignments.

Figure 6.14 shows a standard pie chart followed by a donut chart, with both charts displaying the same measure and dimension object.

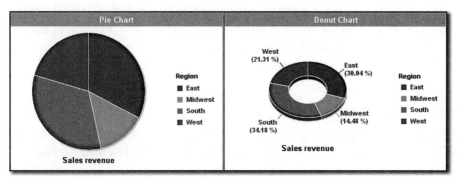

Figure 6.14 Pie Chart and Donut Chart

The donut chart in the example has 3D enabled, displays data labels for the dimensional label, and shows the percent value of each slice. These values are configured by right-clicking on the chart object and selecting FORMAT CHART. Many of the configurable appearance settings are located within the global properties group.

Pie with Variable Slice Depth

A new type of pie chart was introduced in Web Intelligence 4.0 that allows report designers to communicate two values within a single pie chart. This new component provides a depth dimension to pie charts and displays values from a second measure through exploding pie slices.

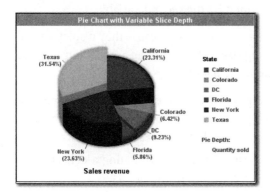

Figure 6.15 Pie Chart with Variable Slice Depth

The chart pictured in Figure 6.15 shows values from the [Sales revenue] and [Quantity sold] measures in a variable slice depth pie chart by state values.

In the figure, the size of each dimensional slice represents each state's sales revenue as a percentage of the whole group of states. The depth dimension in the pie chart illustrates the quantity sold by state. It's easy to see a correlation between the two measures when both measures are represented in the same chart.

Charting in Business Reports

When you use variable slice depth pie charts in reports, make sure that the results can be easily interpreted by the intended audience. Misrepresented or misinterpreted data can lead to costly mistakes and potentially catastrophic situations. Always create thoroughly labeled report elements that describe the measures, dimensions, and context of the information being presented. Formula-driven title labels, legends, category values, and data labels should be used when appropriate to thoroughly communicate information to report consumers.

6.2.4 Point Charts

Use scatter charts to plot the values of two variables and to display the correlation in the style of linear regression. Bubble charts display values similar to scatter charts but with varying sizes of bubbles to represent the values of a third variable. Other types of point charts include polar scatter and polar bubble charts; both of these chart types are used to display data points with a radial axis and an angular axis on a circular charting canvas rather than a standard rectangular canvas. Values are spread over 360 degrees, and data points are plotted between two numbers and then located within bands defined by the second variable.

Polar bubble charts go a step further than polar charts because they display a third value and present the bubbles in varying sizes. The following are the four types of point charts, as described in Web Intelligence 4.0:

▶ Scatter chart: An XY chart displaying plots. Plots are positioned with coordinates given by a pair of values. Each plot may have colored symbols representing the analysis category item associated with the values.

▶ Bubble chart: A two-dimensional chart of points representing a collection of data. Extra variables are represented by the size of the points.

▶ Polar scatter chart: A chart with one radial axis and one angular axis, where each data point is represented with a symbol. Similar to a bubble chart but without the sizing of points.

▶ Polar bubble chart: A two-dimensional chart with one radial axis and one angular axis of points representing a collection of data. Extra variables are represented by the size of the data points.

Scatter Charts

Scatter charts are used to display the correlation of two variables. Depending on the relationship of the charted values, trends can be easily observed that illustrate the strength or weakness in the correlation of the variables used to plot the data points. Many analysts view scatter charts as one of the best components for visualizing data and locating trouble areas to investigate further.

Positive trends are observed when the plotted data points ascend on both the X and Y axes, moving from the lower-left corner of the chart to the upper-right corner. This type of trend is pictured in Figure 6.16. The example shows a linear or straight line trend that proves that when [Quantity sold] increases, the [Sales revenue] also increases. Even though a trend is observed in the plotted points, you can still identify outliers. The screenshot shows that when the plotted values from July are compared to those from November, [Sales revenue] actually decreased, while the amount of [Quantity sold] increased.

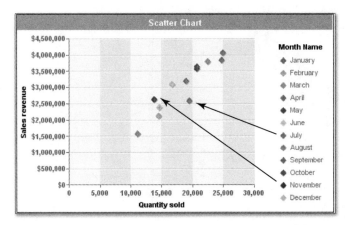

Figure 6.16 Scatter Chart with a Positive Trend Correlating Sales Revenue and Quantity Sold

These findings provide valuable insight into potential revenue issues that deserve additional research. The result of the findings could uncover problems that have caused decreased profits.

Negative trends are observed when one set of data increases while the other decreases. In these scenarios, the plotted data points move in an organized fashion from the upper-left corner of the chart toward the lower-right corner.

If no pattern is observed among the plotted data points, then no relationship exists for the charted variables.

Bubble Charts

Bubble charts produce results very similar to those of scatter charts but with one addition—the potential to add a third variable to the chart to represent the data in bubble sizes. If patterns are observed in the plotted bubbles, then a relationship exists for the variables being charted.

Figure 6.17 shows a bubble chart with the same information displayed in the scatter chart shown in Figure 6.16 but with the addition of increasing bubble sizes to represent the values of a third measure. You can enhance the appearance of the bubbles by making adjustments to several configurable properties available in the Format Chart window. Many of the visual settings can be found when editing settings in the Palette and Style section located in the global chart settings.

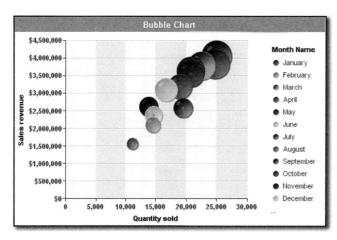

Figure 6.17 Bubble Charts Displaying the Correlation of Two Measures

Polar Charts

Polar charts display a series of values grouped by a dimensional result object on a 360-degree circle. Values are measured by their lengths from the center of the chart. The farther the point is away from the center, the larger the value.

Figure 6.18 shows a polar scatter chart with [Sales revenue] and [Quantity sold] values plotted by [Region]. The chart plots the values on the 360-degree canvas by the amount of quantity sold and within multiple sales revenue bands on the circular background.

Figure 6.19 shows the same values charted on a polar bubble chart but with a third variable. The polar bubble chart displays bubble sizes based on the relative size of the values in the [Margin] object.

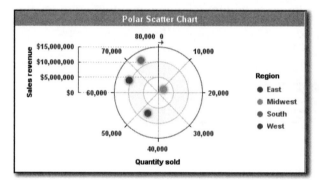

Figure 6.18 Polar Scatter Chart with Two Measures Plotted

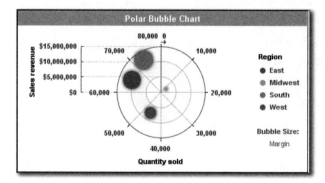

Figure 6.19 Polar Bubble Chart with Three Measures Plotted

6.2.5 Bar Charts

Bar charts produce an effect similar to that of column charts but display information in horizontal bars rather than vertical columns.

You can use bar charts in reports to compare dimensional information with values from at least one measure and dimension object. These chart types are commonly used to present dimensional values so they can be read easier. Figure 6.20 shows a bar chart with the [Sales revenue] measure presented by the [Lines] dimension. Hover over a bar to see the exact measurement values.

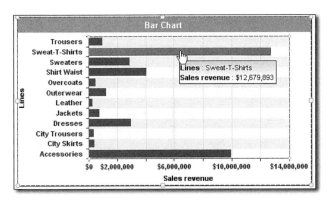

Figure 6.20 Bar Chart

The following bar charts are available for your use:

▶ Bar chart: A chart constructed of horizontally oriented rectangular bars. The height of the rectangles is proportional to the values associated to different category items.

▶ Stacked bar chart: A horizontal bar chart that displays data as a series of bars. It is best used for representing three series of data, where each series is represented by a color stacked in a single bar.

▶ 100% stacked bar: A stacked bar chart with data displayed as parts of a whole (as percentages). A whole is a bar and a series is a subdivision of the bar.

When adding stacked bar charts to reports, include at least two measure objects and at least one dimension or detail object. Without a second measure object, the chart will function as a standard bar chart.

The 100% stacked bar chart requires at least two measure objects. With only a single measure object, every column would convert to 100%. You can use this type of chart to present measures as a percent of whole values by a dimension.

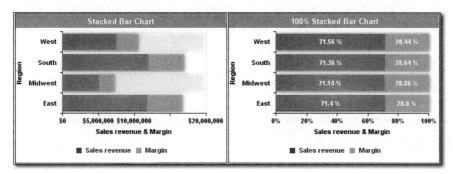

Figure 6.21 Stacked Bar and 100% Stacked Bar Chart

6.2.6 Other Chart Types

Five additional chart types within Web Intelligence 4.0 provide report designers with even more options for displaying data:

▶ Box plot: A box plot is a graphical display of a five-number summary based on the distribution of a dataset: the maximum, the minimum, the first quartile, the third quartile, and the median. It can also show abnormal values called outliers.

▶ Radar: A radar chart (also known as a spider chart) displays several axes starting from a unique origin and with a common scale. Each axis represents an analysis category item. Plots are directly placed on an axis according to the associated values. Plots can be linked by lines.

▶ Tree map: This chart displays values within nested rectangles that can be colored. The levels of nesting correspond to the level of hierarchical breakdown. The size of the rectangles and their color both express a set of values.

▶ Heat map: This map displays values that are represented by colors in a map using a category axis and optionally a second category axis. The colors of the rectangles are determined by a measure value.

▶ Tag cloud: A mono-dimensional visualization representing data as words. A word's font size represents its relative weight in the dataset.

Let's examine each of these further.

Box Plot and Radar Charts

Box plot charts are used to show the distribution of data ranges for a dimension object into five primary groupings. Each chart will also contain a category dimension to axis value. These charts show the following elements of information in a single graphic:

- ▶ Maximum: Highest value, excluding outliers
- ▶ First (or upper) quartile: 25% percent of the values are greater than this value
- ▶ Median: Middle of the dataset
- ▶ Third (or lower) quartile: 75% percent of the values are greater than this value
- ▶ Minimum: Lowest value, excluding outliers

Outliers are displayed in dots and plotted either above the maximum or below the minimum markings. These values can be hidden by checking the HIDE OUTLIERS options located in the Plot Area section available when formatting the chart. Figure 6.22 shows the different segments of a charted box plot. Figure 6.23 shows a box plot chart showing the monthly value ranges for values within the [Quarter] object used as the primary category axis dimension, and compares it to a radar chart.

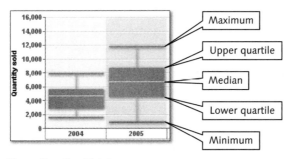

Figure 6.22 Box Plot Ranges

Radar charts are used to quickly convey the "big picture" of one or more variables through a dimensional object. The primary benefit of radar charts is that they allow the user to analyze several different factors related to a single item. The points closest to the center of the axis indicate low values, while the charted points near the edge indicate high values. The right side of Figure 6.23 shows a radar chart displaying [Sales revenue] and [Margin] values by region.

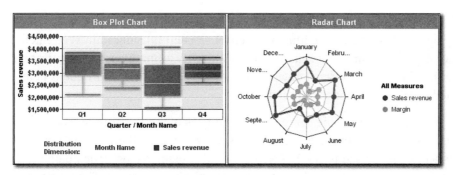

Figure 6.23 Box Plot Chart and Radar Chart

Tree and Heat Map

Tree maps are used for displaying hierarchical data to allow users to quickly identify unexpected patterns, exceptions, and significant factors. Data values are then displayed in rectangular areas of varying sizes, color, and position. Figure 6.24 shows a tree map chart with [Sales revenue] values charted by [Category] and [Lines] values, and also a heat map chart on the right side of the figure. You can mouse over the rectangles to show a tooltip that includes the dimension and measure values of the rectangle.

Heat map charts also display data in rectangular shapes but with a slightly different way of using color. The box style of charted values is also different in the heat map compared to the tree map. Heat maps let you display data from one or more dimensional category axis values and a single measure object; you can add a secondary category axis value when assigning data to a chart.

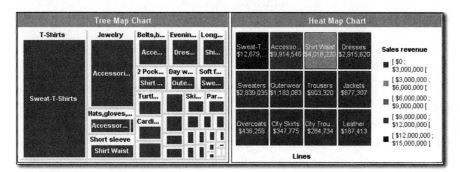

Figure 6.24 Tree Map and Heat Map Charts

Tag Cloud

The tag cloud chart is an exciting new report element introduced in Web Intelligence 4.0. This component is used to represent data values by using only the text data in a dimension or detail object. The size of each dimensional value is determined by the associated measure object.

When assigning data to the component, the Tag Name setting is used to associate a dimension object and the Tag Weight setting is where the measure object is assigned. Objects used in the Tag Name should contain values made up of either single words or very short phrases for clearly displaying results. The purpose of the component is to quickly show the prominence of specific terms. Figure 6.25 shows a tag cloud component created using the [Lines] object and [Sales revenue] object. You can use the component to pass values to other report elements on the canvas with the *add element link* feature or to drill into a hierarchy.

Figure 6.25 Tag Cloud Chart

Another valuable option is to transform one chart into another type, which potentially offers different information.

Converting Chart Types

You can easily convert charts into data tables or other chart types by right-clicking on a chart object while in design mode and selecting TURN INTO. This method of converting an existing chart or table provides seven choices: vertical table, horizontal table, cross table, column, line, pie, and other transformations. Select the MORE TRANSFORMATIONS option to launch a window that gives you the opportunity to convert the existing chart to any chart group, and then choose from any of the 25 chart types or 4 data table types.

Now that we have examined the various types of charts at your disposal, let's transition to the properties that govern those charts.

6.3   Chart Properties

Chart properties in Web Intelligence 4.0 have been dramatically improved over all previous versions of the product. With over 140 different properties available, report designers have more choices than ever to create highly customized and formatted charts and reports. Each chart type contains its own set of properties for displaying data values, changing the presentation effect and style, and applying formatting to titles, legends, and axis values.

To begin customizing the format of a chart, enter design mode and then right-click on the chart to be edited. With the menu displayed, click on FORMAT CHART to launch the chart editor and begin making changes to the properties and attributes. Chart properties are grouped into major categories for logical access: global, title, legend, category axis, value axis, and plot area.

Figure 6.26 displays the categories of a column chart. Here, the global properties are listed, and the other five property categories are minimized at the bottom left of the figure.

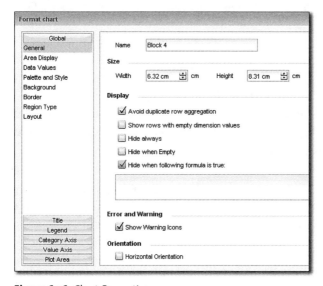

Figure 6.26 Chart Properties

Each category contains specific properties that can be modified to change the style and visual presentation. To access the individual properties, click on the category groupings located on the left side of the format editor.

You can modify individual properties by selecting the subgroup of each property category then manipulating the specific options on the right side of the editor. Property subgroups provide and even more detailed collection of properties.

▶ **Global property category**
Use the global category to revise properties that apply to the entire chart. Eight subgroups are available within the global category:

  ▷ General: Edit the name and size of the chart and enable settings to hide the chart dynamically with a formula.

  ▷ Area Display: Enable or disable a chart title and edit the title label. Use the formula editor to create a dynamic title. Also change the visibility of chart axes, legends, and data values.

  ▷ Data Values: Check SHOW DATA VALUES to display the values being charted. Customize the data type being displayed, data position, orientation, and font properties.

  ▷ Palette and Style: Make visual changes by setting the 3D look, color palette, marker symbols, bar effects, and light and shadow effects. This subgroup of properties provides several advanced capabilities to generate highly customized chart objects.

  ▷ Background: Assign the background color to be RGBA color or gradient.

  ▷ Border: Assign the style, thickness, color, and border type.

  ▷ Region Type: Switch the chart type to bars, lines, or surfaces.

  ▷ Layout: Enable or disable layout properties such as starting on a new page, avoiding page break, repeating on every page, and assigning the relative position to other report elements on the canvas.

▶ **Title property category**
Use this property category to apply a dynamic or static title and edit the layout spacing, orientation, location, layout width, layout height, font properties, and border and background choices.

▶ **Legend property category**
Use this property category to modify properties associated with the legend values or title of the legend. These properties include making it visible and

choosing symbol size, layout location, spacing, orientation, text and font properties, and border and background settings.

▶ **Category axis**

Use this property category to apply visual settings to axis values. Settings include hiding or display the category axis itself and adjusting axis orientation, reverse order on axis, color options, and font properties.

▶ **Value axis**

Use this property category to hide the axis, change the stacking type, modify the scaling method, adjust the layout and orientation, provide changes to color options, edit font properties, and assign a number format.

▶ **Plot area**

Use this property category to make the following adjustments to the plot area settings: invert superimposition order of series, spacing within and between groups, grid and background style, color, and lighting.

Useful Chart Properties

With over 140 adjustable properties, some of the most significant properties can be difficult to locate. Don't overlook these properties when creating charts that engage users and display information in meaningful, actionable and insightful ways:

▶ GLOBAL • PALETTE AND STYLE

　▶ 3D Look Depth: 3D Look—Enhances the visual display of the report element to produce a 3D effect

　▶ Bar Display Effects: Volume Effects—Adjusts the width and brightness in addition to adding volume effects to applicable chart types

　▶ Light and Shadow Effects: Real Lighting and Complex Shadows—Creates the illusion of subtle light with shadows behind the charted values

　▶ Line Display Effects: Volume Effects—Adds thickness to a line to produce a fuller visual impact

　▶ Line Display Effects: Spline Line—Produces lines with smoothed curves at the data point locations (also known as a smoothing spline)

　▶ Region Type: Select surfaces to change chart type to an area chart

　▶ Layout: Relative Positioning

▸ PLOT AREA • BACKGROUND

  ▸ Grid and Background: Striped Background

▸ CATEGORY AXIS • DESIGN

  ▸ Layout: Reverse Order on the Category Axis

Figure 6.27 shows the same basic line chart twice, but several properties have been adjusted on the right. These adjustments include enabling the 3D look, increasing the line width, checking the spline line option in the Line Display Effects section, and selecting the Volume Effects setting.

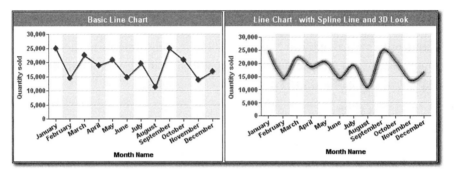

Figure 6.27 Basic Line Chart With and Without Property Changes

Other options are available when right-clicking on an existing chart. These actions are available when you right-click on a chart:

▸ Cut: Remove a chart from a report; paste becomes enabled after CUT has been selected

▸ Copy: Select COPY to begin the copy/paste process of duplicating a chart or data table (you must use this method to copy instead of the commonly used [Ctrl]+[C] command)

▸ Delete: Remove a chart from a report

▸ Turn into: Switch the existing report element to another chart type or data table

▸ Assign data: Assign the dimension, detail, or measure objects to the chart

▸ Linking: Add hyperlinks or element links to other report elements

▸ Start drill: Enable simple filtering to constrain information on reports

▸ Filter: Add a new filter to the selected chart or add a new input control

- Sort: Select Manage Sorts to define a new sort to apply to the object
- Hide: Hide the object, enable the chart to hide when empty, or select Hide When to create a formula and force the object to only be displayed when the criteria defined in the formula is met
- Order: Layer objects, including bring to front, send to back, bring forward, and send backward
- Align: Select two or more objects to align the objects by left, center, right, top, middle, and bottom (also available are relative position, show grid, snap to grid, and grid settings options)
- Format chart: Launch the extensive chart formatting editor
- Publish as web service: Launch the Publish Content window to generate a web service from the values in the selected object and use web services as a data source for SAP BusinessObjects Dashboards

These options are very useful when customizing charts to fit your organization's needs.

6.4 Summary

When you have access to 25 different chart types and over 140 modifiable properties, visually presenting data to users can be a simple or highly customized experience. The chart types include seven column charts, three bar charts, three line charts, four point charts, and three pie charts. In addition, five additional chart types are available for displaying data in a less traditional form with types such as a tree map, heat map, box plot, radar chart, and tag cloud.

Report designers have never had more choices for the customization of reports than with the features available in Web Intelligence 4.0. You can alter charts to include volume effects, a 3D appearance, and several adjustable light and shadowing effects. In addition to formatting reports and reporting elements, you can convert individual charts into other chart types or data tables with as few as three clicks, create a dynamic chart title with formula capabilities, and apply custom formatting to every axis category and title.

Chapter 7 goes a step further and discusses many advanced topics concerning charting.

With the new charting engine in Web Intelligence 4.0, you can produce visual reports that vividly illustrate the data being displayed. Explore the extensive chart properties to create highly customized reports that generate the maximum impact for each unique scenario.

7   Making an Impact with Charts

Web Intelligence is known for its ability to retrieve high volumes of data and produce detailed analytical reports. After data is returned to the Report Panel, analysis is enhanced through the use of features such as simple filters, drilling, and input controls. As of version 4.0, charting can also be included in the list of powerful devices for displaying information and emphasizing important values. The new charting engine upgrades the tool's capabilities to present information in over 24 different customizable and visually engaging chart components. Each chart type provides properties to configure the finest of details, with many charts offering over 200 adjustable settings.

Charts also provide an intuitive method for drilling into results and guiding users to details at lower levels or aggregating up to higher levels in a hierarchy. Navigation can be synchronized when more than one chart is displayed in a report and both contain hierarchical dimension values and when drilling has been enabled.

Displaying hierarchical data in charts is possible for data sourced from either multidimensional or relational data sources. Options are provided to produce visual groupings when more than one dimension object is added to a chart and display multilevel analysis within a single graphic.

This chapter covers all these topics and provides examples to help you make an appropriate visual impact with charts based on the data requirements and audience expectations.

7.1   Properties that Enhance the Display of Data

Whether you're using bar charts, column charts, or scatter charts to display data, the number of available configurable properties varies for each chart type. Properties range from making simple font changes in chart titles to enabling 3D look and applying complex shadows in the Light and Shadow Effects setting in the global Palette and Style property category to maximize the visual impression of data.

These steps explain how you can begin modifying chart properties:

1. Enter design mode.

2. Right-click on the chart to be edited.

3. Select FORMAT CHART.

Before making changes to the visual presentation of a chart, be sure that you understand the business reason behind every modification. Visual changes configured simply to add flair or contrast may be useful in some scenarios but will not be well received in every business setting. In fact, there are several things you should consider planning and making visual changes to charts:

▶ The users' expectations

▶ The client's visual standards

▶ Graphics and colors that enrich the communication of results

▶ Clear display of data that is not confusing and does not misrepresent

▶ Color scheme (colors should not provide meaning because up to 10% of users are colorblind)

Remember that visual attributes should be used to enhance the data being presented rather than distract users or detract from the content being displayed. Information should be easy to read and understand, not confusing or misleading.

Report element placement is also very important when presenting information with charts. Layouts should be well aligned and precisely placed on the report canvas. Consumer confidence is greatly diminished when report elements are misaligned, have inconsistent sizes, or are created with erratic color schemes. You can use the width and height adjustment options in the FORMAT tab and the SIZE subtab to make precise adjustments to chart element widths and heights.

To align two or more charts, hold down the ⌐Ctrl⌐ key and select all the charts that need to be aligned. Then right-click and select ALIGN. Alignment options include align left, center, right, or top, middle, bottom.

Modifying Chart Properties

The Format Chart window in Web Intelligence 4.0 provides a tremendous number of options for configuring charts. With just a few adjustments, standard reports with charts can be elevated to visually stunning report/dashboard hybrids, or dashports. Let's explore configurable options available in the Format Chart window that can be used to change the appearance of a chart. Every chart type contains unique options available only to that chart type, as well as several settings that can apply all chart types.

The settings described next present the options available in column chart.

Global Configurable Options

▶ General: Use this category to rename the chart, adjust the width and height of the entire report element, and assign up to 8 different display options, including settings that show measure or dimension values when empty. From here you can also show error and warning icons when chart drivers encounter incorrect data values and whether you can change the axis orientation when configuring a bar or column chart.

▶ Area Display: Use this category to add a dynamic title label with a formula and also to select a location (top, bottom, left, or right) to display the chart title. Other options include the ability to show or hide category axis labels, values, title, data values displayed on the charted shape, and legend details.

▶ Region Type: Use this category to quickly switch the chart type to bars, lines or surfaces. Select surfaces to convert to an area chart.

▶ Data Values: Check the DATA LABEL DISPLAYING MODE option to display data values on the charted shapes and to configure the appearance of the following data labels:

  ▶ Data Type: Choose from displaying the data by value, label, or percent

  ▶ Data Position: Select the position to display the data label

In a column or bar chart, change the orientation from vertical to horizontal. Configure a variety of font properties, including: font size, border size, border color, spacing, and background color.

► Palette and Style: Enhance your chart with depth, color, and other effects (as seen in Figure 7.1):

  ► Depth: 2D look or 3D look

  ► Palette: 12 different palette combinations and a slider to adjust the transparency effect from 0 to 100% for opaque to invisible

  ► Chart Series Style

    – Bar Effects: None, volume, gradient, glossy, cylinder, or light glossy

    – Light and Shadow Effects: No filter, simple lighting, simple shadows, simple lighting and shadows, real lighting, complex shadows, real lighting and complex shadows, and image embossed with lighting and complex shadows

After you select a LIGHT AND SHADOW EFFECT from the GLOBAL • PALETTE AND STYLE grouping, you have five additional options that enable additional customization and precise adjustments. Figure 7.1 shows the modifiable options available when you select REAL LIGHTING AND COMPLEX SHADOWS:

► LIGHT POWER: Define ranges from –1.00 to 1.00

► SHADOW X OFFSET: Allowable range: 0 to 0.52 cm

► SHADOW Y OFFSET: Allowable range: 0 to 0.52 cm

► FILTER PASS COUNT: Define the complexity of the effect; set from 1 to 9

► FILTER WINDOW SIZE: Determine the smoothness of the shade; set from 1 to 9

► SHADOW COLOR: Choose between RGBA color and gradient

► Background: Choose between RGBA color and gradient

► Border: Select a border style, thickness, color, and border area

► Layout

  ► Start on a Page (enable/disable)

  ► Avoid Page Break (enable/disable)

  ► Relative Position: Set the element's location relative to another object

Figure 7.1 Palette and Style Options on the Global Category

Title Category Options

▶ Design

- ▶ General: Display/hide the title and configure the title label

- ▶ Layout: Select the layout location of the title (top, bottom, left, right) and select the orientation and spacing of the title

- ▶ Text: Define font properties and set a text policy to wrap, truncate, or choose to not wrap long titles

- ▶ Border and Background: Choose a border size (none, thin, medium, thick), border color, and background color

Legend Category Options

▶ Design

- ▶ Set the legend to be visible or not visible (checkbox option)

- ▶ Layout: Select the location of the legend (top, bottom, left, right)

- ▶ Group by Dimension (enable/disable)
- ▶ Spacing: Options range from 0 to 8
- ▶ Orientation: Automatic or vertical lettering
- ▶ Symbol Size: Options range from 4 to 32
- ▶ Text: Define font properties and set a text policy to wrap, truncate, or choose to not wrap long titles
- ▶ Border and Background: Choose a border size (none, thin, medium, thick), border color, and background color
- ▶ Legend Title
  - ▶ Set the legend to be visible or not visible (checkbox option)
  - ▶ Display an automatic title or create a custom title
  - ▶ Layout: Define the spacing and orientation
  - ▶ Text: Define font properties and set a text policy to wrap, truncate, or choose to not wrap long titles
  - ▶ Border and Background: Choose a border size (none, thin, medium, thick), border color, and background color

Category Axis Options

- ▶ Design
  - ▶ Display/hide the category axis (checkbox option)
  - ▶ Layout: Enable/disable the following options:
    - Display axis
    - Reverse order on the category axis
    - Continuous axis layout
    - Show labels
    - Adjust layout: Define the width and height to automatic, fixed, or proportional
    - Display staggered axis labels: Wrap, truncate, or no wrap
  - ▶ Color Options: Choose from RGBA color or gradient for the following: Axis color, grid color, and grid background color.
  - ▶ Text: Define font settings

▶ Title

   ▶ Enable/disable the category axis label and choose a title label type between an automatic or custom title (optionally apply a label separator)

   ▶ Layout: Revise the title spaces within allowable range from 0 to 8

   ▶ Text: Configure font settings

   ▶ Border and Background: Define the border size, color, and background color

Value Axis Options

▶ Design

   ▶ Display/hide the Value Axis (checkbox option)

   ▶ Stacking: Unstacked, stacked, globally stacked chart, scaling, and layout (also use this option to include a Region Color when assigning data to a chart)

   ▶ Scaling: Choose the origin in range from always or automatic and define axis scaling from linear or logarithmic (also use this option to set a minimum and maximum value to the chart and set a unit scale factor that ranges from 0 to 24)

   ▶ Layout: Enable/disable the display axis, show labels, adjust layout, and display staggered axis labels

   ▶ Color Options: Set the axis color to either RGBA color or gradient

   ▶ Text: Define font settings

▶ Title

   ▶ General: Enable/disable the axis title

   ▶ Layout: Revise the title spaces within allowable range from 0 to 8

   ▶ Text: Configure font settings

   ▶ Border and Background: Define the border size, color, and background color

Plot Area Options

▶ Design:

   ▶ Enable/disable the Invert Superimposition order of series setting and set the spacing within groups and spacing between groups with range from −1.00 to 1.00

- ▸ Background
  - ▸ Grid and Background: Set the background of a chart to be either plain background or striped background, and make specific color changes to the following:
    - – Background color
    - – Category axis grid color
    - – Value axis grid color

Additionally, the option to show or hide a dashed line is presented in the section.

Careful configuration of chart properties can make a significant difference in the way data is displayed when presented to users.

7.2 Drilling in Reports with Multiple Charts

It's common for two or more charts to appear on a report canvas and it's crucial that the information remain accurate after drilling occurs. As users begin to drill into charted values and analyze data at a finer granularity, the current dimension value is replaced by the next dimension in the hierarchy setup at the universe level. To further extend drilling capabilities, you need to increase the scope level in the Scope of Analysis pane in the Query Panel to the needed level.

When multiple charts or tables on the same report canvas contain the same dimensional value, drilling can be synchronized between the components when only one value is selected.

To enable synchronized drilling, click on the PREFERENCES link in the BI Launch Pad and then select WEB INTELLIGENCE from the list of preference categories. Scroll down to the DRILL OPTIONS section and check the box labeled SYNCHRONIZE DRILL ON REPORT BLOCKS, as shown in Figure 7.2.

You may want to disable synchronized drilling in some situations, such as when you prefer that other charts or data tables on the canvas remain intact until clicked.

When a charted value is selected while drilling is enabled, the dimension object of the value selected is added to the filter bar and the value is selected. By adding the object to the filter bar, every element in the report will be filtered by the value selected, regardless of whether synchronized drilling has been enabled.

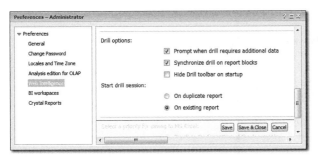

Figure 7.2 Synchronize Drill on Report Blocks Setting

7.3   Hierarchical Charting with Relational Data

Displaying multiple dimensions in a single chart can be achieved in Web Intelligence, whether connected to a relational data source or multidimensional cube. In Web Intelligence 4.0, right-click on a chart; then, while in design mode, select ASSIGN DATA. You can add several dimensions to the Category Axis category. Figure 7.3 shows a column chart built with three dimension objects.

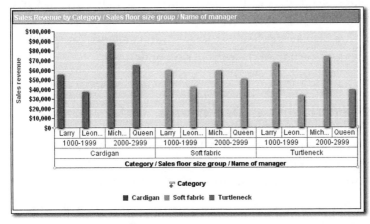

Figure 7.3 Multiple Dimensions Displayed in a Column Chart

Although you can add several additional dimension objects to the Category Axis, you might not be able to display more than three dimensions. This depends on the size of the chart itself and amount of data in each dimension. As Figure 7.4 shows, you can add more than one object to the Region Color section when assigning data to the chart object.

189

Figure 7.4 Assigning Multiple Dimension Objects to a Column Chart

Multiple dimension values are displayed in nested clusters to communicate the hierarchical groupings of the data in the chart. These axis values are clickable when drilling is enabled, which allows for seamless navigation up and down a hierarchy. Tool tips are displayed when you hover over a column, bar, pie slice, or label and provide the direction of the current drill option.

7.4 Reports Functioning as Dashboards

Web Intelligence lets users retrieve well over 100,000 rows of data and produce detailed analytical reports. With version 4.0, you can also present data visually with interactive charting components and in a style that resembles a dashboard.

Several new features in version 4.0 can be used together to create a dashboard experience inside a Web Intelligence report. The following are eight features that can be used to present data visually and in a dashboard format:

► **Element Linking**
Use the Element Linking feature to pass values from one chart component to other dependency components on the same report. This feature allows for

interactivity between components, even when hierarchies have not been set up at the universe level.

▶ **Drill**

Use the Drill feature to perform in-place drilling to analyze dimensional values at different levels. This feature is aided by the Scope of Analysis pane and hierarchies set up in the universe.

▶ **Hide**

Use the Hide and Hide When features to produce dynamic visibility. You can write a formula to show or hide a chart or other report element when specific conditions are met. This feature allows for layers of components to be used in a single report and then only displayed when data conditions are met. These conditions can be the result of simple filter selections, element link selections, drill values, or data retrieved from the data source.

▶ **Scale to Page**

The Fit to Page functionality popularized in Desktop Intelligence has been included in Web Intelligence as Scale to Page. This feature is accessed by going to the primary PAGE SETUP tab then locating the SCALE TO PAGE subtab in the third subtab group. Figure 7.5 shows the options available for scaling a report page:

▶ WIDTH: The default selection is automatic and can be changed from 1 to 9 pages.

▶ HEIGHT: The default selection is automatic and can be changed from 1 to 9 pages.

▶ SCALE: The scale can be changed from 10% to 400% of the current report.

Figure 7.5 Scale to Page Tab

The functionality provided in the SCALE TO PAGE tab works best when used in conjunction with the Page mode selection on the DISPLAY tab. These two choices are displayed in Figure 7.6.

Figure 7.6 Toggling Between the Display Formats: Page and Quick Display

You have two options for the display mode, both found in the DISPLAY tab. The first option, PAGE, is used when a report needs to be analyzed on a single screen or printed report. You should use this setting when creating a Web Intelligence dashboard or exporting to PDF. The second option, QUICK DISPLAY, is used primarily for analysis or exporting to Excel.

▶ **New Chart Engine**
The New Chart Engine in Web Intelligence 4.0 has profoundly improved the data visualization capabilities of the product. Charts can include flashy styles with 3D appearance and complex shadows or be displayed in minimalistic 2D, without unwanted shadows.

▶ **Input Controls**
The Input Controls feature was introduced in Service Pack 2 in XI 3.1 and continues to offer interactive filtering capabilities to Web Intelligence in version 4.0. Use this feature to give users more choices for analyzing data.

▶ **Conditional Formatting**
Known in previous versions as *alerters*, the Conditional Formatting feature allows specific values to be easily identified in data tables when property changes are conditionally applied to values that meet the outlined criteria. Formatting changes are displayed in real time as users explore reporting documents using filters, element links and input controls.

▶ **Additional Report Tabs for Extensive Data Analysis**
This feature amplifies Web Intelligence to become both a data visualization tool and data analysis and reporting tool. By having both capabilities within the same tool, a single document can contain multiple data sources, several dashboards, report/dashboard hybrids or dashports, and also analytical reports containing many thousand records.

You can reach new heights with your reports by combining the features outlined in this section. Scaling the report to fit to a single page, including drilling, Input

Controls, and the Hide When feature, along with uniquely customized charts, can go a long way in engaging users and delivering actionable information to them in the most effective format possible.

7.5   Formatting Tips

With over 200 potential configuration options available for most chart types, it may be difficult to selecting areas that will provide the greatest impact. This section shows a few of the settings that can be easily changed to make a significant impression when the report is viewed by users.

7.5.1   Measure Formatting

You need to assign the correct number format to a measure object in a chart when you assign the data objects. This window is accessed by right-clicking on a chart and selecting ASSIGN DATA.

From the Assign Data window, dimension objects are assigned to appear in the Category Axis and measure objects in the Value Axis sections. Click on the plus (+) symbol located to the right of the object selected to add a second object to the chart.

To configure the number format of a measure object, click on the small downward arrow located immediately to the right of the plus (+) symbol. Clicking on this arrow will display up to nine different options, depending on the number of objects already assigned to the chart. These options are displayed in Figure 7.7. Click on FORMAT NUMBER SELECTION to assign a specific format to the measure object.

The Format Number window lets you choose from 34 pre-set number formats displayed in seven different format groupings.

This window also provides the opportunity to create a custom format if the one you need isn't already provided. Figure 7.8 shows the Format Number window and format groupings available. To set a format, select a grouping from the left side of the window then click on your preferred format on the right side of the window.

Figure 7.7 Formatting the Number of the Value Axis Measure Object

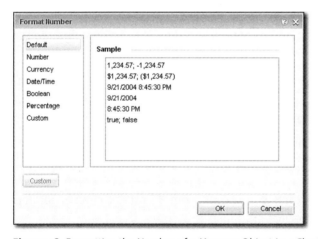

Figure 7.8 Formatting the Number of a Measure Object in a Chart

If the specific format you need isn't found in the list of choices on the right, click on the CUSTOM button to create your own format.

7.5.2   Region Color and Value Axis Stacking

If you'd like each column in a column chart to be displayed with a different color, add a dimension object to the Region Color section when assigning data to a chart. The same dimension object added to the Category Axis section can be used or a completely different object can be selected.

This setting is optional and is used to visually display groupings within the charted values. Figure 7.9 shows the [State] object assigned to a chart that already contains [State] in the Category Axis.

This methodology provides a different color for each state value in the chart.

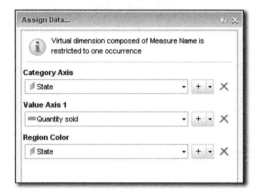

Figure 7.9 Assigning a Region Color to a Chart

Assigning a region color object to a column chart will display the columns in very thin bars, as pictured in Figure 7.10. This result may be acceptable in some scenarios, but it's more likely that users will expect to see the columns in a standard width.

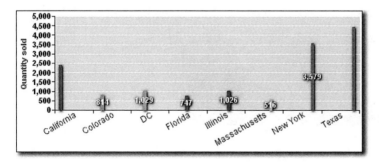

Figure 7.10 Column Chart with a Region Color Object Assigned

To display the columns with a wider width, enter the FORMAT CHART window and revise the STACKING option in the VALUE AXIS grouping. This option is pictured in Figure 7.11. The default setting is UNSTACKED. By changing the stacking selection to either STACKED CHART or GLOBALLY STACKED CHART, the option of converting the chart to a 100% STACKED CHART becomes enabled.

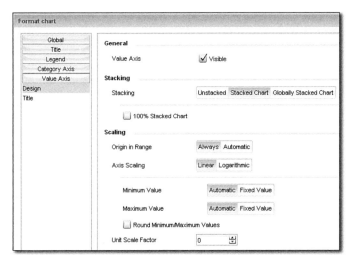

Figure 7.11 Stacking Options

Columns will be presented in a standard width when either STACKED CHART or GLOBALLY STACKED CHART is selected as the stacking option. This setting is useful because it increases the readability of the data presented in the chart.

Figure 7.12 shows the same chart displayed in Figure 7.10 with the only difference being that STACKED CHART was selected as the stacking option as pictured in Figure 7.11. Any dimension object or variable existing in the document can be added to the Region Color section to create visual groupings by color.

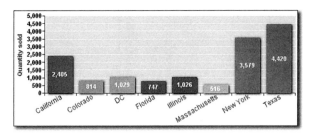

Figure 7.12 Column Chart with Stacked Chart Option Selected

7.6   Summary

Charting in Web Intelligence 4.0 has been elevated to include improved linking and a boardroom-quality appearance. With an extensive array of configurable properties, charts can include changes to over 200 different attributes. You can use the list dashboarding capability features to produce highly effective and visual reporting documents that very closely resemble dashboards while also delivering the data volumes that only Web Intelligence can cleanly consume.

Data analysis is improved by making adjustments to visual settings such as number formats in charts and the stacked chart option when assigning a region color to a chart. The next chapter describes the various report properties and tools available for creating precisely formatted reports.

Web Intelligence 4.0 contains specific metadata about reports, providing report users with a quick and accessible way to modify and interact with them. You can use the various tools and properties in Web Intelligence 4.0 to produce highly configured reports that most effectively communicate information.

8 Report Properties, Tools, and Formatting

This chapter describes the various properties that can be modified in Web Intelligence 4.0 to increase the readability and usability of reporting documents. The new robust reporting interface in version 4.0 gives users quick access to a report's metadata through the tools located in the left pane. The left pane in the report panel contains five sections in design mode, three in reading mode, and one in data mode. Each section delivers useful and relevant information to users for the report viewing scenario. The following sections outline all of the functional capabilities delivered in the left pane of the report panel.

8.1 Formatting Report Properties

The new reporting interface in Web Intelligence BI 4.0 allows for dynamic formatting of report properties. This section explains the ways to access report properties and how to most effectively display reports for different types of report consumers.

The left pane of the report panel was introduced in Chapter 4 and this chapter expands on that introduction by describing all of the functionality available in the pane. This pane plays a critical role in editing existing documents and creating new reports. Notably, it is different for reading mode, design mode, and data mode, so you'll notice that some functionality is not available when viewing a report in reading mode. The differentiation between capabilities in the reading and design modes provides greater control to power users and report developers in design mode. Reading mode provides a cleaner interface designed specifically for report consumers who need only to view, analyze, filter, and export report data.

Table 8.1 shows the properties available in each mode:

Reading Mode	Design Mode	Data Mode
► Document Summary ► Report Map ► Input Controls	► Document Summary ► Report Map ► Input Controls ► Web Services Publisher ► Available Objects ► Document Structures and Filters	► Data

Table 8.1 Properties Listed by Mode

Figure 8.1 Left Pane in Normal Mode

When expanded, the left pane provides report developers with access to available objects, an area for creating new input controls, access to the web service publisher, and a display of report metadata in the Document Summary as shown in Figure 8.1.

The following sections outline the functional options available in the left pane tabs.

8.2 Document Summary

The Document Summary tab includes information about the report such as author, creation date, locale, description, keywords, last refreshed, last modified date, last modified by, duration of previous refresh, and the selections of several document and data options. This report metadata is useful for administrators to see who has created and refreshed published documents. The `duration of previous refresh` setting is helpful to users when refreshing queries. The amount of time the query took to refresh in its last run is used to provide an estimated wait time when the query is refreshed again. If the query has never been run, then this value will be zero.

The following buttons and fields are relevant to the Document Summary tab:

▶ Print: Sends the document properties to the printer.

▶ Edit (design mode only): Allows the document developer to update the general section with metadata about the report. It is important to be specific when entering a description and keywords that accurately describe the report. The Keywords section is used to quickly locate relevant report data by using the search option in the BI Launch Pad. Figure 8.2 shows the properties available in the Document Summary window.

▶ General section: Provides a description of the type of document, author, and creation date. This window also displays descriptions and keywords assigned to the report. Click on Edit at the top of the Document Summary tab to enter new values or make changes to existing information in the description or keywords section. In Feature Pack 3 (Service Pack 4), the document size is also listed.

▶ Statistics: Provides the last refreshed date, last modified date, the user that last modified the report, and the duration of the previous refresh (in seconds). Note that all times are defaulted to GMT.

Figure 8.2 Document Summary

▶ Document options: Indicates the on or off status of six report parameters and describes the default style. These six parameters are ENHANCED VIEWING, REFRESH ON OPEN, PERMANENT REGIONAL FORMATTING, USE QUERY DRILL, ENABLE QUERY STRIPPING, and HIDE WARNING ICONS IN CHARTS. All these options are either on or off and can be set in the Options section after clicking on the EDIT button in the Document Summary.

▶ Data options: Lists three options—DATA TRACKING, AUTO-MERGE DIMENSIONS, and EXTEND MERGED DIMENSION VALUES—followed by whether they have been enabled or disabled in the current report. All three options are listed as either on or off and the latter two can be turned on in the Options section when editing the Document Summary. Data tracking is enabled by navigating to the ANALYSIS tab located above the report panel, then selecting the DATA TRACKING subtab located in the ribbon toolbar. Click on TRACK to choose the tracking method to be applied.

▶ Parameters: Provides prompt name(s) as well as key dates saved with the report.

The DOCUMENT SUMMARY tab provides a significant amount of descriptive report information, including the last refresh time. This information can be used by report designers to troubleshoot any potential performance issues when queries are refreshed. By identifying queries with lengthy refresh times, developers can focus on improving retrieval times and the user experience.

8.3 Report Map

The REPORT MAP tab provides a list of the reports and section values within each report and provides navigation to all of the reports in the document. Figure 8.3 shows a report map with two report tabs (STORE REVENUE ANALYSIS and QUERY RAW DATASET) and all sections associated with the first report tab.

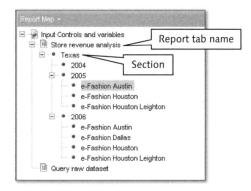

Figure 8.3 Report Map

8.4 Input Controls

This tab allows users to interact with data while reading a report. Filtering reports is easily accomplished by making selections from individual input controls in this tab. In design mode, options include adding new input controls and viewing a detailed list of all objects on the current report with the map selection. A RESET button is available to quickly clear all input control selections.

New input control filters can only be added while in design mode, while the map and reset options are available in both design mode and reading mode. Follow these steps to create a new input control:

1. Enter design mode and select the INPUT CONTROLS tab from the left pane.

2. Click on the NEW button at the top to add a new input control.

3. Select the object or variable to use as the source of the control and click on NEXT.

4. Choose the preferred control type and make modifications to the input control properties. Click on NEXT to proceed.

5. Assign report elements to accept the filter value of the input control and click on FINISH.

The input control map outlines all input controls created for the report. Each input control is assigned a report element at time of creation. The map view allows for report users to see all of the dependencies of each input control. Figure 8.4 shows the map view for all objects on a report. Input controls and their dependencies are easily identified.

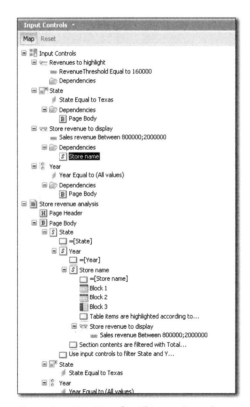

Figure 8.4 Map View for All Input Controls

The RESET button resets all updated input controls to its original defaulted value. Lastly, the up and down arrows (available in design mode only) allow the report designer to sort the input controls in a custom order.

Input controls are one of the most powerful filtering tools you can add to a report to encourage interactivity for report users. This functionality allows users to slice or filter data in a report using retrieved dimensions, measures, or variables. Although the maximum number of input controls is 30 per report, we recommend that each report contain between 2 and 10 input controls depending on the reports requirements. This is because reports with more than 20 input controls can become convoluted and confusing to interpret. Whenever possible, you should revise the input control label to include a name using appropriate business terminology and descriptive terms that fully describe the context of the filter.

Depending on the qualification of the object used in the input control, this powerful interactivity tool can create input controls with the following controls types:

▶ Single value selections
  ▶ Entry field
  ▶ Combo box
  ▶ Radio buttons
  ▶ List box
  ▶ Calendar
  ▶ Entry field
  ▶ Spinner
  ▶ Simple slider
▶ Multiple selections
  ▶ Checkbox
  ▶ List box
  ▶ Double slider

Each control type created from a dimension or detail object contains a label name, description, list of values, default values, and operator selection. This functionality allows for customized user interaction. You'll need to ensure that the label name and description are descriptive enough for the user to understand how to use input controls. Figure 8.5 shows the input control properties for a combo box control named State.

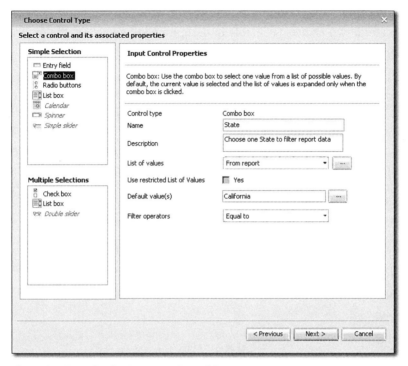

Figure 8.5 State Combo Box Input Control Properties

You can edit existing input controls in design mode by clicking on the wrench icon available on the right side of the header bar. Four icons appear when you hover over the header bar of an input control:

1. EDIT

2. HIGHLIGHT DEPENDENCIES

3. REMOVE

4. COLLAPSE OR EXPAND

Figure 8.6 shows the icons that appear when hovering over an input control title in design mode.

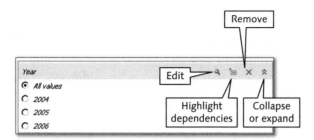

Figure 8.6 Icons Appearing When Hovering Over an Input Control Title in Design Mode

8.5 Web Services Publisher

This tab allows the report designer to create web services using existing components or blocks from Web Intelligence reports. Figure 8.7 shows the Web Service Publisher with a Web Service Definition Language (WSDL) for "Sales_for_Southeast."

Figure 8.7 Web Service Publisher

Let's examine some of the important options here:

▶ MANAGE SERVERS: This button is used to add a web services host to the current document. If you're planning to connect to a web service created by Query as a Web Service, use this tool to retrieve the host name. After adding the host name in the provided text box, the URL is automatically generated.

▶ WEB SERVICES PUBLISHER tab options that are accessed by icons:

  ▶ VIEWS: Allows designer to view created WSDL by the following three options (additionally, an option is presented in the View menu to show web services by query):

    – View by web service

    – View by document and web service

    – View by document and block

  ▶ DELETE: Deletes a selected web service

  ▶ EDIT: Launches the Publish Content wizard to edit an existing web service

  ▶ RENAME: Renames a web service group

  ▶ REFRESH: Refreshes a web service group

  ▶ TEST: Tests the input request and server response for a web service group

  ▶ IMPORT WEB SERVICE QUERY: Displays the web services properties of the query and enables the IMPORT WEB SERVICE QUERY option (available only when the SHOW WEB SERVICES CONTENT option in the View menu is checked)

  ▶ SEARCH: Search for existing web services (this is one reason that WSDL names and descriptions should be descriptive in nature)

▶ Web Services Properties:

  ▶ WSDL URL: Shows the URL associated with the selected web service query (URL is also used to connect to data in Dashboards)

Follow these steps to create a new web service:

1. Right-click on an existing table or chart.

2. Select PUBLISH AS WEB SERVICE.

3. The Publish Content wizard is launched. Click on NEXT to proceed.

4. Click on NEXT on the Identify Duplicate Content window.

5. Enter a descriptive name and description, then click on NEXT, as shown in Figure 8.8.

6. Click on the CREATE button shown in Figure 8.9.

7. Give the new web service a name with no spaces.

8. Add a description for the web service and click on FINISH.

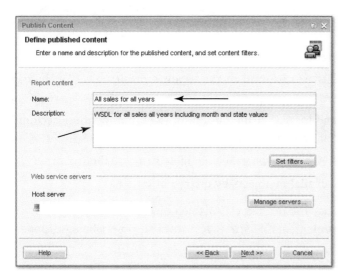

Figure 8.8 Defining a New WSDL Name and Description

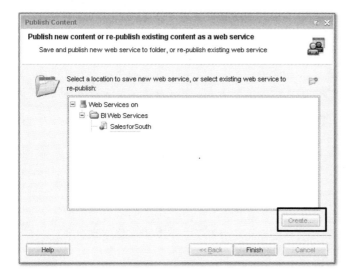

Figure 8.9 Publishing Content as a Web Service

8.6   Available Objects (Design Mode Only)

After you add a data provider and retrieve data from your source, you'll find all result objects available for report consumption in the Available Objects tab. The Available Objects tab contains the following sections and is only available in design mode:

▸ Filter bar: Filters objects by name

▸ List of available objects: Displays all of the report's result objects including locally created variables

▸ Arranged by option and located at the bottom of the window, these sections provide two options for viewing objects:

  ▸ Alphabetical order: Arranges the available objects in alphabetical order

  ▸ Query: Displays all available objects by query name

Report developers can drag and drop any available object onto the report canvas or assign them to report elements. Figure 8.10 shows an object being dropped onto the report canvas.

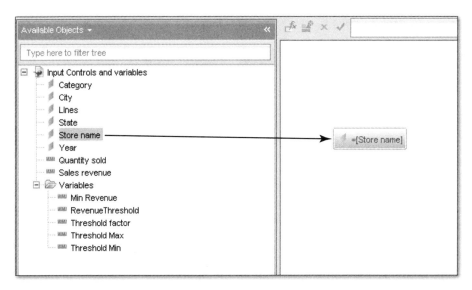

Figure 8.10 Drag and Drop from Available Objects

8.7   Document Structures and Filters

This tab provides a detailed listing of all objects existing within the document and is only available in design mode. Use the DOCUMENT STRUCTURES AND FILTERS tab to access the following sections:

▶ FILTER button: Shows/hides filters that exist on report elements and data blocks within the report

▶ AXIS button: Toggles on and off the report axis found in charts and data tables

▶ Report Structure Elements: Displays the document structure by report tabs.

All report level filters are assigned by a funnel-shaped icon; other report elements also have distinctive icons. It is important to name report elements appropriately in order to easily identify them in this view. Figure 8.11 shows document structure and filters.

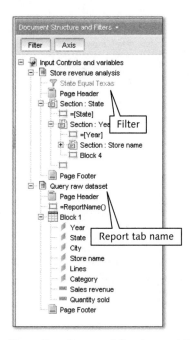

Figure 8.11 Document Structure and Filters

8.8   Data

The DATA tab is only available when data mode is selected. To enter this option click on the DATA button in the upper right corner of the report immediately to the right of the option to enter design mode. This tab shows all data providers and available objects including dimensions, measures, details, and variables.

The following elements are available in the DATA tab:

▸ Filter bar: Filters objects by name

▸ EXPAND and COLLAPSE buttons: Expand and collapse data sources (queries)

▸ Data source and variables list: Displays all queries generated for the report as well as associated variables (you can edit variables by right-clicking on a variable name and selecting EDIT)

Figure 8.12 shows the DATA tab including query name and associated query properties.

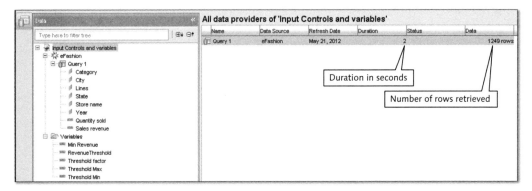

Figure 8.12 Data Tab with Query Information

The purpose of the data mode is to view specific elements of metadata about the data sources in a report. This metadata includes query names, data sources, refresh dates, duration of queries, and the number of rows retrieved.

Figure 8.13 shows actual data retrieved for the query when selecting the query name.

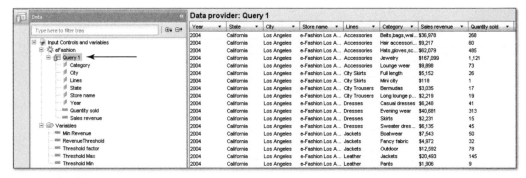

Figure 8.13 Data Provider with Data

8.9 Summary

Web Intelligence 4.0 provides a full spectrum of reporting properties, tools, and formatting. The left pane in the report panel offers easy-to-access tools for reports designers and users to find metadata information about reports. It is important for you to keep report properties up to date with detailed and relevant descriptions so that users can understand the context of the report's content.

Additionally, the left pane allows for robust user interaction by using input controls. Input controls can be created against dimensions, measures or variables and it allows the report user to filter data and change parameters in real time. Lastly, options such as web services allow advanced developers to leverage the speed and security of Web Intelligence to consume data from external applications delivered through a web service.

Chapter 9 describes takes a deep dive into filtering data in both the Query Panel and Report Panel. Now that you've learned how to navigate a report's metadata and properties, next you will learn how to filter data in a report to make reports more meaningful for users.

SAP BusinessObjects Web Intelligence 4.0 provides several different ways to filter data and present specific information for answering business questions. Whether you are restricting data in the Query Panel or filtering results in the Report Panel, you have many options for displaying detailed and accurate company information.

9   Filtering Data in the Query and Report Panel

Filtering and restricting data is done to produce reporting documents that provide business users with pertinent and contextually relevant information.

You can restrict the amount of information returned to your report by applying query filters in the Query Panel. Query filters translate to the where clause of the generated SQL statement and help you minimize the amount of information returned to the microcube in a Web Intelligence 4.0 document.

After running or refreshing a query in a Web Intelligence document and retrieving data, you can filter your results to produce reports with data tables and charts containing subsets of the data returned.

Several different types of filters can be applied to reports and report elements, including the types found in the filter bar, filters applied directly to specific report elements, input control filters, and conditionally hidden report elements.

This chapter covers these data filtering methods and offers screenshots to help explain how each method is accomplished in Web Intelligence 4.0.

9.1   Filtering in the Query Panel

Query filtering restricts the amount of information retrieved from a data provider when a query is refreshed. Query filtering is achieved by including any of three filter types when creating a query:

- Predefined filters: Filter objects created in the universe
- User-defined filters: Filters defined in the Query Panel
- Prompted filters: Filter objects that prompt users for input

Let's examine each of these more closely.

9.1.1 Predefined Filters

Predefined filters are objects that have been previously set up in the universe. These filter types are symbolized with a yellow funnel icon and contain SQL syntax that assigns a value to an object or contains formula to calculate the value.

Figure 9.1 shows four predefined filters in a query sourced from the eFashion universe. This example shows how predefined filter objects appear to users in the Query Panel of a Web Intelligence 4.0 document. These filter objects are often aliased with descriptive terms that easily communicate the function of the filter to business users for intuitive report filtering.

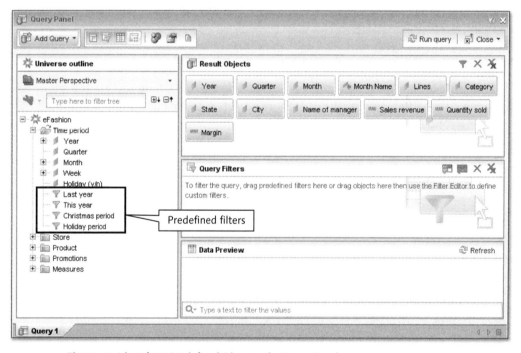

Figure 9.1 Identifying Predefined Filters in the Query Panel

The contents of a predefined filter generally contain the assignment of a specific value or set of values and also a description. Figure 9.2 shows the filter object definition for the [Christmas period] object in the eFashion universe while editing the properties of the object in the Universe Design Tool of Web Intelligence 4.0.

The key element in a predefined filter is the Where section in the filter definition. Figure 9.2 sets the Where section of the Christmas Period filter for the Calendar_year_lookup.Week_In_Year to be between week number 46 and 53. Whenever this object is used in a query, the data returned will have occurred between this weekly timeframe.

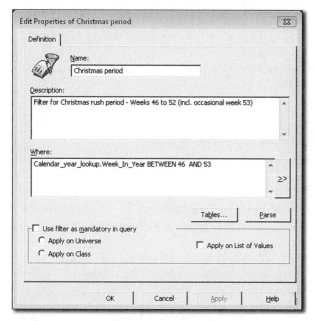

Figure 9.2 Properties of the Predefined Christmas Period Filter Object

The DESCRIPTION field of a filter object plays an important role because it communicates additional information about the object to the user when creating a query.

Mouse over a predefined filter in the Query Panel to see the filter's description. Figure 9.3 shows the description of the [Christmas period] object that appears when you hover over it in the Query Panel.

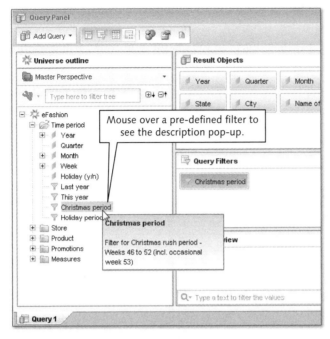

Figure 9.3 Predefined Filter Descriptions

In many cases, predefined filters need to be applied by default to every query created from a specific universe. This can be accomplished by checking the USE FILTER AS MANDATORY IN QUERY option when creating or editing the filter object properties in the Universe Design Tool.

Figure 9.4 shows the option that forces the filter object to be inserted into every query created from the universe.

As a universe designer, you'll have the opportunity to set a predefined filter to be applied on either the entire universe or the class where the filter is saved, as is shown in Figure 9.4. These options become enabled when the USE FILTER AS MANDATORY IN QUERY checkbox is checked.

A single predefined filter can either include the assignment of values to multiple objects or contain a variety of complex formulas. By adding a predefined filter to a Web Intelligence query, you ensure that the data returned to the microcube will be restricted by the conditions defined in the filter.

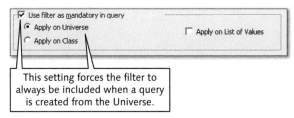

Figure 9.4 Applying Filter as Mandatory Query

When creating a predefined filter object, make sure that you name the object with a term or short phrase that clearly describes the purpose of the filter with terminology known by the user community and anticipated audience.

9.1.2   User-Defined Filters

User-defined filters are created in the Query Panel by adding dimension, detail, or measure objects to the Query Filters pane. Objects are added to the Query Filters pane by dragging them from the universe outline and dropping them in the Query Filters pane.

After adding an object to the Query Filters pane, you need to select an operator for the object. By default, the operator assigned by Web Intelligence is In List. Change the operator by clicking on the small down arrow located immediately to the right of the existing operator. Figure 9.5 shows the [Quarter] object after it has been added to the Query Filters pane.

Once an operator has been selected, click on the icon to the right of the input box to select the assignment type.

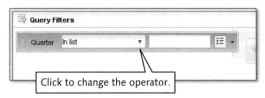

Figure 9.5 Viewing a Dimension Object in the Query Filters Pane

The following operators are available for creating filters with detail, dimension, or measure objects:

- ▶ In list
- ▶ Not in list
- ▶ Equal to
- ▶ Not Equal to
- ▶ Greater than
- ▶ Greater than or Equal to
- ▶ Less than
- ▶ Less than or Equal to
- ▶ Between
- ▶ Not Between
- ▶ Is null
- ▶ Is not null
- ▶ Matches pattern
- ▶ Different from pattern
- ▶ Both
- ▶ Except

Figure 9.6 shows the assignment type choices available in Web Intelligence 4.0 when creating a user-defined filter. The default assignment type selection is CONSTANT.

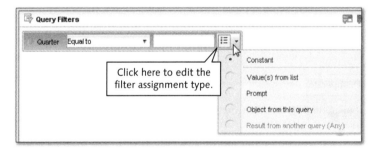

Figure 9.6 User-Defined Filter Assignment Types

The following are filter assignment types:

▶ CONSTANT: Allows the user to type a constant value

▶ VALUE(S) FROM LIST: Launches the List of Values dialog box to select one or more values from a distinct list of values for the selected object

▶ PROMPT: Prompts for user input when a query is refreshed

▶ OBJECT FROM THIS QUERY: Selects from the available objects and variables (not enabled when the `In List` or the `Not In List` operator is selected)

▶ RESULTS FROM ANOTHER QUERY: Selects a value from a different query within the same document

When a measure object is added to the Query Filters pane, a small calculator icon appears inside the value box. This icon is used to launch a calculator panel and provide users with the capability to add a specific number without using their keyboard. Figure 9.7 shows this calculator panel with a measure object.

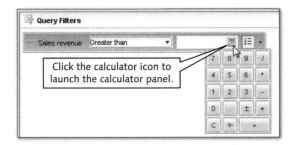

Figure 9.7 Calculator Panel in Measure Filter

Remove Filter Objects from the Query Filters Pane

To remove filter objects, choose any of these methods:

▶ Select the filter and press `Delete`.

▶ Drag the filter from the Query Filters pane and drop it in the universe outline panel.

▶ Select the filter and then click on the X in the upper-right corner of the pane.

▶ Click on the REMOVE ALL button in the upper-right corner of the pane.

Figure 9.8 shows the icons located in the upper-right corner of the Query Filters pane. Use these icons to remove a single filter or to remove the entire set of query filters. You'll be prompted with a dialog box asking, `Are you sure you want to delete all filters?`

If you click on YES, all of the filters will be removed without an option to undo the changes.

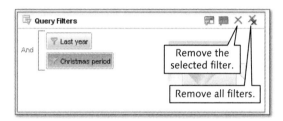

Figure 9.8 Removing One or All Filters

9.1.3 Value(s) from List

When VALUE(S) FROM LIST is selected as the filter assignment type, a full distinct list of the values that belong to the object being filtered will be displayed.

Lists of values (LOVs) are either enabled or disabled when the objects are created in the universe. Custom LOVs can also be created in the universe to provide cascading prompted filtering to report consumers.

To select values from the List of Values dialog box, follow these steps:

1. Select VALUES from the list of distinct values to be included.

2. Click on the > button to add the values to the Selected Value(s) box.

3. Click on OK to accept.

9.1.4 Prompted Filters

Use prompted filters to require report consumers to provide input when refreshing a report. The user's response will be passed into the `where` clause when the SQL statement is generated.

When a Web Intelligence 4.0 reporting document is saved with the document property option REFRESH ON OPEN selected, and the document includes prompted filters, users will be required to answer the prompt(s) as the report opens.

If PROMPT is selected as the filter's assignment type, a PROMPT PROPERTIES icon will be displayed to provide options for configuring the prompt (see Figure 9.9).

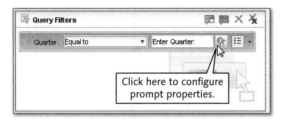

Figure 9.9 Locating the Prompt Properties Icon

Prompt Filter Properties

When a prompted filter object is included in a query, report developers have the opportunity to revise a variety of properties for each filter object.

Figure 9.10 shows the Prompt Properties window that is launched when you define a prompt. The following are the associated properties:

▶ PROMPT TEXT: A prompt text is added by default. This property is important if the document and filter will receive values passed to it with a hyperlink. This will be discussed in detail in Chapter 14.

▶ PROMPT WITH LIST OF VALUES: This property displays a distinct list of values for the object being filtered.

▶ KEEP LAST VALUES SELECTED: This property defaults to the last value selected.

▶ SELECT ONLY FROM LIST: This property requires the selection to be made only from the provided list of value(s) rather than allowing freehand entry.

▶ OPTIONAL PROMPT: This property permits the prompt to be optional rather than required.

▶ SET DEFAULT VALUES: This property allows a default value to be added to the filter.

The next section describes the process of applying several different types of filtering in the Report Panel.

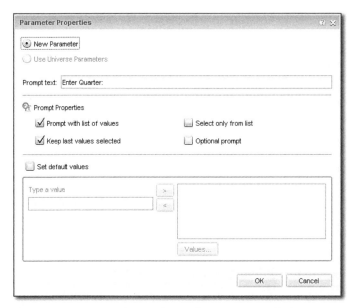

Figure 9.10 Prompt Dialog Box for Configuring Prompted Filters

9.2 Filtering in the Report Panel

Report filtering provides business users with the capability to display a small subset of data in a report rather than everything returned from the query and stored locally within the microcube.

It's very common for business requirements to call for Web Intelligence reports that contain charts for specific values in a data set along with additional charts or data table elements that display diverse divisions of the values.

This type of functionality is possible in Web Intelligence 4.0 by applying different report filters to each element (chart, table, or section) within a report.

When values are filtered in a report, the data is hidden only from the user and remains within the microcube for use in other report tabs within the document. This way, business users can insert new report tabs and set up new filters without affecting other reports in the same document.

Filtering report data can be achieved by performing the following actions:

▶ Adding simple filters to entire reports by assigning values to objects on the filter bar

▶ Adding filters to specific elements in a report by assigning values to objects in the Report Filter Panel

▶ Interacting with report data by using input controls

9.2.1 Simple Filtering with the Filter Bar

Simple report filters are easily added to a reporting document by clicking on the FILTER BAR shortcut icon in the reporting toolbar while in design mode.

The ideal method of adding simple report filters entails the following three steps:

1. Enter design mode.

2. Select the ANALYSIS tab.

3. Click on the FILTER BAR icon located on the INTERACT subtab.

Figure 9.11 shows the FILTER BAR icon on a report in design mode. Enabling the filter bar lets you drop objects onto the bar for simple report filtering.

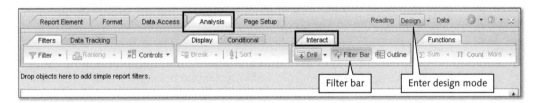

Figure 9.11 Enabling the Filter Bar in Design Mode

Even though the FILTER BAR icon is present in reading mode, simple filters can only be added while in design mode. This toggle is primarily used in reading mode to turn off simple report filters. Figure 9.12 shows the filter bar with objects added for filtering.

Figure 9.12 Report Filter Bar with Objects Added

Simple report filters are added by dragging and dropping result objects onto the filter bar. Distinct lists of the object values will be displayed in dropdown components and provide a flexible method of filtering the entire report.

Simple filtering can be toggled on or off by selecting the REPORT FILTER TOOLBAR icon located on the default toolbar.

9.2.2 Element Filters

Element filters in Web Intelligence 4.0 can be added to single data blocks, charts, sections, or to entire reports. This type of filtering is applied to reports while in design mode only.

Take the following steps to add a filter to a specific report element:

1. Right-click on the element and select FILTER from the list of choices.
2. Select ADD FILTER to launch the Report Filter window.
3. From the Filter Map pane in the Report Filter window, select the report element to assign the new filter to and click on ADD FILTER.
4. Choose from the list of available objects to begin creating the filter.
5. Select the operator for the filter.
6. Assign or enter a value and then click on OK.

Figure 9.13 shows the menu displayed when right-clicking on a report element.

Choosing ADD FILTER allows you to place a filter on the element selected or switch to another element on the current Report Panel. From this menu you'll also have the opportunity to edit or remove existing filters or to add a new input control filter.

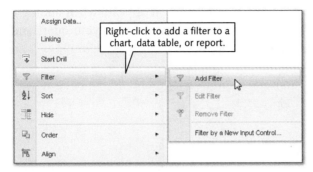

Figure 9.13 Adding a Filter to a Report Element

Every element (chart, table, section, or report) on the Report Panel can be assigned one or more unique filters for the creation of highly customized reports.

The new Report Filter window introduced in Web Intelligence 4.0 lets you assign filters to every element on the Report Panel without having to right-click on each element individually. Select the element from the Filter Map pane that you'd like to assign the filter to and then click on ADD FILTER.

Notice that charts, data blocks, sections, and even entire reports are displayed in the Filter Map pane for easy configuration of filters.

Figure 9.14 shows the Filter Map pane within the Report Filter window.

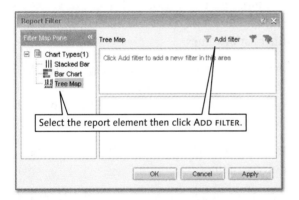

Figure 9.14 Report Filter Window and the Filter Map Pane

After you select ADD FILTER, the list of objects available in the existing report will be displayed. Select an object and click on OK to proceed with creating the filter.

Figure 9.15 shows the Available Objects window as it appears when adding a report filter. This window will display all objects retrieved from your query and also existing variables created within the report.

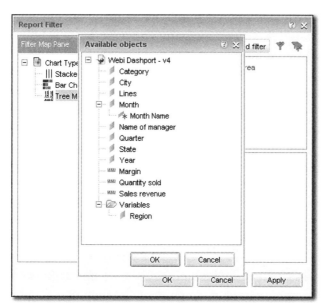

Figure 9.15 Available Objects for Creating a Report Filter

After selecting a dimension or measure and clicking on OK, you can select an operator for the filter. The default operator is In list and allows for multiple selections to be made from a distinct list of values.

Twelve different operators are available for this type of filtering. Figure 9.16 shows a chart element with a single filter assigned to it. In the example below, the [State] object has been selected along with the In list operator. The list of available state values is displayed at the bottom of the screen.

Double-click on or select values followed by clicking on the > symbol to assign a value to the filter. Click on APPLY • OK to accept.

In the next section we will cover how to use input controls to control data results.

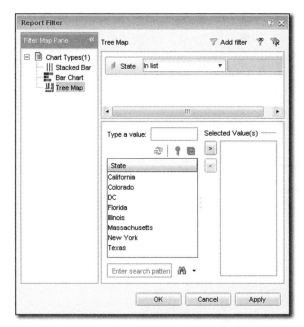

Figure 9.16 Assigning an Operator to a Chart Filter

9.2.3   Filtering with Input Controls

Input controls provide users with the flexibility to interact with and analyze report data in several different ways. You can choose from four different components for filtering single value dimension objects or two components for multiple-value dimension filtering.

Similar to report element filters, input controls can be assigned to charts, tables, sections, or entire reports. They must be created while in design mode.

To create an input control, enter design mode and right-click on a report element. Then click on FILTER • FILTER BY A NEW INPUT CONTROL. Figure 9.17 shows a portion of the menu displayed when you right-click on a report element with FILTER selected.

Another way to add a new input control is by clicking on the ANALYSIS tab, the FILTERS subtab, and then clicking on CONTROLS. This method of adding a new input control is also available only in design mode and is pictured in Figure 9.18.

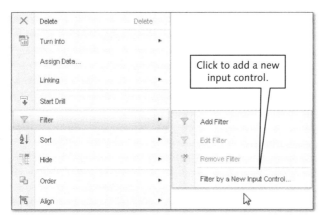

Figure 9.17 Adding a New Input Control When Right-Clicking on a Report Element

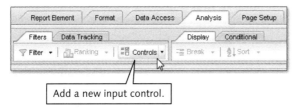

Figure 9.18 Adding a New Input Control from the Toolbar

After selecting FILTER BY A NEW INPUT CONTROL, the Define Input Control window will appear and prompt you to select a report object as the basis for the new input control filter. The objects can be arranged alphabetically or by query. This option is helpful when filtering reports sourced from multiple data sources.

You may also want to create input controls with objects existing in the selected block (chart or data table). This is accomplished by checking the INCLUDE OBJECTS FROM SELECTED BLOCK ONLY box at the bottom of the window. Figure 9.19 shows these options at the bottom of the Define Input Control box.

Figure 9.20 shows the types of input controls available for single-value and multiple-value dimension objects.

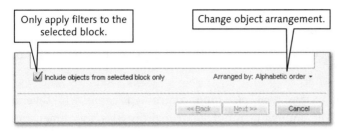

Figure 9.19 Properties When Defining a New Input Control

Figure 9.20 Input Control Properties for a Dimension Object

The following input control properties are single-value control types for dimension objects:

▶ Entry field: Allows for user input without a consistency check

▶ Combo box: Allows users to select from a list of possible values with the selected value being displayed in the box

▶ Radio buttons: Enable users to select from a list of possible values (the selected value is displayed as checked)

▶ List box: Enables users to make several selections from a list of possible values

The following input control properties are multiple value control types for dimension objects:

- ▶ Checkboxes: Provide users with the ability to make several selections from a list of possible values (the selected values are shown as checked)
- ▶ List box: Provides users with the ability to make several selections from a list of possible values

Except for the entry field control type, each input control type comes with several modifiable properties. The following input control properties for dimension objects can make a big difference in terms of how data is returned and how the control is presented to users:

- ▶ Label: This property is the revisable name of input control. The default entry is the object name.
- ▶ Description: This is an optional area for entering a full description of the input control filter. We recommend that you add a complete description of the input control, including the blocks it's assigned to and the business meaning of the filter.
- ▶ List of Values: This property allows for a custom or restricted list of available values to be used. This is a good practice for creating regulated reports that allow users to view and interact only with limited values.
- ▶ Use restricted List of Values: This property is used in combination with the List of Values property when a custom list of values has been selected.
- ▶ Default value(s): This property lets you select a default value.
- ▶ Operator: This property provides you with the following six operators for filtering data:
  - ▶ Equal to
  - ▶ Not Equal to
  - ▶ Less than
  - ▶ Less than or Equal to
  - ▶ Greater than
  - ▶ Greater than or Equal to
- ▶ Number of lines: This property allows designers to set the number values that will be displayed when the input control is viewed. The default setting is 5.

After choosing the control type, the next step is to assign it to report elements.

Assigning Dependencies to Input Controls

After selecting the control type and configuring the properties of the control, you need to assign the control filter to elements on the report. Figure 9.21 shows the Assign Report Elements window.

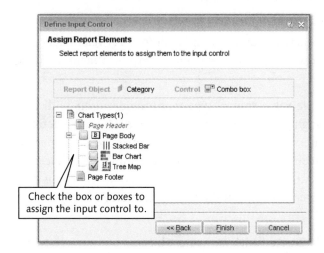

Figure 9.21 Assigning Report Elements in an Input Control

Click on NEXT >> on the Choose Control Type window to proceed to the Assign Report Elements window. This is where report elements are selected to have the new input control filter assigned.

Available elements to assign the input control filters to include the report page body, sections, charts, and data tables. The boxes indicate that the elements can be selected and explicitly assigned to the input control filter.

When a top-level box is selected (for example, the report page body or section), all elements nested within that object will be checked by default and greyed-out. To uncheck a specific child element, you need to uncheck the top-level element and then explicitly check the box of the element(s) requiring the input control assignment.

Adding Input Controls on Measure Objects

Because measures and dimensions need to be filtered differently, defining input controls on measure objects is accomplished with a different set of control types and properties. Several control types are available for filtering numerical values rather than descriptive data.

The following are single value control types:

▶ Entry field: Allows for user input without a consistency check

▶ Spinner: Allows users to enter or adjust values with arrows

▶ Simple slider: Provides users with a slider component to select values between a defined interval (requires a minimum, maximum, and increment value at time of creation)

The double slider is a multiple value control type that provides users with two sliders for selecting and changing the range of values existing between a defined minimum and maximum interval. This functionality lets users focus on specific data elements that fall between a range defined by the position of the sliders. It requires a minimum and maximum value to be defined when the control is created and also requires an increment value at the time of creation.

Properties of Input Controls Created with Measure Objects

It's important to know that the minimum and maximum values must be set on the spinner, simple slider, and double slider input controls. The filter operator is also adjustable, allowing you to change the default *Equal to* operator if the input control requires a different operator such as *Less than* or *Greater than*.

Figure 9.22 shows the available control types and properties for an input control created with a measure object.

Once you've created one or more input controls, it's time to save your document to the BI Launch Pad and share your report with other users to begin exploring and analyzing the results.

Interacting with Input Controls

Users can interact with input controls while reading reports without a need for editing or working in design mode. By default, input controls are located on the left side of the Report Panel.

Figure 9.22 Adding a New Input Control on a Measure Object

Report data updates instantly as users interact with input control values, thus providing a fluid analysis experience. Figure 9.23 shows a report with two input controls viewed in reading mode.

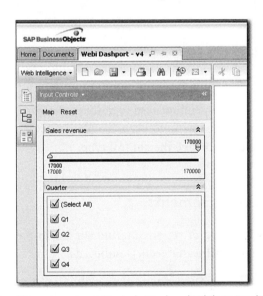

Figure 9.23 Input Controls Displayed While in Reading Mode

Editing or Removing an Input Control

To edit the properties of an existing input control, begin by entering design mode and then locating the input control to be updated. With appropriate permissions, you'll be able to edit and remove any input control existing within the report.

Mouse over the input control title of the control to be modified to display three shortcut icons previously not visible. These icons allow you to edit, show dependencies, or delete the control. Figure 9.24 shows these icons on the title bar of the input control for easy editing or removal.

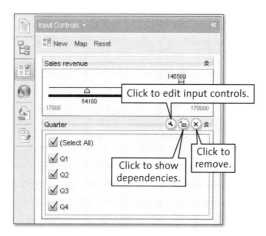

Figure 9.24 Editing or Removing an Input Control

Editing an input control will return you to the window used to define the control and its properties during creation. From this screen, you can change the filter's dependencies, modify its properties, or even change the control type.

9.3 Conditionally Hiding Report Elements

Conditionally hiding report elements is a type of report filtering similar to the dynamic visibility feature available in SAP BusinessObjects Dashboards.

This type of conditional formatting provides designers with the capability of creating reports that resemble and function as dashboards in many ways. This includes adding layers of components onto a single report, and then triggering the appropriate components to be displayed based on the result of custom formulas. It may also mean hiding report elements when they are empty.

There are two ways to conditionally hide report elements; both are enabled when in design mode. Figure 9.25 shows the menu that appears when you right-click on a report element. Click on HIDE • HIDE WHEN... to write a formula to allow for conditional visibility.

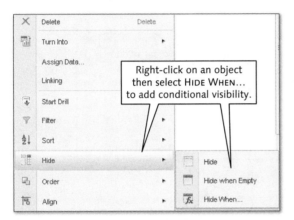

Figure 9.25 Setting Conditional Visibility with the Hide When Feature

Another method for selecting HIDE WHEN is to right-click on a report element and then click on FORMAT TABLE. Both methods will take you to the GENERAL tab of the Format Table window (shown in Figure 9.26, along with the area to enable the HIDE WHEN feature).

The Hide menu is available to any chart type, data table, or section within a report. A common reason for enabling Hide When conditional formatting is to display different customized charts based on the number of dimensions being viewed.

As users begin to analyze refined data sets by drilling into results through the use of the filter bar and input controls, the number of dimensions that meet the criteria will shrink significantly, which changes the way the data is displayed. For robust reporting documents that resemble the functionality of dashboards, use the Hide When feature to display appropriate report elements that match the amount of data being viewed at any given time.

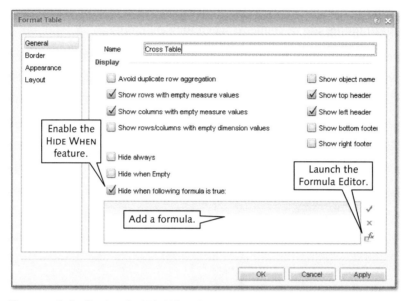

Figure 9.26 Configuring the Hide When Feature

9.4 Summary

Filtering data in Web Intelligence 4.0 is both flexible and easy to apply. Begin filtering your documents by restricting the amount of data returned in a query by including predefined, user-defined, or prompted filters in the Query Panel.

After data is returned to the microcube in a Web Intelligence document, you can fine-tune your reports by adding element filters to precisely display subsets of data. Or you can create a series of input controls to put the power of filtering results in the hands of business users.

An extensive list of operators in both the Query Panel and Report Panel give report developers the tools to meet any business requirement. Whether filtering the available data in your data source or limiting data from being displayed in the Report Panel, as a report developer you have many choices for creating highly functional reporting documents.

You can use the filter bar to provide dimension and detail values in selectable dropdown lists to quickly filter entire reports, and can conditionally hide charts, data tables and sections based on the result of a custom designed formula. This new functionality can transform the way data is delivered in a report and how users interact with reporting documents.

The next chapter will explain how the Scope of Analysis section works in the Query Panel to produce drillable hierarchies when analyzing data. This topic is important because it dictates the drill paths and interactive capabilities of report data.

Drill functionality puts the power of analysis into the end users' hands by enabling them to filter down on report tables and charts with the click of the mouse. New features allow users not only to drill down, but to drill up, drill by, and drill upon bars and data points in a chart, making Web Intelligence a powerful end user reporting tool.

10 Scope of Analysis and Drilling Down

By drilling down on a report, you can see levels of data beyond your original query. For instance, let's say that you receive a monthly report summarizing sales revenue by state. Upon review of the report, you discover that sales revenue seems high for the state of Massachusetts in the year 2006, as shown in Figure 10.1. Exploring this anomaly further to determine its root cause would normally require running numerous additional detailed reports or even requesting a customized query to get your desired result.

Sales Revenue by State

	California	Colorado	DC	Florida	Illinois	Massachusetts
2004	$1,704,211	$448,302	$693,211	$405,985	$737,914	$238,819
2005	$2,782,680	$768,390	$1,215,158	$661,250	$1,150,659	$157,719
2006	$2,992,679	$843,584	$1,053,581	$811,924	$1,134,085	$887,169
Totals:	$7,479,569	$2,060,275	$2,961,950	$1,879,159	$3,022,658	$1,283,707

Figure 10.1 Sales Revenue for Massachusetts is High for the Year 2006

This process means that a report request is made and another query generated, which produces another report showing sales revenue results at a monthly level by state. If this *still* didn't answer your questions, you'd need to make another request to produce another query to further drill down the data to a lower level (perhaps City or Week) in order to pinpoint the reason for the revenue results. You can see how this process could become lengthy and cumbersome.

Here's the good news: A report developer can avoid these extra steps and, by setting scope of analysis and enabling drilling on a report as shown in Figure 10.2, put the ownership back into your hands as an end user.

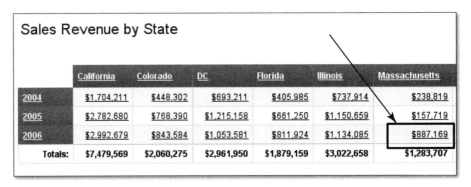

Figure 10.2 Enabling Drill on the Table to Explore the Data Further

10.1 Setting the Scope of Analysis in the Query Panel

The first step to enabling the drill feature is to set the *scope of analysis* in the Query Panel. This tells Web Intelligence to return additional data beyond the results specified in the Result Objects pane. The additional data returned does not appear in the initial report displayed upon execution of the query, but you can see the objects returned in the data pane of the report view, as shown in Figure 10.3.

Scope of analysis is the defined drill path for a data element in the universe and is applicable only for dimension objects. The default scope of analysis for a universe object is defined by the order of the objects within a class. For example, in the Store class, the objects are ordered from top to bottom as State, City, Store Name, so the hierarchy for the scope of analysis would be by STATE, CITY, and STORE NAME, as shown in Figure 10.4. The universe designer can also overwrite these defaults and define custom hierarchies in the universe. (Setting up hierarchies in the universe is discussed in further detail in Chapter 23.)

Figure 10.3 Available Objects Pane in the Report Manager—Result Objects and Scope of Analysis Objects

Figure 10.4 Default Object Hierarchy Defined by Order or Objects in the Universe

To view the defined hierarchies in the universe, go to the Query Panel by editing the data provider in the Web Intelligence report. In the Universe outline box, select the dropdown arrow next to MASTER PERSPECTIVE. Select the radio button for DISPLAY BY NAVIGATION PATHS to view the defined object hierarchies for the selection universe (see Figure 10.5).

In order to set scope of analysis, you must first define the result objects for the query in the Query Panel. After creating the initial query by adding result objects into the Result Objects pane and adding any filters into the Query Filters pane, select the SCOPE OF ANALYSIS PANEL button on the query panel toolbar, as shown in Figure 10.6.

Figure 10.5 Display by Navigation View in Query Panel

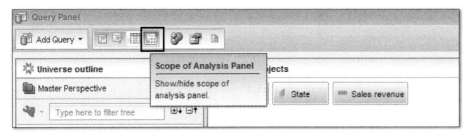

Figure 10.6 Scope of Analysis Button on the Query Panel Menu Bar

This will display the Scope of Analysis panel, as shown in Figure 10.7.

Notice that each of the dimension objects from your query appears in this pane. The additional objects shown after the result objects are the objects included in the hierarchy set up in the universe. In the Scope of Analysis panel, Figure 10.7 shows a hierarchy for state that includes STATE, CITY and STORE NAME, and a hierarchy for Year that includes YEAR, QUARTER, and MONTH. These are the applicable levels of drill-down that can be enabled for each dimension object included in the Result Objects pane shown in Figure 10.8.

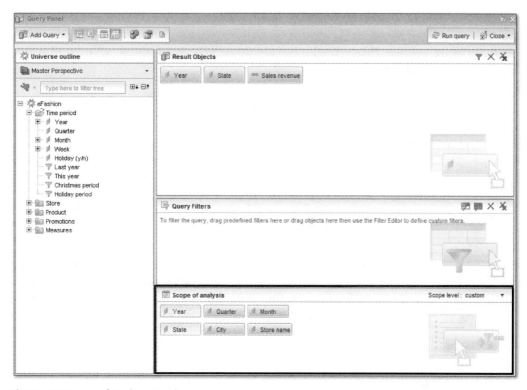

Figure 10.7 Scope of Analysis Panel

In the top right corner of the Scope of Analysis panel is a scope level list drop-down box that is used to define the number of levels of drill-down that should be returned with the query. The options include NONE, ONE LEVEL, TWO LEVELS THREE LEVELS, and CUSTOM, as shown in Figure 10.8.

Figure 10.8 Scope Level Options

Let's look at these options further. If NONE is selected, as it is in Figure 10.9, then only the result objects shown in the Result Objects pane will be returned in the query results. There will be no additional objects returned with the query to enable drill down.

Figure 10.9 Scope Level: None

If ONE LEVEL is selected, as shown in Figure 10.10, then only one level of drill down will be enabled. This will return the dimension object from the Result Objects pane as well as the next one dimension object listed in the scope of analysis. For the result object of State, the query would return State and City.

Figure 10.10 Scope Level: One Level

If TWO LEVELS is selected, as in Figure 10.11, then two levels of drill-down will be enabled. This will return the dimension object from the Result Objects pane as well as the next two dimension objects listed in the scope of analysis.

For the result object of State, the query would return State, City, and Store Name.

If THREE LEVELS is selected, as in Figure 10.12, then three levels of drill-down will be enabled. This will return the dimension object from the Result Objects pane as well as the next three dimension objects listed in the scope of analysis. For the result object of Year, the query would return Year, Quarter, Month, and Week.

Figure 10.11 Scope Level: Two Levels

Figure 10.12 Scope Level: Three Levels

For the State object, only two levels of hierarchy exist in the universe; therefore, only two will show in the Scope of Analysis panel.

If CUSTOM is selected, as in Figure 10.13, then all objects added manually into the Scope of Analysis panel as well as those objects in the Result Objects pane are returned.

In Figure 10.13, the custom scope of analysis is defined without Quarter. Consequently, when you drill down on the report, the Year objects will drill down directly to Month, skipping the Quarter level.

This is useful if certain levels of drilling are not applicable for reporting on certain business questions.

Note
When setting scope of analysis, remember that each new level of drill-down increases the size of the microcube returned with the query results. The larger the microcube, the longer it will take to run the report and the larger the file size maintained in the repository.

Figure 10.13 Scope Level: Custom

While scope of analysis can add value to a report, it can also be a hindrance if end users must wait an unusual amount of time for their report data to populate. Report developers should gather appropriate reporting requirements to determine whether drill-down capability would be a value addition for a report or whether this functionality should not be enabled. If end users will only be viewing one level of drill-down, then it is important to explore the idea of creating two reports or two report tabs to achieve this result. The appropriate choice would depend on each individual report, based on factors such as end user requirements, data being returned, purpose of the report, and output medium.

10.2 Drill-Down Setup in the Report Panel

Once the scope of analysis has been set up in the Query Panel, the query results will return the additional data required to perform drill analysis. Once the data is available at the report level, the user can drill within the report against the report's microcube. No further queries are necessary to run against the database to gather more information as long as drill remains within the defined scope.

10.2.1 Enabling Drill

You can enable the drill feature at the report level either as the report designer in the Web Intelligence report or as the end user in the BI Launch Pad toolbar.

As the Report Designer

The first step to enabling drill functionality in the Report Panel is to check that you are in drill mode. In Web Intelligence, go to design mode on the report that you would like to drill upon. Select the DRILL button on the ANALYSIS tab under the INTERACT section, as shown in Figure 10.14.

Figure 10.14 Drill Button on Web Intelligence Toolbar

Upon selecting the DRILL button, you'll see a drill icon appear on the REPORT tab. If your Web Intelligence options have been set up in BI Launch Pad to open a new report for drilling, then a duplicate report will open in a new window. We will discuss how to personalize your drill settings later in this chapter.

As the End User

If the report designer did *not* enable drill functionality, the end user can enable drill-down on a report in BI Launch Pad from the BI Launch Pad toolbar. After you have selected to view a report in BI Launch Pad, the DRILL button appears on the toolbar, as shown in Figure 10.15. When the user enables the drill feature, his Web Intelligence preferences specify whether the report will open in a new window or whether drill will be enabled in the current window.

Figure 10.15 Drill Button on BI Launch Pad Reading Toolbar

10.2.2 Drill Toolbar

The drill toolbar is enabled at the top of our report to display the drill path. Figure 10.16 shows the drill toolbar display when a user has drilled on Year and State on a table in the report. The drill toolbar shows what path has been taken. These dropdown boxes can also be used to drill back up in the hierarchy by selecting a different option from the list box.

The drill toolbar shows the filters applied to your report. You can also use the drill toolbar to filter additional data elements within your report by dragging the object from the Available Objects pane to the drill toolbar. This functionality works like a report level filter and filters all elements in the report.

Figure 10.16 Drill Toolbar Showing State and Year Drill Filters

10.2.3 Drilling on Dimensions

When Web Intelligence projects the data elements of a query into the report, the measures are calculated based on the dimension objects placed in the same table or chart.

This concept is called calculation context. Figure 10.17 shows a table where SALES REVENUE has been calculated by STATE and STORE NAME because the state and store name objects appear in the table with the measure. State and store name is the context for this calculation.

State	Store name	Sales revenue
California	e-Fashion Los Angeles	$4,220,929
California	e-Fashion San Francisco	$3,258,641
Colorado	e-Fashion Colorado Springs	$2,060,275
DC	e-Fashion Washington Tolbooth	$2,961,950
Florida	e-Fashion Miami Sundance	$1,879,159
Illinois	e-Fashion Chicago 33rd	$3,022,658
Massachusetts	e-Fashion Boston Newbury	$1,283,707
New York	e-Fashion New York 5th	$2,960,367
New York	e-Fashion New York Magnolia	$4,621,854
Texas	e-Fashion Austin	$2,699,673
Texas	e-Fashion Dallas	$1,970,034

Figure 10.17 Table with Sales Revenue Calculated by State and Store Name

Figure 10.18 shows what happens to the calculation of a measure object when the STORE NAME dimension object is removed from the table. Now the measure recalculates and is displayed for each state.

The measure recalculates automatically based on the dimension objects contained in the table with it.

State	Sales revenue
California	$7,479,569
Colorado	$2,060,275
DC	$2,961,950
Florida	$1,879,159
Illinois	$3,022,658
Massachusetts	$1,283,707
New York	$7,582,221
Texas	$10,117,664

Figure 10.18 Table Including State and Sales Revenue Objects

This same concept exists when performing a drill on a report table. As the user drills on a dimension object in a report table or chart, the measure or measures included in that table or chart are recalculated.

There are three forms of drill available on dimension objects: drill down, drill up, and drill by. The concept of calculation context applies to each method.

Drill Down

Once a report has been opened in drill mode, the objects in the tables appear with an underline. The underline indicates which objects are available for drill. To drill down on a dimension object, you need to click on the object name in the table. The drill toolbar will appear, showing the dimension object that has been filtered. You can continue to drill down to the lowest level of grain that was set up in your scope of analysis.

Drill down can be completed by selecting the underlined data element in the report, as shown in Figure 10.19, or by right-clicking on the data element and selecting the DRILL DOWN option from the menu, as shown in Figure 10.20.

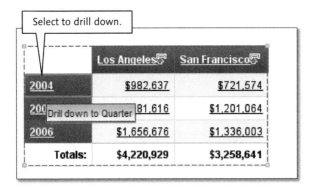

Figure 10.19 Selecting Underlined Data Element in Report to Drill Down to Next Level in Hierarchy

Figure 10.20 Right-Clicking and Drilling Down on a Data Element

In order to drill beyond the objects that were set up in the scope of analysis, the user must extend the scope of analysis. The right to extend a scope of analysis is set up by your BusinessObjects administrator, so not all users will retain this right.

If you have the authority to extend scope of analysis, then when you hover over the object at the end of your scope of analysis, a tooltip will specify the next object that requires a new query, as seen in Figure 10.21.

If your Preferences have been set to prompt before extending the scope of analysis, then a dialog box will appear allowing you to select what filters to apply to the next drill level.

In this example, the scope of analysis only included through Month, so Week is selected to include in further analysis. At this point, you can extend the scope to include Holiday if you know that you will want to include another level of drill as well. As you extend to these levels, the new objects are shown in the Available Objects pane.

Section 10.5 offers further discussion regarding setting your drill preferences.

Figure 10.21 Tooltip to Extend Scope of Analysis

If you select to drill on Year for a scope of analysis of two levels, then you would have to extend the scope of analysis when you reach the dimension of Month.

Figure 10.22 shows the table results of using the extend scope of analysis option in this example.

Drill Up

Drill up enables the user to drill from a lower level of aggregation to a higher level of aggregation. After drilling down to a lower level, you may want to drill back up to a higher grain. You can right-click on the dimension and select DRILL UP from the dropdown menu, as shown in Figure 10.23.

Figure 10.22 Table Results for Extended Scope of Analysis to Include Week

Figure 10.23 Dropdown List to Select Drill Up Option

Another option is to click on the small arrow next to the name of the dimension that appears once you have has drilled down at least one level, as shown in Figure 10.24.

Figure 10.24 Selecting Arrow to Drill Up in Hierarchy

Drill By

The drill by function is found on the right-click menu when the user selects on a dimension object in a report block.

If you go back to the report example shown in Figure 10.17, you are viewing sales revenue by State and Store Name. Drill down and drill up functionality will not answer your business question if your desired result is to view sales revenue for this year by State. In this case, Year is not an option in the drill path for either the State or Store Name objects.

By viewing the scope of analysis, the report developer can see that Year is a separate drill path. You can change from Store Name to Year by switching the drill path using drill by functionality, as shown in Figure 10.25.

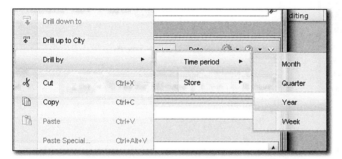

Figure 10.25 Right-Click Menu to Drill by a Dimension Object

When you right-click on STORE NAME and select DRILL BY from the menu, another menu appears with the available choices to drill by. In this example, the choices are TIME PERIOD or STORE, as shown in Figure 10.25.

Once you select TIME PERIOD, another menu appears, showing the available objects in the time period hierarchy to drill by. If you select Year, the measure recalculates for the new dimension object of Year contained within the table.

10.2.4 Drilling on Measures

There is a slight difference seen when drilling on measures. When selecting a measure to drill down or drill up in the hierarchy, Web Intelligence automatically drills all dimensions contained in the table with the measure by one level. Then the measure recalculates for the new dimension objects in the table with it.

Figure 10.26 shows a table with sales revenue calculated by Year and State. When you select the measure object from the table to drill down, then both the State and Year objects are drilled down to the next level of hierarchy. Therefore, the new table appears as shown in Figure 10.27 with sales revenue calculated for City and Quarter.

Figure 10.26 Drill Down on Measure Object

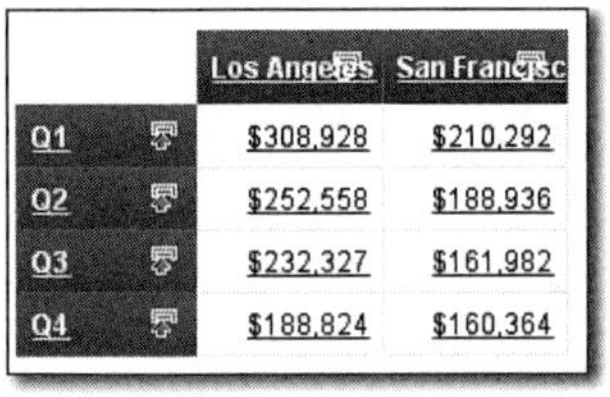

	Los Angeles	San Francisco
Q1	$308,928	$210,292
Q2	$252,558	$188,936
Q3	$232,327	$161,982
Q4	$188,824	$160,364

Figure 10.27 Table After Drill Down on Measure Object

10.2.5 Drilling on Charts

Users can drill on charts in the same ways that they can drill on tables: drill down, drill up, and drill by. Exciting chart drill features that provide a more user-friendly experience to the report consumer are available in Web Intelligence.

Dimensions on Chart Axis

Drill functionality is available on dimensions included in the chart axis. For example, a vertical bar chart containing cities along the X-axis and dollars of sales revenue along the Y-axis details the amount of sales revenue for the respective city.

The user can click on one of the cities on the X-axis to drill down to the next level in the hierarchy. A pop-up box appears showing the next level of drill available, as shown in Figure 10.28.

The same principles for drill up apply as for the tables: You can right-click on the dimension to drill up in order to drill back to the Year dimension or select the up arrow. The user can also select to drill by an object by selecting the DRILL by option from the right-click menu when selecting on a dimension. This functionality works the same as it does with a table. In some cases the chart has multiple dimensions on the axis, as shown in Figure 10.29. In this case, drill by functionality will not be available on the axis of the chart.

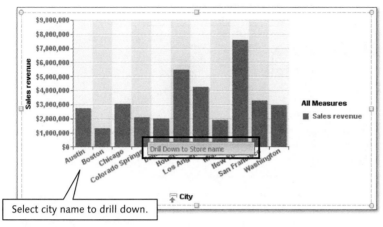

Figure 10.28 Drill Down on Chart Axis Label

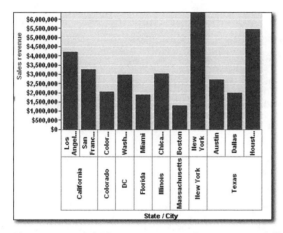

Figure 10.29 Multiple Dimensions on Category Axis of Chart

Dimensions on Legends

Drill functionality is also available on dimensions included in the chart legend as long as the legend is viewable in the report. This feature can be especially helpful for pie charts, for which can it sometimes be difficult to determine which slice belongs to what data element, as shown in Figure 10.30.

In this example, the user can click on one of the states listed in the legend to drill down to the next level in the hierarchy. A pop-up box showing the next level of drill available appears.

257

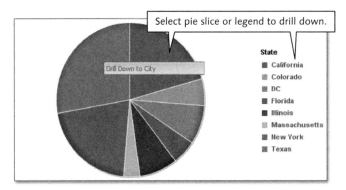

Figure 10.30 Pie Chart Showing Sales Revenue by State

The user can right-click on the dimension to drill up in order to drill back to the State dimension, as done with drill functionality on a chart axis.

The user can also choose to drill by an object by selecting the DRILL BY option from the right-click menu when selecting on a dimension. This functionality works the same as it does with a table.

In some cases the chart has multiple dimensions on the axis as shown in Figure 10.29. In this case, drill by functionality will not be available on the legend of the chart.

Measures on Chart Bars and Markers

An exciting charting feature in Web Intelligence is the ability to select the bar or marker in a chart to drill up or down. This functionality is available on bar charts, pie charts, line charts, and radar charts. For bar charts, users drill on the bars. On pie charts, users drill on the pie slices. Drilling on line and radar charts is done by drilling on the line markers, as shown in Figure 10.31. The bars, slices, or markers of a chart consist of the measure data elements; therefore, the drill functionality is the same as drilling on a measure in a table.

When drilling on a measure, all dimension objects placed with it are drilled down by one level and the measure is recalculated to match the new data elements.

To drill down on the chart bars and markers, select the appropriate bar and click to enable the drill down to the next level in the hierarchy. To drill *up* on the charts and markers, right-click on the bar or marker and select DRILL UP to reach the next highest level in the drill hierarchy.

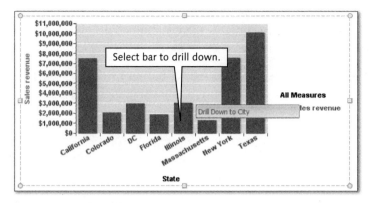

Figure 10.31 Drill on Chart Bars

There are some limitations to drilling on measures in chart bars and markers. Certain chart types—such as 2D and 3D area charts, stacked area charts, radar charts, and scatter charts—do not drill down on all dimensions included in the chart when selecting on the chart measure bars or markers. When drilling on these charts, only the dimension included in the chart legend is drilled upon and therefore the measure object recalculates for this dimension change only.

> **Note**
>
> Measures cannot be drilled upon in 3D area charts.

10.3 Query Drill Option

The query drill feature lets the user drill upon a report without maintaining all the data within the data provider, thereby minimizing the refresh time and the amount of space taken up by the report.

The query drill is also essential when report measures must be calculated at the database level and cannot be calculated properly through normal drill mode. Examples of these measure calculations are ranks, percentages, distinct counts, standard deviations and variances, running aggregates, and lead and lag functions.

These measures would not recalculate correctly if recalculated at the report level during drill down. In this case, you'd need to use the query drill to perform the calculation correctly at the database level. This can be especially useful for data-bases such as Oracle 9i OLAP, which contains aggregate functions not supported at the report level in Web Intelligence.

In order to enable query drill, select the DOCUMENT button from the Properties menu. Select the checkbox for USE QUERY DRILL, as shown in Figure 10.32.

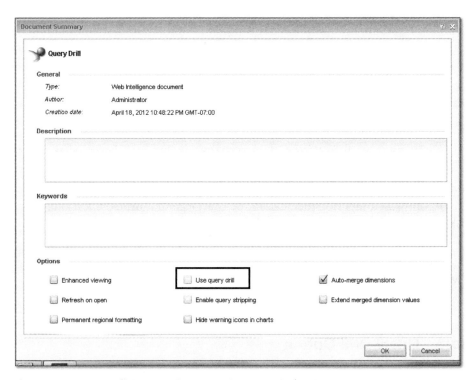

Figure 10.32 Query Drill Option in Document Properties Dialog Box

The query drill works differently than standard drill mode. When a user selects to drill down on Year and selects the year 2001, Web Intelligence not only applies the drill filter to limit the results at the report level, but also applies a query filter to limit the results at the query level.

This means that the user can no longer use the dropdown boxes in the drill tool-bar to change the filter because only the year 2001 exists in the report. Also, the new query filter will affect the entire report. The entire report is now filtered for only the year 2001.

Caution
The query drill applies the drill filter to the report query, so all report tabs will be affected by the drill.
If you drill from Year to Quarter in query drill mode, then the Year object will be removed from your query and replaced with the Quarter object. Therefore, the Year object will be removed from all report tabs in your Web Intelligence report.

10.4   Taking a Snapshot

When performing report analysis using drill functionality, the user may need to refer back to the current state of drill at a later date. Web Intelligence enables the user to take a *snapshot* of the current view of the report for future reference. Once you enable drill functionality from the INTERACT menu in the Analysis ribbon, you'll find the drill menu option to select SNAPSHOT, as seen in Figure 10.33. By selecting this option, a copy of the current report at the current state of drill down is opened in a new report tab. You can save this report snapshot and reference it later.

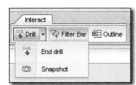

Figure 10.33 Snapshot Option

10.5   User Settings for Drill Down

Users can specify their own settings for drill in their Preferences menus located on the BI Launch Pad toolbar, as shown in Figure 10.34.

Figure 10.34 Preferences Option on BI Launch Pad Toolbar

Your drill options are found on the WEB INTELLIGENCE PREFERENCES tab, as shown in Figure 10.35. Each of these options can provide a more personalized drill experience based on your drill preferences. The overall capability for each of these options is determined by the administrator in the Central Management Console, so not all options may be available to use based on these user rights.

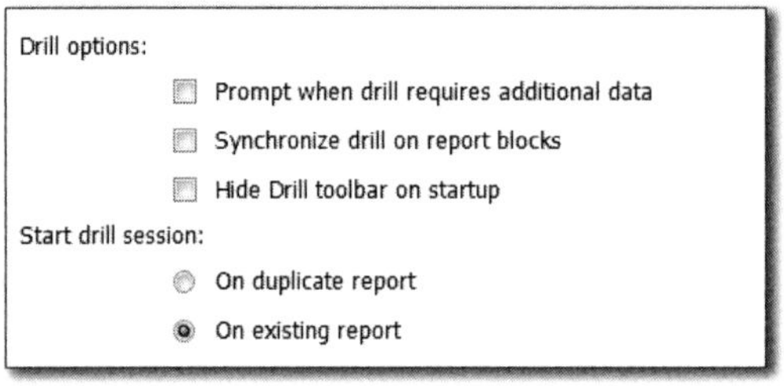

Figure 10.35 Drill Preferences

10.5.1 Prompt When Drill Requires Additional Data

When you need to extend the scope of analysis to view a higher or lower level of drill than was set up in the report scope, then you must run a query to retrieve the additional data. If the PROMPT WHEN DRILL REQUIRES ADDITIONAL DATA option is selected, then you'll be prompted to ensure that you want to run a query before the query is run. If this option is not selected, then a query will automatically be run if you choose to extend the scope of analysis by drilling beyond the designated scope.

10.5.2 Synchronize Drill on Report Blocks

The SYNCHRONIZE DRILL ON REPORT BLOCKS option lets you drill on all report blocks simultaneously. A report block can include tables or charts. If you enable synchronized drill in your Web Intelligence preferences, then when you choose to drill on an object that is contained in more than one report block, the object changes in all report blocks in which it is contained.

If the option is not enabled, then when you select to drill on an object that is contained in more than one report block, the object changes only in the block in which you selected to drill.

10.5.3   Hide Drill Toolbar on Startup

When drill is enabled on a report, a toolbar appears at the top of the screen that shows dropdown boxes with the selected drill filters. You can change the filters by using these boxes and see which filters you've chosen in your drill path by referencing the boxes shown in the drill toolbar.

The drill toolbar can be hidden so it does not show when drill is enabled. In order to set this option, select the checkbox next to HIDE DRILL TOOLBAR in the Web Intelligence Preferences.

10.5.4   Start Drill Session

The START DRILL SESSION option sets whether drill is completed within the current report or whether a new report is opened in a new browser to complete drill mode. The two options are to START DRILL SESSION ON EXISTING REPORT or to START DRILL SESSION ON DUPLICATE REPORT.

10.6   Summary

Drill functionality is an important feature that puts the power of analysis in the end user's hands. It enables users to quickly and easily answer the important business questions by performing drill down, drill up and drill by functions, either by viewing a report in BI Launch Pad or editing a report in Web Intelligence. The report designer can set up reports to provide drill objects within the report's data cube or enable query drill to perform live queries as drill analysis is completed by the end user.

Users can also create snapshots of their results for further analysis or distribution. It is important to know your audience and how the report will be used in order to set up the drill preferences appropriately for your audience. Chapter 11 delves further into the use of formulas and variables in your reports to provide added value to the end consumer.

Create complex calculations by using data objects retrieved from your database along with more than 160 built-in reporting functions and nearly 40 operators in the Formula Editor. By using formulas and variables to transform data into analytical information, you'll be able to make better business decisions.

11 Using Formulas and Variables

Formulas and variables are commonly used structures that allow you to create calculations using the data retrieved from a query. Variables are used to store the calculation syntax of a formula in reusable objects that are saved in Web Intelligence reporting documents.

Variables can be used in reports to perform a variety of tasks that display your data in different ways than when retrieved by queries. Variables can be used to insert `If-Then-Else` logic into a column or chart, contain complex calculations that produce precise views of information, or create analytical formulas that solve difficult business problems—all within a single object that can be used throughout a reporting document.

The *formula bar* provides the capability to quickly revise the definition of an object within a toolbar, similar to Microsoft Excel. The Formula Editor or Create Variable windows can be used to create extensive and detailed formulas with the convenience of viewing all available data elements, functions, and operator types in the same window.

The next several sections will introduce you to the Formula Editor, explain the syntax used in creating formulas and variables, and provide examples to help you get the most out of the editor when creating unique calculations.

11.1   Formulas and Variables

The first step in creating a formula or variable or modifying the definition of an existing field is to enable either the formula bar or Formula Editor. Regardless of the viewer set in the Web Intelligence preferences, the formula bar is accessible only while in design mode. The second step is to understand the syntax used in the Web Intelligence report panel. We'll begin by editing an existing report and describing the various ways to access the Formula Editor, also known as the Create Variable window.

To add a new variable to a reporting document without placing it directly in a data table, select the DATA ACCESS tab provided in the ribbon of tabs located above the report. Next, select the DATA OBJECTS tab in the second set of subtabs. Figure 11.1 shows the New Variable icon accessible inside the DATA OBJECTS tab. The default variable type is dimension. Select the small down arrow immediately to the right of the NEW VARIABLE button to choose between dimension, detail, or measure as the new variable type.

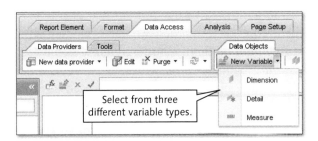

Figure 11.1 Creating a New Variable Object from the Tab Ribbon

11.1.1   Converting In-Place Objects into Formulas

Formulas are calculations created to transform data retrieved by your queries for producing results that solve business problems. These formulas can be created as variables and then used in data tables and charts throughout a Web Intelligence document rather than creating single instances of the formula.

Every object added to a table or chart in a report contains a formula definition, even if the object added comes directly from objects retrieved by the query. Figure 11.2 shows the dimension object selected in a cross table with the formula bar displayed. Notice that the formula for the selected object is =[State].

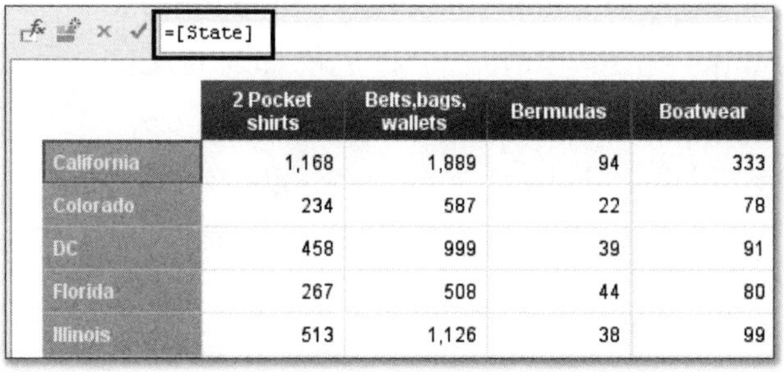

	2 Pocket shirts	Belts,bags, wallets	Bermudas	Boatwear
California	1,168	1,889	94	333
Colorado	234	587	22	78
DC	458	999	39	91
Florida	267	508	44	80
Illinois	513	1,126	38	99

Figure 11.2 Formula of the Selected Dimension Object

The formula or definition of a selected object in a table can be edited by changing the definition in the formula bar. An example of a revision that can be applied to the selected object is displayed in Figure 11.3, in which the `[State]` object was replaced with a formula by modifying the object definition in the formula bar.

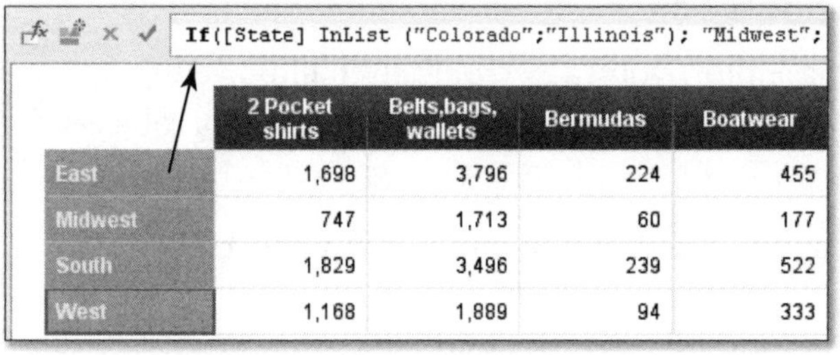

	2 Pocket shirts	Belts,bags, wallets	Bermudas	Boatwear
East	1,698	3,796	224	455
Midwest	747	1,713	60	177
South	1,829	3,496	239	522
West	1,168	1,889	94	333

Figure 11.3 Revised Formula in the Selected Dimension Object

Editing the definition of an object in the formula bar will result only in modifying the specific instance of the object. To use the formula in other report elements within the document, click on the CREATE VARIABLE icon to transform the formula into a variable usable throughout the document.

Tip

Clicking on the CREATE VARIABLE icon located to the left of the formula bar launches the Formula Editor and gives you access to available objects, functions, and operators for creating even more complex and powerful formulas.

Figure 11.4 shows the other commands to use when editing an object definition or formula:

▶ Formula Editor: Launch the Formula Editor by clicking on the Fx icon

▶ Create Variable: Transform the existing formula into a reusable variable

▶ Cancel: Cancel the revisions made to a calculation in the formula bar

▶ Validate Formula: Validate the formula by clicking on the green check icon

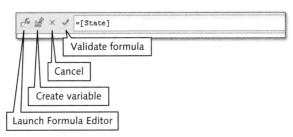

Figure 11.4 Revising the Formula of a Selected Object in a Cross Table

11.1.2   Exploring the Formula Editor

After launching the Formula Editor, you can graphically build or edit your formula by using elements from the following three categories of objects for advanced formula creation:

▶ Data: All result objects and variables that exist within the document

▶ Functions: More than 140 functions are available to be used in formulas

▶ Operators: Nearly 40 operators are available to be used in formulas

Figure 11.5 shows the Formula Editor window, which is used for creating and editing formulas graphically, writing freehand syntax, or a combination of both.

Formulas can be edited manually, by dragging and dropping, or by double-clicking on available objects, formulas, and operators and then placing them in the Formula area. To validate the syntax of the statement created in the formula, click on the green checkmark to the right of the Formula Editor window. If the formula is incorrect, the position of the first invalid identifier will be displayed.

For a quick example of the proper syntax to be used for a function or operator, click on the object and then view the contents of the description box located at the bottom of the formula editor. A brief description of the function or operator will appear, followed by the proper syntax structure of the object selected.

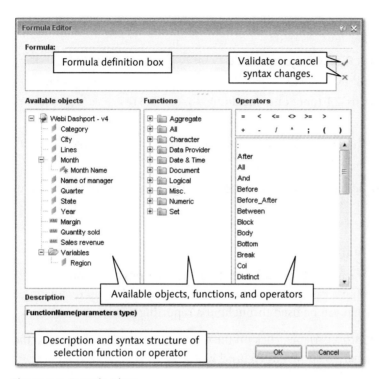

Figure 11.5 Formula Editor

Functions in the formula editor are presented in nine different categories. A tenth category is also provided that contains all 160+ functions. These nine functional groups are listed here along with a few commonly used functions.

▸ Aggregate: Contains 24 functions, including `Average()`, `Min()`, `Max()`, `Sum()`, `Median()`, `Percentage()`, `RunningSum()`

▸ Character: Contains 24 functions, including `Char()`, `FormatNumber()`, `Concatenation()`, `LeftTrim()`, `Pos()`

▸ Date and Time: Contains 17 functions, including `CurrentDate()`, `CurrentTime()`, `LastDayOfMonth()`, `Year()`, `Month()`

▸ Document: Contains 13 functions, including `DocumentAuthor()`, `ReportFilter()`, `DrillFilters()`, `PromptSummary()`

▸ Data Provider: Contains 17 functions, including `UserResponse()`, `Connection()`, `UniverseName()`, `NumberOfRows()`

269

▶ Misc.: Contains 28 functions, including `If()`, `Else`, `Then`, `BlockName`, `CurrentUser()`, `ForceMerge()`, `NameOf()`

▶ Logical: Contains 9 functions, including `Even()`, `IsDate()`, `IsNull()`, `IsNumber()`, `IsString`, `IsTime()`, `Odd()`

▶ Numeric: Contains 23 functions, including `Abs()`, `Ceil()`, `Cos()`, `Floor()`, `Power()`, `Rank()`, `ToNumber()`

▶ Set: Contains 7 functions, include `Ancestor()`, `Children()`, `Descendants()`, `IsLeaf()`, `Lag()`, `Parent()`, `Siblings()`

Section 11.2 provides additional information about and examples of these formulas.

11.1.3 Creating Variables

Variables simply are in-place formulas that have been converted into reusable objects. By promoting a calculation or formula into a variable, you're creating a local result object that can be used throughout a reporting document.

To turn a formula into a variable, click on the CREATE VARIABLE icon located to the left of the formula bar, as shown in Figure 11.6.

Figure 11.6 Create Variable Icon to Convert the Formula into a Variable

The Create Variable window allows you to perform all of the same tasks as the Formula Editor with the addition of being able to assign a name and qualification to the variable. If DETAIL is selected as the qualification type, you also have the opportunity to assign an associated dimension to the object. The following are the modifiable sections in the variable definition section of a new variable:

▶ Name: Provide a descriptive and user-friendly term or short phrase to uniquely identify and clearly describe the variable.

▶ Qualification: Select DIMENSION, MEASURE, or DETAIL as the variable qualification type (if DETAIL selected, choose a dimension that the new detail object should be associated with).

▶ Formula: Review the syntax of the formula to be used in the variable.

Figure 11.7 shows the Create Variable window used to name and set the qualification of a new variable object being converted from a formula.

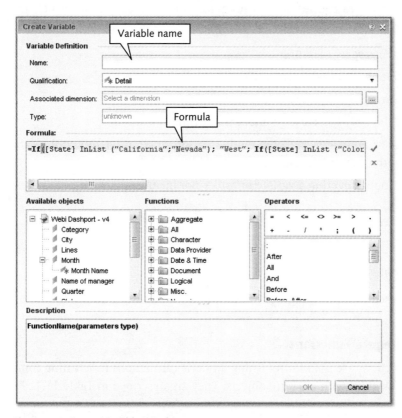

Figure 11.7 Create Variable Window

11.2 Reporting Functions and Operators

Web Intelligence 4.0 provides an even more extensive set of reporting functions with which you can create very detailed and complex formulas for producing advanced reporting documents.

This section introduces you to the full list of reporting functions available for creating formulas and variables in the Report Panel. More than 140 reporting functions can be easily located within nine functional categories.

The broad collection of operators used in formulas and variables is also described here. With more than 40 available operators, report developers can create precise formulas that leverage the full set of built-in reporting functions.

The nine function categories for creating formulas in the Report Panel are reviewed here:

- Aggregate: Aggregate measures
- Character: Functions that interact with character data
- Date and Time: Functions created with date data
- Document: Identify information about the current document
- Data Provider: Functions available to identify information relating to the data provider in the current document
- Misc.: Functions covering a variety of topics not included in the other categories
- Logical: Logical Boolean functions
- Numeric: Numerical related functions
- Set: Multidimensional functions

Let's look at each function category in more detail.

11.2.1 Aggregate Functions

Aggregate functions are used for returning numeric calculations for creating commonly used formulas with measure objects. They are described in Table 11.1.

Function	Description
Aggregate (measure,set)	Used in a reports sourced from BEx queries to aggregate values by set
Average (measure;IncludeEmpty)	Returns the average value of a measure

Table 11.1 Aggregate Functions

Function	Description
Count (dimension|measure; IncludeEmpty;Distinct|All)	Returns the number of values in a dimension or measure
First (dimension|measure)	Returns the first value in a data set
Interpolation (measure; PointToPoint|Linear; NotOnBreak;Row|Column)	Calculates empty measure values by interpolation
Last (dimension|measure)	Returns the last value in a dimension or measure
Max (dimension|measure)	Returns the largest value in a dimension or measure
Median (measure)	Returns the median (middle value) of a measure
Min (dimension|measure)	Returns the smallest value in a dimension or measure
Mode (dimension|measure)	Returns the most frequently occurring value in a data set
Percentage (measure;break;row|col)	Expresses a measure value as a percentage of its embedding context
Percentile (measure;percentile)	Returns the (nth) percentile of a measure
Product (measure)	Multiplies the values of a measure
RunningAverage (measure; Row|Col;IncludeEmpty;reset_dims)	Returns the running average of a measure
RunningCount (dimension| measure;Row|Col; IncludeEmpty;reset_dims)	Returns the running count of a number set
RunningMax (dimension| measure;Row|Col;reset_dims)	Returns the running maximum of a dimension or measure
RunningMin (dimension| measure;Row|Col;reset_dims)	Returns the running minimum of a dimension or measure
RunningProduct (dimension| measure;Row|Col;reset_dims)	Returns the running product of a measure

Table 11.1 Aggregate Functions (Cont.)

Function	Description
RunningSum (dimension|measure;Row|Col;reset_dims)	Returns the running sum of a measure
StdDev (measure)	Returns the standard deviation of a measure
StdDevP (measure)	Returns the population standard deviation of a measure
Sum (measure)	Returns the sum of a measure
Var (measure)	Returns the variance of a measure
VarP (measure)	Returns the population variance of a measure

Table 11.1 Aggregate Functions (Cont.)

11.2.2 Character Functions

Character functions are primarily used for performing tasks that manipulate dimension objects (see Table 11.2).

Function	Description
Asc (string)	Returns the ASCII value of a character
Char (ascii_code)	Returns the character associated with an ASCII code
Concatenation (first_string; second_string)	Concatenates (joins) two character strings
Fill (repeating_string; num_repeats)	Builds a string by repeating a string n times
FormatDate (date;format_string)	Formats a date according to a specified format
FormatNumber (number; format_string)	Formats a number according to a specified format
HTMLEncode (html)	Applies HTML encoding rules to a string
InitCap (string)	Capitalizes the first letter of a string
Left (string;num_chars)	Returns the leftmost characters of a string

Table 11.2 Character Functions

Function	Description
LeftPad (padded_string; length;left_string)	Pads a string on its left with another string
LeftTrim (trimmed_string)	Trims the leading spaces from a string
Length (string)	Returns the number of characters in a string
Lower (string)	Converts a string to lowercase
Match (string;pattern)	Determines whether a string matches a pattern
Pos (string;pattern)	Returns the starting position of a text pattern in a string
Replace (replace_in; replaced_string;replace_with)	Replaces part of a string with another string
Right (string;num_chars)	Returns the rightmost characters of a string
RightPad (padded_string; length;right_string)	Pads a string on its right with another string
RightTrim (trimmed_string)	Trims the trailing spaces from strings
Substr (string;start;length)	Returns part of a string
Trim (trimmed_string)	Trims the leading and trailing spaces from a string
Upper (string)	Converts a string to uppercase
URLEncode (html)	Applies URL encoding rules to a string
WordCap (string)	Capitalizes the first letter of all of the words in a string

Table 11.2 Character Functions (Cont.)

11.2.3 Date and Time Functions

Date and Time functions allow developers to extract date elements from date objects and calculate date differences (see Table 11.3).

275

Function	Description
CurrentDate()	Returns the current date formatted according to the regional settings
CurrentTime()	Returns the current time formatted according to the regional settings
DayName (date)	Returns the day name from a date from the data passed to the function
DayNumberOfMonth (date)	Returns the day number in a month from the data passed to the function
DayNumberOfWeek (date)	Returns the day number in a week from the data passed to the function
DayNumberOfYear (date)	Returns the day number in a year from the data passed to the function
DaysBetween (first_date;last_date)	Returns the number of days between two dates passed into the function
LastDayOfMonth (date)	Returns the date of the last day in a month
LastDayOfWeek (date)	Returns the date of the last day in a week
Month (date)	Returns the month name in a date
MonthNumberOfYear (date)	Returns the month number in a date
MonthsBetween (first_date;last_date)	Returns the number of months between two dates
Quarter (date)	Returns the quarter number in a date
RelativeDate (start_date;num_days)	Returns a date relative to another date
ToDate (date_string;format)	Returns a character string formatted according to a date format
Week (date)	Returns the week number in the year from the date passed to the function
Year (date)	Returns the year in a date from the date passed to the function

Table 11.3 Date and Time Functions

11.2.4 Document Functions

Document functions, which are shown in Table 11.4, let you identify various attributes of a reporting document.

Function	Description
DocumentAuthor ()	Returns the logon of the document creator
DocumentCreationDate ()	Returns the date on which a document was created
DocumentCreationTime ()	Returns the time when a document was created
DocumentDate ()	Returns the date on which a document was last saved
DocumentName ()	Returns the document name
DocumentOwner ()	Returns the logon of the user that last saved the document
DocumentPartiallyRefreshed ()	Determines whether a document is partially refreshed
DocumentTime ()	Returns the time when a document was last saved
DrillFilters (object|separator)	Returns the drill filters applied to a document or object in drill mode
PromptSummary ()	Returns the prompt text and user response of all prompts in a document
QuerySummary (query_name)	Returns information about the queries in a document
ReportFilter (object)	Returns the report filters applied to an object or report
ReportFilterSummary (report_name)	Returns a summary of the report filters in a document or report

Table 11.4 Document Functions

11.2.5 Data Provider Functions

Data Provider functions (shown in Table 11.5) let you create formulas that retrieve various details about the query, retrieved result set, and universe used to build the query.

Function	Description
Connection ([query_name])	Returns the parameters of the database connection used by a data provider
DataProvider (object)	Returns the name of the data provider containing a report object
DataProviderKeyDate ([query_name])	Returns the keydate of a data provider
DataProviderKeyDateCaption ([query_name])	Returns the keydate caption of a data provider
DataProviderSQL ([query_name])	Returns the SQL generated by a data provider
DataProviderType ([query_name])	Returns the type of a data provider
IsPromptAnswered ([query_name];prompt_string)	Determines whether a prompt has been answered
LastExecutionDate ([query_name])	Returns the date on which a data provider was last refreshed
LastExecutionDuration ([query_name])	Returns the time in seconds taken by the last refresh of a data provider
LastExecutionTime ([query_name])	Returns the time at which a data provider was last refreshed
NumberOfDataProviders ()	Returns the number of data providers in a report
NumberOfRows ([query_name])	Returns the number of rows in a data provider
RefValueDate ()	Returns the date of the reference data used for data tracking
RefValueUserResponse ([query_name]; prompt_string;index)	Returns the response to a prompt when the reference data was the current data

Table 11.5 Data Provider Functions

Function	Description
ServerValue ([measure])	Returns the value of a measure calculated by the database
UniverseName ([query_name])	Returns the name of the universe on which a data provider is based
UserResponse ([query_name]; prompt_string;index)	Returns the response to a prompt

Table 11.5 Data Provider Functions (Cont.)

11.2.6 Misc. Functions

A wide variety of functions are included in the Misc. category that returns details about components and features of a report (see Table 11.6).

Function	Description
BlockName ()	Returns the block name
ColumnNumber ()	Returns the column number
CurrentUser ()	Returns the login of the current user
[member].Depth	Returns the depth of a specified member in a hierarchy
Else (false_value)	Returns a value from the If function when the test expression is false
ElseIf (test_value)	Used to nest an If function within another If function
ForceMerge (measure)	Includes synchronized dimensions in measure calculations when the dimensions aren't in the measure's calculation context
GetContentLocale ()	Returns the locale of the data contained in the document (the Document Locale)
GetDominantPreferredViewing Locale ()	Returns the dominant locale in the user's Preferred Viewing Locale group

Table 11.6 Misc. Functions

Function	Description
GetLocale ()	Returns the user's locale used to format the Web Intelligence interface (the Product Locale)
GetLocalized (string;comment)	Returns a string localized according to the user's Preferred Viewing Locale
GetPreferredViewingLocale ()	Returns the user's preferred locale for viewing document data (the Preferred Viewing Locale)
If (boolean_value;true_value; false_value)	Returns a value based on whether an expression is true or false
[member].Key	Returns the key of a member
LineNumber ()	Returns the line number in a table
[member].Name	Returns the name of a member
NameOf (object)	Returns the name of an object
NoFilter (object;all|drill)	Ignores filters when calculating a value
NumberOfPages ()	Returns the number of pages in a report
Page ()	Returns the current page number in a report
Previous (dimension|measure| Self; reset_dims; offset; NoNull)	Returns a previous value of an object
RefValue (object)	Returns the reference value of a report object when data tracking is activated
RelativeValue (measure|detail; slicing_dims;offset)	Returns previous or subsequent values of an object
RepFormula	Appears when a document has been converted from Desktop Intelligence and previously used a function not supported in Web Intelligence, such as BlockNumber()
ReportName ()	Returns the name of a report
RowIndex ()	Returns the number of a row

Table 11.6 Misc. Functions (Cont.)

Function	Description
Then true_value	Returns a value from the If function when the test expression is true
UniqueNameOf (object)	Returns the unique name of an object

Table 11.6 Misc. Functions (Cont.)

11.2.7 Logical Functions

Logical functions determine whether an object is true or false by returning either a 1 or 0 (see Table 11.7).

Function	Description
Even (number)	Determines whether a number is even
IsDate (object)	Determines whether a value is a date
IsError (object)	Determines whether an object returns an error
IsLogical (object)	Determines whether a value is Boolean
IsNull (object)	Determines whether a value is null
IsNumber (object)	Determines whether a value is a number
IsString (object)	Determines whether a value is a string
IsTime (object)	Determines whether a variable is a time variable
Odd (number)	Determines whether a number is odd

Table 11.7 Logical Functions

11.2.8 Numeric Functions

Numeric functions allow you to manipulate and measure values in a variety of ways, as shown in Table 11.8.

Function	Description
Abs (number)	Returns the absolute value of a number
Ceil (number)	Returns a number rounded up to the nearest integer
Cos (angle)	Returns the cosine of an angle
EuroConvertFrom (euro_amount; curr_code;round_level)	Converts a Euro amount to another currency
EuroConvertTo (noneuro_amount; curr_code;round_level)	Converts an amount to Euros
EuroFromRoundError (euro_amount; curr_code;round_level)	Returns the rounding error in a conversion from Euros
EuroToRoundError (noneuro_amount; curr_code;round_level)	Returns the rounding error in a conversion to Euros
Exp (power)	Returns an exponential (e raised to a power)
Fact (number)	Returns the factorial of a number
Floor (number)	Returns a number rounded down to the nearest integer
Ln (number)	Returns the natural logarithm of a number
Log (number;base)	Returns the logarithm of a number in a specified base
Log10 (number)	Returns the base 10 logarithm of a number
Mod (dividend;divisor)	Returns the remainder from the division of two numbers
Power (number;power)	Returns a number raised to a power
Rank (measure;ranking_dims; Top|Bottom;reset_dims)	Ranks a measure by dimensions
Round (number;round_level)	Rounds a number
Sign (number)	Returns the sign of a number
Sin (angle)	Returns the sine of an angle
Sqrt (number)	Returns the square root of a number

Table 11.8 Numeric Functions

Function	Description
Tan (angle)	Returns the tangent of an angle
ToNumber (string)	Returns a string as a number
Truncate (number;truncate_level)	Truncates a number

Table 11.8 Numeric Functions (Cont.)

11.2.9 Set Functions

A series of set functions have been added to the Report Panel to get more information from data retrieved by BEx queries. Use these functions to identify ancestral information relating to hierarchical members, including parents, children, siblings, and ancestors of a specific member.

Many of these functions are used primarily in the input parameter in aggregate functions to specify a member to be aggregated and cannot be used as stand-alone functions. When using a member in a function, you need either to specify the member explicitly or provide the full hierarchical path of the member.

Table 11.9 provides a list of the set functions followed by a description of each.

Function	Description
Ancestor (member;level|distance)	Returns an ancestor member of a member by either level or distance
[member].Children	Returns the child members of a specified member or member path
Descendants (member;level | distance;desc_flag)	Returns the descendant member of a specified member by either level or distance; optionally, in the desc_flag position, use either Self, Before, After, Self_Before, Self_After, Before_After, Self_Before_After, or Leaves.
[member].IsLeaf	Determines whether a member is a leaf member; returns either True or False.

Table 11.9 Numeric Functions

Function	Description
[member].Lag (distance)	Returns the members before or after a specified member; use a negative distance to identify the member before; use a positive number to identify the member after
[member].Parent	Returns the parent member of a specified member
[member].Siblings	Returns the sibling members of a specified member

Table 11.9 Numeric Functions (Cont.)

11.2.10 Operators

Operators are symbols used in formulas and variables to indicate the type of operation you want to perform. More than 35 operators are available for creating formulas in Web Intelligence reporting functions.

Formulas can contain several different combinations of operators, which are used to solve a variety of business problems.

Report operators are grouped into the following six categories, each of which has a corresponding table:

- Mathematical (see Table 11.10)
- Conditional (see Table 11.11)
- Logical (see Table 11.12)
- Function-specific (see Table 11.13)
- Extended syntax operators (see Table 11.14)
- Extended syntax keywords (see Table 11.15)
- Hierarchical operators (see Table 11.16)

Operator	Description
-	Subtraction
+	Addition

Table 11.10 Mathematical Operators

Operator	Description
*	Multiplication
/	Division

Table 11.10 Mathematical Operators (Cont.)

Operator	Description
=	Equal to
>	Greater than
<	Less than
>=	Greater than or equal to
<=	Less than or equal to
<>	Not equal to

Table 11.11 Conditional Operators

Operator	Description
And	Links Boolean values, commonly used in IF statements
Or	Links Boolean values, commonly used in IF statements
Not	Returns the opposite of a Boolean value
Between	Determines whether a value is between two values
InList	Determines whether a value is within a list of values

Table 11.12 Logical Operators

Operator	Description
All	Used as an optional parameter in many functions to calculate All or Distinct values
Drill	Used with the NoFilter function to ignore report filters
Bottom	Ranks values in ascending order

Table 11.13 Function-Specific Operators

Operator	Description
Break	Forces the `Percentage` function to calculate within table breaks
Col	Optionally used to set the calculation direction in the following functions: `Percentage, RunningAverage, RunningCount, RunningMax, RunningMin, RunningProduct, RunningSum`
Distinct	Used as an optional parameter in many functions to calculate Distinct or All values
IncludeEmpty	Optionally used to tell an aggregate function to include empty values
Index	Used by the `UserResponse` and `RefValueUserResponse` functions to return the database primary key of a prompt response
Linear	Used by the `Interpolation` function to use linear regression
NoNull	Tells the `Previous` function to ignore null values
NotOnBreak	Optionally used by the `Interpolation` function to ignore section and block breaks
PointToPoint	Used by the `Interpolation` function to use point-to-point to account for missing values
Row	Optionally used to set the calculation direction in the following functions: `Percentage, RunningAverage, RunningCount, RunningMax, RunningMin, RunningProduct, RunningSum`
Self	Refers the `Previous` function to the previous cell when it doesn't contain a report object
Top	Ranks values in descending order
Where	Restricts the data to calculate a measure

Table 11.13 Function-Specific Operators (Cont.)

Operator	Description
In	Specifies an explicit list of dimensions to use in the context
ForAll	Removes dimensions from the default context
ForEach	Adds dimensions to the default

Table 11.14 Extended Syntax Operators

Operator	Description
Block	Refers to data within an entire block, ignores breaks, respects filters: Sum([Revenue]) In Block
Body	Displays the value of the data presented in a block and can be used in a footer, header, or body: Sum([Revenue]) In Body
Break	Calculates the total for the dimension used in a break: Sum([Revenue] In Break
Report	Displays all report data: Sum([Revenue]) In Report
Section	Calculates the section total of a measure when section has been set in a report: Sum([Revenue]) in Section

Table 11.15 Extended Syntax Keywords

The hierarchical operators are used in place of the *desc_flag* keyword in the Descendants function to specify the distance of the descendant in relation to the specified member.

Operator	Description
After	Returns the descendants *after* the level or distance is specified in the Descendants function
Before	Returns the descendants *before* the level or distance is specified in the Descendants function
Before_After	Returns the current member and all descendants except those specified by the level|distance parameter in the Descendants function
Leaves	Returns all members between the current member and the level or distance specified for members that do not have child members
Self_After	Returns the current member and all descendants at and *after* the level or distance specified in the Descendants function
Self_Before	Returns the current member and all descendants at and *before* the level or distance specified in the Descendants function
Self_Before_After	Returns the current member and all descendants

Table 11.16 Hierarchical Operators

11.3   Formula Syntax

The first step in writing formulas and creating variables is to understand the Web Intelligence formula syntax. You must follow a few basic rules to create a valid formula. Once you understand how to apply these basic rules, the task of writing a formula will no longer be a challenge. You can then focus your efforts on writing formulas and building analytical Web Intelligence reports that provide the greatest value to your client.

11.3.1   Primary Formula Syntax Rules

Consider these primary rules:

1. Each formula must begin with the equals symbol (=).
2. Data objects used in a formula must be encapsulated by brackets ([ ]).
3. Use a semicolon to represent `Else` in an `If-Then-Else` statement (;).
4. Use a semicolon to represent `Then` in an `If-Then-Else` statement (;).
5. Every statement with an open parenthesis must also include a closing parenthesis.
6. Click on the green checkmark button to validate the syntax of the formula or variable.
7. Change the qualification type when creating a measure or detail variable.
8. Assign a commonly used business term or phrase with the proper naming convention as the variable name.

11.3.2   If – Then – Else Syntax

Figure 11.8 shows a simple formula entered into the Formula Editor window. Several key areas of the formula are labeled in the screenshot, including three of the most important rules:

1. Begin a formula with the equals symbol (=).
2. Use a semicolon for `THEN` (;).
3. Use a semicolon for `ELSE` (;).

(You'll notice that these rules are repeated from the list of primary syntax rules.)

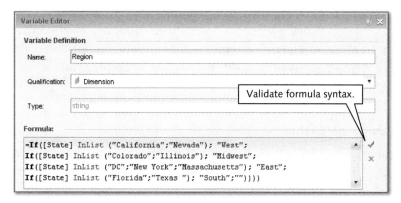

Figure 11.8 Example of Variable Syntax in a Formula

The formula in Figure 11.8 is listed as

```
=If([State] InList ("California";"Nevada"); "West"; If([State] InList (
"Colorado";"Illinois"); "Midwest"; If([State] InList ("DC";"New York";
"Massachusetts"); "East"; If([State] InList ("Florida";"Texas ");
"South";""))))
```

This statement is translated into English as the following:

> *If the State data object contains values of California or Nevada, then assign the value to West. If the State data object contains values of Colorado or Illinois, then assign the value to Midwest. If the State data object contains values of DC, New York, or Massachusetts, then assign the value to East. If the State data object contains values of Florida or Texas, then assign the value to South. If the State data object contains values other than the nine items states previously listed, then return an empty string. An empty string is symbolized with two double quotes: "".*

11.3.3 Saving a Variable

Before clicking on OK in the Formula Editor and saving a formula, click on the green checkmark button located to the right of the formula. This button validates the syntax in the formula.

If the syntax is valid, a small statement beneath the formula will appear that reads "The formula is correct." Click on OK to at the bottom of the Formula Editor to proceed.

If there's an error in the syntax, the formula cannot be validated. To close the formula editor, all modifications will either have to be discarded or revised to include the correct syntax. If an error in the formula is present, the position of the first occurrence will be displayed beneath the formula when the syntax is validated.

11.3.4 Modifying a Variable

When a variable is created in a Web Intelligence report, the new object will be added to the Available Objects section for use in report elements throughout the document. The variable will appear along with all of the existing result objects returned from the query. Figure 11.9 shows the region variable created in the previous section.

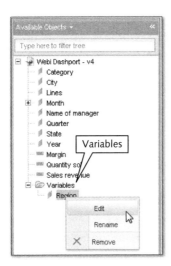

Figure 11.9 Right-Clicking on a Variable to Edit, Rename, or Remove

All variables created in a document are easily identified because they're automatically added to a variables folder. To modify a variable, right-click on the object and select EDIT. Editing a variable will launch the Variable Editor, in which you can modify the formula, name, or qualification of the object.

11.4   Summary

Functions and variables allow report developers to provide valuable analytical insight by using business data to create calculations. Data retrieved by a Web Intelligence query can be used in combination with over 160 functions and almost 40 operators to create complex and precise formulas.

Formulas can be converted into variables, used throughout an entire reporting document, and saved within a document to provide ongoing and maintenance-free analysis.

You can use result objects returned by your queries to create functions that aggregate data, extract information from dates, or dissect string values by using character functions.

You can create formulas and variables to calculate data at an even more detailed level of analysis by using a unique set of operators. Examples of these operators include filtering values with the `Where` operator and aggregating values by block, section, or report.

Chapter 12 discusses how to extend Query Panel functionalities.

You can apply complex filtering strategies when retrieving data to create reports with highly customized and refined data sets. Use advanced querying techniques to produce highly focused reporting documents.

12   Extending Query Panel Functionality

All reporting requirements begin with a business question and end with a refined set of data displayed in a report that delivers a clear business answer. You can achieve your reporting objectives and make more informed decisions when data is transformed into actionable information. SAP BusinessObjects Web Intelligence 4.0 allows report viewers and report writers to achieve these goals by providing several different query filtering options for producing highly constrained data sets.

You can retrieve data and create powerful and interactive reports by using many advanced techniques in the Query Panel. These techniques include modifying the generated SQL with freehand SQL, creating complex and nested filters, and prompting the user for input with optional filters.

When queries are refreshed and data is returned, each Web Intelligence document stores the data in its own microcube. After data is in the microcube, you can create reports by adding result objects to a variety of available components. Chapters 3 through 9 provided very detailed information on creating and filtering reports.

Visually tracking data changes in a report is discussed later in this chapter. Data tracking is used to assist users with identifying revised or updated data from the most recent refresh compared to the previously refreshed instance.

We'll start the discussion of extending the Query Panel with information on the complex filtering options available, and then move to cascading prompts, tracking data changes, and previewing a sample of data before running the query.

12.1   Complex Filtering Options

Several techniques can be employed in the Query Panel to filter data retrieved by a query. Chapter 2 discussed the use of combined queries and subqueries in the Query Panel.

This section covers additional methods of filtering queries to produce reports that contain the data needed for solving specific business problems.

12.1.1   Filtering with Wildcards

You can use wildcards to help you filter an object when the entire value isn't known, such as when the exact spelling of the intended filter is uncertain.

Wildcards are created by using the matches pattern operator. Figure 12.1 shows the [State] object using the matches pattern operator and % wildcard to return all states that begin with C.

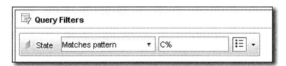

Figure 12.1 Query Filter Using Matches Pattern and the % Wildcard

Use the underscore character for each character to be represented in a filtered value. For example, if you want to filter an object to return the color BEIGE, use both wildcards in combination with the known characters.

Figure 12.2 shows two different wildcards with the [Color] object, in which a percentage sign is used to represent any number of characters, and an underscore is used to represent a single character.

Figure 12.2 Custom Filter Containing the Wildcards _ and %

The matches pattern operator is converted to LIKE when the SQL statement is generated. Figure 12.3 shows the SQL translation of the operator in combination with the % wildcard.

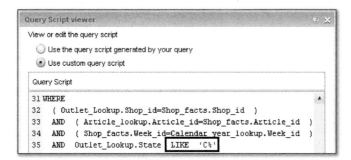

Figure 12.3 Matches Pattern Converted to LIKE in Generated SQL

Figure 12.4 shows the SQL generated by the matches pattern operator that includes an underscore wildcard and a % wildcard.

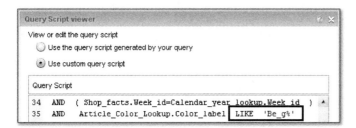

Figure 12.4 SQL Generated by the Matches Pattern Operator

12.1.2 Nested Query Filters

You can use nested query filters to group a series of targeted constraints that return a precise data set.

When you nest filters, dimensions and measures can be grouped into several combinations by using the AND or OR operators. Nested filters can be applied to many layers of grouped objects with the AND or OR operator. This method of filtering is very easy to set up.

Adding and Nesting Query Filters

To add and nest query filters, follow these steps:

1. Drag and drop predefined filters, prompted objects, or standard results objects into the Query Panel.

2. Drop the filter directly on top of an existing filter object to nest the filter.

3. Drop the filter immediately beneath an existing filter to apply filtering outside of a nested relationship.

4. Double-click on the AND and OR operator located immediately to the left of the nested group to toggle the operator type.

Figure 12.5 shows several query filters included at the same level in a Web Intelligence document grouped by default with the AND operator. If a query containing the filters in the screenshot were executed, the result would include only results from the current year's [Christmas period], [owned stores] only, and for color lines that begin with "be". The results must meet all criteria in order for results to be returned.

But if the filters were grouped using the OR operator for the nested collection of filters, the SQL statement would be generated differently and results would be returned relating to any of the four filters rather than all four.

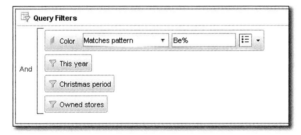

Figure 12.5 Query Filters Without Nesting

Note

The default group operator is AND. Double-click on it to change it to OR. Query filters can be grouped by both AND and OR in the same document.

Nesting Filters

Figure 12.6 shows the exact same filters listed in the previous screenshot but the results from the two queries are quite different. The SQL statement generated with this set of query filters returns rows that meet the criteria from two pairs of filters separated by the OR operator. Results from [This year] or when the [Color] object begins with "Be" make up the first pair of filters; the second pair limits the results to either [Owned stores] or [Christmas period].

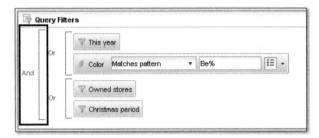

Figure 12.6 Nested Query Filters

Query filters can be added to a nested group with objects that have already been added to the Query Filters pane or by dragging and dropping new custom or pre-defined filter objects into the Query Filters pane.

Creating a Nested Group

To create a nested group, drop an object on top of an existing filter in the Query pane. A thin vertical line will be displayed to the left of two or more filters to denote that a nested group has been created with the filters. Double-click on AND to the left of the thin vertical line to switch the nested group to the OR operator.

This can also be achieved with existing filters by dragging and dropping an object on top of another filter to add it to an existing group. Figure 12.7 shows the pre-defined [Christmas period] filter being dropped onto the [Owned stores] filter to create a new nested filter group.

Figure 12.7 Creating a New Nested Group with Existing Query Filters

Un-Nest Query Filters

To remove a query filter from a nested group, drag and drop it to a different location. This can mean moving it to a different nested group or removing it completely from all nested groups.

Figure 12.8 shows the [This year] object being moved from a nested group and dropped to the bottom of the query filters.

Figure 12.8 Removing a Query Filter from a Nested Group

12.1.3   Database Ranking

Database ranking is used in a reporting document to return only the rows meeting the ranking criteria. By pushing ranking onto the database instead of performing ranking locally, you can significantly minimize the amount of data retrieved in a Web Intelligence document.

However, you can use database ranking only if your database supports it. These databases include Oracle, DB2, Teradata, and SQL Server. The addition of a database ranking shortcut icon will be disabled if your database doesn't support ranking.

Adding Database Ranking

You can add database ranking to a document by clicking on the ADD A DATABASE RANKING button located in the upper right corner of the Query Filters pane, as shown in Figure 12.9. Click this icon to configure the database ranking parameters. The default setup is arranged to return the Top 10 <dimensions> based on a <measure>. Below are details about the options available when adding a database ranking.

▶ Rank direction: The default ranking number is set to 10 but can be adjusted up or down:

  ▷ Top: Returns the top 10 <dimension> object values based on the <measure>, with the number 10 being adjustable

  ▷ Bottom: Returns the bottom 10 <dimension> object values based on the <measure>, with the number 10 being adjustable

  ▷ % Top: Returns the top 10% of the <dimension> object based on the <measure>, with 10 being adjustable

  ▷ % Bottom: Returns the bottom 10% of the <dimension> object based on the <measure>, with 10 being adjustable

▶ Ranked number: Use the default number of 10, change to a different constant value, or prompt the user for a value

▶ Context for ranking: Insert a dimension object to be used in the ranking by dragging and dropping it into the database ranking structure

▶ Ranking based on: Drop a measure object as the basis for the ranking

▶ Optional rank: Add another dimension object to rank by

▶ Ranking filtering: Drop predefined filters or objects for custom filters to restrict the dataset returned by the ranking query

Figure 12.9 Adding Database Ranking in the Query Panel

The Database Ranking Parameters filter will be added to the Query Filters pane when add a database ranking is clicked. Figure 12.10 shows the database ranking parameter filter object.

Figure 12.10 Database Ranking Parameters

Enabling Database Ranking

To complete the parameters for database ranking, follow these steps:

1. Select a ranking direction (top or bottom).

2. Enter the number of records to be ranked, or click on the small down arrow beside the value box to select PROMPT. The default value is Constant.

3. Drop a dimension object for the context of the ranking.

4. Drop measure object to be ranked in the BASED ON box.

5. (Optional) Specify additional calculation context by clicking the small arrow to the right of the BASED ON measure to expand the ranking parameters box and display a FOR EACH (dimension) option.

Whenever possible, apply complex filtering options at the query level rather than at the report level to produce a result set that already meets the business requirements. Simple filters added in the Report Panel can be easily removed and can potentially misrepresent the information. By restricting the results at the query level, only the needed information is returned.

Filters can also be added at the query level that prompts users for input when the report is opened or refreshed. The next section describes how to set up optional prompts that present users with a list of available values to select from.

12.2   Cascading and Optional Prompts

Cascading prompts are used to assist users with selecting values in prompted Web Intelligence reports. Use the Universe Design Tool to create and modify cascading prompts for dimension objects by creating a cascading List of Values (LOVs).

Figure 12.11 shows the steps for opening the Create a Cascading List of Values window. Use the following menu path to begin setting up cascading lists of values: TOOLS • LISTS OF VALUES • CREATE CASCADING LISTS OF VALUES.

Figure 12.11 Create Cascading Lists of Values in Designer

12.2.1 Defining a Cascading List of Values in the Universe Design Tool

Figure 12.12 displays the Create Cascading List of Values window. You can use this utility to provide users with a hierarchical structure for selecting values in prompted reports. By providing a functional context of the dimensional values, users have a better understanding of the data in a report that uses a cascading list of values in the prompted filter.

To add dimensional objects to a cascading list, double-click on dimension objects or select them from the list of available objects, and click the > icon. LOVs should be created from logical hierarchies previously set up in the universe.

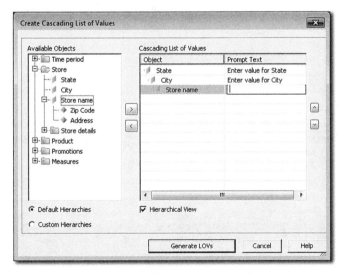

Figure 12.12 Cascading Lists of Values Dialog Window

To create a cascading LOV, follow these steps:

1. Select objects to generate a cascading list of values.

2. Click the > symbol to add objects to the Cascading List of Values section.

3. Revise the prompt text of each object (optional).

4. Click GENERATE LOVs to accept the selections and create the cascading list.

12.2.2   Using a Cascading List of Values Object as a Prompted Filter in a Report

After you create a cascading LOV in the universe, you can use any object in the list of values as a prompted filter by following these steps:

1. Drop the object onto the Query Filters pane.

2. Select PROMPT as the filter type (see Figure 12.13).

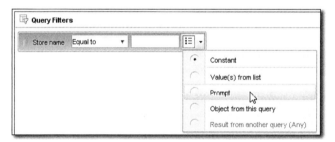

Figure 12.13 Using Cascading Objects as a Prompted Filter

3. After selecting the PROMPT filter type, click the SETTINGS button to view the prompt settings.

4. Be sure to check the PROMPT WITH LIST OF VALUES checkbox, as shown in Figure 12.14.

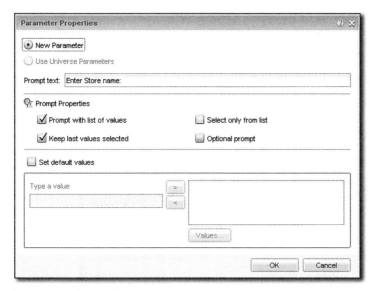

Figure 12.14 Prompt Properties

12.2.3 Refreshing a Report with a Prompted List of Values Object Filter

Cascading prompted filters become useful when refreshing reports. All objects in the cascading list will appear in the prompted values list in tree form. Navigate into the tree to select the values you want.

As an example, Figure 12.15 shows the order of the cascading list of objects. Notice that the [Store name] object is at the bottom of the hierarchy, the [City] object is one level up, and the [State] object is at the top of the hierarchy.

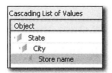

Figure 12.15 Hierarchy of Cascading List of Values

When the [Store name] object is added as a prompted filter and the report is refreshed, you'll be prompted to select a value from the list of available customer objects.

When the object being filtered is at the bottom of the hierarchy in a cascading LOV, you need to expand the object values above it in the hierarchy until you get down to the level of the object.

In this example, the [Store name] object prompts the user to expand a [State] value, followed by expanding a [City] within the state selected, and finally selecting the [Store name] value (see Figure 12.16). Click on the > symbol to add the value to the list, and then click RUN QUERY.

The RUN QUERY button becomes enabled when at least one value is added.

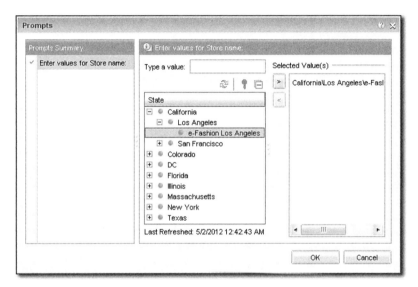

Figure 12.16 Prompted Filter of Cascading List of Values Object

12.2.4 Optional Prompts

Check the OPTIONAL PROMPT checkbox to make a prompted filter object optional when answering prompts rather than requiring the user to select or enter a value.

To access this setting, set the filter type to PROMPT, and then launch the PROMPT PROPERTIES dialog box. Figure 12.17 shows the OPTIONAL PROMPT selection in the PROMPT PROPERTIES section of the Parameter Properties window.

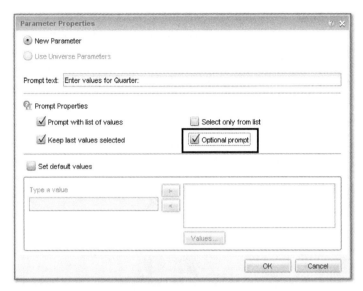

Figure 12.17 Making a Prompt Filter Optional

12.3   Using Custom Freehand SQL

Freehand SQL can be used in a Web Intelligence 4.0 report to enable report developers to rewrite, revise, or completely replace the SQL generated by the Query Panel.

You can edit a Web Intelligence document to view the SQL generated by the result objects and query filters in the Query Panel (see Figure 12.18).

Figure 12.18 Viewing SQL Button in the Query Toolbar

Viewing a Generated Query Script

The Query Script Viewer is used to display the SQL generated by the objects in your query. The SQL syntax is displayed in light gray lettering until the USE CUSTOM QUERY SCRIPT button is selected.

Figure 12.19 shows the Query Script Viewer with the generated SQL syntax displayed. The Undo and Validate buttons are disabled unless changes are made to the SQL generated by Web Intelligence.

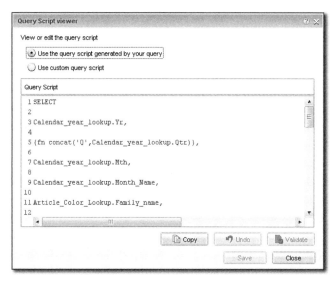

Figure 12.19 SQL Viewer Displaying Generated SQL

Use Custom Query Script

Select the Use custom query script option to enable the text area that displays the generated SQL statement. The code is then displayed in black lettering and is editable.

Figure 12.20 shows the Query Script Viewer with a customizable SQL statement. Modify or replace the existing SQL and then click on Validate to test the syntax of your changes.

If no errors were found after validating the syntax, click on Save to overwrite the SQL generated by the Query Panel.

The two requirements for editing the generated SQL are listed here:

1. The number of items in the Select section of the edited SQL statement must match the number of result objects originally placed in the query.

2. The data type of the objects in the edited Query Script Viewer must match the data type of the result objects originally placed in the query

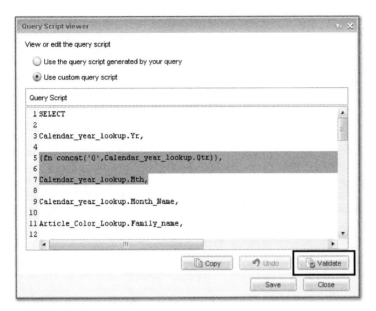

Figure 12.20 SQL Viewer with Custom SQL

Figure 12.21 shows an error message received when attempting to add a twelfth object to the `Select` section in the query script generated by the Query Panel when only eleven objects are in the Result Objects pane.

Figure 12.21 Error When Modifying Generated SQL

12.4 Visually Tracking Data Changes in the Report Panel

Tracking data changes allows you to visually identify data changes at a glance when a query is refreshed. Many viewing options can be modified to customize the appearance of data values that have changed when a report is refreshed.

To compare the changes in data, you must first set a reference point. Two options are available when setting the reference point:

1. Compare with last data refresh (default).

2. Compare with data refresh from (select from several recent refresh dates from a dropdown menu).

Data tracking is toggled on or off by clicking the TRACK button located on the DATA TRACKING subtab, which is found on the ANALYSIS tab in the Report Panel. The button to activate data tracking is shown in Figure 12.22.

Figure 12.22 Track Data Changes Button

Let's examine a few other actions that relate to data changes.

12.4.1 Showing and Hiding Data Changes

After clicking on TRACK and toggling data tracking on, you'll see that a SHOW CHANGES button becomes enabled. This button allows you to either show or hide the data changes found by the data tracking tool without deactivating tracking. Once tracking has been deactivated, you won't be able to compare the current data with the reference data.

Figure 12.23 shows the default data tracking formatting when values from the reference point are different from the values in the latest refresh. Different background colors, font colors, and font types can be configured to represent increased values, decreased values, insertions, deletions, or changes.

City	Sales revenue	Quantity sold	Margin
Austin	$13,517	73	$5,749
Boston	$8,420	44	$3,608
Chicago	$12,079	61	$5,626
Colorado Springs	$7,013	37	$3,099
Dallas	$9,569	54	$3,911
Houston	$33,269	180	$14,128
Los Angeles	$17,046	89	$7,525

Figure 12.23 Visible Changes When Tracking Data Changes

12.4.2 Data Tracking Options

You can launch the Data Tracking Options dialog box by clicking on the button to the right of the HIDE/SHOW CHANGES tracking button on the default toolbar in the Report Panel. Formatting can be applied to modify a variety of font- and background-related attributes. Figure 12.24 shows the five options to visually display data changes (insertions, deletions, changes, increased values, and decreased values).

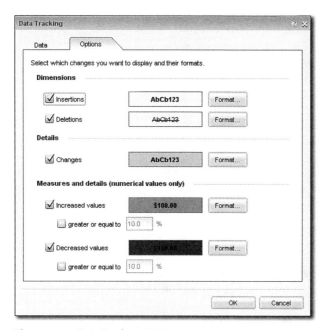

Figure 12.24 Data Tracking Options

Data tracking can be applied to every report in a Web Intelligence document or to only specific report tabs. Click on the DATA tab when configuring data tracking to select the context for comparing the refreshed data and also for selecting which reports to include data tracking.

It's common for one tab to have data tracking enabled but all other tabs to have data tracking disabled. Other scenarios require that all tabs have data tracking enabled. Figure 12.25 shows the DATA tab in the Data Tracking menu. Use this screen to define the instance to compare data against and also which reports should show data tracking. Check REFRESH DATA NOW to refresh the query immediately after clicking on OK.

Figure 12.25 Data Tracking Settings

12.4.3 Purging Data

The option to purge data is commonly used before publishing Web Intelligence reports to the server that may contain restricted information.

You can purge data in the Query Panel and Report Panel. Figure 12.26 shows the PURGE icon located on the default toolbar in the Report Panel.

Figure 12.26 Purge Data

12.4.4 Identify and Modify Partial Results

If a query refreshes successfully but returns partial results, the bottom right corner of the report will display a yellow icon containing an exclamation point, as shown in Figure 12.27. This icon indicates that only partial results have been retrieved.

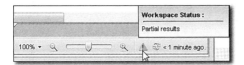

Figure 12.27 Yellow Icon Indicating Partial Results

Partial results leave reporting documents incomplete and should be resolved before publishing, printing, or exporting a report locally or to the CMS.

The three most common scenarios that cause partial results are listed below:

▶ MAX ROWS RETRIEVED setting in the Limits category of the Query Properties window in the Query Panel, as shown in Figure 12.28

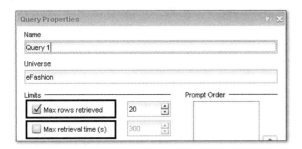

Figure 12.28 Max Rows Retrieved and Max Retrieval Time Settings

▶ MAX RETRIEVAL TIME setting in the Limits category of the Query Properties

▶ CONTROLS tab in the Universe Parameters dialog box, as shown in Figure 12.29

To modify the maximum number of rows retrieved in the query, take the following steps:

1. From the Report Panel, click the DATA ACCESS tab to enter the Query Panel.

2. Click the QUERY PROPERTIES shortcut icon located at the top of the screen.

3. Check or uncheck the MAX ROWS RETRIEVED setting. If checked, modify the number of rows.

4. Check or uncheck the MAX RETRIEVAL TIME setting. If checked, modify the time value.

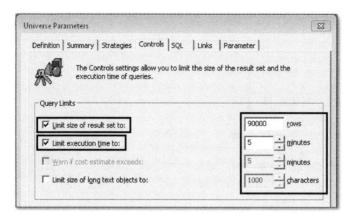

Figure 12.29 Controls Tab in the Universe Parameters

Use the following steps to modify the maximum number of retrievable rows at the universe level:

1. Launch the Universe Design Tool.

2. Open the Universe Parameters dialog box.

3. Click on the CONTROLS tab.

4. Check or uncheck the LIMIT SIZE OF RESULT SET TO, and then modify the maximum number of rows to be retrieved.

The capability to visually track the changes from a previous report instance to a recently refreshed instance gives users the opportunity to quickly spot increases or decreases that otherwise may not be as easy to spot. Before running a new query or re-running an existing one, preview the data while you're still in the Query Panel.

12.5 Data Preview

The Data Preview pane is a new addition to the Query Panel in Web Intelligence in version 4.0. This new panel lets you preview a sample of the data based on the existing result objects and query filters before actually running a query.

To view a preview of the data, open the Data Preview panel and click on the REFRESH icon located in the upper right corner of the panel. A sample of the result data will be displayed inside the panel, as pictured in Figure 12.30.

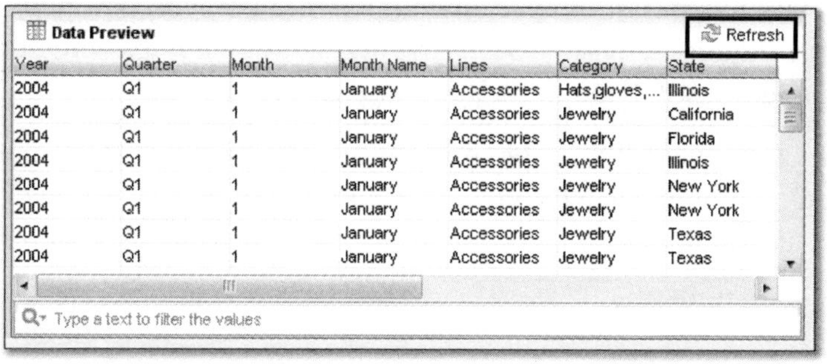

Figure 12.30 Data Preview

Filter Preview Data

While reviewing data in the Data Preview panel, you have the option to further restrict the result set by creating a query filter for a specific value. To do this, right-click on a value in the panel and select CREATE SIMPLE FILTER. This selection will add the object and value to the query filters panel. Click on REFRESH in the Data Preview panel again to preview the updated data set.

Figure 12.31 shows the Data Preview panel if you right-clicked on 3 in the [Month] column. Select the option displayed in the screenshot (CREATE SIMPLE FILTER: MONTH EQUAL TO 3) to dynamically create a custom filter object in the query filters panel.

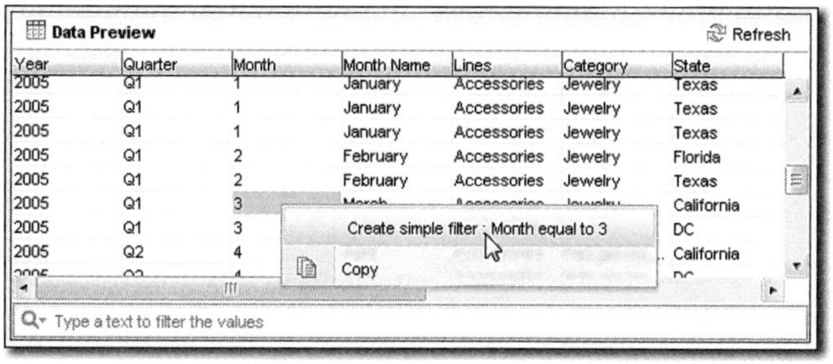

Figure 12.31 Creating Simple Filters from the Data Preview Section

Using Search to Filter Data Preview Values

If you're looking for a specific value in a data set but are unable to locate it in the Data Preview panel, click in the search window located beneath the panel and begin entering your term or phrase. The box will search through every row in the panel and immediately filter the results. Searching begins when a single letter or number is entered and every column in each row is searched.

Figure 12.32 shows the letters "Ch" entered in the search bar. The data in the Data Preview panel was immediately filtered and the following values were located: Chicago in the [City] column, and Michelle and Richards in the [Name of manager] column.

Figure 12.32 Dynamically Filtering Preview Data

By previewing a sample of the data set, you can identify areas to improve the query and further refine the information set to be retrieved from the data source.

12.6 Additional Queries and New Data Providers

Adding additional queries to a Web Intelligence document while working in the BI launch pad offers three different data source types:

▶ FROM UNIVERSE

▶ FROM BEX

▶ FROM ANALYSIS VIEW

These data source types are accessed by selecting NEW DATA PROVIDER from the DATA ACCESS tab and DATA PROVIDERS subtab in the Report Panel, as shown in Figure 12.33.

These same data source types are also available when ADD QUERY is selected from the Query Panel, as shown in Figure 12.34.

Figure 12.33 Adding a New Data Provider from the Report Panel

Figure 12.34 Adding a New Query from the Query Panel

In addition to the three primary sources, three additional data sources (custom data providers) can be used to create Web Intelligence 4.0 documents while working in the Web Intelligence Rich Client application: text, web services and Microsoft Excel. When Rich Client is launched, users have the opportunity to create reporting documents from six different source types: text, web services, universe, Microsoft Excel, BEx, and Analysis View. All six sources are displayed in Figure 12.35.

Figure 12.35 Data Source Types Available in Web Intelligence Rich Client

12.6.1 Text Files as a Data Source

When Text is selected as the data source, the Custom Data Provider—Text window is launched and provides a BROWSE button for searching for local text files in the .TXT format. Options are provided for the Data Separator and Text Delimiter of the source text file. Other options include assigning the first row of the file as column names, selecting the locale, charset, and date format. Figure 12.36 shows the window creating documents with text files as the data source.

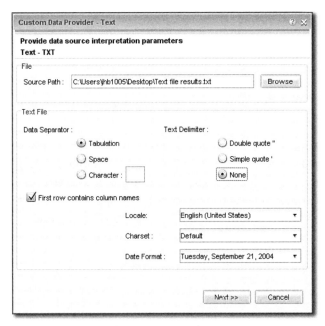

Figure 12.36 Options for Using a Text File as a Data Source

12.6.2 Web Services as a Data Source

You can also create Web Intelligence documents using web services as the data source. These web services can be created from Query as a Web Service, data blocks published as web services from other Web Intelligence documents, or generic web services. After selecting web services as the data source, the Custom Data Provider—Web Services window will be launched as pictured in Figure 12.37. To get started, paste your web service URL into the source path box and click on SUBMIT. Selections should be made in the SERVICE NAME, PORT NAME, and OPERATION NAME settings located in the SERVICE DETAILS group.

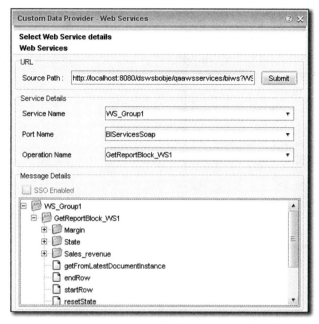

Figure 12.37 Options for Using a Web Service as a Data Source

12.6.3 Microsoft Excel Files as a Data Source

Web Intelligence documents can be sourced from Excel files when working in Rich Client. Figure 12.38 shows the Custom Data Provider—Excel window opened when creating a document with Excel as the data source. Click on Browse to locate a local .XLS file and then select the sheet name that contains the data. Next select between using all fields, defining a range definition, or selecting a range name. Additionally, you can check or uncheck the option to accept the first row in the spreadsheet as column names.

Custom data providers let business users leverage the extensive capabilities of Web Intelligence 4.0 to display data found in Excel files, text files, and web services in unique and powerful ways.

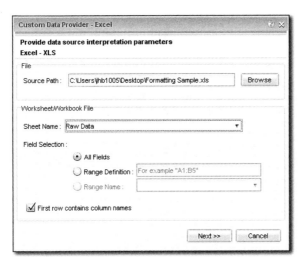

Figure 12.38 Options for Using an Excel File as a Data Source

12.7 Summary

You can get the most out of your queries by including complex nested filters, prompted filters with cascading lists of values, database ranking, and custom SQL in a Web Intelligence report. You can produce the most accurate, valuable, and actionable reports possible for your clients by using the extensive features available in the Query Panel.

Use a variety of data tracking features in a report to easily identify changes in company data compared to values from a specified reference point. With the addition of the Data Preview panel, you can catch a glimpse of a dataset before running a query. And while you are reviewing preview data, custom query filters can be created with just two clicks. Then you can move on to Web Intelligence Rich Client and create documents from Excel files, text files, and web services to leverage all the strengths of the Web Intelligence application with local data in an Excel file.

Chapter 13 explains how to use multiple data sources and merge dimensions in a Web Intelligence document. Reports created with multiple queries sourced from different data sources can produce highly actionable information in areas such as cost analysis, variance analysis, and other analytical comparisons that's only possible when combining data from disparate sources.

Integrate data from multiple sources into a single Web Intelligence document to produce powerful and analytical reports. You can join unrelated results by merging compatible dimension objects from disparate sources.

13 Using Multiple Data Sources

SAP BusinessObjects Web Intelligence 4.0 lets you combine data retrieved from separate queries into a single reporting document. Several different queries can be added to a single document by querying the same universe, querying different universes, or accessing other data sources such as text files, Microsoft Excel files, BEx queries, Analysis workspaces, or web services.

Chapter 2 briefly discussed the use of multiple data sources in a single report. This chapter will take you deeper into the processes of working with multiple queries, synchronizing data by merging dimensions, and using local data providers to bring data into a document with Web Intelligence in BI Launch Pad or Web Intelligence Rich Client. First, we will explain how you can create a Web Intelligence document with multiple queries to the same universe. Next, we will explain how to create a Web Intelligence document using multiple queries to different universes, which requires common dimensions to be manually synchronized. Finally, we will show you how to create a Web Intelligence document that combines data from a universe with local data from a Microsoft Excel spreadsheet.

13.1 Combining Multiple Queries from Same Data Source

Our first example involves combining two data providers, both from the same eFashion universe, using Web Intelligence in the BI Launch Pad. This can also be done using the Web Intelligence Rich Client.

> **Note**
>
> With Web Intelligence 4.0, you can query BEx and Analysis View data sources in addition to universes. The Rich Client adds local files and web services, which will be examined later in the chapter.

For the first data provider, you need to create a query using the Store name, Sales revenue, and Margin objects. The results should appear similar to Figure 13.1.

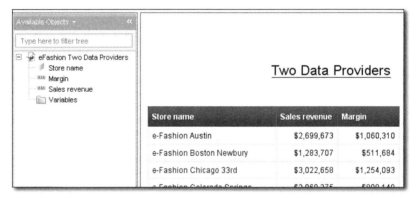

Figure 13.1 Single Query from eFashion Universe

Next, add a second data provider to the Web Intelligence document. Begin by choosing the Data Access tab and then choosing Edit from the Data Providers subtab, which opens the Web Intelligence Query Panel. From the Query Panel, click on the Add Query button in the top left corner and select From Universe, as shown in Figure 13.2.

Figure 13.2 Adding Query from Web Intelligence Query Panel

As an alternative method, choose NEW DATA PROVIDER directly from the DATA PRO-VIDERS subtab and select FROM UNIVERSE, as shown in Figure 13.3.

Figure 13.3 Adding New Data Provider Directly from Web Intelligence Main Window

Adding a query using this method will add the data in a new table to the current report. It may be preferable to add the new data provider from the Edit Query window, as it has more options for controlling the display of data.

In either case, choose the eFashion universe again for the second data provider. Add STORE NAME and QUANTITY SOLD objects to the Query Panel, as shown in Figure 13.4.

Figure 13.4 Result Objects in a Second Query

Notice that the RUN QUERY button now displays RUN QUERIES, indicating that multiple queries exist in the Web Intelligence document, as shown in Figure 13.5, to refresh the data providers.

Figure 13.5 Running Both Queries

As new data providers are added to the Web Intelligence document from the Query Panel, you will be prompted to instruct Web Intelligence where to place the data from the new query, as shown in Figure 13.6.

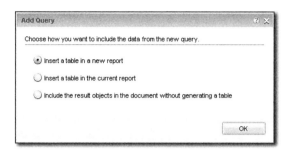

Figure 13.6 Options for Placement of Query Data

There are the three possibilities:

▶ INSERT A TABLE IN A NEW REPORT: Creates a new report tab with data shown in standard vertical table

▶ INSERT A TABLE IN THE CURRENT REPORT: Adds a new table on currently active report tab, alongside any existing tables and charts on report

▶ INCLUDE THE RESULT OBJECTS IN THE DOCUMENT WITHOUT GENERATING A TABLE: Projects data from Report Manager later in report

To continue our example, you should choose the third option, INCLUDE THE RESULT OBJECTS IN THE DOCUMENT WITHOUT GENERATING A TABLE.

Available objects are displayed in alphabetical order by default, as shown in Figure 13.7.

Figure 13.7 Available Objects Arranged by Alphabetical Order

When working with multiple data providers, it is often helpful to display available objects by query, as shown in Figure 13.8.

Figure 13.8 Available Objects Arranged by Query

Because both data providers included the Store Name object, Web Intelligence altered its appearance after the second data provider was added. A special icon showing two overlapping dimension objects, shown in Figure 13.9, is used to indicate a merged dimension. By default, multiple data providers from the same source are automatically synchronized.

Figure 13.9 Automatically Merged Dimension

Because the data providers were automatically merged, you can add the QUANTITY SOLD measure from the second query to the table containing objects from the first query, as shown in Figure 13.10.

Store name	Sales revenue	Margin	Quantity sold
e-Fashion Austin	$2,699,673	$1,060,310	17,078
e-Fashion Boston Newbury	$1,283,707	$511,684	7,676
e-Fashion Chicago 33rd	$3,022,658	$1,254,093	17,976
e-Fashion Colorado Springs	$2,060,275	$808,149	12,787 =[Quantity sold]
e-Fashion Dallas	$1,970,034	$754,862	12,365
e-Fashion Houston 5th	$2,202,102	$929,226	12,016

Figure 13.10 Combining Measures from Two Queries into Single Table

323

Let's turn our attention to how automatic merging of dimensions works.

Data synchronization allows a report developer to combine measures from multiple queries into a single table without worrying about data accuracy. For example, the total sales revenue for the `eFashion Austin` store is perfectly synchronized with the quantity sold for `eFashion Austin` even though it came from a separate query.

Two requirements govern merging dimensions:

▶ The result objects to be merged must have the same data type.

▶ The result objects to be merged must contain compatible and related data.

Both of these requirements are met when objects from a single universe appear in multiple queries. In the next section, you'll learn how to manually merge dimensions when the queries come from different sources.

In certain instances, it may be desirable to disable the automatic merging of dimensions feature. Choose DOCUMENT SUMMARY • EDIT FROM THE LEFT PANEL. From the dialog box that appears (shown in Figure 13.11), clear the AUTO-MERGE DIMENSIONS option. Any previously merged dimensions will remain merged and must be manually unmerged, if desired.

Figure 13.11 Web Intelligence Document Options

Unlike combining data from a single universe, data providers from different sources are not automatically synchronized, so you'll learn the steps required in the next section.

13.2 Combining Data from Different Universes

In this section, we'll explain how to combine data from different universes. Figure 13.12 shows Web Intelligence document with two data providers from two different universes. The REVENUE query was created using the eFashion universe and the HEAD COUNT query was created using the eStaff universe. Because data from two different sources is not automatically synchronized, the results are not accurate. Notice that each row in the table shows 143 employees, the total for the entire eFashion organization. Because the data providers are not synchronized, Web Intelligence does not understand how to take the sales revenue from the eFashion Austin store and combine it with the employee count for the Austin store. Therefore, it combines a single store's revenue with the employee count for all stores, which is not correct.

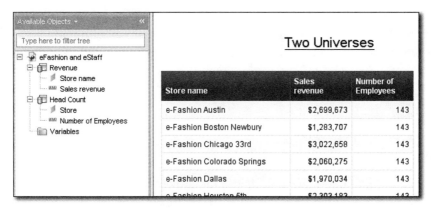

Figure 13.12 Two Unsynchronized Queries

Note
When working with multiple queries, it's worth the extra effort to rename them with useful, plain-English names.

The STORE NAME dimension from eFashion and the STORE object from eStaff meet the two requirements merging dimensions:

▶ The result objects to be merged have the same data type (character).

▶ The result objects to be merged contain compatible and related data (eFashion Austin, eFashion Boston Newbury, etc.)

To manually synchronize the data providers and merge their dimensions, select the DATA ACCESS tab and click on the MERGE button on the DATA OBJECTS subtab, as shown in Figure 13.13.

Figure 13.13 Merge Data Providers Button on Toolbar

From the list of available objects, shown in Figure 13.14, choose the desired dimension, STORE NAME, from the REVENUE query.

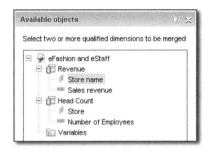

Figure 13.14 Choosing the First Dimension to be Merged

While holding down the Ctrl key, choose the STORE dimension from the HEAD COUNT query, as shown in Figure 13.15. Then choose OK.

Figure 13.15 Choosing the Second Dimension to be Merged

The appropriate dimensions in both queries have been merged and the data is properly synchronized. Now the number of employees from the eStaff universe displays the correct results when placed in the same table as the other objects from the eFashion universe, as shown in Figure 13.16.

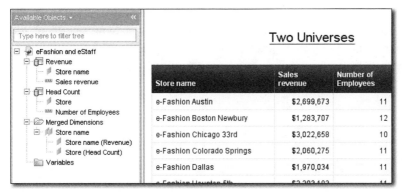

Figure 13.16 Data Providers Synchronized

In this simple example, only a single pair of dimensions needed to be merged. In practice, additional dimensions shared among multiple data providers must be merged by repeating this technique.

13.3 Query Local Data Sources Using Web Intelligence Rich Client

Web Intelligence in the BI Launch Pad permits users to build queries from universes, BEx queries, and Analysis workspaces. Using the Web Intelligence Rich Client adds support for local desktop data sources such as text files and Microsoft Excel spreadsheets. Rich Client users can also create and consume web service queries. The New Data Provider menu is shown in Figure 13.17.

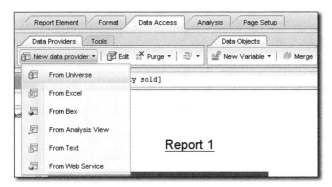

Figure 13.17 New Data Provider in Web Intelligence Rich Client

Additional data providers can also be added via the Web Intelligence Query Panel. Select the ADD QUERY button and choose desired data source from the dropdown menu, as shown in Figure 13.18.

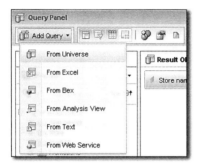

Figure 13.18 Adding Query from Query Panel

Microsoft Excel Files

The ability to work with local data sources such as Microsoft Excel is a key benefit of deploying the Web Intelligence Rich Client in your organization. For example, Web Intelligence users can compare sales forecast numbers stored in a spreadsheet against actual sales figures stored in an enterprise data warehouse.

To begin, choose FROM EXCEL from either the NEW DATA PROVIDER or the ADD QUERY dropdown menus. You'll be asked to browse to the location of Microsoft Excel document, as shown in Figure 13.19.

Figure 13.19 Selecting the Microsoft Excel Data Source

Web Intelligence 4.0 introduces support for .XLSX files created by Microsoft Excel 2007 and Microsoft Excel 2010, in addition to the older .XLS file format. In our example, eFashion Forecast.xlsx is chosen, as shown in Figure 13.20.

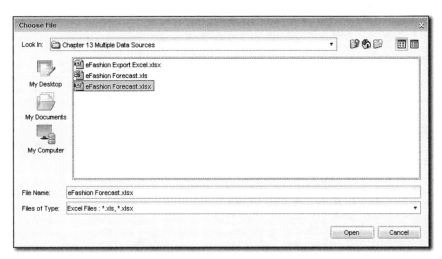

Figure 13.20 Choosing the Desired Microsoft Excel File

Next, you are asked which worksheet to import from the Microsoft Excel document, as shown in Figure 13.21. You can specify data from the entire worksheet or name a smaller range.

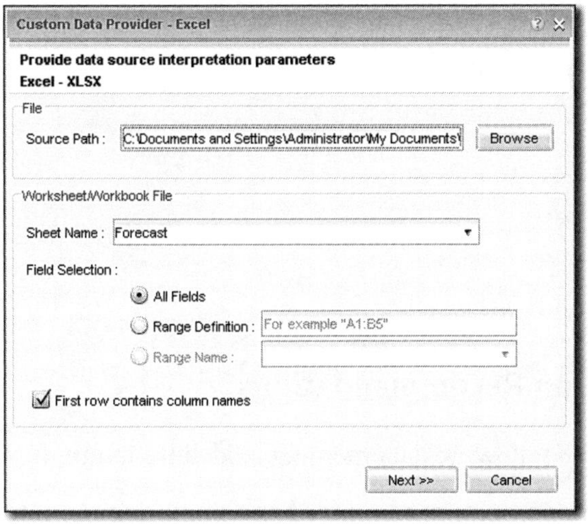

Figure 13.21 Providing Data Source Interpretation Parameters

Once a Microsoft Excel data provider has been created, the properties of individual objects can be adjusted from the Web Intelligence Query Panel shown in Figure 13.22.

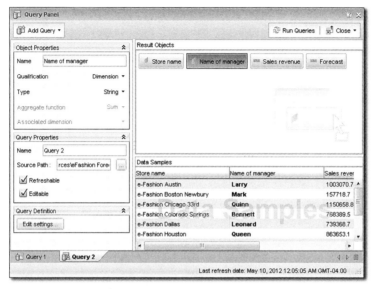

Figure 13.22 Microsoft Excel Query Properties in Query Panel

Text Files

In addition to Microsoft Excel files, the Web Intelligence Rich Client can use the following desktop file types as query sources:

▶ Text *.TXT

▶ Comma Separated Value *.CSV

▶ Text formatted for printers *.PRN

▶ ASCII *.ASC

13.4   Data Synchronization Recommendations

We recommend that you keep the following data merging guidelines in mind:

▶ Multiple queries from the same universe can be added to a single document to include results with different result objects and query filters.

▸ Multiple queries can be inserted using different universes.

▸ Dimensions to be merged must have the same data type.

▸ When manually merging dimensions, only the data type of the selected objects is required to create the merged dimension. Both objects should, however, contain compatible data. The object has no bearing.

▸ An unlimited number of data sources can exist within a single document.

▸ An unlimited number of data source dimensions can be merged.

You can use the Extend Merged Dimension Values setting in the Document properties to perform a full outer join of merged dimension objects. This setting allows for all of the values from both data sources to be merged into the newly created merged dimension object.

You can use the `forceMerge()` formula to provide synchronization to data providers with different aggregation levels. The `forceMerge()` formula works when the dimensions merged have objects above it in the hierarchy. Figure 12.21 displays the Store Name object and its location in the hierarchy. This allows both measures to display accurate results when using any of the following objects: State, City, or Store Name.

Figure 12.22 shows the same vertical table as in Figure 12.18, but the `[Quantity sold]` measure has been encapsulated in the `ForceMerge()` formula.

> **Note**
>
> Filtering in reports can't be applied to merged dimension objects. The premerged dimension objects must be used when adding report filters. When a filter is added to a report that was used to create a merged dimension, the filter is applied to all synchronized data providers.

13.5 Summary

This chapter builds on the information presented in Chapter 2 to provide you with advanced techniques for creating powerful queries in the Query Panel. You can use multiple data sources in a single document to expand the capabilities of your reports by combining data from a variety of sources.

Report writers and developers can include the results from multiple queries sourced from the same universe, different universes, and other data sources such as BEx queries, Analysis workspaces, Microsoft Excel files, various text formats, and web services.

Data synchronization is the key to combining the results from multiple data sources. This is achieved by auto-merging dimensions or manually merging dimension objects through the Merge Dimensions Editor. You can use the `force-Merge()` function to synchronize data providers with different aggregate levels if the dimensions objects have other dimensions above it in the hierarchy.

Embed hyperlinks into Web Intelligence reports to connect to multiple document types, including SAP BusinessObjects Dashboards, and other Web Intelligence 4.0 documents. You can add element links to create interactivity between reporting components or to create hyperlinks to pass variables to prompted reports using the openDocument() function and associated syntax.

14 Linking in Web Intelligence 4.0 Reports

Hyperlinks enable report developers to create comprehensive and cohesive reporting solutions that connect SAP BusinessObjects documents with single-click navigation. This feature can be used to provide business users with a form of guided analysis by connecting to reports and dashboards that tell a different story with the information. Strategically inserted links in Web Intelligence reports expand on the data being viewed by opening and refreshing other reporting documents.

Hyperlinks allow reports to be connected for a variety of purposes. They can launch reports to open in a printer-friendly PDF format, connect to SAP Business-Objects Dashboards for interactive visualizations, or provide additional information in detailed reports associated by specified parameters in prompted documents.

One of the most significant and exciting benefits of hyperlinking is opening and refreshing reports that pass values to prompted Web Intelligence documents. This feature gives business users access to live data in reports that are refreshed at the moment the link is clicked. Links can also go outside of the SAP Business-Objects BI 4.0 platform to intranet or public-facing websites.

New in version 4.0 is the feature of element linking. This capability allows report designers to add interactivity between individual components or groups of report elements to create a more cohesive solution with guided analysis.

This chapter describes how to link to other reports graphically while working in the Web viewer or manually in the Rich Internet Application viewer. We'll explain the relative advantages and disadvantages and describe manual hyperlink creation in detail.

14.1 Linking to Documents with the Web Viewer

You can easily add hyperlinks to existing Web Intelligence documents when in design mode and when you have selected the Web viewer in the Web Intelligence preferences. (This viewer provides an additional feature that's not available when the view and modify preferences are set to the Rich Internet Application viewer.) This feature provides the ability to link to a document published to SAP Business-Objects BI 4.0 with the Add Document Link option.

The next several sections discuss how to add hyperlinks to reports and how to customize and add additional parameters to hyperlinks using both the Web viewer and Rich Internet Application viewer.

14.1.1 Adding Hyperlinks to Published BI 4.0 Documents

To add a hyperlink to a document published to the SAP BusinessObjects BI 4.0 platform with the Web viewer, right-click on a row, column, or cell in a data table and then select the LINKING option from the menu. From this menu, you can add a hyperlink, document link, or element link to an existing reporting document.

Figure 14.1 shows the menu that appears when you right-click on a column in a data table while in design mode. The same hyperlink options appear when right-clicking on a freestanding cell. Select ADD DOCUMENT LINK to create a connection to another document published to the BI 40 platform.

After you click on ADD DOCUMENT LINK, the CREATE HYPERLINK window will open with options divided into two tabs:

▶ LINK TO WEB PAGE
▶ LINK TO DOCUMENT

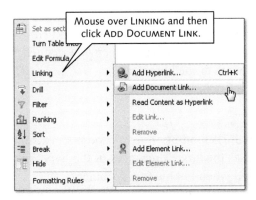

Figure 14.1 Adding a Hyperlink While Viewing a Report with the Web Viewer

If you right-click on a cell or column that already contains a hyperlink, the ADD HYPERLINK and ADD DOCUMENT LINK options will be disabled and the options to EDIT LINK and REMOVE will be enabled so that you can make changes to an existing hyperlink.

After a hyperlink has been created, the READ CONTENTS AS HYPERLINK setting will be checked, indicating that the cell contains an enabled link. Unchecking this option will disable the link but not get rid of the link completely. Use the REMOVE option to completely disable and delete a hyperlink.

Another Method for Adding Hyperlinks

When using the Web viewer, select a row, column, or cell in a data table or free-standing cell, and then locate the linking icons in the tabbed ribbon running across the top of the report. To do this, click on the REPORT ELEMENTS tab, followed by the LINKING tab in the third set of subtabs. Notice that the icon to add a document link is available while working within the Web viewer, as shown in Figure 14.2.

Figure 14.2 Linking Options in the Web Viewer

The three linking icons you see enable you to create hyperlinks, document links, and element links. Each link provides to option to create a new link and edit or remove an existing link. The same options are also available when you right-click on a report element to be used as the source of the hyperlink.

Browsing for Documents

With the LINK TO DOCUMENT tab selected, click on BROWSE to choose an existing document on the BI 4.0 platform to set as the target document of the hyperlink. Figure 14.3 shows the window displayed when linking to a document.

Figure 14.3 Linking to a Document in the Web Viewer

> **Note**
>
> The option to LINK TO DOCUMENT is available only when you have selected the Web viewer in the Preferences section for Web Intelligence.

Clicking on BROWSE launches the Choose a Document window, where you'll see a full list of reporting documents that you have the rights to access and link to. These documents include:

- Web Intelligence documents
- Crystal Reports
- BI workspaces
- Analysis workspaces
- SAP BusinessObjects Dashboards

Figure 14.4 shows the window opened when browsing for a document. Follow these steps to select a document to link to while viewing a report:

1. From the left side of the window, select the storage location of the target document. Options include:

   ▶ MY DOCUMENTS

   ▶ FOLDERS

   ▶ CATEGORIES

2. From the right side of the window, select the document to link to and then click on OPEN to confirm.

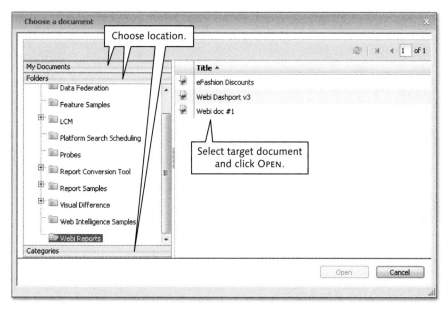

Figure 14.4 Choosing a Document to Link To

Setting Hyperlink Properties

After selecting a document, you have the opportunity to revise four properties and three or four settings depending on whether the target document contains a prompted filter. Figure 14.5 shows the available hyperlink properties after a document has been created. Properties of the new hyperlink are broken down into three categories:

▶ HYPERLINK PROPERTIES

▶ DOCUMENT PROMPTS (displayed only when linking to a report that contains a prompted filter)

▶ CUSTOMIZE THE LOOK AND BEHAVIOR OF THE HYPERLINK

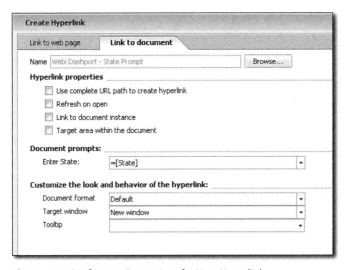

Figure 14.5 Configuring Properties of a New Hyperlink

Any of the four hyperlink properties can be selected to provide the following types of functionality. All four are unchecked by default.

▶ USE COMPLETE URL PATH TO CREATE HYPERLINK: Includes the web server name and port number in the hyperlink

▶ REFRESH ON OPEN: Sets the linked report to refresh on open (recommended when connected to a prompted document)

▶ LINK TO DOCUMENT INSTANCE: Used when linking to a scheduled instance

▶ TARGET AREA WITHIN THE DOCUMENT: Provides the option to link to a specific report tab if multiple reports exist in the linked document as well as the capability to link to a report part

Figure 14.6 shows the options available when the TARGET AREAS WITHIN THE DOCUMENT property is selected. Set the target document to open to a specific REPORT NAME or select the REPORT PART option to target a specific chart or data table within a report.

Both options are helpful for creating connections that guide users directly to the information needed for specific scenarios.

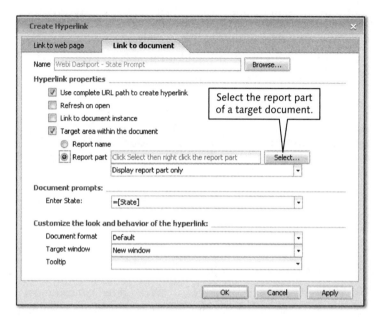

Figure 14.6 Linking to a Target Area or Report Part

If a target document contains a prompted filter, a document prompt property will be presented in the list of LINK TO DOCUMENT properties. Use this entry to define what is passed to the prompted filter in the linked document.

The best practice for linking to a prompted report is to set the hyperlink on a column or value that contains the same object as the prompted filter.

You can use one of the following five choices to pass values to a prompt:

▶ Select object

▶ Build formula

▶ Enter a constant

▶ Prompt user at runtime

▶ Use document default

Three settings are provided to customize the look and behavior of the target document:

▶ Document Format: Choose from default, HTML, PDF, Excel, and Word

▶ Target Window: Open documents in the current or new Window

▶ Tooltip: Type a message, select object, or build a formula to display specific information when a user hovers above an active link

We'll discuss document prompts shortly.

Note

After checking property boxes and making selections from the behavior dropdowns, click on APPLY • OK to accept the changes and set the hyperlink.

When a hyperlink has been applied to a cell or column in a data table, the values will be displayed with a blue text color and underlined by default.

14.1.2 Insert a Hyperlink to a Web Page

The second type of hyperlinking that can be added to a Web Intelligence report is to a web page. This setting allows you to create and embed hyperlinks to your company websites, blogs, or other types of web pages.

Figure 14.7 shows the LINK TO WEB PAGE selection in the CREATE HYPERLINK window. Click on PARSE after adding the URL to view the components of the link and any dynamic elements in the URL.

Figure 14.7 Adding a Hyperlink to a Web Page

After a URL has been entered, click on PARSE to display additional link settings. The URL can be broken down into three parts:

▶ MAIN

▶ CUSTOMIZE URL PARAMETERS

▶ CUSTOMIZE THE LOOK AND BEHAVIOR OF THE HYPERLINK

Figure 14.8 shows the expanded CREATE HYPERLINK window that enables you to modify two default link behavior settings:

▶ TARGET WINDOW: Specify here whether documents are to be opened in a new window or the current window

▶ TOOLTIP: Enter a tooltip to be displayed when you mouse over the hyperlink and use dropdown options to assign a formula or object as the tooltip

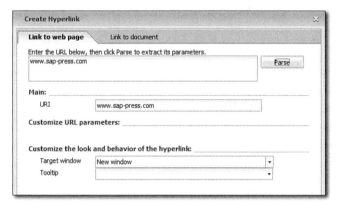

Figure 14.8 Customize the Look and Behavior of Web Page Links

14.1.3 Adding Hyperlinks to Prompted Documents

When a prompted Web Intelligence document is selected in the Choose a Document window, an additional set of options is displayed for DOCUMENT PROMPTS. This section allows you to pass values to a prompted filter in the linked document.

The DOCUMENT PROMPTS section of the link properties displays a list of all prompted filters listed by the prompt text for each filter in the linked document.

By default, the object in the column or cell that contains the link will be passed to the prompted filter. Additionally, five options (shown in Figure 14.9) are provided to allow different ways of dynamically passing values to a prompted filter in the linked document:

▶ SELECT OBJECT: Selects an object or variable from the source document

▶ BUILD FORMULA: Opens the Formula Editor for custom formula creation

▶ ENTER A CONSTANT: Allows manually entered values

▶ PROMPT USER AT RUNTIME: Prompts the user at runtime

▶ USE DOCUMENT DEFAULT: Uses the default prompt value selection type

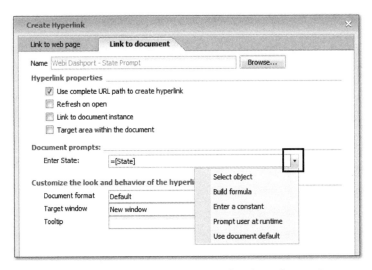

Figure 14.9 Creating a Hyperlink to a Prompted Web Intelligence Report

---

Note

If a prompted document contains two or more prompted filters and is selected as the linked document, a Select Prompts window will present you with both prompted filters, allowing you to choose which object will receive the value.

Figure 14.10 shows the Select Prompts window when a new hyperlink has been created based on the [State] object in a data table and linked to a document containing two prompted filters. Choose the prompt filter to receive the value.

Figure 14.10 Select Prompts Window

Passing a Selected Object to a Prompted Report

An excellent way of linking Web Intelligence reports is to create a hyperlink based on the value of a selected object. This type of linking works best when the target report contains a single prompted filter that contains compatible values. This is most commonly used when creating a hyperlink on a dimension object when the same object serves as the prompted filter in another document.

An example of this type of linking is shown in Figure 14.11, in which you right-click on a column in a vertical table that contains the [State] object as the basis for the hyperlink. Mouse over the Linking option to display the available linking choices and then select Add Document Link to create a connection to another document. The selected value in the [State] object will be used as the basis for the new link. If the target document contains a prompted filter, then by default the value selected will be passed to the prompted filter in the linked document.

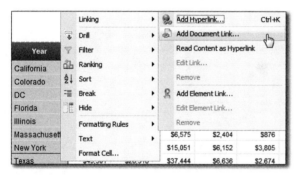

Figure 14.11 Creating a Hyperlink Based on the State Object

> **Note**
>
> The result of setting up a hyperlink containing this parameter-passing feature is that any [State] value selected in the data table is dynamically passed as part of the hyperlink to the target document when the value is clicked.

14.2   Linking with the Rich Internet Application Viewer

You can also add hyperlinks to reports while designing documents in the Rich Internet Application viewer. With this viewer, you'll notice that the right-click menu and the overall look and feel of creating a hyperlink are slightly different.

Similar to adding links to reports using the Web viewer, you must be in design mode to add hyperlinks.

When adding hyperlinks using the Rich Internet Application viewer, it's important to note that the option Add Document Link is not available. Adding hyperlinks to other documents published to the BI 4.0 platform is much more of a manual process than in the Web viewer and requires writing the full URL to create a link to another document. Figure 14.12 shows the linking options available when right-clicking on a report element while in the Rich Internet Application viewer and in design mode. Select LINKING from the available options then click on ADD HYPERLINK to launch the Hyperlinks window.

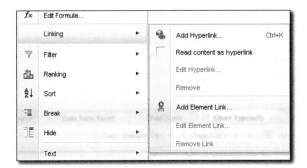

Figure 14.12 Adding a New Hyperlink While Editing a Report

Clicking on ADD HYPERLINK provides the capability of linking to another document or web page. The result of this selection is pictured in Figure 14.13.

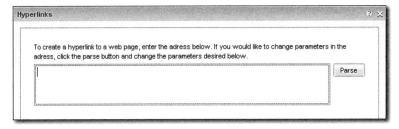

Figure 14.13 Adding a New Hyperlink in the Rich Internet Application Viewer

Paste or type a URL, and then click on PARSE to display the dynamic elements of the URL entered in the provided text area.

Alternate Method of Adding Hyperlinks

Another way of adding hyperlinks is with the shortcut icons provided in the multilayer tabbed ribbon located across the top of the report. To add a hyperlink using these icons, begin by selecting a report element, freestanding cell, or value in a data table and then clicking on the REPORT ELEMENT tab. Next, select the LINKING tab located in the third set of subtabs, as shown in Figure 14.14.

Figure 14.14 Adding Hyperlinks Using Icons in the Ribbon

> **Note**
>
> Notice that only the icons for creating a hyperlink and element link are available in the Rich Internet Application viewer.

To link to a web page while using the Rich Internet Application viewer, use the standard URL structure. An example of this format is *www.sap.com*.

Linking to Documents Published to the BI 4.0 Platform

To link to documents published to the BI 4.0 platform, use this basic format below for constructing your URL and using the OpenDocument syntax:

```
http://<server>:<port>/BOE/OpenDocument/opendoc/openDocument.jsp?
```

> **Note**
>
> Unlike XI 3.x, SAP BusinessObjects BI 4.0 supports only a Java deployment. This means you'll need to use openDocument.jsp when creating document hyperlinks.

One of the easiest ways to familiarize yourself with the structure of a hyperlink URL is to analyze the syntax generated when the Web viewer is used to add a document link. To do this, take the following steps:

1. Add a document link using the Web viewer and check the option to USE THE COMPLETE URL PATH TO CREATE THE HYPERLINK.

2. Select the cell or column that contains the new hyperlink and view it in the formula bar while in design mode.

3. Copy the full URL beginning with `http://` and ending at the final double-quote symbol located before the title parameter.

4. Change the viewer to Rich Internet Application and add a new hyperlink.

5. Paste the full URL retrieved from the previous step into the hyperlink box and click on PARSE.

Consider this example of the full URL created when a link to another Web Intelligence document is added:

```
="<ahref=\"http://localhost:8080/BOE/OpenDocument/opendoc/
openDocument.jsp?iDocID=AYSsA1E0e4hAhUXUssDC6OA&sIDType=CUID&
sType=wid&sRefresh=N\"title=\"\"target=\"_blank\"nav=\"doc\">"+
[State]+"</a>"
```

Recognize that the URL within the statement begins with `http://` and ends with the final slash before the quotation mark and title parameter. To use this URL to link to another document, switch to the Rich Internet Application viewer and create a new hyperlink. Paste the URL into the hyperlink box and click on PARSE.

Figure 14.15 shows the dynamic elements of the URL after adding it to the hyperlinks box and clicking on PARSE. The syntax used in the URL is broken into three different groupings:

▶ MAIN: Uses the openDocument.jsp application

▶ CUSTOMIZE THE FOLLOWING DYNAMIC ELEMENTS OF THE URL: Contains the dynamic identifier parameters of the target document

   ▶ IDocID

   ▶ sIDTYPE

   ▶ sTYPE

▶ CUSTOMIZE THE VISUAL AND INTERACTION PROPERTIES OF THE HYPERLINK

   ▶ TOOL TIP: Manually enter a constant, select an object, or build a formula to provide a tooltip or mouse over message to the user

   ▶ TARGET WINDOW: Specify where to open the target window (for example, current window or new window)

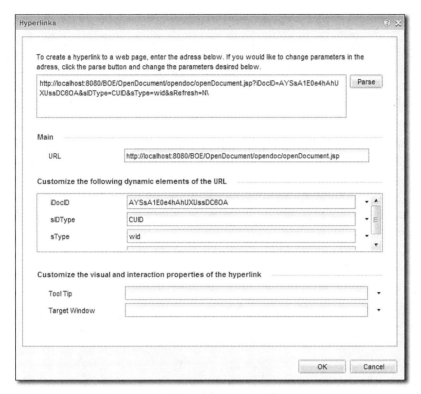

Figure 14.15 Hyperlink Parsed in the Rich Internet Application Viewer

14.2.1 Manually Creating Links Using the OpenDocument Syntax Structure

Let's focus our attention briefly on the parameters used in the URL displayed in Figure 14.15. By understanding the syntax generated in a link to another report, you'll be able to manually create your own links or edit existing ones.

Although the sType and sRefresh parameters were included in the URL, neither element is required.

Full OpenDocument URL example: `http://localhost:8080/BOE/OpenDocument/opendoc/openDocument.jsp?iDocID=AYSsA1E0e4hAhUXUssDC6OA&sIDType=CUID&sType=wid&sRefresh=N\`

Main URL: `http://localhost:8080/BOE/OpenDocument/opendoc/openDocument.jsp?`

Document ID: `iDocID=AYSsA1E0e4hAhUXUssDC6OA`

Figure 14.16 shows the document ID of the hyperlink's target document. This property is used in conjunction with the sIDType parameter and CUID value. The document ID can be found by right-clicking on a published document's name in the BI Launch Pad and then selecting properties.

Figure 14.16 Locating the iDocID or CUID of Web Intelligence Document

Document Type: sType=wid. This is an optional parameter that's still generated when adding Web Intelligence document links while working in the Web viewer.

Refresh: sRefresh=N. Include a Y to force the target Web Intelligence document to refresh when opened. The use of N to open the target document without refreshing is optional.

14.2.2 Adding a Hyperlink to an SAP BusinessObjects Dashboard

Hyperlinks to dashboards can be created by adding as few as a single parameter to the end of the main URL. This can be achieved by using the sDocName parameter, followed by the name of the target document.

Use a plus (+) symbol to represent spaces between words in the document title, as in this working URL that links to a dashboard: *http://localhost:8080/BOE/Open-Document/opendoc/openDocument.jsp?sDocName=Simple+Dashboard*

Whether linking to a report by using the Web viewer or Rich Internet Application viewer, understanding the syntax of document link is crucial to being able to edit it and expand on it. The next section introduces the various parameters available for customizing a document link using the OpenDocument syntax.

14.3   OpenDocument Syntax

The OpenDocument syntax can be used to pass a wide variety of parameters to the document being opened with the OpenDocument URL hyperlink.

Parameters are grouped into three different categories:

▸ Document identifier parameters

▸ Input parameters

▸ Output parameters

14.3.1   Document Identifier Parameters

The platform parameters are described in Table 14.1.

Parameter	Description	Mandatory	Additional Information
`iDocID`	Document identifier	Yes*	Document ID located in document properties
`sDocName`	Document name	Yes*	Use the plus symbol to represent spaces between words
`sIDType`	CMS Object ID type	Yes*	Values: `CUID`, `ParentID`, `InfoObjectID`
`sType`	File type of target document	No	Values: `wid`, `rpt`, `car`, `flash`

Table 14.1 Document Identifier Parameters

Parameter	Description	Mandatory	Additional Information
sInstance	Open the latest instance owned by the current user, latest instance of the report, or latest instance of report with matching parameter values.	No	Values: user, last, param

Table 14.1 Document Identifier Parameters (Cont.)

▶ *iDocID is required if the sDocName parameter isn't used
▶ *sDocName is required if the iDocID parameter isn't used
▶ *sIDType is required in conjunction with the iDocID parameter

14.3.2 Input Parameters

The input parameters are described in Table 14.2.

Parameter	Description	Additional Information
lsC	Specifies a contextual prompt if there is an ambiguity during SQL generation (SAP BusinessObjects and Web Intelligence documents only).	Resolves ambiguity of generated SQL by providing a prompt value.
lsM[Name]	Specifies multiple values for a prompt. [NAME] is the text of the prompt.	Allows multiple prompt values to be passed to a prompt filter. Values are separated by commas.
lsR[Name]	Specifies a range of values for a prompt. [NAME] is the text of the prompt.	A range of values are passed to the prompt, separated by a double period (..). Use no_value to ignore an optional prompt.
lsS[Name]	Specifies a value for a single prompt. [NAME] is the text of the prompt.	Pass single values using the lsS parameter, multiple values using lsM.

Table 14.2 Input Parameters

Parameter	Description	Additional Information
sPartContext	Used when linking to a Crystal Report. Use with sReportPart.	Data context of report part.
sRefresh	Indicates whether a refresh should be forced when the target document is opened.	Use Y to force the document to refresh on open.
sReportMode	For Crystal Report targets only, indicates whether the link should open the full target report or just the report part specified in sReportPart.	Use Full or Part as the report mode.
sReportName	Identifies the report to open if the target document contains multiple reports.	Use the report name in a Web Intelligence document.
sReportPart	Indicates which specific part of the target Crystal Report to open.	Name of the report part. Easily selected when creating a hyperlink and selecting a report part while viewing a report in InfoView.

Table 14.2 Input Parameters (Cont.)

The only required input parameter is for sPartContext when a sReportPart parameter has been included in a URL.

14.3.3 Output Parameters

The output parameters are described in Table 14.3.

Parameter	Description	Additional Information
NAII	Forces the display of the prompt selection page. Web Intelligence only.	Document ID located in document properties
sOutputFormat	Defines the format of target document.	H (HTML), P (PDF), E (Excel), W (Word)

Table 14.3 Output Parameters

Parameter	Description	Additional Information
sWindow	Specifies window of target report.	Same (current window), New (new window)
sViewer	Specifies the selected report viewer.	Available viewer types: html, part
sViewer	Forces Web Intelligence target documents to open in Design mode.	Use the value of true to force the report to open in design mode.

Table 14.3 Output Parameters (Cont.)

By knowing the available parameters that can be used with the OpenDocument function and the syntax required for using them, you can create complex links to meet unique business requirements. Links can contain several input parameters, output parameters, and document identifier parameters. Remember to separate every parameter and value combination with an ampersand (&) symbol.

The next section introduces a capability new in Web Intelligence 4.0 known as element linking. Use this feature to link charts and tables and create a cohesive and interactive experience for report consumers.

14.4   Element Linking

Element linking lets you create an interaction between a chart or data table and one or more report elements. This new functionality allows report designers to produce a form of guided navigation by using a chart value or object in a data table to filter other report elements.

This form of linking bears a similarity to drilling and also resembles the type of interaction experienced with input controls. But element linking performs much differently by allowing a component to pass filters to other elements on a report. This new functionality leads to the creation report/dashboard hybrids and can be accomplished within the Web viewer or Rich Internet Application viewer.

14.4.1 Adding Element Linking

Two methods for adding element links are available. The first step in both methods is to select the source element to be used as the basis for the document link. This can be a chart or object in a data table.

▶ Right-click on the element to be used as the source of the element link.

▶ Select LINKING from the menu and then select ADD ELEMENT LINKING.

The second method of adding linking is by selecting the ADD ELEMENT LINK icon from the tabbed property ribbon. Click on the REPORT ELEMENT tab, followed by selecting the LINKING subtab to reveal the icons for the available linking types.

Figure 14.17 shows the ADD ELEMENT LINK option available when right-clicking on the source element and selecting LINKING from the menu.

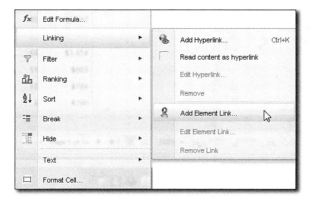

Figure 14.17 Adding Element Linking

After selecting ADD ELEMENT LINK, the Define Input Control window will open so you can select the report objects used to filter data in the dependency elements. Change the default selection from ALL OBJECTS to SINGLE OBJECT to pass the value from a single object to filter the dependency sections.

This option will display all the dimension and detail objects used in the report element creating the document link. Select the object to filter data in the dependency elements and then click on NEXT to proceed.

Figure 14.18 shows the Define Input Control window, which you'll use to select the report objects that filter and connect data to the dependency components.

Figure 14.18 Selecting Objects Used to Filter Data in Element Linking

You can make changes to the label name or add a description to the source component of the element link in the next window. Updates to this screen are optional. Figure 14.19 shows the Set Control Properties window as it appears after you select the report object to be used in adding an element link.

Figure 14.19 Setting Control Properties of Element Link

The final screen in the process is where you'll assign the report elements to be filtered by the selections made in the element link. These report elements, shown in Figure 14.20, are also known as dependency objects. Notice that only one object is unavailable for selection. That's because block 5 is the object that the element link is based on in this example.

Report elements that can be dependencies of an element link include:

▸ Page body
▸ Sections
▸ Charts
▸ Data tables

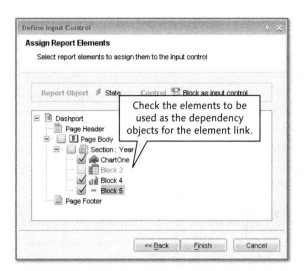

Figure 14.20 Selecting Report Elements as Dependencies of Element Link

14.4.2   The Impact of Element Linking

After an element link has been added to an object in a report, the chart or table containing the link will display a small icon in the upper right corner of the object to indicate that an element link has been added.

This can be seen in the Sales Revenue by City chart in Figure 14.21. In the example, the tag cloud chart contains the element link and all three of the other elements display data related to the Texas selection made by the user.

Valid and accurate labeling is very import when developing dynamic and interactive reports. Because of the filtering capabilities of element links, we recommend that you label dependency charts with the filtered value used in the link.

As an example, use the steps below to add the filtered value to a dependency chart's title.

1. Right-click on a dependency chart object and select FORMAT CHART.

2. Navigate to the Title section in the Format Chart window.

3. Edit the Title Label to include the dynamic filtered value.

4. Click on the green checkmark to validate the syntax.

5. Click on APPLY • OK.

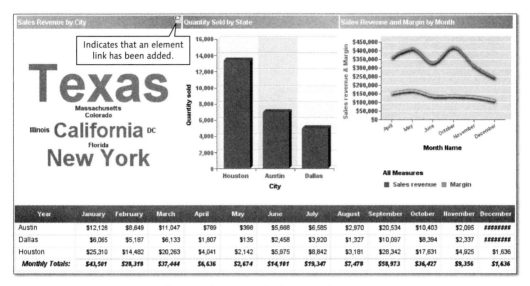

Figure 14.21 Series of Report Elements with Element Linking

Figure 14.22 shows the edited title of a dependency chart with the [state] object used as the filter object.

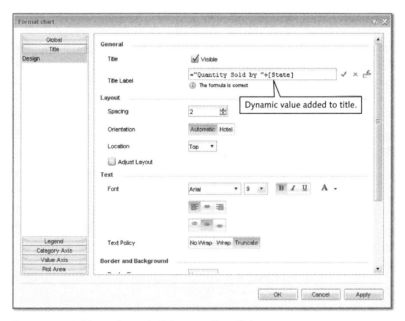

Figure 14.22 Adding a Dynamic Value to a Chart Title

Adding the filtered object used in creating the element link to the title of a dependency chart will provide a better context for users viewing the report. An example of a dynamic title can be seen in Figure 14.23 using the following formula in the title label:

```
="Quantity Sold in "+[State]+" Cities"
```

Use this formula to produce a valid title when the state object is used as a simple filter. The purpose of this formula is to display "Quantity Sold by City" if a value has not been selected and "Quantity Sold in Alabama Cities" if the value selected in the state filter object is Alabama:

```
=If(Count([State])>1;"Quantity Sold by City"; "Quantity Sold in "+[State]+"
Cities")
```

In Figure 14.23, the Tag Cloud object contains the element link. The values being charted in the column chart are associated with the state selected in the tag cloud.

The [State] object has also been included in the title of the column chart.

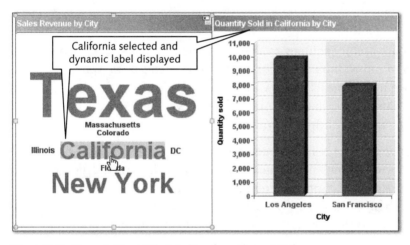

Figure 14.23 Dynamic Chart Title Resulting from Element Link

If you need to reset an element link value to remove the filters from the dependency charts, locate the Input Controls menu on the left side of the page and click on CLEAR FILTERS for the block containing the element link. This action will release the filter and return the dependency charts to their original state. The CLEAR

FILTERS button is pictured in Figure 14.24. After the filter has been cleared, the message below the button will change to No FILTER APPLIED.

Figure 14.24 Clearing Element Link Filters

> **Note**
>
> Element linking cannot be used when it's added to a chart that contains a dimension object that's part of a hierarchy and when drill mode has been enabled. This is because drill mode will force the chart to drill either up or down the hierarchy rather than functioning as an element link.
>
> Disabling drill mode will allow the element link to function as designed.

14.5   Summary

Hyperlinks are useful additions to Web Intelligence reports. They allow report developers to embed links to other reporting documents or to web pages. Links can be added to documents while working in the Web viewer through document linking or with the Rich Internet Application viewer and Web Intelligence Rich Client using the OpenDocument syntax.

Guided analysis to deeper information can be easily added to reports by strategically inserting hyperlinks and element links that contain related data at different hierarchy levels and featuring different dimension objects. Use element linking to produce a cohesive collection of report elements that encourage interaction. This new feature allows developers to produce reports that function similar to dashboards.

One of the biggest benefits of inserting hyperlinks in reports is the capability of passing dynamic values to prompted filters. This feature allows entire columns to serve as hyperlinks that pass only the selected value to a prompted filter in a Web Intelligence document. Reporting documents can also be refreshed and opened to display up-to-the-minute data—all with a single click.

An extensive list of input, output, and document identifier parameters are available for passing values to linked reports published to the SAP BusinessObjects BI 4.0 platform. These parameters are appended to URLs created with the Open-Document syntax structure that connect to target documents.

Chapter 15 provides details on working within the BI Launch Pad, which was introduced in the SAP BusinessObjects BI 4.0 platform.

The BI Launch Pad web portal used to access Web Intelligence documents provides you with a fully integrated interface for organizing, viewing, analyzing, and sharing business intelligence content. The added functionality and ease of use of the interface make the BI Launch Pad a powerful tool for end users and report writers alike.

15 Working in the BI Launch Pad

Web Intelligence reports are accessed using the BI platform web portal named the *BI Launch Pad* (formerly InfoView). The BI Launch Pad portal gives you access to a variety of business content outside of Web Intelligence reports, including Crystal Reports, dashboards, Microsoft Office documents, and so on. This gives business users one secure location to view business intelligence content. You can also publish and distribute content to other users in Web Intelligence, Excel, PDF, SAP StreamWork, and MHTML format from within the BI Launch Pad. All users, from casual users to advanced power users, must be familiar with working within the BI Launch Pad in order to consume report content. From viewing documents to on-report analysis, the BI Launch Pad provides a single user interface for working with your documents.

15.1 Navigating in BI Launch Pad

Figure 15.1 shows the default view when you log on to the BI Launch Pad. The initial view shows the HOME tab, which can be customized in General Preferences (discussed in Section 15.2). The initial view is divided into three sections by default: Header panel, tabs, and HOME tab view. The Header panel includes the BI Launch Pad toolbar with menu options applicable across the BI Launch Pad. The tabs display the default HOME and DOCUMENTS tabs as well as any tabs pinned to the BI Launch Pad interface. Additional tabs may be available by default depending on your configuration. If your environment is integrated with SAP Stream-Work, you may see a tab for the feeds.

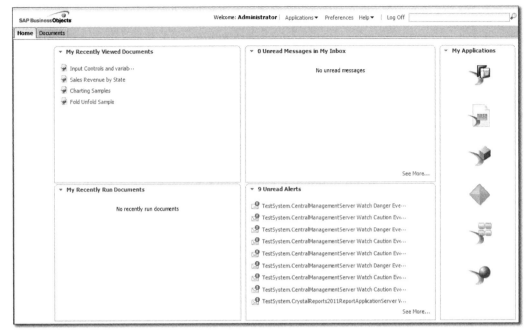

Figure 15.1 BI Launch Pad Initial View

Let's begin by zeroing in on the Header panel.

15.1.1 Header Panel

The Header panel menu options may vary depending on any customization that may have been applied to your environment (see Figure 15.2).

Figure 15.2 Header Panel

The Header panel includes the customizable top header section with the SAP BusinessObjects logo and the Header panel menus. A number of menu options are available by default, though availability of these options will depend on your access rights. The header also displays the name of the user account that is currently logged on.

The following are various menus found in the Header panel:

▶ HOME tab

Selecting the HOME tab brings you back to the initial view as seen in Figure 15.1. Your HOME tab can be customized in your General Preferences, as discussed in Section 15.2.

▶ DOCUMENTS tab

Selecting the DOCUMENTS tab enables you to view the drawers with the folders and categories organization structure as well as the documents available within these folders and categories.

▶ APPLICATIONS

Upon selecting the APPLICATIONS menu from the Header panel, a dropdown list appears listing the available types of applications that can be opened within the BI Launch Pad, as shown in Figure 15.3. These options will vary based on the settings in your environment as well as your user rights.

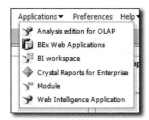

Figure 15.3 Applications Menu on Header Panel

▶ PREFERENCES

Selecting the PREFERENCES menu opens up the personal preferences available to customize the BI Launch Pad and Web Intelligence for your user account. Further discussion regarding setting preferences is in Section 15.2.

▶ HELP

Selecting the HELP menu provides the About page with the specific product information about your environment as well as access to additional help resources.

▶ LOG OFF

Selecting the LOG OFF option ends your current BI platform session. It is important to log out of the BI Launch Pad rather than close the browser because your session will remain open until the default time-out period set up by your SAP BusinessObjects administrator. Depending on your company's licensing structure, numerous open sessions may restrict your access to the BI Launch Pad. If you experience this problem, contact your SAP BusinessObjects administrator to re-enable your access.

Home Tab

The default HOME TAB, which is shown in Figure 15.1, features icons for quick access to applications as well as four panels:

▶ MY RECENTLY VIEWED DOCUMENTS
The first quadrant includes links to the ten last viewed documents sorted by view date with the most recent at the top of the list.

▶ UNREAD MESSAGES IN MY INBOX
The second quadrant displays the ten most recent unread messages in your BI inbox. Selecting the SEE MORE... link at the bottom right of the box will bring you to your BI inbox to view the unread messages.

▶ MY RECENTLY RUN DOCUMENTS
The third quadrant lists the last ten documents that you scheduled or ran. It also includes the status of each instance. You may select the document name to open the instance.

▶ UNREAD ALERTS
The fourth quadrant includes a listing of unread alert messages that you are subscribed to in your alert subscriptions. Selecting the SEE MORE... link at the bottom right of the box will bring you to your Alerts to view the unread messages.

Documents Tab

The second default tab in the initial workspace is the DOCUMENTS tab shown in Figure 15.4, which contains the drawer menus and objects such as folders, categories, Web Intelligence documents, and publications for your use in the BI Launch Pad.

The expandable panes on the left of the screen in the DOCUMENTS tab are called drawers. Depending on your access rights, not all objects in the drawers may be visible to you. The following drawer menus are available:

▶ **My Documents**

The items included in the MY DOCUMENTS drawer include objects which are visible *only to you*. It also has a MY FAVORITES folder, in which you can store your personal documents as well as temporary files saved from a timeout. You can create additional folder hierarchies within your MY FAVORITES folder to further personalize and organize your documents. Other folders include your BI INBOX, MY ALERTS, SUBSCRIBED ALERTS, and PERSONAL CATEGORIES.

▶ **Folders**

The FOLDERS drawer includes the public folders visible to all users, although which specific folders are available depends on access rights.

▶ **Categories**

The CATEGORIES drawer includes the categories available for public consumption. These will be discussed in Section 15.3.

▶ **Search**

The SEARCH drawer includes the search box discussed in further detail in Chapter 17.

Figure 15.4 Documents Tab

If you select the DOCUMENTS tab instead of the HOME tab, you'll see the drawers for navigation, the folders, or the categories set up within the BI Launch Pad.

Figure 15.5 shows a sample navigation panel structure within the Folders drawer. The navigation panel within each organization will be customized to their needs, so your navigation panel will be different from this view. Along with the folder hierarchy in the navigation panel, you will see the list of documents in the list panel as well as the toolbar and details panel. Figure 15.5 shows a sample view of the list panel after selection of PUBLIC FOLDERS from the Folders drawer.

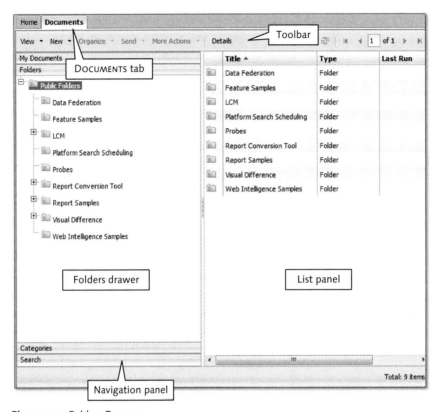

Figure 15.5 Folders Drawer

When you have selected the DOCUMENTS tab from the BI Launch Pad, you can access the documents toolbar, shown in Figure 15.6.

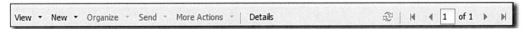

Figure 15.6 Documents Toolbar

The toolbar includes the following items:

▶ VIEW

As shown in Figure 15.7, you have several options when you select the VIEW menu: view the document, view latest instance, or properties. To activate the menu options, you must first select a document from the list panel. The view option will open the document in reading mode within the BI Launch Pad. The VIEW LATEST INSTANCE option will open the latest scheduled instances in the reading mode. If there are no saved instances, then this option will not show as active in the menu options. The PROPERTIES option displays the document properties with specific information regarding the selected report.

Figure 15.7 View Menu

▶ NEW
When you select the New menu from the toolbar, a dropdown list displays the available options, as shown in Figure 15.8. The available options will depend on your environment and user settings.

Figure 15.8 New Menu

▶ ORGANIZE
The Organize menu contains options that are standard in a number of programs, such as cut, copy, copy shortcut, paste, and delete, as shown in Figure 15.9. The ORGANIZE button will only become enabled when selecting a folder where your rights allow you to perform this action. When selected on a document in the list panel, it also contains the option to CREATE SHORTCUT IN MY FAVORITES.

▶ SEND
The Send menu contains options for sending a document to other users across the enterprise, including to another user's BI inbox.

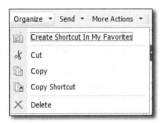

Figure 15.9 Organize Menu

▶ More Actions

The More Actions menu displays only after you select an object from the work-space panel. This menu contains a number of actions you can perform upon a Web Intelligence document from within the BI Launch Pad.

▶ Modify: Allows you to modify the object. For a Web Intelligence report, selecting the Modify option will open the report in Web Intelligence in design mode to make any necessary changes.

▶ Schedule: Allows you to schedule to a designated distribution. Refer to Chapter 18 for detailed information on scheduling reports.

▶ History: Displays the schedule history. Refer to Chapter 18 for detailed information on scheduling reports.

▶ Categories: Allows you to select which categories within which an object should display.

▶ Document Link: Provides the open document hyperlink information. Chapter 14 provides further information on utilizing document linking.

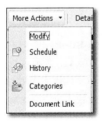

Figure 15.10 More Actions Menu

▶ Details

The Details button opens the details panel (shown in Figure 15.11), which provides information about the document. A drawer menu is also available on the DETAILS tab to open the discussions panel. These topics are discussed in further detail in Chapter 18.

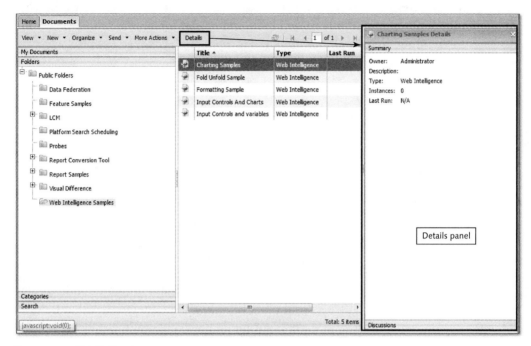

Figure 15.11 Details Panel

▶ REFRESH
Selecting the REFRESH button refreshes the DOCUMENTS tab. This can be helpful when a new report is added to the BI Launch Pad or after creating a new folder or category.

▶ PAGE NAVIGATION
Page Navigation includes the current page number of the navigation panel with arrows allowing you to quickly navigate between pages. The default number of items displayed per page is set in the general preferences, as discussed in Section 15.2.

15.1.2 List Panel

The list panel displays the objects selected in the navigation panel.

15.1.3 Tabs

Additional tabs may be available to you, depending on your environment. The SAP BusinessObjects administrator can designate specific default tabs for your organization. Also, if your implementation includes integration with SAP Stream-Work, you may see a tab for the SAP StreamWork feeds. You can also select the PIN THIS TAB option to pin a selected document to your initial view, as shown in Figure 15.12.

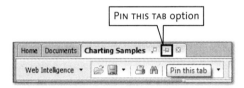

Figure 15.12 Pin This Tab Option

15.2 Setting BI Launch Pad Preferences

The majority of user settings are set by the SAP BusinessObjects administrator in the Central Management Console, but there are some preferences that the user can set. These include preferences for the BI Launch Pad, Web Intelligence, and possibly Crystal Reports or BI workplace. Refer to Chapter 1 for a more substantial discussion of Web Intelligence preferences. Settings that are specific to the BI Launch Pad environment are defined within your general preferences.

15.2.1 General Preferences

General preferences include settings for your BI Launch Pad environment. The checkbox for USE DEFAULT SETTINGS (ADMINISTRATOR DEFINED)—which enables you to naturally inherit default settings—is selected by default. You can define your own custom preferences if you uncheck this box.

The first setting allows you to define the BI Launch Pad Start Page, whose options are shown in Table 15.1.

The DOCUMENTS tab preferences allow you to select the default view of either folder or categories that will display in your workspace. We'll discuss the differences between folders and categories in further detail in the next section.

HOME **tab**	The HOME tab is the default setting as shown in Figure 15.1. You can select the default home tab or browse the repository for a custom home tab.
DOCUMENTS **tab**	
MY DOCUMENTS • MY FAVORITES	The FAVORITES option opens the BI Launch Pad with the navigation panel selected on your Favorites folder and the list panel showing the contents of your Favorites folder.
MY DOCUMENTS • PERSONAL CATEGORIES	The PERSONAL CATEGORIES option opens the BI Launch Pad with the navigation panel selected on your personal categories and the list panel showing the contents of your categories.
MY DOCUMENTS • MY INBOX	The INBOX option opens the BI Launch Pad with the navigation panel selected on your BI inbox and the list panel showing the contents of your inbox.
FOLDERS	The FOLDERS option shows the Tree View set to the folder you specify in the Browse folder box and the workspace detail panel showing the contents of the selected folder.
CATEGORIES	The CATEGORY option shows the Tree View set to the category you specify in the Browse category box and the workspace detail panel showing the contents of the selected category.

Table 15.1 BI Launch Pad Start Page Options

The DOCUMENTS tab display option allows you to select which columns will be displayed by default when viewing the DOCUMENTS tab in the list panel. Select the checkbox to display the property according to your preference. Options include: type, last run, instances, description, created by, created on, location (categories), received on (inbox), from (inbox).

The document viewing location property specifies how you will view documents upon selection of VIEW from the toolbar in the BI Launch Pad.

The available options include:

▶ In the BI Launch Pad portal as tabs
▶ In multiple full screen browser windows, one window for each document

The final general preferences option allows you to set the maximum number of objects to show at one time per page in the workspace details panel of the BI Launch Pad. The default setting is set to 50 items per page. Increasing the number of objects shown per page can have an impact on performance, so exercise caution when changing these settings.

15.2.2 Locales and Time Zone Preferences

Additional properties specific to your locale are shown in Figure 15.13. Locale-specific properties are usually defined in the Central Management Console by your SAP BusinessObjects administrator. If you prefer to use customized personal properties, then the option is available in general preferences.

The following are locale-specific properties:

▶ PRODUCT LOCALE: The default setting uses the locale of your browser.

▶ PREFERRED VIEWING LOCALE: The default setting uses the locale of your browser.

▶ CURRENT TIME ZONE: The default setting uses the time zone of the web server used by SAP BusinessObjects.

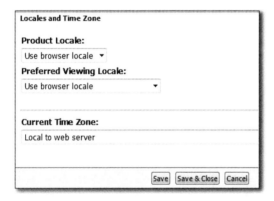

Figure 15.13 Locales and Time Zone Preferences

15.2.3 Changing Your Password

The ability to change your password will depend on your authentication type. If you are set to Enterprise authentication and the administrator has enabled this right, then you can change your password. The Change Password preferences are shown in Figure 15.14.

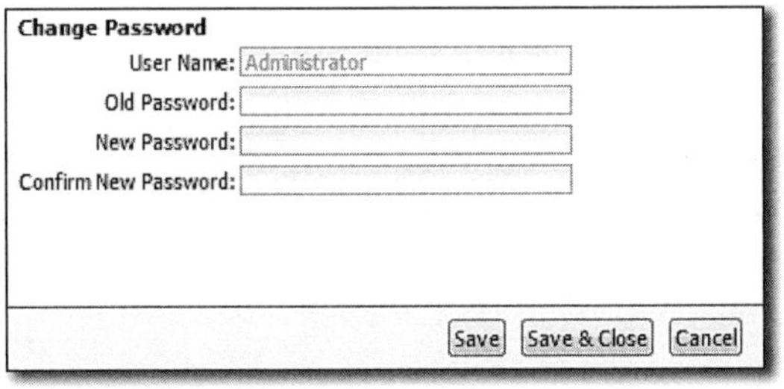

Change Password

User Name:	Administrator
Old Password:	
New Password:	
Confirm New Password:	

[Save] [Save & Close] [Cancel]

Figure 15.14 Change Password Preferences

> **Note**
>
> The options that are available to you in preferences may vary depending upon the settings in the Central Management Console set by your SAP BusinessObjects administrator as well as your specific SAP BusinessObjects deployment.

15.3 Organizing in Folders versus Categories

There are two ways to organize your documents within the BI Launch Pad: folders and categories. The key difference between folders and categories is that every document must belong to a folder, but a document does not have to belong to a category. Categories are a way to organize your documents into logical groupings without having to create copies or shortcuts of your documents. The documents contained within categories are not duplicates, but the same original document organized in a different way. For example, your public folders may be organized by region so that each region is restricted to see their folder alone. The category structure could be organized by logical grouping of time when reports are normally viewed or run: yearly, monthly, weekly, or daily. This helps the users quickly see which reports to view using categories, but also lets them navigate through the folders based on their company structure.

15.3.1 Folders

There are two types of folders: public and personal. Public folders are usually set up by the SAP BusinessObjects administrator and restricted in terms of who can set up new public folders. They also can be restricted as to who can publish documents to the public folders in order to maintain a system of testing and quality assurance before reports are published out for public consumption. They are contained in the Folders drawer.

In contrast, only you or users with administrative access can view documents contained in personal folders. Each user has his own personal folders to organize documents for his own personal use. These documents are not available for public consumption. They are found in the My Documents drawer.

Personal folders include the My Favorites documents and the user's BI inbox. Users across an organization can share documents by sending them to each other's inbox. More detail on sharing documents is discussed in Chapter 18. My Favorites consists of personal documents for the user's own consumption. You can create additional personal folders within your favorites to further organize your documents provided you have been given the appropriate rights. Figure 15.5 shows a sample folder structure in the BI Launch Pad.

15.3.2 Categories

Categories are created to help organize documents in a way that is different from the folder view. A report can belong to only one folder, but it can belong to numerous categories. But, like folders, categories can include both personal and corporate. Corporate categories are available across an organization while personal categories are only available to the specific user. Figure 15.15 shows a sample category view in the BI Launch Pad available in the Categories drawer in the Documents tab. You can access personal categories from the My Documents drawer.

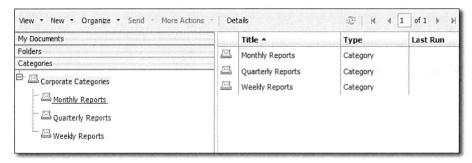

Figure 15.15 Sample Category View

15.3.3 Organizing Objects

Objects such as Web Intelligence documents are organized in the BI Launch Pad using folders and categories. Depending on your user rights, you can create new folders and categories, move and copy existing folders and categories, sort objects within folders and categories, delete unneeded folders and categories, and set folder and category preferences. Let's explore all of these options further.

Creating New Folders and Categories

To create a new folder, it is necessary to be in the Folder drawer or selected in My Favorites in the My Documents drawer. Select NEW from the BI Launch Pad workspace toolbar and choose FOLDER from the dropdown list.

To create a new category, it is necessary to be in the Categories drawer or selected on Personal Categories in the My Documents drawer. Select NEW from the BI Launch Pad workspace toolbar and choose CATEGORY from the dropdown list.

Moving Objects in Folders and Categories

Use the CUT • PASTE option from the Organize menu to move an object in a folder or category. First select the object to be moved. Then select the Organize menu from the BI Launch Pad workspace toolbar and choose CUT. This will remove the object from its current location and allow you to paste it into the new location. Navigate to the new folder or category location and select PASTE from the Organize menu.

> **Note**
>
> Any shortcuts that have been applied to an object will be maintained when copying and pasting objects to a new location.

Copying Objects in Folders and Categories

To copy an object in a folder or category to another location, highlight the object to be copied and select COPY from the Organize menu on the DOCUMENTS tab toolbar. Then navigate to the new folder or category to add the object to the new location and select PASTE from the Organize menu. This will create another instance of this object in the new location. If you make changes to one object, you also need to make them to the other object to maintain consistency. If you want the second instance to automatically reflect any changes made to the original object, then you should use the shortcut function discussed in Chapter 18.

Sorting and Filtering Objects in Folders and Categories

You can sort objects from within folders and categories into ascending or descending order by selecting the heading of the column of the workspace panel. The default setting is to sort objects from A to Z by title. When hovering over the title bar, a funnel icon will appear. Select this icon to filter content in the list, as shown in Figure 15.16. Reselect the FILTER icon and select the CLEAR FILTER checkbox to remove the content filter.

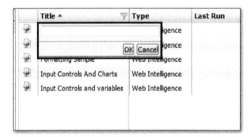

Figure 15.16 Column Filters Option

Deleting Objects from Folders and Categories

To delete an object from a folder or category, select the object and choose the DELETE option from the Organize menu. Whether you are authorized to delete objects will depend on your user rights. Usually users are authorized to delete only objects in their personal folders or categories unless they have administrative level access.

Setting Object Properties

To set object properties, highlight the object in the workspace panel and select PROPERTIES from the View menu. The Properties box allows you to define the object title, description, and keywords.

15.4   Viewing, Printing, and Saving Objects in the BI Launch Pad

You can view, print, and save Web Intelligence documents within the BI Launch Pad without having to edit them in Web Intelligence. From within the list panel, select the Web Intelligence document that you wish to view within the BI Launch Pad and select VIEW from the Actions menu on the BI Launch Pad workspace toolbar. You can also double-click on the name of a report to open it in reading mode, or select VIEW from the right-click menu when selected on a document. (The View option also opens the Web Intelligence document in reading mode. How the document opens within reading mode will be dependent on your preferences, as discussed in Section 15.3.) When viewing a Web Intelligence document within the BI Launch Pad, the Web Intelligence Viewer toolbar shown in Figure 15.17 will appear with the options available to you.

Figure 15.17 Web Intelligence Viewer Toolbar in Reading Mode

Let's examine this toolbar closely.

15.4.1   Web Intelligence Viewer Toolbar

The first menu on the Web Intelligence Viewer toolbar is the Web Intelligence menu, where you can select options for your toolbar views. This includes toggling on or off the filter bar, outline view, left pane, report tabs, and status bar.

The following toolbar options are shown in Figure 15.17:

▸ OPEN: Enables you to select from the DOCUMENTS tab to open another Web Intelligence report in reading mode

▸ SAVE: Saves any changes made to the report

▸ SAVE AS: Saves any changes made to the report as a new name and/or to a new location

▸ PRINT: Exports the report to PDF format for printing. Web Intelligence documents must first be exported to PDF before they can be printed (Once you select the EXPORT TO PDF button, you will be prompted to open the PDF or save it. You don't need to save the PDF to create a printed copy, but you may wish to save the PDF for further reference)

- ▶ FIND: Searches for text in tables and cells on the page being viewed of the report

- ▶ HISTORY: Lists dates corresponding with the history of the scheduled instances of the document

- ▶ EXPORT: Enables you to export a document in PDF, Excel, Excel 2007, or CSV format

- ▶ SEND TO: Allows you to send to email, BI inbox, or FTP location

- ▶ UNDO: Undoes the previous action

- ▶ REDO: Redoes the previous action

- ▶ REFRESH: Refreshes selected queries or all queries used by the report

- ▶ TRACK: Activates or deactivates the data tracking mode (to be discussed shortly)

- ▶ DRILL: Enables drill mode, as discussed in Chapter 10

- ▶ FILTER BAR: Displays the filter bar on the report

- ▶ OUTLINE: Shows or hides the outline providing the ability to use fold/unfold features on the report

- ▶ READING MENU: Lets you switch between different modes such as HTML and PDF for viewing the document

- ▶ DESIGN MENU: Lets you edit the document in Web Intelligence by selecting DESIGN WITH DATA or STRUCTURE ONLY

- ▶ HELP: Opens the online help

Other menu options extend Web Intelligence Viewer functionality.

15.4.2 Additional Menu Options

The left side panel includes additional toggle menu options, including Document Summary, Navigation Map, Input Controls, and User Prompt Input. Document summary details the properties of the Web Intelligence document. The navigation map shows the sections of the document including the content on each report tab. The input controls (which were discussed in Chapter 9) let you specify values or move selectors to change the content of the report. This option is only available if this feature has been enabled and set up by the report designer. The user prompt input box, which is shown in Figure 15.18, shows the prompt values and enables you to change the prompt values to refresh a report.

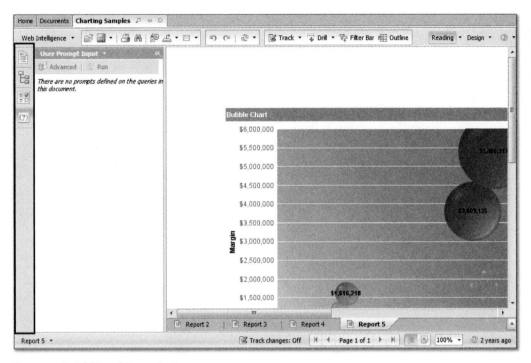

Figure 15.18 Additional Menu Options

15.5 Summary

The BI Launch Pad portal provides a multifunctional interface for the casual user to organize, view, print, and share Web Intelligence documents. Additional features discussed in Chapter 18 (such as tracking data changes and robust search capabilities) make the BI Platform interface a powerful tool for collaboration across the business. Chapter 17 discusses the use of the BI workspaces to create custom pages for viewing your report content.

Using BI Workspaces, users can create multitabbed dashboards that combine multiple types of BI content.

16 Using Web Intelligence with BI Workspaces

BI Workspaces is a web application that allows users to define multitabbed workspaces to organize related objects from the BI platform for an integrated viewing experience. BI Workspaces can combine Crystal Reports, Analysis edition for OLAP workspaces, Web Intelligence documents, and Dashboards (formerly known as Xcelsius) with agnostic content such as static text, HTML, or web pages external to the BI platform. You can also integrate existing BI workspaces into new BI workspaces. Once created, BI workspace can be accessed on demand or set as the default home tab to be seen when users log on to the BI Launch Pad.

In this chapter, we'll explore the BI Workspaces application and learn how to combine Web Intelligence documents and report parts into a single, cohesive BI workspace.

> **Note**
>
> This chapter has been written using SAP BusinessObjects Business Intelligence 4.0 Feature Pack 3 (Service Pack 4), as it contains new BI Workspaces features not present in previous releases of the BI 4.0 platform.
>
> In versions prior to SAP BusinessObjects Business Intelligence 4.0, the BI Workspaces application was known as Dashboard Builder.

16.1 Introducing BI Workspaces

The BI Workspaces application can be launched from the Applications menu in the BI Launch Pad, as shown in Figure 16.1.

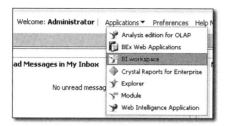

Figure 16.1 BI Workspaces Application

Within the BI Workspaces application, there is a large canvas for laying out the design of the workspace. At the top of the canvas you'll find the BI Workspaces toolbar. On its left side is the Module Library. In the next sections, we'll explore how to use the BI Workspaces toolbar and the Module Library to add content to the workspace canvas.

16.1.1 BI Workspaces Toolbar

The BI Workspaces toolbar appears across the top of the BI Workspaces application, as shown in Figure 16.2. It presents the following options:

▶ NEW: Creates a new BI workspace

▶ OPEN: Opens an existing BI workspace

▶ SAVE: Updates the repository with the latest BI workspace changes

▶ SAVE AS: Saves a new BI workspace with a different name or location than the original

▶ SHOW MODULE LIBRARY: Opens the Module Library sidebar

▶ REVERT CHANGES: Returns BI workspace to the last saved revision

▶ CONTENT LINKING: Enables content linking between different modules in the BI workspace

▶ LAYOUT: Organizes the canvas by columns, template, or freeform layout

▶ EXIT EDIT MODE: Exits the edit mode (any unsaved changes will be lost)

Note

Other options appear on the toolbar depending on which layout (column, template, or freeform) is chosen.

Figure 16.2 BI Workspaces Toolbar

A BI workspace consists of a primary, or home, tab. This HOME tab can be extended with a series of tabs and subtabs, permitting a two-layer hierarchy to be constructed, as shown in Figure 16.3.

Figure 16.3 Two-Layer Hierarchy

The options for each tab or subtab can be modified by right-clicking on the desired tab or subtab. There are five options, as shown in Figure 16.4:

▶ RENAME: Renames the current tab or subtab

▶ DUPLICATE: Duplicates the current tab or subtab

▶ DELETE: Deletes the current tab or subtab

▶ PROPERTIES: Modifies the properties of the current tab or subtab

▶ SET AS DEFAULT: Sets the current tab or subtab as the default, meaning it will appear first when the user selects BI WORKSPACE

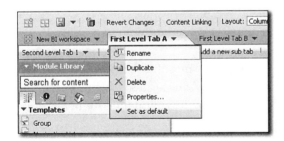

Figure 16.4 Tab Options

Each tab or subtab can display multiple objects from the BI platform. There are three different layout options available from the BI Workspaces toolbar: column layout, template layout, and freeform layout.

Column layout, shown in Figure 16.5, organizes the content into multiple columns for an orderly appearance.

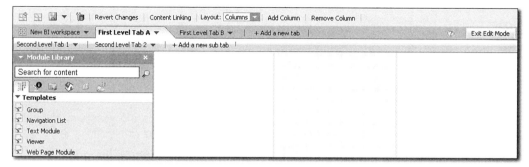

Figure 16.5 Column Layout

Template layout, shown in Figure 16.6, provides several predefined templates with options for either rows or columns.

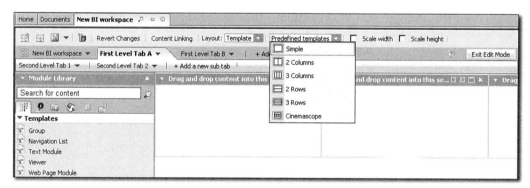

Figure 16.6 Template Layout

Freeform layout, shown in Figure 16.7, offers the most flexibility of the three layout options. BI workspace authors can choose a visible grid to assist with module placement, and can even choose to snap modules to the grid lines for better organization.

The BI Workspaces Module Library is a left-hand pane found underneath the BI Workspaces toolbar.

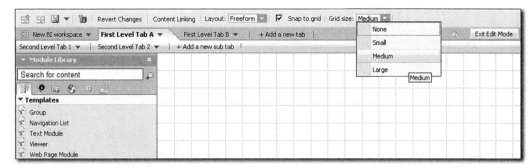

Figure 16.7 Freeform Layout

16.1.2 BI Workspaces Module Library

The BI Workspaces Module Library offers six different sources of business intelligence content: templates, BI Launch Pad modules, public modules, private modules, BI workspaces, and Document Explorer. Let's explore each of these now.

Template Modules

The five types of templates that can be used with BI workspace are shown in Figure 16.8:

▸ GROUP: Provides a box outline. This outline can improve the appearance of other modules.

▸ NAVIGATION LIST: Can be used as a table of contents. It can be paired with a Viewer module using module variables.

▸ TEXT MODULE: Displays either plain text or formatted HTML. Text modules are useful for documentation or navigation when neither presently exist on an external web page.

▸ VIEWER: Displays content from the BI platform, such as a Web Intelligence document. Content can also be selected using the Public and Private modules, which are covered later in this chapter.

▸ WEB PAGE MODULE: Displays the contents of a web page. An example is the contents of a corporate intranet such as a help page.

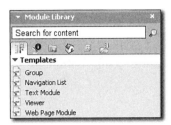

Figure 16.8 Template Modules in the Module Library

BI Launch Pad Modules

The modules available from the BI LAUNCH PAD MODULES tab should be familiar to even the most casual SAP BusinessObjects user, as they appear on the default home page tab in the BI Launch Pad. The following modules are shown in Figure 16.9:

▶ MY ALERTS: Displays alerts from the BI platform

▶ MY APPLICATIONS: Displays icons for applications if the user has rights to access them

▶ MY INBOX: Displays the contents of the user's BI inbox.

▶ MY RECENTLY RUN DOCUMENTS: Displays documents recently run (or, in other words, scheduled) by the user

▶ MY RECENTLY VIEWED DOCUMENTS: Displays documents recently viewed by the user

▶ SAP STREAMWORK FEED: Displays the user's SAP Streamwork feed (requires SAP Streamwork to be integrated with the BI Platform)

Figure 16.9 BI Launch Pad Modules in the Module Library

Public Modules

As shown in Figure 16.10, the Public Modules tab displays all of the business intelligence content available from the public folders. To access them, simply navigate to the desired public folder, identify the desired module, such as a Web Intelligence document, and drag it to the BI workspace canvas.

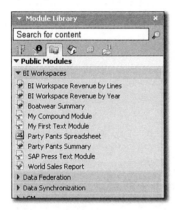

Figure 16.10 Public Modules in the Module Library

Private Modules

The Private Modules tab of the Module Library, shown in Figure 16.11, displays the modules present in the BI workspace author's personal folders, such as eFashion and eStaff and eFashion Expert Excel. These modules can only be used for personal BI workspaces that will be saved in the user's personal folders because other users do not have sufficient rights to private modules to use them.

Figure 16.11 Private Modules in the Module Library

BI Workspaces

Tabs and subtabs from other BI workspaces can be reused by choosing them from the BI WORKSPACES tab in the Module Library, as shown in Figure 16.12. In our example, you can see that a single BI workspace, named the Web Intelligence 4.0 BI Workspace, exists in the repository. That BI workspace contains two tabs (BY LINES and BY YEAR), which can be added to the currently open BI workspace canvas.

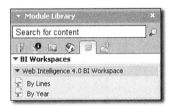

Figure 16.12 BI Workspaces in the Module Library

Note
We strongly recommend that you replace default module names in BI workspaces with meaningful names. This action will make it easier for other BI workspace authors to find useful pre-existing content for their own BI workspaces without reinventing the wheel.

Document Explorer

The DOCUMENT EXPLORER tab in the Module Library, shown in Figure 16.13, provides an easy way to add an entire public folder to a BI Workspaces tab or subtab. Document explorers for personal lists such as the inbox or Query Panel are also available.

16.1.3 Setting BI Workspaces Preferences in the BI Launch Pad

Only a single setting, default style, is available in the BI Launch Pad preferences, as shown in Figure 16.14. Several of these styles are carried over from previous versions of the BI platform for backwards compatibility, so the appearance is outdated. You might prefer the newer BI Launch Pad style for new BI workspaces.

Figure 16.13 Document Explorer in the Module Library

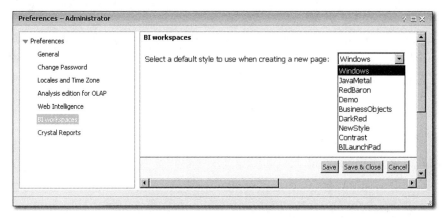

Figure 16.14 BI Workspaces Preferences in the BI Launch Pad

16.1.4   Setting Web Intelligence Preferences in the BI Launch Pad

The ability to include a single report part from a Web Intelligence document is a useful feature of Web Intelligence 4.0 that will be explored later on in the chapter. It is important to choose the Web viewer (VIEW setting) in the Web Intelligence preferences because the Java-based Rich Internet Application viewer does not permit the selection of report parts, but it makes no difference to the BI Workspaces application which version of Web Intelligence is used to create and modify Web Intelligence documents (MODIFY setting). For example, in Figure 16.15, the Web application has been specified for viewing but the Rich Internet Application has been specified for modification.

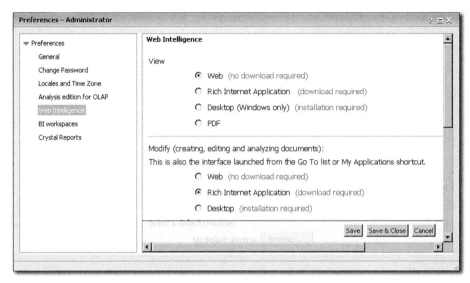

Figure 16.15 View and Modify Options

16.2 Working with Modules

The BI Launch Pad application menu also offers an application to create modules is available to you; this Module application is shown in Figure 16.16.

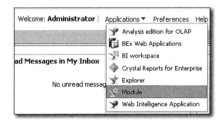

Figure 16.16 BI Launch Pad Module Application

Two types of modules can be created in this manner: text modules and compound modules. Let's take a closer look at both of these.

Text Modules

Text modules can contain either plain text or formatted HTML. They can be useful for annotating BI workspaces with simple documentation or hyperlinks to locations outside of the BI platform when a pre-existing web page that performs those functions does not exist.

To begin, chose TEXT MODULE from the NEW MODULE tab, as shown in Figure 16.17.

Figure 16.17 Text Modules and Compound Modules

Next, choose either REGULAR (plain) or HTML text, which has been selected in Figure 16.18.

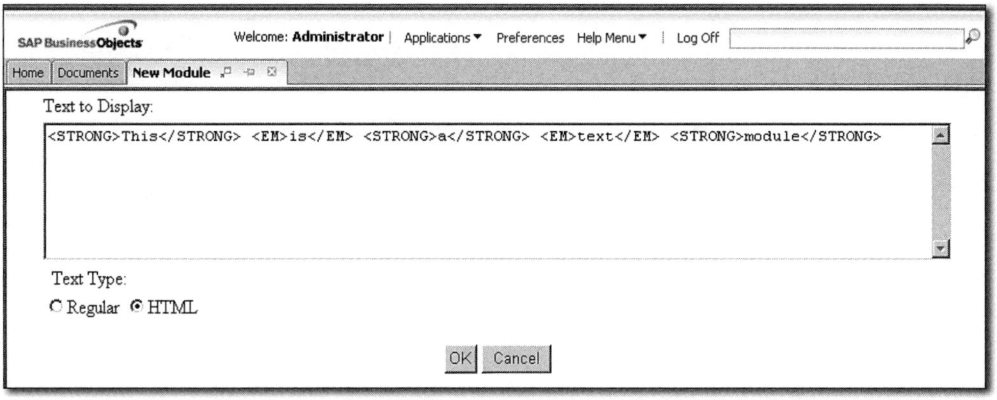

Figure 16.18 Creating a Text Module Using HTML

The formatted HTML, shown in Figure 16.19, can be saved as a module in a personal or public folder.

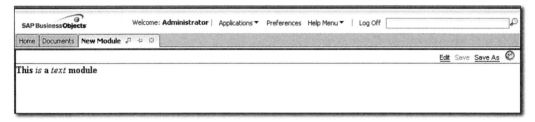

Figure 16.19 Viewing a Text Module Using HTML

Compound Modules

In contrast to text modules, a compound module is a simplified BI workspace that does not contain tabs and subtabs. Compound modules are useful for reusing content in multiple tabs or subtabs of the same BI workspace or even across multiple BI workspaces. For example, it may be beneficial to create a compound module containing corporate branding elements for BI workspaces.

16.3 Working with Web Intelligence Report Parts

Although entire Web Intelligence documents can be placed inside a viewer on a BI workspace, it can be more effective to place a single report part (either a table or chart) on a single tab or subtab. In this section, we will place a tag cloud chart from a Web Intelligence 4.0 document on a subtab of an existing BI workspace (see Figure 16.20).

The existing BI workspace is called eFashion BI Workspace. As shown in Figure 16.21, it already contains a tab named PARTY PANTS with a subtab named BUBBLE, which is where the bubble chart report is found. To begin editing an existing BI workspace, click on the EDIT BI WORKSPACE button in the top right corner.

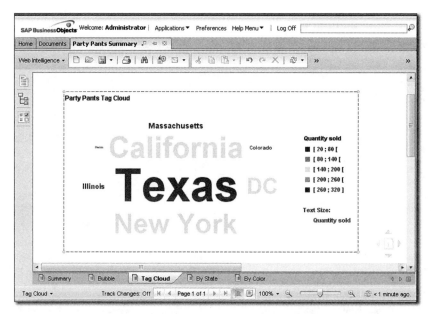

Figure 16.20 Web Intelligence Document with a Tag Cloud Chart

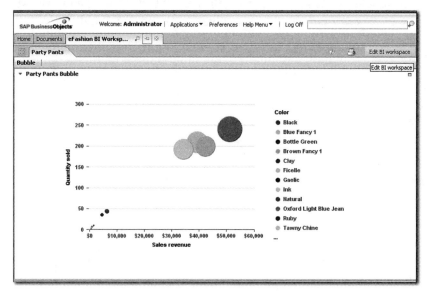

Figure 16.21 Editing an Existing BI Workspace

Next, add a new subtab next to the BUBBLE subtab by clicking on + ADD A NEW SUBTAB, as shown in Figure 16.22.

Figure 16.22 Adding a New Subtab

Next, assign the subtab a name by replacing the default text "New subtab," shown in Figure 16.23. In our example, the new subtab is named Tag Cloud.

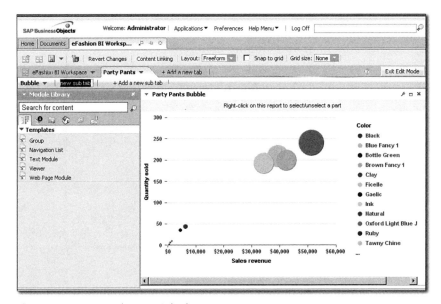

Figure 16.23 Naming the New Subtab

The next step is to choose the layout of your new subtab. In our example, we've selected the freeform layout, as shown in Figure 16.24.

Figure 16.24 Choosing the Layout

Next, you need to choose the PUBLIC MODULES tab from the Module Library. In our example, we navigate to the public folder BI WORKSPACES and drag the PARTY PANTS SUMMARY Web Intelligence document from the Module Library to the BI Workplace canvas, as shown in Figure 16.25.

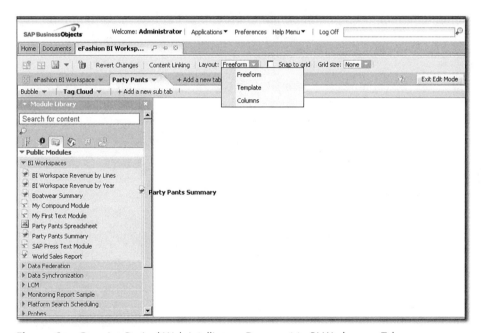

Figure 16.25 Dragging Desired Web Intelligence Document to BI Workspaces Tab

By default, the entire Web Intelligence document is placed on the subtab. However, we prefer to select a single report part (a tag cloud chart), which is located on a Web Intelligence report tab named TAG CLOUD. Right-click on the desired chart and choose SELECT THIS REPORT PART from the menu, as shown in Figure 16.26.

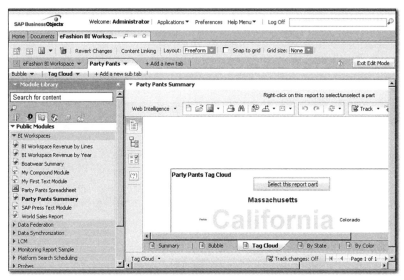

Figure 16.26 Right-Clicking on Desired Report Part

The report part is now part of the BI WORKSPACES subtab. Notice that, by default, the subtab is labeled with the name of the Web Intelligence document, PARTY PANTS SUMMARY, as shown in Figure 16.27. To modify this label and other properties, click on the EDIT (wrench) icon in the top right corner of the subtab.

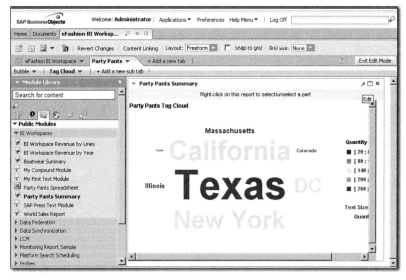

Figure 16.27 Editing the Report Part

When you edit the report part, you'll find that module properties are located on two tabs: CONTENT and LAYOUT (see Figure 16.28). On the CONTENT tab, notice that the DISPLAY MODE is set to SELECTED REPORT PART. Notice that the report content can be loaded on demand, from the latest instance (selected), or from the latest instance of a specific user. This functionality allows the BI workspace designer to take advantage of Web Intelligence documents that were previously scheduled— a useful feature particularly for long-running Web Intelligence documents.

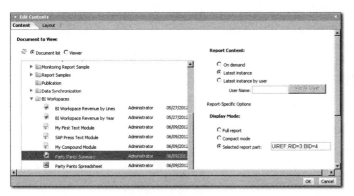

Figure 16.28 Review Properties on Content Tab

On the LAYOUT tab, you can change the default title (the name of the Web Intelligence document). In the example shown in Figure 16.29, we have changed the title to "My Tag Cloud."

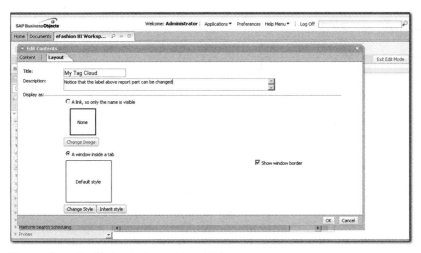

Figure 16.29 Modify Properties on Layout Tab

Once all modifications are complete, click on EXIT EDIT MODE in the top right corner of the BI WORKSPACES subtab, as shown in Figure 16.30.

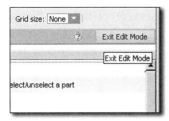

Figure 16.30 Exit Edit Mode

To finish, click on the SAVE icon on the BI Workspaces toolbar to update the BI workspace with all modifications, as shown in Figure 16.31.

Figure 16.31 Saving Changes on BI Workspaces Toolbar

You'll receive a message indicating that the BI workspace was saved, such as the one shown in Figure 16.32.

Figure 16.32 Saved BI Workspace

16.4 Using a BI Workspace as Default Home Tab

If desired, you can replace your default home tab with a custom BI Workspaces tab. To begin, open the BI Launch Pad preferences. The GENERAL tab is active by default. Uncheck the box labeled USE DEFAULT SETTINGS (ADMINISTRATOR DEFINED) and choose SELECT HOME TAB from the HOME TAB menu. Next click on the BROWSE HOME TAB button, as shown in Figure 16.33.

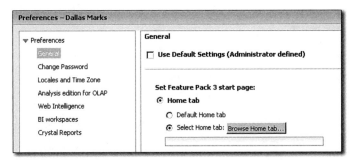

Figure 16.33 Setting Custom Home Tab in BI Launch Pad General Preferences

Next, browse to the folder containing the desired BI workspace. For our example, we've selected the eFashion BI Workspace from the public folder BI Workspace, as shown in Figure 16.34.

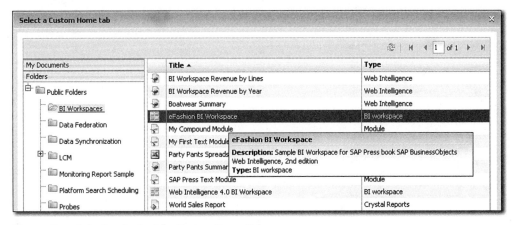

Figure 16.34 Selecting Content for Custom Home Tab

Notice that the selected BI workspace appears in the general preferences screen, as shown in Figure 16.35. Save and close the BI Launch Pad preferences.

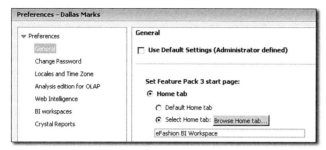

Figure 16.35 Workspace Selected as Custom Home Tab

The user will see the customized HOME tab the next time he logs on to the BI
Launch Pad, as shown in Figure 16.36.

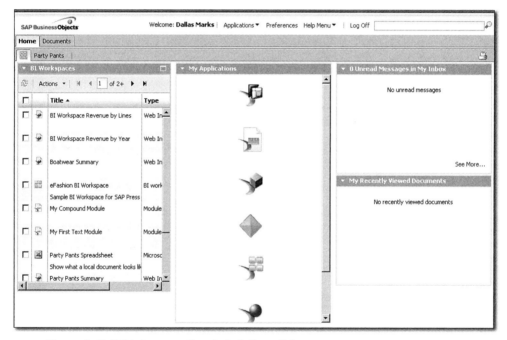

Figure 16.36 BI Workspace as New Default Home Tab

16.5 Summary

The BI Workspaces application provides you with a powerful way to mash up
multiple types of content into a cohesive user experience within the BI Launch

Pad. Although this book focuses on Web Intelligence, BI workspaces can additionally contain Crystal Reports, Analysis for OLAP workspaces, Dashboards, and content such as web pages from outside the BI platform.

You can use a custom BI workspace in place of the default HOME tab, and it is immediately visible once users log on to the BI Launch Pad.

Many features and functionalities are available for navigation within the BI Launch Pad, making it a powerful tool for end user report consumption. Report consumers utilize this interface to implement powerful reporting capabilities including hyperlinks, tracking data changes, sorting, filtering, discussions, and alerts.

17 Interaction from a User's Perspective

The casual user navigates within the BI Launch Pad to consume Web Intelligence documents and other content. These users usually do not develop their own documents; instead, they refresh canned reports already created and contained within the BI platform. Report consumers can create shortcuts and hyperlinks, track data changes within reports, complete powerful searches, sort and filter content, leverage discussions regarding reports, and manage alerts. In this chapter, we will explore these functions.

17.1 Creating Shortcuts and Hyperlinks

One method of organizing content within the BI Launch Pad is to create a hyperlink or a shortcut to another location or document. This enables quick collaboration and ease of updating without having to update numerous copies of the same report.

17.1.1 Shortcuts

Creating a shortcut can help organize documents that are viewed by different security profiles without having to maintain numerous copies of the same report.

To create one, you can select the report and then select COPY SHORTCUT from the Organize menu on the BI Launch Pad toolbar, as shown in Figure 17.1. You can then navigate to the folder location to paste the shortcut. Another option is to select CREATE SHORTCUT IN MY FAVORITES from the Organize menu when you have a document selected. This will automatically create a shortcut to the selected document in your My Favorites folder. Both of these options are also available from the right-click menu when the report name in the workspace is selected.

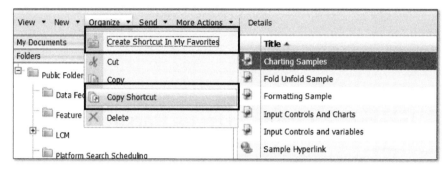

Figure 17.1 Shortcut Options from Organize Menu

17.1.2 Hyperlinks

Hyperlinks can be helpful in sharing online help resources or internal help resources for quick reference. You can create hyperlinks within the BI Launch Pad to reference other important web pages or information resources. To create a hyperlink, select the NEW button on the BI Launch Pad toolbar and choose the HYPERLINK option from the dropdown menu, as shown in Figure 17.2.

Figure 17.2 Hyperlink from New Menu on BI Launch Pad Toolbar

A box will appear to enter the properties, URL address, and categories for the hyperlink, as shown in Figure 17.3. The hyperlink will appear as an object in the designated folder, categories, or both.

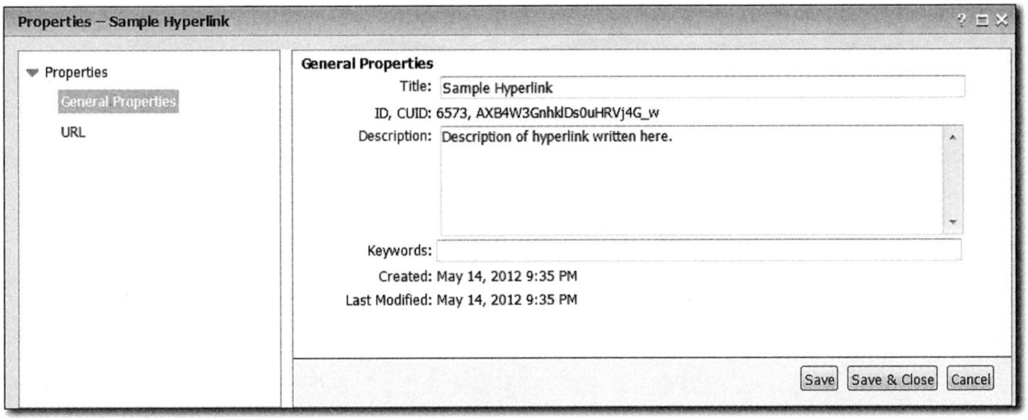

Figure 17.3 Hyperlink Properties

Shortcuts and hyperlinks provide enhanced functionality for organizing content within the BI Launch Pad. Additional features are available within this environment to enable more robust data analysis for the report customer.

17.2 Tracking Data Changes

The ability to track data changes is an exciting feature in Web Intelligence. This functionality enables you to easily pinpoint changes to data to make informed decisions in a timely manner. Reference data is chosen during setup and used to make the changes; these are highlighted in your reports based on your selections. You can also use formulas and functions within Web Intelligence and build custom alerts to highlight changed data.

The following data changes can be tracked within a Web Intelligence report, as shown in Figure 17.4:

▸ Added data
▸ Removed data
▸ Modified data
▸ Increased data
▸ Decreased data

	Q1	Q2	Q3	Q4	Sum
Increased					
Decreased					
Changed					
Inserted					
~~Removed~~		Product Line Sales for 2006			
Sweat-T-Shirts	1,967,328.20	2,121,860.20	1,506,478.90	1,863,826.20	7,459,493.50
Accessories	357,834.80	526,371.10	645,054.70	370,144.10	1,899,404.70
Sweaters	337,200.70	426,442.70	525,878.30	370,518.60	1,660,040.30
Shirt Waist	495,577.90	377,973.70	391,807.80	388,999.10	1,654,358.50
Dresses	295,717.80	355,629.50	564,570.30	192,677.30	1,408,594.90
Jackets	109,943.30	51,513.60	70,667.70	72,555.80	304,680.40
Trousers	60,114.60	87,518.50	71,101.20	53,702.00	272,436.30
City Skirts	19,634.30	55,353.90	103,390.20	17,906.60	196,285.00
Overcoats	40,269.40	518.20	22,308.70	7,915.60	71,011.90

Figure 17.4 Sample Report with Data Tracking

The setup of the reference data and display of the changes is completed from within Web Intelligence.

17.2.1 Setting Reference Data

When you enable tracking of data changes, you select a particular data refresh as your reference point. This data is known as your reference data. If you make changes to your data provider, the reference data is lost; consequently, data tracking will not be available. These actions will cause changes that will render the current version of the document incompatible with the reference data, making data tracking misleading.

> **Note**
>
> An asterisk will appear on the report tab when changed data tracking is activated on the report.

The following actions are incompatible with data tracking:

- Drill out of scope
- Query drill
- Deleting a query

▶ Any changes to the SQL generated by the data provider

▶ Modifications to security rights that will affect the SQL generated

▶ Purging the document data

▶ Refresh on Open (prior data is purged when document is refreshed on open)

Reference data is set from within Web Intelligence. To set reference data, select the DATA TRACKING tab from the Analysis menu on the Web Intelligence document. There are two options available for the selection of reference data, as shown in Table 17.1.

Compare with Last Data Refresh	The data existing before the REFRESH DATA button is selected becomes the reference data and the new data after the refresh is tracked against this prior refresh.
Compare with Data Refresh from [Select Date]	The data selected becomes the reference data and remains the reference data after each refresh regardless of the number of times the data is refreshed. The newly refreshed data is tracked against the fixed reference data.

Table 17.1 Data Tracking Options

Select the TRACK button on the BI Launch Pad Viewer toolbar to activate data tracking from within the BI Launch Pad. From within Web Intelligence, select the TRACK button on the DATA TRACKING tab of the Analysis ribbon from within design mode. This will display the Data Tracking dialog box. This box will display the options to either compare with last data refresh or compare with a specific refresh date instance.

17.2.2 Formatting Changed Data

The default setting for the formatting of changed data is defined by the Business-Objects administrator in the Central Management Console. You have the ability to overwrite these defaults by setting your formatting within the Data Tracking Options dialog box, as shown in Figure 17.5. Select the FORMAT tab to specify your formatting dependent on the type of changed data.

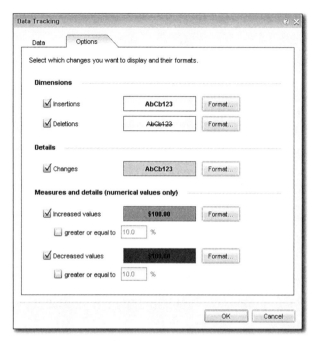

Figure 17.5 Data Tracking Options Dialog Box

The following changes are available for configuration of formatting:

▸ Inserted dimension and detail values

▸ Deleted dimension and detail values

▸ Changed dimension and detail values

▸ Increased measure values

▸ Decreased measure values

Changed data is displayed differently in blocks, sections, breaks, charts, and reports with merged dimensions.

Displayed Data in Blocks

If data is removed from a row in a block, deleted data formatting is applied to all cells as defined in the Data Tracking properties. If a measure increases for a row, increased data formatting is applied to the Measure cell. If a measure has decreased, decreased data formatting will be applied to the Measure cell. New data appearing in a block will show inserted data formatting on all cells. The following example details how these formatting changes will appear given a block of sample data.

Let's look at an example. The sample reference data in Table 17.2 shows sales revenue by year and by state.

Year	State	Sales Revenue
2008	Arizona	$1,100,000
2009	Arizona	$1,200,000
2007	California	$1,100,000
2007	New York	$1,150,000

Table 17.2 Example Reference Data

The changed data in the Table 17.3 shows the comparison data used for the data tracking.

Year	State	Sales Revenue
2009	Arizona	$1,300,000
2008	California	$1,900,000
2007	New York	$1,000,000
2009	Washington	$1,700,000

Table 17.3 Example Changed Data

When data tracking is enabled, the reference and changed data are compared and formatting is applied to the resulting data block as per the options selected in the data tracking dialog box (see Table 17.4).

Year	State	Sales Revenue	Formatting
2008	Arizona	$1,100,000	[deleted data formatting on all cells]
2009	Arizona	$1,300,000	[increased data formatting on the Revenue cell]
2007	California	$1,300,000	[deleted data formatting on all cells]

Table 17.4 Example with Data Tracking Activated and Results Displayed

Year	State	Sales Revenue	Formatting
2008	California	$1,900,000	[inserted data formatting on all cells]
2007	New York	$1,150,000	[decreased data formatting on Revenue cell]
2009	Washington	$1,700,000	[inserted data formatting on all cells]

Table 17.4 Example with Data Tracking Activated and Results Displayed (Cont.)

Displayed Data in Sections

The data in the section header can be displayed two possible ways, depending on whether the entire section data changed or just some of the rows within in the section:

▶ If all rows in the section have changed in the same way, the section header format will be the same as all the rows.

▶ If only some rows in a section have changed or the rows have changed in different ways, the section header will stay in its default format.

Displayed Data in Breaks

If the CENTER VALUE ACROSS BREAK option is applied to the break in the properties, the same formatting rules apply as with sections.

▶ If all rows in the break for the centered value have changed in the same way, the centered break value format will be the same as all the rows.

▶ If only some rows in a centered break section have changed or the rows have changed in different ways, the centered break value will stay in its default format.

Displayed Data in Charts

Tracked data is not displayed within a chart. When data tracking is applied to a chart, an icon will appear above the chart. Select the icon to display the tracked data changes. The chart will be converted to a table to allow you to see the details of the tracked data changes.

Displayed Data in Reports with Merged Dimensions

When using merged dimensions, Web Intelligence does not show that a new data element was added to a block unless the data element has been added to all dimensions participating in the merge.

17.2.3 Displaying Tracked Data

Select the HIDE CHANGES/SHOW CHANGES button to the right of the TRACK button on the toolbar in report mode or the BI Launch Pad Viewer toolbar to display tracked data.

17.2.4 Advanced Tracking Techniques

Several formulas are available for use within Web Intelligence in order to perform advanced techniques with the data tracking functionality. Two are shown in Table 17.5.

RefValue	RefValue returns the value of the reference data.
RefValueDate	RefValueDate returns the date of the reference data.

Table 17.5 Web Intelligence Functions for Data Tracking

These functions can be used in a formula to find the difference between changed data and reference data. For example:

```
=[Sales Revenue] - RefValue([Sales Revenue])
```

If the current refresh returned sales revenue equal to $2.5 million and the reference data showed sales revenue equal to $1.5 million, then this difference formula would return a result of $1 million.

17.3 Searching within the BI Launch Pad

Web Intelligence documents, Crystal reports, Microsoft Excel, Microsoft Word, RTF, PDF, PowerPoint, and text files are all searchable if they are contained within the BI Launch Pad environment. The metadata of additional object types are also searchable. The files that you can search will depend on your access rights. The data regarded by a search is different for each document type.

Searches are performed within the BI Launch Pad from the Documents tab in the search drawer, as shown in Figure 17.6. You can type the words to locate in the search box. If you pause while typing in the search box, the quick search functionality is prompted and the top six matches are displayed.

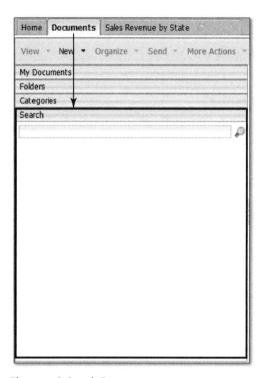

Figure 17.6 Search Drawer

When you finish typing your search criteria, select the Search icon. The search results are shown in the list panel and additional facets appear in the Search drawer as shown in Figure 17.7. To view a result, double-click on the object link in the list panel or click on a facet in the Search drawer and double-click on the generated object link. When the document opens, the viewer will scroll to the location of the first match to your search criteria.

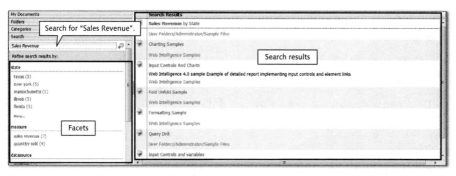

Figure 17.7 Search Drawer Results Sample

17.3.1 Search Facets

Facets are different attributes about your documents that help to provide further filtering of your search content. These appear in the Search drawer as seen in Figure 17.7. The following facets may appear:

▶ Location
▶ Type
▶ Refresh time
▶ Author
▶ Data source

17.3.2 Searchable Object Types

A large number of object types are available for search within the BI Launch Pad. There are also a number of attributes that are searched within your commonly consumed document types, which enable thorough search capabilities:

▶ Web Intelligence documents
  ▶ Report title
  ▶ Report description (as defined in report properties)
  ▶ Universe filter names
  ▶ Universe object names
  ▶ Data contained in the report as saved data
  ▶ Constants in filter conditions that are defined in a document
  ▶ Static text contained within the report

- Crystal Reports
  - Report title
  - Report description (as defined in report properties)
  - Selection formulas
  - Data contained in the report as saved data
  - Text fields
  - Parameter values
  - Subreports
- Microsoft Excel and Word documents
  - Data
  - Document properties
  - Header and footer text
  - Numerical values
  - Calculation or formula values (Excel only)
  - Date/time values (Excel only)

These attributes are not available for document search.

- Text fields only
  - Rich Text Format (RTF)
  - Portable Document Format (PDF)
  - Microsoft PowerPoint
  - Text files (TXT)
- Metadata only
  - Agnostic objects
  - Analysis Views
  - BI workspaces
  - Dashboards and Xcelsius objects
  - Discussions
  - Events
  - Adobe Flash objects
  - Hyperlinks

- Lifecycle management console jobs

- Metadata from Information Designer

- Modules

- Object packages

- Profiles

- Program objects

- Publications

- Queries from QAAWS

- Universes

- Widgets

- Workspaces created in SAP BusinessObjects Analysis, OLAP edition

17.3.3   Search Techniques

Certain techniques are recommended when you search content within the BI Launch Pad. For example, separate search terms using spaces, which implies the AND separator. Table 17.6 defines key techniques.

Technique	Description
Space	Space between words implies the AND separator (Ex: sales revenue)
Asterisk *	Asterisk returns results with any number of characters in its place (Ex: 19*)
Question mark ?	Question mark represents a single character (Ex: Sm?th)
Quotations " "	Quotations are used to indicate an exact phrase that should be found in the documents returned by the results.
Plus sign +	Plus sign forces the inclusion of a search term (Ex: sales + revenue)
Minus sign -	Minus sign removes results that have the indicated term (Ex: sales – revenue)
OR	OR returns results when the word before or after the word OR are found in the document (Ex: income OR profit statement)

Table 17.6 Search Techniques

You can perform attribute searches by typing the name of the attribute with a colon and then the term to be searched. You may also combine search techniques from the table above for more specific results.

17.4   Sorting and Filtering Content

Objects within BI Launch Pad are sorted alphabetically by the title. Of course, your access to the content depends on whether you have the appropriate access rights to view in each folder or category. It may be useful to customize these views to sort by different criteria or filter for your desired results.

Selecting the column heading resorts the list by that heading in ascending order. Selecting the heading again sorts the list in descending order. When you hover over a column heading, you will notice that a FILTER icon (a yellow funnel) appears, as shown in Figure 17.8.

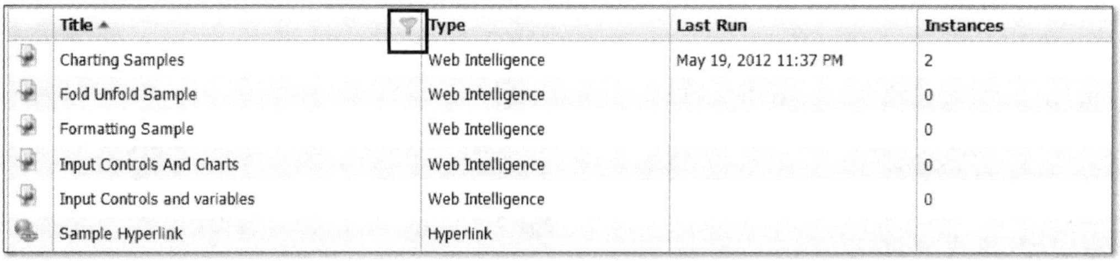

Title ▲	Type	Last Run	Instances
Charting Samples	Web Intelligence	May 19, 2012 11:37 PM	2
Fold Unfold Sample	Web Intelligence		0
Formatting Sample	Web Intelligence		0
Input Controls And Charts	Web Intelligence		0
Input Controls and variables	Web Intelligence		0
Sample Hyperlink	Hyperlink		

Figure 17.8 Filter Icon on Column Heading

Click on the icon to filter the content in the list. After applying the filter, the filtered results will only display in the list view as shown in Figure 17.9.

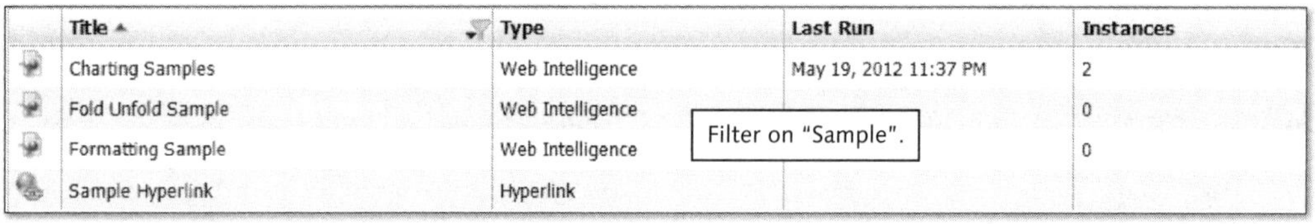

Title ▲	Type	Last Run	Instances
Charting Samples	Web Intelligence	May 19, 2012 11:37 PM	2
Fold Unfold Sample	Web Intelligence		0
Formatting Sample	Web Intelligence	Filter on "Sample".	0
Sample Hyperlink	Hyperlink		

Figure 17.9 Filters Results in List View

To remove the filter, select the title bar again and select the CLEAR FILTER checkbox.

17.5   Creating Discussions

Users can create *discussions* for BI platform documents in order to post document-relevant information. These discussions can be organized in threads or as notes in a document. Figure 17.10 shows a sample discussion.

Figure 17.10 Sample Discussion

Discussions must first be enabled by your SAP BusinessObjects administrator in order for them to be created against your Web Intelligence documents in the BI Launch Pad. If you are integrated with SAP StreamWork, you can post comments and participate in online discussions with other StreamWork users from within BI Launch Pad.

Discussions are located in the Details panel of the selected document. Select the Discussions drawer at the bottom of the Details panel to view the notes and discussion threads.

17.5.1 Notes

To add a note, select the NEW MESSAGE icon, type the subject and message as relevant. You may also change the level of importance from low to high, which will create a flag indicator on the note, as shown in Figure 17.11.

You can edit notes you've created by selecting an already existing note and making any modifications to the previous text as necessary. If a note has replies in a discussion thread, then you may no longer modify it unless you have administrative rights. The same is true for deleting a note, which you would do by clicking on its DELETE icon.

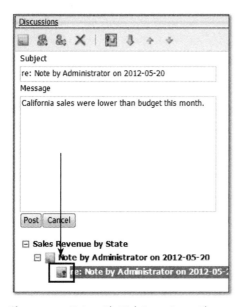

Figure 17.11 Note with High Importance Flag

17.5.2 Discussion Threads

You can create a *discussion thread* by replying to an existing note, as shown in Figure 17.12. After selecting a note, you have the option to select to reply to group or reply to sender. The REPLY TO GROUP option makes your response visible to everyone, while the REPLY TO SENDER displays your comments to only the sender of the note. After completing your comments and selecting POST, the note will display in the hierarchy of the conversation. The plus (+) sign indicates that there is a discussion thread associated with a note.

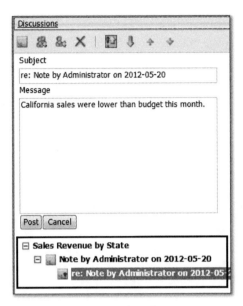

Figure 17.12 Discussion Thread

17.6 Summary

A variety of functionalities are available to the end user within the BI Launch Pad portal to customize the user experience. Creating hyperlinks, tracking data changes, searching within the environment, and managing discussions provide extra features to go above and beyond the capability of only reviewing a static report.

Chapter 18 discusses methods of sharing your Web Intelligence document with other users inside and outside the organization. From basic copy and paste functionality to robust scheduling, the BI Launch Pad offers a variety of options to answer the need for collaboration.

The core functionality of Web Intelligence involves querying, reporting, analyzing, and sharing information across the enterprise. The ability to share information quickly and easily is vital to successful business intelligence reporting. Web Intelligence 4.x provides enhanced sharing capabilities to schedule, publish, and burst your information to your internal and external audience.

18 Sharing a Web Intelligence Report

So far in this book you've learned how to create a Web Intelligence report, use advanced query techniques and multiple data providers, create unique charts, and format your report to create the most meaningful output for your audience. Now that your report design is complete, it is time to share your results with others.

Web Intelligence provides a variety of ways to distribute and share your reports across the organization, including many new features to enhance the publishing capabilities. From the enhanced ability to copy and paste data between Web Intelligence reports to the ability to create publications and burst them out for end user consumption, you have a wide variety of options for sharing reports from within Web Intelligence or the BI Launch Pad. We will review each of these methods in this chapter to give you a thorough understanding of each of the options available to you.

18.1 Copying and Pasting

The most basic way to share a Web Intelligence report is a method used often in numerous tools: *copy and paste*. This powerful tool for sharing reports enables the end user to bring report parts into other applications and between Web Intelligence documents.

18.1.1 Copying and Pasting Between Applications

Report parts can be pasted into spreadsheets, presentations, and word processing documents to integrate with additional business content.

From within the *Report Panel* on a Web Intelligence document, right-click on the report part that should be copied to display the menu options, as shown in Figure 18.1. Select to either Cut or Copy your content.

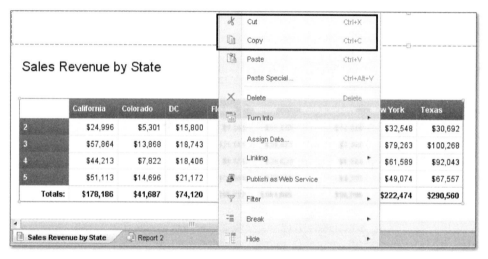

Figure 18.1 Copy Options in Web Intelligence

Copying will copy the data contained within the report block in the format as it appears on your screen. When pasting into your destination application, you can select to paste with or without formatting. This feature is useful when copying the report part into a Word document or within a PowerPoint presentation so it will maintain its formatting.

Pasting as text will convert all elements to a text format. Paste is helpful to copy the data itself into the columns in the spreadsheet without the formatting to perform further manipulation of the data within Excel. Figure 18.2 displays the copy options in Microsoft Excel.

Paste without formatting

⊿	A	B	C	D	E	F	G	H	I
1									
2		California	Colorado	DC	Florida	Illinois	Massachu	New York	Texas
3	2	$24,996	$5,301	$15,800	$6,040	$11,438	$13,296	$32,548	$30,692
4	3	$57,864	$13,868	$18,743	$21,166	$38,487	$7,398	$79,263	$100,268
5	4	$44,213	$7,822	$18,406	$8,576	$28,620	$8,849	$61,589	$92,043
6	5	$51,113	$14,696	$21,172	$19,949	$23,440	$9,255	$49,074	$67,557
7	Totals:	$178,186	$41,687	$74,120	$55,732	$101,985	$38,798	$222,474	$290,560
8									
9									
10									
11		California	Colorado	DC	Florida	Illinois	Massachusetts	New York	Texas
12	2	$24,996	$5,301	$15,800	$6,040	$11,438	$13,296	$32,548	$30,692
13	3	$57,864	$13,868	$18,743	$21,166	$38,487	$7,398	$79,263	$100,268
14	4	$44,213	$7,822	$18,406	$8,576	$28,620	$8,849	$61,589	$92,043
15	5	$51,113	$14,696	$21,172	$19,949	$23,440	$9,255	$49,074	$67,557
16	**Totals:**	**$178,186**	**$41,687**	**$74,120**	**$55,732**	**$101,985**	**$38,798**	**$222,474**	**$290,560**
17									
18									
19									
20									

Paste with formatting

Sheet1 / Sheet2 / Sheet3

Figure 18.2 Copy Options in Microsoft Excel

18.1.2 Copying and Pasting Between Web Intelligence Documents

New capabilities in Web Intelligence allow you to copy and paste report parts between Web Intelligence documents. Select the report content that you would like to copy into a new or existing report, and then select COPY from the right-click menu. Figure 18.3 shows the initial chart before it is copied into a new document using the NO DATA SOURCE option.

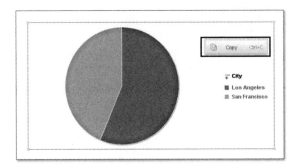

Figure 18.3 Copy on Right-Click Menu

After creating your new Web Intelligence document or navigating to an existing document, select PASTE from the right-click menu on your report canvas to paste your copied content, as shown in Figure 18.4.

Figure 18.4 Paste on Right-Click Menu

Figure 18.5 shows the copied results, including the objects available in the data pane when pasting the initial chart from Figure 18.3. In this example, additional data is shown since drill was enabled on the original report.

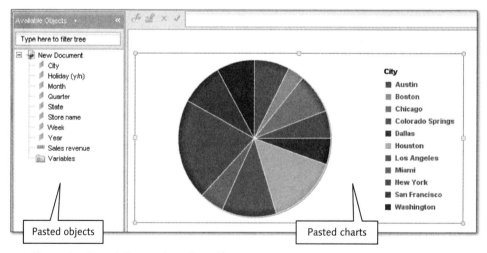

Figure 18.5 Pasted Chart and Resulting Objects

The query used in the report block is also brought over with the content, as seen in Figure 18.6. This is a powerful tool for leveraging current content among different reports and expediting report creation.

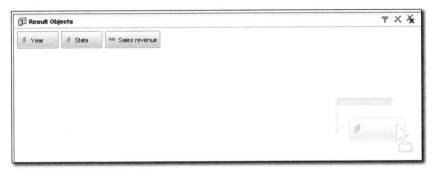

Figure 18.6 Query Results Copied between Web Intelligence Documents

The copy and paste functionality available in Web Intelligence 4.x provides a wealth of time savings for the report designer.

18.2   Using the Send Feature in the BI Launch Pad

You can easily share reports from within the BI Launch Pad portal provided that you have been given the rights by the SAP BusinessObjects administrator. Another option available in the BI Launch Pad is the ability to send Web Intelligence reports.

> **Note**
>
> Chapter 16 discusses how to view a Web Intelligence report in the BI Launch Pad; refer to it for a review of this and other features within the BI Launch Pad.

In order to activate the SEND option on the BI Launch Pad toolbar, you must first select the report to be sent so that it is highlighted in the Workspace panel. The SEND button will become active.

Select the SEND button to display the dropdown list options shown for sending a document: BI INBOX, EMAIL, FTP LOCATION, FILE LOCATION, or SAP STREAMWORK. The options available will depend on your configuration, so we'll examine them further.

18.2.1 BI Platform Inbox

You can send a Web Intelligence document to another BI platform user's inbox. The report will be displayed in his My Documents drawer in the inbox, as shown in Figure 18.7. The new report will be listed in the Unread Messages in My Inbox panel on the Home tab.

Figure 18.7 BI Inbox

Upon selecting the option to send a report to a BI inbox, a dialog box appears to indicate the Send options, as shown in Figure 18.8. When marking the Use default settings checkbox at the top of the dialog box, the user will not be able to complete any custom settings. The default settings for distribution will be used as defined by the SAP BusinessObjects administrator. To select personalized settings for the report destination, proceed to the settings below.

Figure 18.8 shows the selection of users and *Send To* inbox settings.

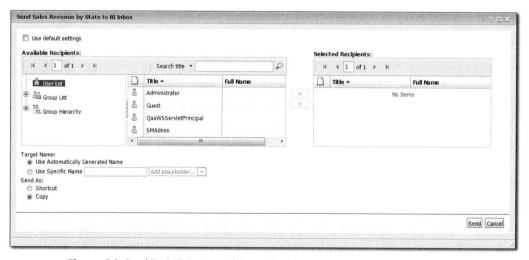

Figure 18.8 Send To SAP BusinessObjects Inbox Settings

You will be prompted to select the destination SAP BusinessObjects Inbox from the User List or from the Group List. Selecting from the Group List will enable you to select all members of a group to receive the same report in his BI inbox. A search box is also available to aid in finding the appropriate name from the user or group list. Select the arrows to move the names into the Selected Recipients box.

The next option is to designate a target name by selecting one of the options.

▶ Use Automatically Generated Name: This will use the current name of the document selected as the name of the report as it appears in the recipient's inbox.

▶ Use Specific Name: This will enable you to generate a unique name to use for the report name as it will appear in the inbox. There is also a dropdown list to add placeholder values, which are shown in Table 18.1.

Title	Inserts the title as it exists when the report is sent
ID	Inserts the unique identifier number for the report as it exists in the system at the time the report is sent
Owner	Inserts the name of the owner of the document as it appears in the properties
Date andTime	Inserts the current date and time when the report is sent
Email Address	Inserts the email address the report is being sent to
User Full Name	Inserts the user's full name
Document Name	Inserts the document name as it exists when the document is sent
File Extension	Inserts the file extension of the document type

Table 18.1 Placeholder Values

Note
Use caution when sending a shortcut. If the recipient does not have the right to view reports in the folder where the original report resides, he will be unable to view the report.

An example would be if you sent a report to another user that resides in your My Documents drawer (i.e., Favorites or Inbox). Unless he had administrative level access to this location (unlikely), the recipient would not have the right to view these reports. |

The final option enables you to select whether the recipient will receive a shortcut or copy of the report. Once these options have been marked, select SUBMIT to send your document to the recipient's BI inbox.

18.2.2 Email

A Web Intelligence report can be sent to an email address for the user to view outside of the BI Launch Pad. If Web Intelligence format is sent by email, the user must have a BI platform user account to view the Web Intelligence report because he will need to enter his credentials to log on to the BI platform.

There is an additional placeholder in the list for the message body from those mentioned in Section 18.2.1. The placeholder of the viewer hyperlink allows you to insert a hyperlink into the report within the BI Launch Pad environment. The user would select the hyperlink and log on to the BI platform environment to view the report. Figure 18.9 provides a view of the *Send To* email options.

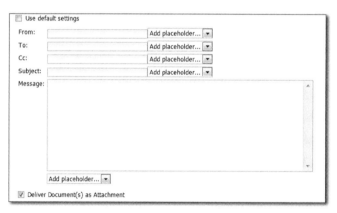

Figure 18.9 Send to Email Options

18.2.3 FTP Location

Send to FTP location enables the user to send a Web Intelligence document to a File Transfer Protocol location. An FTP location is a standard network protocol location used to exchange files over a network.

Specific information regarding the FTP location must be specified in the options box, including host, port, user name, password, account, and directory. This information is specific to the FTP location the document is being sent to.

Once the FTP specific properties are set, the file name properties are specified, including whether the report is automatically generated or uses a specific name with placeholder options. Figure 18.10 shows the options for sending documents to FTP locations.

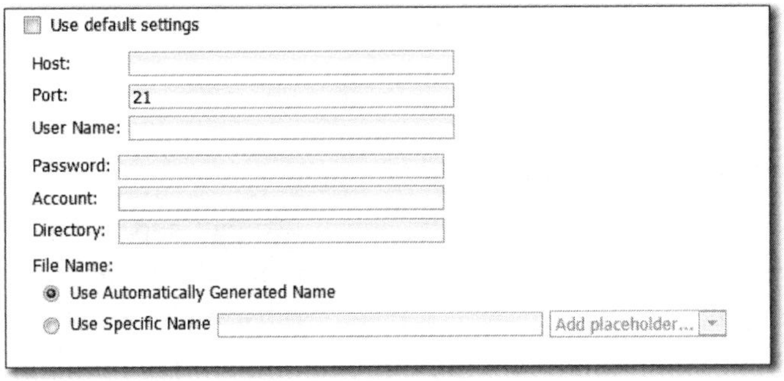

Figure 18.10 Send to FTP Location Options

18.2.4 File Location

The final possible location to send a report is a *file location*. Sometimes the best option may be to send PDF or Excel versions of Web Intelligence documents to a location on a share drive that can be viewed by numerous users for collaborative purposes and ease of access.

When specifying a file location, the directory path must be specified as well as a user name and password for that directory if applicable. Then the file name property can be set to use an automatically generated name or a specific name with placeholder options. Figure 18.11 shows the file location options when scheduling a report.

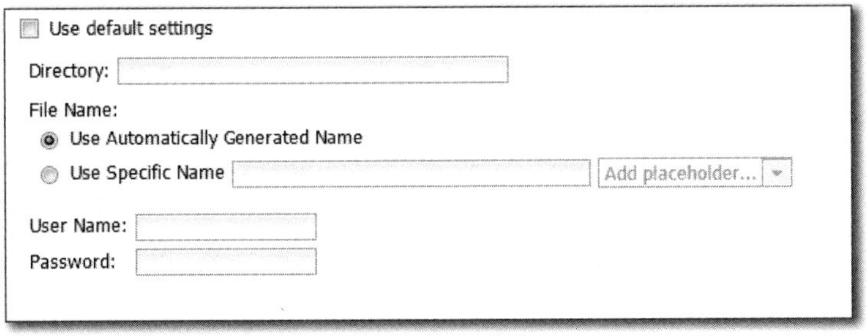

Figure 18.11 File Location Options

18.3 Exporting a Web Intelligence Report

Business users are often required to analyze company data in Excel for even more detailed analysis or to distribute reports in PDF format. Web Intelligence provides report consumers with the capability to export report data retrieved from the universe and database into one of the following file formats: Microsoft Excel, PDF, or CSV.

18.3.1 Export Options in the BI Launch Pad

The export options available to you within the BI Launch Pad will depend upon your user settings created by the SAP BusinessObjects administrator. There are dropdown menu options on the BI Launch Pad Viewer toolbar when viewing a Web Intelligence report in the BI Launch Pad. The Save As menu, as shown in Figure 18.12, includes the export options of Microsoft Excel, Microsoft Excel 2007, and PDF in the file type dropdown list shown in Figure 18.13.

Figure 18.12 Export Options on the BI Launch Pad Viewer Toolbar

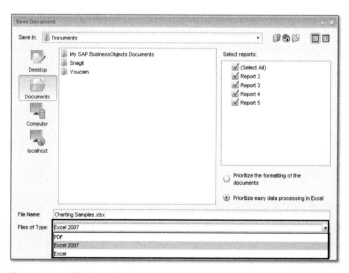

Figure 18.13 File Type Options

Microsoft Excel

Saving in Microsoft Excel format will convert the Web Intelligence report into Excel format and allow you to open or save the report. The data in the tables of the Web Intelligence document will drop into the columns and rows of the Excel spreadsheet, as you saw with the paste without formatting option. Further manipulation of the data will be available in this format.

Microsoft Excel 2007

The Excel 2007 option allows the user to save the document into the .XLSX format—effectively enabling up to one million rows of data to export into the spreadsheet. The previously mentioned Excel option saves the report into .XLS format, which limits the resulting rows to 65,000.

PDF

Selecting to save in Adobe Acrobat PDF format will convert the Web Intelligence report into PDF format and allow you to open or save the report. The report will appear similar to a picture, so further manipulation of the data will not be available. This is a preferable format when you would like to maintain the report formatting and ensure the data cannot be manually changed in the future.

CSV

The CSV export option saves the Web Intelligence report in Comma Separated Value format. This enables you to import the report into a number of different programs outside of Excel. The CSV format gives you additional options for customizing the format of your comma separated value output file, letting you designate the specific format to make the CSV file compatible with the end program where you may be importing your data.

18.3.2 Export Options in Web Intelligence

The same options for export are also available within Web Intelligence. From the Report Panel, select the arrow next to the disk icon on the report toolbar. Upon selecting the SAVE TO MY COMPUTER AS option, a menu will display the options of Excel, Excel 2007, PDF, or CSV as your file output format for export, as shown in Figure 18.14.

Figure 18.14 Save As in Web Intelligence Report Panel Toolbar

18.4   Scheduling a Web Intelligence Report

The processes discussed so far have included manually generated methods of sharing Web Intelligence reports. A document can also be scheduled to be distributed out to recipients in a variety of formats and methods. This scheduling ability is available within the BI Launch Pad, from which you can schedule a report, view the latest instance of a scheduled report, and view the scheduling history of the report.

18.4.1   Scheduling in the BI Launch Pad

After selecting the report to be scheduled in the Workspace panel, navigate to the More Actions menu on the BI Launch Pad toolbar, as shown in Figure 18.15. Select the SCHEDULE option to set the scheduling properties.

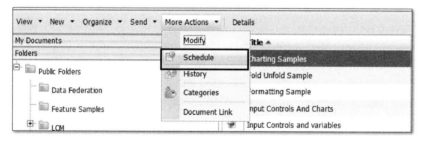

Figure 18.15 Select Schedule from the Actions Menu on the BI Launch Pad Toolbar

You will be prompted to complete the following items:

▶ INSTANCE TITLE
Type in title for this instance of the report or use the default title already entered.

▶ RECURRENCE

Numerous options are available in the dropdown menu for selection dependent upon your report distribution requirements.

  ▶ Now: The Now option runs your report schedule immediately upon completion of your scheduling properties and selecting the SUBMIT button.

  ▶ ONCE: The ONCE option runs your report schedule once during the time frame specified in the recurrence properties box, as shown in Figure 18.16.

Figure 18.16 Once View

  ▶ HOURLY: The HOURLY option shown in Figure 18.17 runs the report at the hourly increments specified in the hours and minutes boxes in the recurrence properties. The start and end date/time are also specified.

Figure 18.17 Hourly View

  ▶ DAILY: The DAILY option shown in Figure 18.18 runs the report daily for *N* number of days as specified in the recurrence properties. The start and end date/time are also specified.

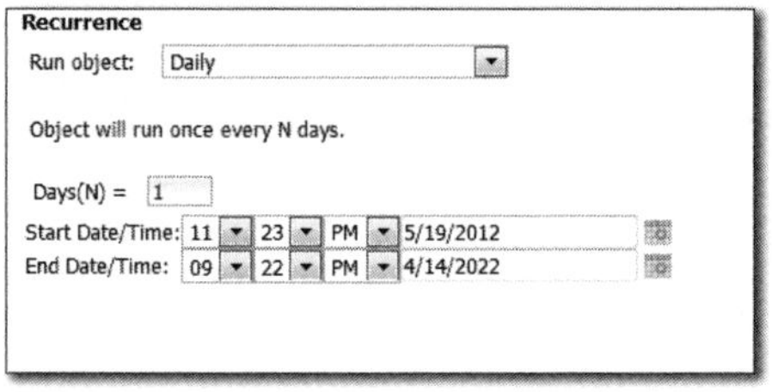

Figure 18.18 Daily View

433

► WEEKLY: The WEEKLY option shown in Figure 18.19 runs the report weekly on the day or days specified by the checkboxes. You also specify the start and end date/time for when the schedule will start and end.

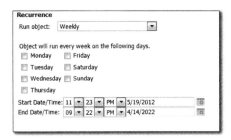

Figure 18.19 Weekly View

► MONTHLY: The MONTHLY option shown in Figure 18.20 will run the report monthly EVERY N MONTHS, as specified. A start and end date and time are also specified for this schedule.

Figure 18.20 Monthly View

► NTH OF MONTH: The NTH OF MONTH schedule shown in Figure 18.21 allows you to specify the exact day of the month to run the schedule. This can be especially useful for financial reports run for month-end reporting. A start and end date/time is also specified for the schedule.

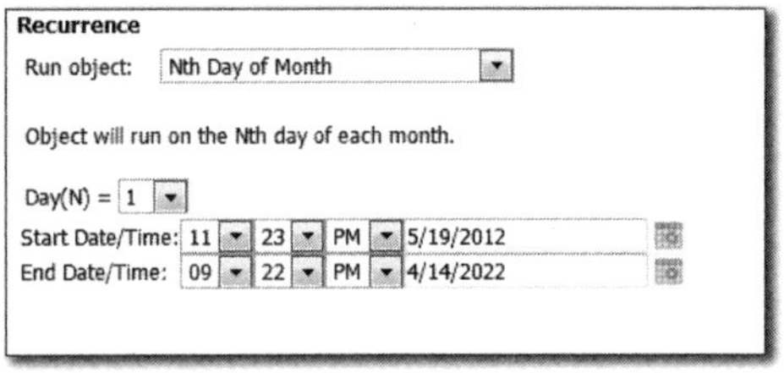

Figure 18.21 Nth of Month View

▶ 1ST MONDAY OF MONTH: This schedule allows you to run the report on the first Monday of every month. This can be useful for monthly reports to maintain consistency in the run date. You will also specify the schedule start and end date/time. This can be seen in Figure 18.22.

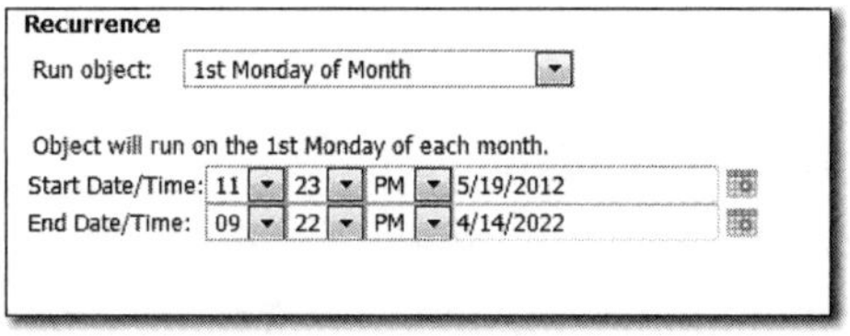

Figure 18.22 1st Monday of Month View

▶ LAST DAY OF MONTH: The LAST DAY OF THE MONTH option will run the report on the final day of each month. You will specify the schedule start and end date/time. Figure 18.23 shows the options available when selecting the LAST DAY OF MONTH recurrence option.

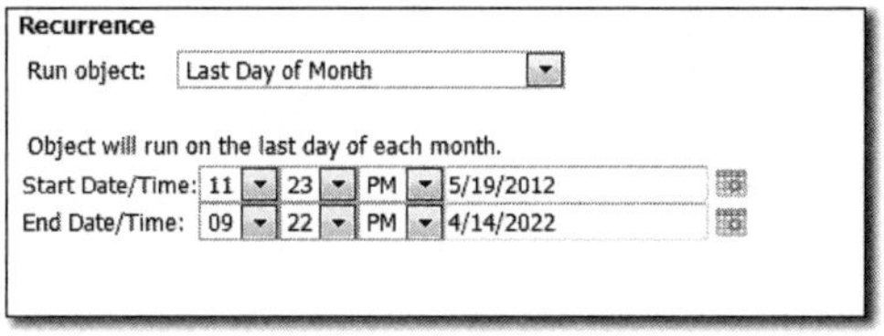

Figure 18.23 Last Day of Month View

▶ X DAY OF NTH WEEK OF THE MONTH: This schedule, as shown in Figure 18.24, enables you to specify the week and day of each month that the schedule should be run. For example, you can specify to run the report on the third Thursday of each month. In this case, you would specify week number 3 and the day of Thursday. You will also specify when the schedule should start and end by date/time.

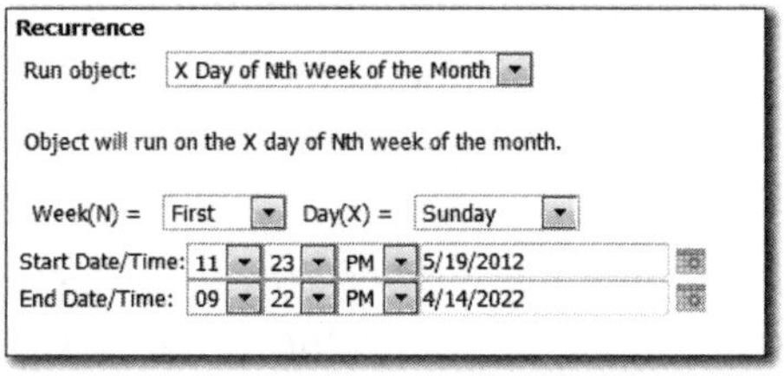

Figure 18.24 X Day of Nth Week of the Month View

▶ CALENDAR: Calendars need to be set up in the CMC by the SAP Business-Objects administrator in order for them to be seen here. If a customized calendar is set up, you can specify to use them here as seen in Figure 18.25. These enable you to have more specific options on dates to run the report.

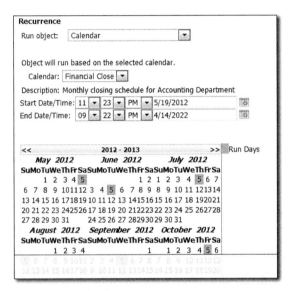

Figure 18.25 Calendar View

▶ FORMATS AND DESTINATIONS
Output formats include Web Intelligence, Microsoft Excel, and Adobe Acrobat. Available destinations include the BI inbox, file locations, FTP server, and email recipients.

Destination options and settings change depending on the output format details selected in the Output Format and Destination section. These settings are the same as discussed in Section 18.2.

When you check the box for CLEANUP INSTANCE AFTER SCHEDULING, the instance will be removed from the history after it has been sent out to the selected recipients. This removes unnecessary extra copies of the report to maximize disk space.

▶ CACHING
Select the formats to be used to preload the cache when scheduling (only applicable if scheduling in Web Intelligence format). Available formats to cache

include: Microsoft Excel, standard HTML, and Adobe Acrobat. Select the formatting locales to be used to preload the cache when scheduling. The available locales will show in left box. You must select the arrow to move to selected locales box in order to specify your selection.

▶ EVENTS

Events are set up by your SAP BusinessObjects administrator in the Central Management Console. Available events are listed in the box on the left. Select the arrows to move your selections to the EVENTS TO WAIT FOR box. You may also select the event in the AVAILABLE SCHEDULE EVENTS box to move to the EVENTS TO TRIGGER on completion. This will specify which events must occur in order for the job to be triggered. This can be useful to ensure a nightly data load job has completed loading the new data before the report is run.

▶ SCHEDULING SERVER GROUP

This option enables you to specify a specific server group to use when scheduling your document. The usual setting is to use the first available server. Note that if a specified server is busy, your job will likely fail. The SCHEDULING SERVER GROUP options are detailed in Figure 18.26.

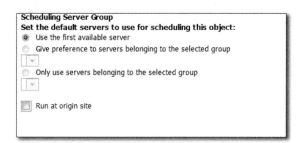

Figure 18.26 Scheduling Server Group Box

18.4.2 Viewing Latest Instance

After scheduling a report, you can view the latest instance of the report. After selecting the report name in the Workspace panel, select the More Actions menu on the BI Launch Pad toolbar to view the dropdown list options. Figure 18.27 displays the actions available when viewing a report.

If a report has been scheduled previously, then the VIEW LATEST INSTANCE option will appear in the menu. The latest instance shows you the last scheduled version of the report as distributed to your selected recipients.

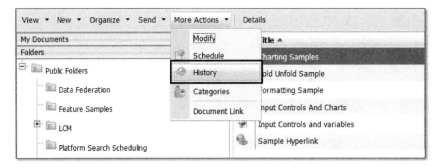

Figure 18.27 Action Menu Options

18.4.3 Viewing History

You are also able to see the history of all instances scheduled for a report by selecting HISTORY from the ACTIONS dropdown list. The history view will show a listing of all scheduled reports including the date/time of the instance, title, run by, parameters (if applicable), format, and status.

In Figure 18.28, the instance in the history view is showing a status of RUNNING. This indicates that the report schedule is currently running and not yet complete to view. Additional radio buttons and checkboxes at the top of the history view can aid you in filtering a longer list of instances to customize your view. These options include SHOW ALL, SHOW COMPLETED, SHOW ONLY INSTANCES OWNED BY ME, and FILTER INSTANCES BY TYPE.

Figure 18.28 History View

18.5   Summary

The collaboration features available in Web Intelligence 4.x make it a powerful business intelligence reporting tool. The manual sharing capabilities of copy and paste or sending to a user or group enable quick and easy collaboration. Scheduling enables the user to automate the process. The powerful new features available for creating and subscribing to publications has added a plethora of new possibilities for the Web Intelligence report designer and report consumer to share reports with ease across the organization.

Chapter 19 discusses another exciting feature available for sharing report content: publications. Publications provide a powerful tool for creating robust, customized distributions of documents contained within the BI platform.

SAP BusinessObjects Business Intelligence 4.0 can be harnessed to distribute personalized reports, known as publications, to subscribers, either inside or outside of your organization.

19 Report Scheduling and Distribution with Publications

The primary strength of SAP BusinessObjects Web Intelligence is that it allows business users to query and manipulate corporate data with minimal assistance from corporate IT. However, the SAP BusinessObjects Business Intelligence platform also includes powerful capabilities for automatically distributing data to business users utilizing a feature called *publications* and known more generically in the business intelligence industry as *report bursting*.

A *publication* is a collection of documents intended for distribution to a mass audience, often personalized to target this group specifically. You can define the publication metadata surrounding these documents, such as document sources, recipients, and personalization rules, from either the BI Launch Pad or the Central Management Console (CMC). Publication subscribers can view publications through the secure BI Launch Pad portal or via email.

Publications have been part of the BusinessObjects platform since an add-on product named Broadcast Agent Publisher was introduced on the classic (pre-XI) BusinessObjects platform. Beginning with SAP BusinessObjects Enterprise XI Release 2, when Desktop Intelligence was reintroduced to the platform (XI Release 1 did not include Desktop Intelligence), publications could be created only in the Desktop Intelligence format. Additionally, a recipient required an SAP BusinessObjects BI license to receive a publication.

SAP BusinessObjects Enterprise XI 3.0 added significant new capabilities to publications. For the first time, publications could be created using Crystal Reports or Web Intelligence in addition to Desktop Intelligence. Also, a new feature called dynamic recipients permitted organizations to schedule and distribute publications via email for users who were not license holders on the BI platform. This enhancement was particularly useful for distributing publications to customers outside the traditional walls of the organization. Dynamic recipients also made the distribution of publications more cost effective, as no user license was required.

SAP BusinessObjects Business Intelligence has since replaced the Enterprise series. The BI 4.0 platform continues the features introduced in XI 3.0, but no longer supports Desktop Intelligence. Existing publications that use Desktop Intelligence as the source document format must be modified to use a Web Intelligence document instead. Desktop Intelligence documents can be converted to the Web Intelligence format using the Report Conversion Tool.

The focus of this chapter is publications created using SAP BusinessObjects Web Intelligence. For publications that utilize Crystal Reports, refer to the SAP PRESS book *100 Things You Should Know About Reporting with SAP Crystal Reports* by Coy W. Yonce, III (2012).

Publications allow critical business information such as corporate sales figures to be pushed directly to recipients and complement the self-service features of the business intelligence platform. As necessary, each recipient can receive a personalized version of the publication that displays only data of interest to him; this personalization can also serve as a security measure, limiting access to sensitive data. For example, employees in the Asia Pacific region will receive a publication with only their data; data for the Americas and EMEA regions will not appear in their copy of the publication.

One of the key features of publications is its efficient use of database resources during personalization, known as single-pass report bursting. Instead of executing unique database queries for each publication recipient, the publication executes non-personalized database queries. By applying one or more report filters to the source document, you can make sure that the data is personalized after it is retrieved from the database. Because publications use Web Intelligence report filters, one popular practice is to distribute publications in a neutral format such as Adobe PDF or Microsoft Excel, because a savvy user could potentially remove the report filtering from the original document and view sensitive corporate data.

As we look ahead to the publication creation process, let's begin by understanding the various roles that are involved.

19.1 Publication Roles

There are four roles involved in the creation and consumption of a publication: administrator, report designer, publisher, and recipient. The first three roles can be filled by a single person with access to both the BI Launch Pad and CMC. In larger organizations, these roles are often divided among multiple people.

▶ Administrator: The SAP BusinessObjects administrator ensures that the BI environment is functioning, that security roles are defined, and that desired destinations such as email are configured. These tasks are performed in the CMC.

▶ Report designer: This individual will use the techniques outlined in this book to create one or more Web Intelligence documents to form the foundation of a publication. These Web Intelligence documents can be created using either Web Intelligence from the BI Launch Pad or the Web Intelligence Rich Client.

▶ Publisher: This individual creates the publication and configures its metadata, including the personalization information. Publications can be created by users from the BI Launch Pad or administrators from the CMC.

▶ Recipient: This individual receives the publication, typically via email, although the BI Launch Pad inbox can also be used.

Let's examine each of the four roles in greater detail.

19.1.1 The SAP BusinessObjects Administrator

The SAP BusinessObjects administrator has several important tasks. First, he is responsible for ensuring that the user account used to schedule the publication has access to the public folders containing the publication source documents and the universes and connections on which those documents are based. He must also ensure that the desired destination (inbox, email, FTP, file system) is properly configured on the publication job server. Lastly, the administrator will create and manage profiles that are used to personalize publications for enterprise recipients. Each of these administrative tasks requires access to various management areas of the CMC.

19.1.2 The Web Intelligence Report Designer

The report designer is responsible for creating one or more source documents for the publication. (Although Crystal Reports can be used for publications, our focus here is limited to Web Intelligence.)

All documents in the publications must be of a single type—in other words, they must all be Web Intelligence documents—because it is not possible to combine Web Intelligence documents and Crystal Reports into the same publication.

Although the report designer does not need to understand the inner mechanics of the publication mechanism, the report designer must understand the reporting requirements and the personalization requirements. Personalization is applied by the publication server to documents as report filters, which are presented in Chapter 9 of this book.

19.1.3 The Publication Designer

The publication designer uses either the CMC or the BI Launch Pad to build a new publication. This chapter focuses mainly on this role.

19.1.4 The Recipient

The publication recipient has the easiest responsibilities of the four roles. The recipient simply checks his SAP BusinessObjects BI inbox or corporate email inbox to see whether a publication has been sent. A recipient can also subscribe or unsubscribe to a publication from the BI Launch Pad, a procedure that will be described later in the chapter.

19.2 Creating a Publication

We will use a single Web Intelligence document as the basis of our publication. The document will use the eFashion universe and format the eFashion Store name object from Chapter 16. The sample document is shown in Figure 19.1.

The query in the publication source will retrieve all eFashion stores; however, the publication's metadata will ensure that each recipient only receives data for one store by applying a report filter to the Store name object in the report section.

SKU by Color for Party pants			
e-Fashion Austin			$22,066

SKU desc	Color	Quantity sold	Sales revenue
Clown Printed Satin Trousers	Ficelle	16	$2,678
	Ink	14	$2,888
	White	19	$4,333
Clown Printed Satin Trousers			
	Sum:	49	$9,898

Figure 19.1 Sample eFashion Publication

To begin creating a new publication, open the BI Launch Pad and choose PUBLICA-TION from the New menu on the main toolbar, as shown in Figure 19.2.

Figure 19.2 Select Publication from the New Shortcut Icon in BI Launch Pad

19.2.1 Naming the Publication

First you must give the publication a name. The sample publication is called eFashion Publication Dynamic, as shown in Figure 19.3. Adding a description and keywords that help identify the publication is optional.

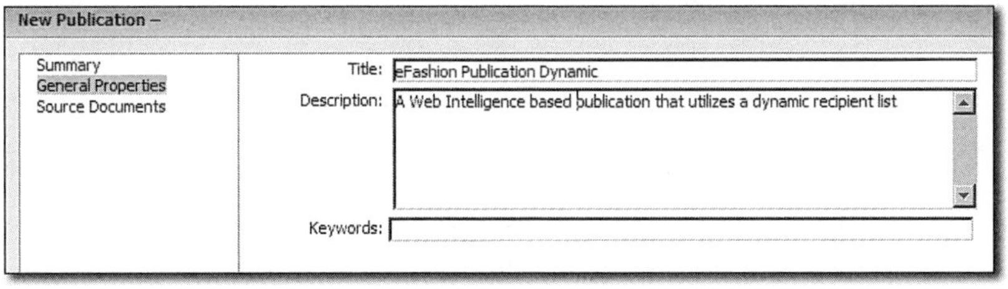

Figure 19.3 Publication General Properties

19.2.2 Choosing the Source Documents

Choose one or more source documents from the SOURCE DOCUMENTS box shown in Figure 19.4.

Figure 19.4 Source Documents

Now choose one or more Web Intelligence documents. Our example uses a single document named Analysis by SKU by Category, as shown in Figure 19.5.

Figure 19.5 Source Documents

Once you've entered the general properties and source documents, you'll see additional menus on the left side of the screen, as shown in Figure 19.6.

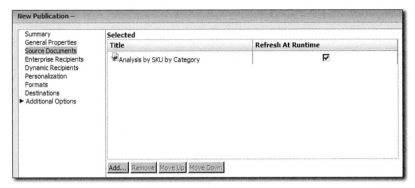

Figure 19.6 Source Documents

19.2.3   Choosing Enterprise Recipients

A publication may have enterprise recipients, dynamic recipients, or both. You can add enterprise recipients as individual users or as groups using the selection box, shown in Figure 19.7. In our example, a group named eFashion has been chosen.

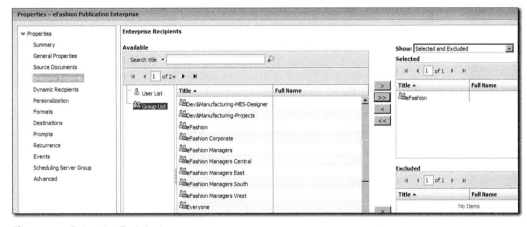

Figure 19.7 Enterprise Recipients

> **Note**
>
> Keep in mind that users that have access to the folder containing the publication can subscribe or unsubscribe themselves via the BI Launch Pad, which will be described later in the chapter.

Personalization with a Global Profile

If the SAP BusinessObjects administrator has created a suitable profile in the CMC, it may be applied to the publication. The administrator must also grant viewing rights to the profile to the publication author; otherwise, the profile will not appear in the author's dropdown list. In Figure 19.8, the profile eFashion Manager Profile is used to personalize the publication.

The details concerning the profile and delineation of which universes and objects are filtered can only be examined using the CMC.

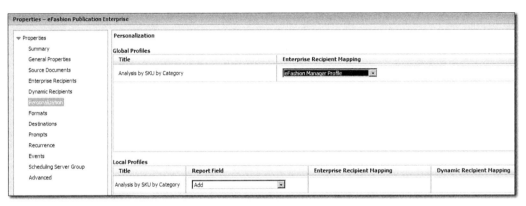

Figure 19.8 Personalization with a Global Profile

Personalization Using a Local Profile

Personalization for enterprise recipients can also be accomplished by a local profile, as shown in Figure 19.9. A local profile filters a report field in the Web Intelligence source document. Although local profile filters can be used to filter universe objects, they are typically employed when the source document contains a report variable to be filtered that is not present in the universe.

19.2.4 Choosing Dynamic Recipients

Dynamic recipients are specified using a dynamic recipient provider, which is a report authored using either Crystal Reports or Web Intelligence. In this example, we've selected Web Intelligence as the Web Intelligence Report Dynamic Recipient Provider, as shown in Figure 19.10.

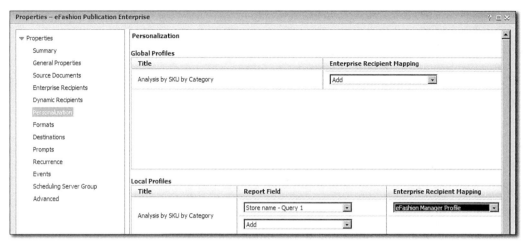

Figure 19.9 Personalization with a Local Profile

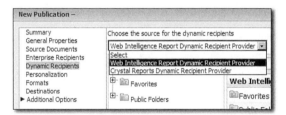

Figure 19.10 Web Intelligence Report Dynamic Recipient Provider

Next, you need to select the desired Web Intelligence report. Figure 19.11 shows eFashion Dynamic Recipient List as our selection.

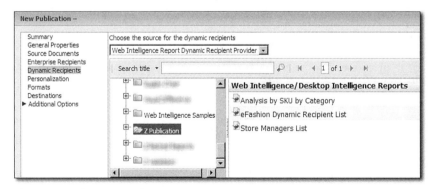

Figure 19.11 Choosing eFashion Dynamic Recipient List Report

Once the dynamic recipient provider report is selected, choose the data provider containing the dynamic recipient list, as shown in Figure 19.12. In our example, the default Query 1 contains the dynamic recipient list.

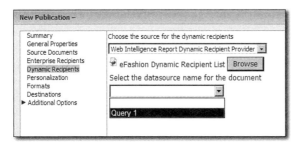

Figure 19.12 Selecting the Data Source Name for the Document

Once the data provider is chosen, three fields appear for the RECIPIENT IDENTIFIER, FULL NAME, and EMAIL address of the recipients, respectively. These fields should be mapped to the proper objects in the data provider, as shown in Figure 19.13.

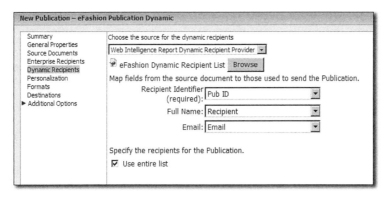

Figure 19.13 Map Fields from the Source Document

Personalization with a Local Profile

Once the dynamic recipients are specified, the publication can be personalized for each recipient using additional fields in the Dynamic Recipient Provider report, as shown in Figure 19.14. In our example, each recipient will receive a publication for a single store name.

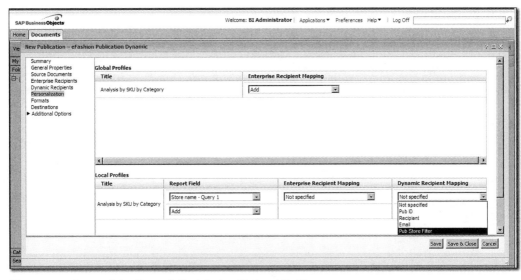

Figure 19.14 Personalizing Dynamic Recipients with Local Profile

19.2.5 Setting Publication Properties

A variety of settings are available to format your publication with your audience in mind.

Formats

Publications can be delivered in four formats: Web Intelligence, Microsoft Excel, Adobe Acrobat (PDF), and MHTML, as shown in Figure 19.15.

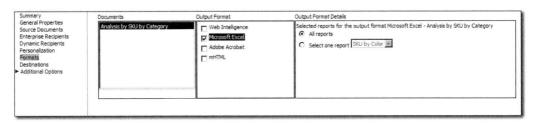

Figure 19.15 Formats

Destinations

As with any scheduled job, you can send publications to the five standard destinations: DEFAULT ENTERPRISE LOCATION, BI INBOX, EMAIL, FTP SERVER, AND FILE SYSTEM, as shown in Figure 19.16. Except for the default enterprise location, the other destinations may require additional configuration by the SAP Business-Objects administrator.

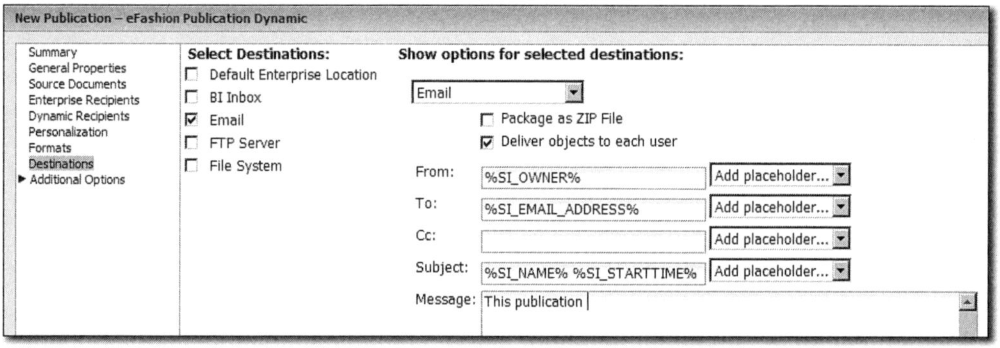

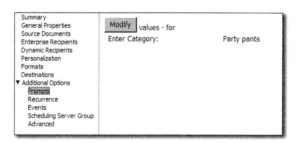

Figure 19.16 Destinations

Prompts

If any of the source documents contain prompts, they can be modified. Figure 19.17 shows a default value of "Party pants" for the publication source document.

Figure 19.17 Prompts

Recurrence

Publications support all of the standard recurrence intervals of the BI platform, as shown in Figure 19.18. For more information about scheduling recurrence options, see Chapter 18.

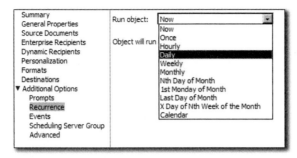

Figure 19.18 Recurrence

Events

Publications support all of the standard event types (file, schedule, and custom) of the BI platform, as shown in Figure 19.19. Again, see Chapter 18 for more information.

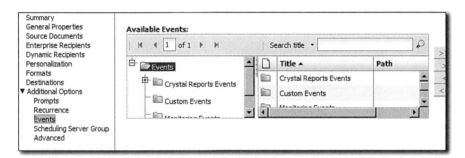

Figure 19.19 Events

Scheduling Server Group

Server groups are created and managed by the SAP BusinessObjects administrator to specify specific resources in the BI platform cluster, as shown in Figure 19.20. For example, as an administrator, you can create a special server group for long-running jobs that specifies job servers located on larger, faster machines than the rest of the cluster.

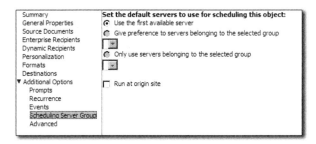

Figure 19.20 Scheduling Server Group

Advanced Options

Advanced options is where you control profile resolution, display of users who have no personalization applied, and the method for report bursting, as shown in Figure 19.21.

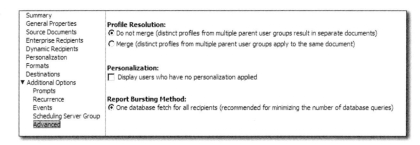

Figure 19.21 Advanced Options

Let's briefly examine these options.

Profile Resolution

In certain cases, an enterprise recipient may be defined in more than one profile. The profile resolution specifies how the publication should behave for these recipients. If DO NOT MERGE is chosen, the recipient will receive multiple distinct documents for each profile in which they are defined. If MERGE is chosen, the distinct profiles will be combined and the recipient will receive a single document.

Personalization

By selecting the DISPLAY USERS WHO HAVE NO PERSONALIZATION APPLIED box, publishers can see which subscribed recipients have no personalization applied, meaning that those recipients will see the entire unfiltered source documents.

Depending on business requirements, it may be totally appropriate for corporate executives and senior managers to appear on this list, as their role in the organization dictates that they should have visibility to all corporate operations.

Report Bursting Method

Publications based on Web Intelligence can only have the option of one database fetch for all recipients. Additional report bursting methods exist for publications based on Crystal Reports.

Summary

Once the publisher has completed the publication setup, it is helpful to return to the SUMMARY screen, shown in Figure 19.22, to review all options you have selected.

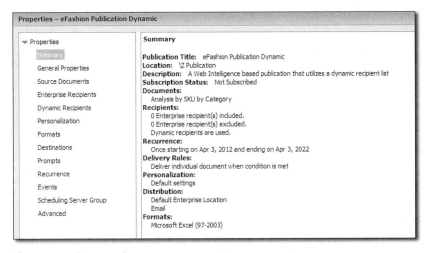

Figure 19.22 Summary Screen

19.2.6 Testing the Publication

Test mode, shown in Figure 19.23, allows the publisher to validate a publication before sending it to actual recipients. All instances of the publication will be sent to the publisher—not the actual recipients—so the publication behavior can be tested. Testing the publication is an important step to ensure that sensitive corporate data is not inadvertently revealed by the publication.

Figure 19.23 Test Mode

19.3 Summary

Publications allow organizations to complement self-service reporting by publishing personalized content directly to users, both inside (enterprise recipients) and outside (dynamic recipients) the organization.

Of the four roles involved in publications (the administrator, report designer, publication designer, and recipient), this chapter has focused on the role of the publication designer. The publication designer builds a publication using one or more Web Intelligence documents and assigning personalization through either a global profile (a reusable profile managed in the Central Management Console) or a local profile (unique to a single publication).

Publications use the same destinations and scheduling options available to other document types on the BI platform. The most common destination is email, as it allows publications to serve customers outside the walls of an organization. For additional information about publications, consult the BI Launch Pad User Guide for SAP BusinessObjects Business Intelligence 4.0.

The next chapter will cover Web Intelligence Rich Client, which enables the use of local data providers to create reports.

Web Intelligence Rich Client puts the power of Web Intelligence reporting on the user's local machine. It provides all the same capabilities while working in offline or standalone mode—with no Central Management Server required.

20   Web Intelligence Rich Client

Prior to the release of Web Intelligence 3.x, Web Intelligence reporting existed over the web only. Users were required to log on to the web portal of the BI Launch Pad to view, create, modify, and share Web Intelligence report content. With the introduction of this thin-client version, Web Intelligence 3.x provides you with the ability to utilize all the functionality of Web Intelligence from your local personal computer, completely unconnected from the CMS. Web Intelligence documents can be stored locally, which offers you with another means for backing up your reports. Local data providers can be used to create reports with Web Intelligence Rich Client.

There are two ways to install Web Intelligence Rich Client: using the BI platform CD to install it as part of a client installation, or selecting INSTALL Now in the Web Intelligence Preferences to install it from the BI Launch Pad.

This chapter will explore the unique functionality available within Web Intelligence Rich Client as well as the differences in navigation when working in the desktop product rather than the online version.

20.1   How Rich Client is Different

Web Intelligence Rich Client, or *Rich Client,* enables you to access Web Intelligence from a Windows-based application installed on your local computer. The familiar interface of Rich Client, which is shown in Figure 20.1, makes it a favorite destination for report writers. Access to the Central Management Console is not required. Documents can be saved to your local computer, and you can use local data providers when building queries. Timeouts or web-based issues will not create interruptions to your Web Intelligence report writing and viewing. These features provide exciting new capabilities for the Web Intelligence report consumer.

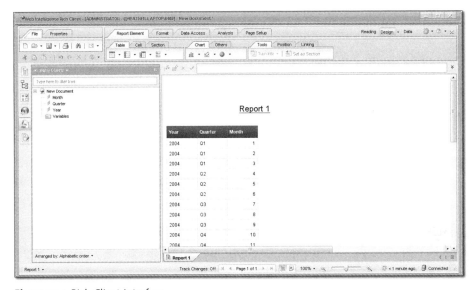

Figure 20.1 Rich Client Interface

Compelling reasons for users to turn to Web Intelligence Rich Client for their reporting needs include the following:

▶ Rich Client can work offline without a connection to the CMS.

▶ Rich Client performs calculations locally—rather than on the server—for improved performance.

▶ Rich Client can be used in standalone mode when there is no CMS or application server installed.

▶ When the data source is contained in Excel, CSV, text or web services, you can use Rich Client as a local data source.

Note that all of the features of Web Intelligence via the BI Launch Pad are available in Rich Client. Additional available features will be discussed in further detail in this chapter, though for the purposes of this chapter, we will not duplicate our discussions in other chapters on the core functionality of Web Intelligence. Instead, we will discuss only the differences found when using Rich Client for your Web Intelligence reporting needs.

There are two ways to access Rich Client: locally or through the BI Launch Pad. After Rich Client is installed in your local machine, go to Start • Programs • SAP BusinessObjects BI Platform 4.0 • SAP BusinessObjects BI Platform Client Tools • Web Intelligence Rich Client; this path is seen in Figure 20.2. To launch Rich Client from the BI Launch Pad, set your Web Intelligence preferences to use Desktop as your default creation/editing tool.

Figure 20.2 Rich Client Program Path

When you open Rich Client, you are presented with the initial screen to create a new document or open an existing document. At the bottom left of the screen is an option for Blank Document, as shown in Figure 20.3. Selecting this option will open Rich Client without establishing a connection to the repository; therefore, a login screen will not appear. With this option, you default to enter Rich Client in offline mode. You may begin working with a blank Web Intelligence document now and add queries and connections at a later time.

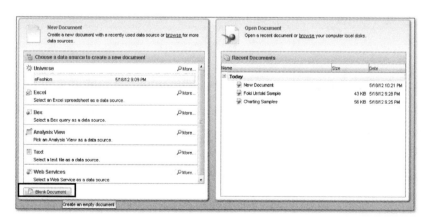

Figure 20.3 Initial Options when Opening Rich Client

After selecting a connected option, the login screen will appear. At this point, you may select to log on to the repository or log on in standalone mode. You have three options when accessing Rich Client: offline, connected, and standalone.

20.1.1 Working in Offline Mode

The first new option available is the USE IN OFFLINE MODE checkbox, as seen in Figure 20.4. *Offline mode* utilizes the security of the CMS stored on your local machine. The first time you log on to Rich Client, you will have to log on using connected mode in order for the CMS security information to be downloaded to your local machine. Every document and universe stored locally on your machine carries an access control list that stores the groups and users that have access rights to the object. Therefore, when working in offline mode, you are not connected to the CMS, but CMS security is applied. You have the ability to work with secured or unsecured local documents and universes. When creating or refreshing documents, you will need a local universe and local connection server.

Figure 20.4 Offline Mode

20.1.2 Working in Connected Mode

Working in *connected mode* enables you to import documents and universes from the CMS as well as export Web Intelligence documents back to the CMS. This capability is not available in offline or standalone modes. There are two options for logging on in connected mode. From within the BI Launch Pad, set your Web

Intelligence preferences to use Desktop as your default creation/editing tool. When you select to edit an existing Web Intelligence document from or create a new Web Intelligence document form the BI Launch Pad, Rich Client is launched on your local computer. When you use this method, Web Intelligence connects to the CMS in client-server mode and database middleware is needed on your local machine.

Another method involves logging on to Rich Client by launching Web Intelligence Rich Client from your programs on your local machine. When presented with the login dialog box, select the CMS and select the same authentication type used when logging on to the BI Launch Pad.

20.1.3 Working in Standalone Mode

To log on using *standalone mode*, select STANDALONE from the system list when entering your login credentials, as shown in Figure 20.5. Standalone mode does not connect to the CMS, and security is not enforced as in offline mode. While in connected and offline mode, you can work with secured or unsecured documents and universes; in standalone mode, you can work with secured documents and universes only. This requires the appropriate database connection middleware in order to enable you to create and refresh documents with local universes.

Figure 20.5 Standalone Mode

20.2   Data Provider Options

Multiple types of data sources are available in Rich Client: Universe, Excel, BEx, Analysis View, text, and web services. The universe data source includes all universes stored within the CMC, as discussed in previous chapters. Other data sources include Excel, Text or web services. When you select the text and Excel options, the personal data provider dialog box will open. Personal data providers include the following file types:

► *.TXT

► *.CSV

► *.PRN

► *.ASC

► *.XLS

After selecting the file type, you are prompted to define further options for selection of your data source. Refer to Chapter 12 for further details on creating queries with a personal data provider.

Another data source available is the use of a web service. When selecting these options from the other data sources menu, you are prompted to enter your source URL as well as additional pertinent information about your web service. This functionality can be used to bring in real-time information to your Web Intelligence document. Data from Query as a Web Service or BI Services can be integrated into your Web Intelligence Rich Client document. Refer to Chapter 12 for further details on utilizing a web service as your custom data provider.

20.2.1   Importing a Universe from the CMS

When creating a new Web Intelligence report in Rich Client, you are prompted to select your data source. When selecting a universe as a data source, you have the option to choose a local universe or a universe saved in the CMS. Note that you can use a universe in the CMS only if you are working in connected mode. If you would like to store additional universes locally for use in unconnected sessions, you can use TOOLS • IMPORT UNIVERSE to import universes from the CMS. Upon selecting UNIVERSES from the Tools menu, you receive a list of available universes, as shown in Figure 20.6. Select the universe to be imported locally and click on the IMPORT button.

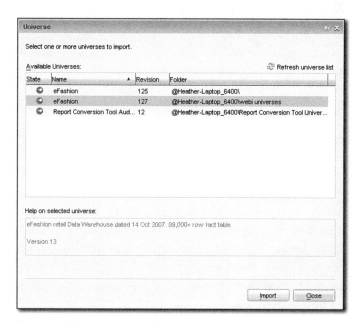

Figure 20.6 Import Universe Dialog Box

20.2.2 Query Panel in Rich Client

In Rich Client, select EDIT from the Data Access menu to view the Query Panel. This is the same workflow as operating from within the web-based interface. Upon selecting EDIT, the Query Panel dialog box appears. Make any appropriate changes to the query from this panel and then select RUN QUERY to see your changes reflected in your report. This functionality works the same as within web-based Web Intelligence.

20.3 Working with Web Intelligence Reports

When working in Rich Client, the same ribbon and menu exist as seen when working with Web Intelligence reports over the web. This provides a familiar source of organization for the options available for use when designing Web

Intelligence reports. Figure 20.7 shows the menu options as seen in Web Intelligence Rich Client.

Figure 20.7 Rich Client Menu

20.3.1 Opening Documents from the CMS

To import a report from the CMS, you first must be in connected mode. Select OPEN from the File menu. (You may also select the OPEN FROM option.) The Open a Document dialog box will appear, as shown in Figure 20.8. Select the name on your BI platform from the left panel. Navigate through your personal and public folder or categories to select the name of the document from the document list. You may also search for the document by using the search box at the top of the dialog box. These search options are similar to that seen within the BI Launch Pad. You can select one or many documents to be opened on your local machine. After selecting a document, click on the ADD button to move the document to your list of documents to be imported locally. When complete, click on the OPEN button at the bottom of the dialog box.

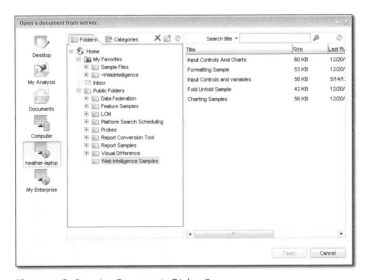

Figure 20.8 Opening Documents Dialog Box

The new document will open by default in a new window in reading mode.

20.3.2 Saving Reports Locally

To save a Web Intelligence Rich Client document locally, you can select SAVE or SAVE As from the File menu. SAVE will save the document as its original name to its original location. SAVE As has a number of options including: Web Intelligence Document, Excel, or PDF. These documents will not be viewable in the BI Launch Pad. The next step depends on which file type you save the document as; these file types are located in the dropdown menu at the bottom of the dialogue box.

The SAVE AS A WEB INTELLIGENCE DOCUMENT option opens another dialog box, which is shown in Figure 20.9.

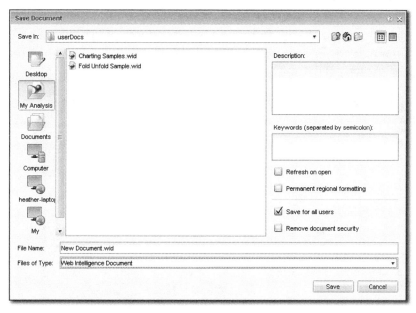

Figure 20.9 Web Intelligence Document Dialog Box

Enter the Web Intelligence document name, descriptions, and keywords as you would like them to appear within the BI Launch Pad. You also can indicate whether to refresh the document upon open by selecting the checkbox. Another checkbox indicates that it will maintain permanent regional formatting rather than adjusting per the user's settings. The new options that are available when saving a Web Intelligence document within Rich Client include:

▶ SAVE FOR ALL USERS: Saves the document for all users to view and enables the Web Intelligence report to be moved between environments

▶ REMOVE DOCUMENT SECURITY: Saves the document as unsecured so it can be viewed in standalone or offline mode

After selecting available options and indicating the report name, description, and keywords, you can select a location to save the document outside of the BI platform environment. The default location is to save to your userDocs folder. The path for this folder is defined within your Rich Client options, as discussed in Section 20.4.

The SAVE AS EXCEL or EXCEL 2007 option changes the dialog box properties as shown in Figure 20.10. When saving a Web Intelligence document as an Excel file, you have the option to convert all report tabs to Excel or select only certain report tabs for export. You can also select the option on how to prioritize the processing of the Excel document. The default setting for these preferences are defined in the Rich Client options in the Tools menu. Further information on these options has been discussed in previous chapters.

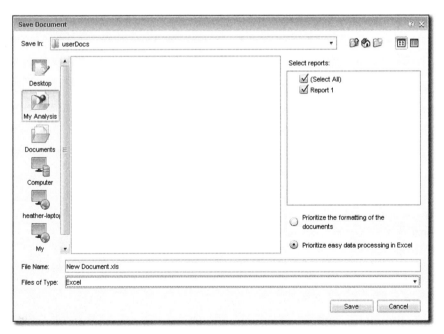

Figure 20.10 Save as Excel Option

The SAVE AS PDF option opens another dialog box, as shown in Figure 20.11. When saving as a PDF, you are given the option to define which reports and pages to include in your PDF.

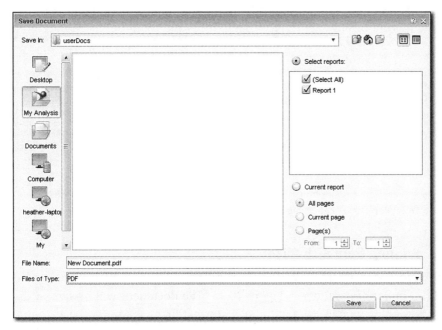

Figure 20.11 Save as PDF Option

The SAVE AS CSV (DATA ONLY) option opens another dialog box where you can define the text qualifier, column delimiter, and character set for the CSV file.

20.3.3 Exporting Reports to CMS

In order to view these documents within the BI Launch Pad and share with other users in the web portal, you have to save your report to the CMS. To export your document to the CMS, you must first be in connected mode. Then select PUBLISH TO CMS from the Save dropdown list. Select the folder and categories to export your document for viewing within the BI Launch Pad and select the SAVE button, as shown in Figure 20.12. Additional export options are available by selecting the ADVANCED button in the dialog box. This enables options to SAVE FOR ALL USERS or REMOVE DOCUMENT SECURITY, as mentioned above.

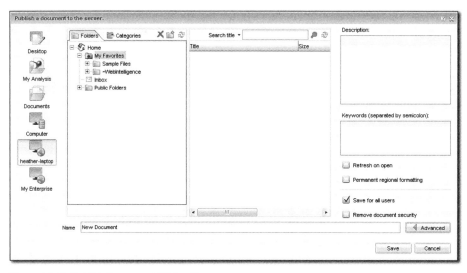

Figure 20.12 Publish Document Dialog Box

20.3.4 Printing from Rich Client

To print from Rich Client, select PRINT from the File menu. You are presented with print options, as shown in Figure 20.13. The document will be sent to the printer without having to open within PDF format first.

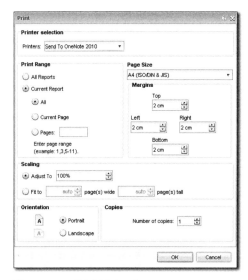

Figure 20.13 Print Dialog Box

20.3.5 Sending Reports as Email Attachments

Another option is available in Rich Client is the ability to send a report as an email attachment is available from the File menu. Select SEND BY EMAIL ATTACHMENT from the File menu. You have the choice to send the document in a number of formats, including Web Intelligence document, unsecured Web Intelligence document, Excel, PDF, and CSV (data only).

20.4 Setting Preferences in Rich Client

Preferences are available in Rich Client, as seen in the Web Intelligence preferences in the BI Launch Pad. These options are available from the Properties ribbon under APPLICATION or from the Tools menu under OPTIONS. Preferences can be defined for Drilling, Locales, Viewing and General Preferences. These are defined separately in Rich Client to what is defined for Web Intelligence documents viewed in the BI Launch Pad.

20.5 Summary

Web Intelligence Rich Client brings the features of web-based Web Intelligence onto your desktop, opening up new features that are instrumental to the report writer. Former SAP BusinessObjects Desktop Intelligence users will appreciate the new thin client capabilities of Web Intelligence provided within Web Intelligence 4.x. The ability to work whether connected or disconnected from the CMS, save universes and documents locally, and use local data providers offers additional capabilities to aid the report designer in the report creation, consumption, and sharing processes.

Chapter 21 discusses the ability to bring Web Intelligence report content into Microsoft Office documents using another tool called Live Office. This provides another familiar interface for report writers and consumers alike to work with data within the easy-to-use environment of programs such as Microsoft Excel.

Live Office is a powerful tool that enables the use of business intelligence content within Microsoft Office documents. Live Office allows a larger audience to consume, query, analyze, and visualize Web Intelligence content in a familiar interface.

21 Connecting Live Office to Web Intelligence 4.0

With Live Office, you can work with your business intelligence content within Microsoft Office applications such as Word, Excel, PowerPoint and Outlook. This functionality allows you to quickly and easily collaborate with other users across your organization. It also empowers users of different skill sets or comfort levels to manipulate their Web Intelligence query results within other mediums. This chapter will review the core functionality, basic settings, and usage of the Live Office product with Web Intelligence documents. Live Office 4.0 is compatible with Microsoft Office 2003, 2007, and 2010. The menu options may appear different in the various versions than those shown in this chapter.

21.1 Introduction to Live Office

Live Office is an Excel plugin that can be installed on a client machine. After Live Office has been installed, a new Live Office ribbon will appear on your toolbar when you are in Microsoft Office applications (Word, Excel, PowerPoint, or Outlook), as shown in Figure 21.1. Live Office allows you to bring report data from Web Intelligence reports, Crystal Reports, and universe queries to do further manipulation within the Microsoft Office application. Excel is frequently used with Live Office because it lets users perform further analysis of the data in a familiar place. Users in finance departments are often very familiar with Excel, and Live Office gives them a tool that works within their comfort zone and requires little additional training.

Figure 21.1 Live Office Ribbon from within Microsoft Excel

21.1.1   Integration with Web Intelligence Reports

Live Office enables you to insert Web Intelligence report content into your Microsoft Office document as tables, charts, or freestanding cells.

Excel is the most common destination for Web Intelligence content because it uses a tabular interface and enables further manipulation of the data. A user who is not fully trained in how to use Web Intelligence can easily create a report using Web Intelligence content from within Live Office.

Web Intelligence content involves report objects, report instances, and reports parts. *Report objects* are the actual Web Intelligence reports contained within SAP BusinessObjects Business Intelligence. *Report instances* are the versions of reports created when a report is scheduled. Report instances will contain data from a specified report refresh with the prompt values used at the time of that refresh. Lastly, *report parts* are the various elements of the report (such as the tables and charts) contained within the report. It is important to understand each of these elements when using the Live Office Wizard for specification of the Web Intelligence content to integrate in your Office document.

21.1.2   Live Office Ribbon Menu

The *Live Office ribbon menu* is available from within your Word, Excel, Power-Point, or Outlook document beginning with Microsoft Office 2007. In Microsoft Office 2003, these options appear in the toolbar. The ribbon menu, which is shown in Figure 21.1, enables quick access to the most commonly used functions available within Live Office.

The following options are available on the Live Office ribbon menu, and are organized by pane:

- ▶ INSERT

  - ▶ CRYSTAL REPORTS: This option opens the Live Office Wizard to define the options available for inserting content from a Crystal Report.

  - ▶ INTERACTIVE ANALYSIS (WEB INTELLIGENCE CONTENT): This option opens the Live Office Wizard to define the options available for inserting content from a Web Intelligence report.

  - ▶ UNIVERSE QUERY: This option opens the Live Office Wizard to define the options available for creating a universe query to insert results into your destination Office document.

- ▶ OBJECT ACTIONS

  - ▶ REFRESH ALL OBJECTS: This option lets you refresh all objects contained in your Live Office document.

  - ▶ GO TO OBJECT: This option enables you to go to a specific object in your Live Office document.

  - ▶ MODIFY OBJECT: This option allows you to modify the properties for a specific object.

  - ▶ REFRESH OBJECT: This option enables you to refresh a specific object only.

- ▶ EXPLORE

  - ▶ SELECTION: This is new functionality available in Live Office 4.0. It enables you to export a selection in your Live Office document to SAP Business-Objects Explorer for further analysis (new to Live Office 4.0).

  - ▶ SHEET: This feature enables you to export an entire sheet in your document to SAP BusinessObjects Explorer for further analysis.

- ► PUBLISHING

  - ► OPEN FROM REPOSITORY: This option allows you to open a Live Office document saved to the SAP BusinessObjects repository.

  - ► SAVE TO REPOSITORY: This option saves the Live Office document to the SAP BusinessObjects Business Intelligence platform to share and collaborate with others in your organization.

  - ► SAVE AS NEW TO REPOSITORY: This option allows you to save as a different name or to a different location for a Live Office document existing in the SAP BusinessObjects Business Intelligence platform.

  - ► CREATE SNAPSHOT: This option enables you to create a snapshot of the document in the current state to save for further reference. More information on snapshots is discussed in Chapter 10.

- ► SETTINGS (more details in Section 21.3)

  - ► OBJECT PROPERTIES: This option allows you to define object-specific properties.

  - ► REFRESH OPTIONS: This option allows you to define refresh options for the Live Office document.

  - ► APPLICATION OPTIONS: This option allows you to define Live Office application options.

- ► VIEW

  - ► OBJECT IN BROWSER: This option opens the object in a browser window.

  - ► HELP: This option opens the Live Office Help dialog box.

  - ► ABOUT LIVE OFFICE: This option shows the version information for your current Live Office installation.

Now that you're familiar with the Live Office basics, let's shift our attention to how to create documents in this tool that contain valuable web intelligence information.

21.2 Creating Live Office Documents with Web Intelligence Content

The integration of Web Intelligence content within Live Office provides a powerful tool for the end user and report writer alike. To integrate Web Intelligence content, a Web Intelligence report must already exist in the repository for access within Live Office. This report content can be brought into Word, Excel, Power-Point, or Outlook. For the purpose of this section, we'll assume that we are using Excel to integrate our Web Intelligence content.

21.2.1 Accessing the Live Office Wizard

Navigate to the appropriate cell where you would like the content to be dropped in your Excel worksheet. From the Live Office ribbon menu, select the INSERT WEB INTELLIGENCE/INTERACTIVE ANALYSIS CONTENT button. If you have not already logged on or selected auto-authentication, then the login dialog box will appear. After authentication, the Live Office Wizard will display.

21.2.2 Selecting the Web Intelligence Document

The first option in the Live Office Wizard is to select the Web Intelligence document to use for content in your Excel document. Figure 21.2 shows the CHOOSE DOCUMENT screen in the Live Office Wizard.

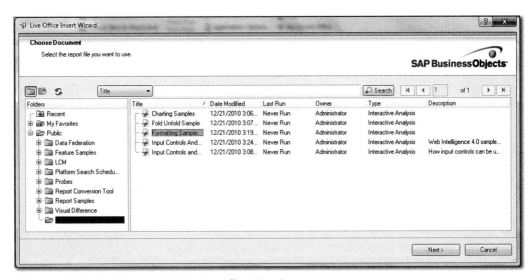

Figure 21.2 Choosing Document in the Live Office Wizard

The screen displays the Web Intelligence documents available for integration within the repository. This view displays the folders and categories in the BI Launch Pad. You can navigate by folders or categories by selecting the icons at the top. You can also search by title, keyword, content, or all fields to find a document, and you can include Web Intelligence objects, instances, or publications in Live Office. Highlight the name of your chosen document and select Next.

21.2.3 Setting Context

If more than one context exists for the Web Intelligence report, you will be prompted to set context as part of the Live Office Wizard. After choosing the appropriate context, select Next.

21.2.4 Configuring Prompt Values

The option to configure prompt values will appear only if prompts are set up on the Web Intelligence report. If no prompts exist, then this option will not appear. The prompt properties allow you to select the prompt value from a list or set to be prompted to enter the prompt value each time the data is refreshed. After specifying prompt values, select Next.

21.2.5 Selecting Report Content

After choosing the Web Intelligence document, you need to select the report content to be included in the Live Office document. Select each report block to include it in the report. All selected blocks will be brought into your Live Office document starting at the cell where you placed your cursor. Figure 21.3 shows the Choose Data dialog box. After making all selections of relevant report parts, select Next.

21.2.6 Creating the Summary

Upon selection of the report parts to be included in your Live Office document, you will be shown the Summary. At this time, you'll give a name to your particular Live Office content before selecting Finish. Figure 21.4 shows Web Intelligence report content in an Excel document using Live Office.

21.2.7 Adding More Content

Once your selected report content is displayed within Excel, you may wish to add in more report blocks from the same report. To add additional content, right-click on the report content within Excel to display the right-click menu. Select the Live Office option to view the available options as shown in Figure 21.5.

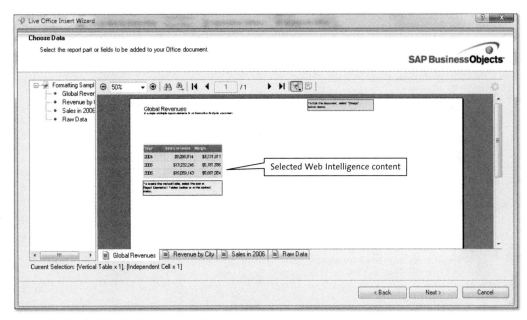

Figure 21.3 Choosing Data in the Live Office Wizard

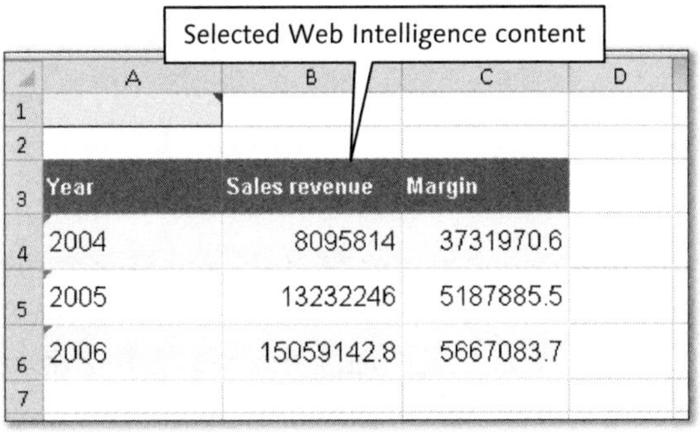

Figure 21.4 Web Intelligence Live Office Content in Excel

You'll have the option to insert or remove rows and columns within your Live Office object. Using these menu items ensures that you do not use your object mapping. You can refresh or set options from the right-click menu as well. To add a more content from the same report, select the option New Object from Same Report. The Live Office Wizard will appear to select the relevant options using the same Web Intelligence document.

To insert new content from a new Web Intelligence document, select the INSERT WEB INTELLIGENCE DOCUMENT from the Live Office toolbar and select the appropriate new report in the Live Office Wizard.

Figure 21.5 Live Office Menu Options

21.3 Setting Preferences

You can customize your session using a number of preferences within Live Office. Preferences apply to application options, refresh options, object properties, and prompt binding options.

21.3.1 Application Options

Application options enable you to define default settings for all your Live Office documents within the application. To define application options, select APPLICATION OPTIONS from the Live Office ribbon menu. The dialog box tabs define three types of application options: General, View, and Enterprise.

General

GENERAL tab properties will vary depending on the Office application. In the GENERAL options tab from Excel (shown in Figure 21.6), you can define the Shortcut menu options. In addition, options for the treatment of Live Office cells and refresh options are available. If you select the option to PROMPT BEFORE OVERWRITING LIVE OFFICE CELLS, you will be prompted before you are enabled to type over content that is being fed by your business intelligence content. If you select the option to REFRESH LIVE OFFICE CONTENT WHEN BINDING CELL CHANGES, the content will refresh when you bind your business intelligence content to cells in your Excel spreadsheet. If you choose to REFRESH LIVE OFFICE OBJECT ON DOCUMENT OPEN, then Live Office will go to the business objects repository and return the most recent results for your specified content. The COPY AND PASTE WITH LIVE OFFICE CONNECTIVITY option enables you to move bound ranges without losing the connectivity to Live Office. If this is disabled, then only the results will move and the copied content will not be refreshed when the Live Office content is refreshed.

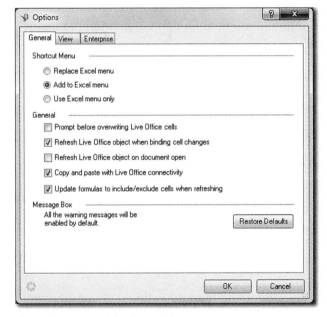

Figure 21.6 General Application Options

View

The VIEW tab options apply to how the data will be displayed in your Live Office document. The APPEARANCE options are set to determine whether the formatting from the original report should be maintained. The APPEARANCE options also allow you to set whether to show filters as comments in the Live Office document and to alert you when a time-consuming operation occurs that will affect a defined number of cells.

The VIEW tab options also define how cells will display for default cell values of NO DATA, DATA ERROR, and CONCEALED DATA. You can also define column headings to be set to the FIELD NAME, FIELD DESCRIPTION, or BOTH by default. These options are shown in Figure 21.7.

Figure 21.7 View Application Options

Enterprise

The ENTERPRISE tab options allow you to define your login criteria, as shown in Figure 21.8. The appropriate criteria should be given by your SAP Business-Objects administrator. The USER NAME and PASSWORD will be your SAP BusinessObjects Business Intelligence user name and password. The AUTHENTICATION and SYSTEM will be the same as well. The WEB SERVICES URL is defined as follows: *http://webserver:portnumber/dswsbobje/services/session*. Web server and port number should be replaced with the appropriate information for your SAP BusinessObjects deployment. The last setting in this tab allows you to define the open document URL for viewing content in a web browser.

Figure 21.8 Enterprise Application Options

21.3.2 Data Refresh Options

The data in a report can be set to refresh based on the original report, an instance, or on demand. The available options for refresh consist of the following:

▶ Latest Instance: The first option in the Refresh Options box shown in Figure 21.9 is to refresh data based on the latest instance of a scheduled report. Therefore, the Live Office data will refresh as the scheduled report data refreshes. The Live Office object will use the latest instance of the report for its data.

▶ On Demand: This option enables you to manually refresh the Live Office document when you want updated data. The source of the update will come from the database rather than the original Web Intelligence report or instance.

▶ Use Report Saved Data: This option refreshes the Live Office objects with the data saved in the original Web Intelligence report contained in the SAP BusinessObjects Business Intelligence platform environment.

▶ Specific Instance: This option enables you to use one of the scheduled instances of a Web Intelligence report as the source data for the Live Office report.

Figure 21.9 Refresh Options Box

21.3.3 Object Properties

The Object Properties box shown in Figure 21.10 allows you to specify properties that are specific to an object contained in your Live Office document. An object is defined as one of the report parts from the Web Intelligence report.

In the sample report, there are two report objects as shown in the objects of the report box. When you click on each object, detailed information about the object is shown on the right of the box. Specific details on the Web Intelligence report used in the Live Office document are also contained within the Objects/Reports box at the top. By clicking on each of these objects, you can see the properties display to the right.

To set refresh properties for the object, select the object from the Objects of the Report box on the bottom right, and then select the appropriate properties in the Refresh tab, shown in Figure 21.11. Available properties include whether to Apply report format when refreshing, Conceal data on saving, and Refresh Setting. Conceal data on saving enables you to secure the data so that a refresh must be made before a user can view the data. This will ensure that the user is seeing only the data that he is allowed to access, given his security settings.

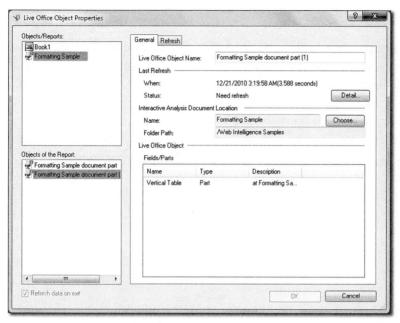

Figure 21.10 General Object Properties Box

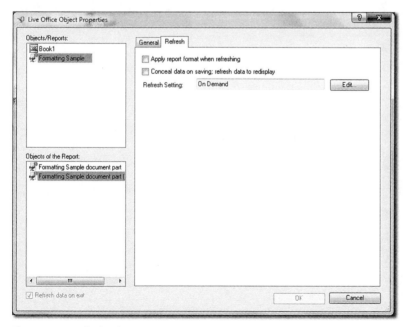

Figure 21.11 Refresh Object Properties Box

21.4   Summary

Live Office is a powerful tool that enables the consumption of Web Intelligence report content within Microsoft Office documents. This combines the power of business intelligence queries in a comfortable, familiar setting for end users and report writers alike. The next chapter will discuss another powerful tool to customize your Web Intelligence reporting experience. BI Mobile allows users to create customized mobile reporting to be shared on mobile devices—one more step toward a completely integrated business intelligence reporting experience.

Because the mobile landscape has changed significantly in recent years, business intelligence must respond accordingly to provide advanced analytics available on mobile devices. SAP BusinessObjects Web Intelligence answered this need through on-device mobile integration with the BI Mobile application.

22   On-Device Mobile Integration: BI Mobile

The ability to quickly and easily view, analyze, and interact with key metrics while performing day-to-day activities is a requirement for today's organizations. For everyone from executives to operational employees, business analytics provide a consumable source of data on the current status of the company, enabling them to respond quickly to business needs. Web Intelligence documents can be easily created for mobile consumption and available on a variety of mobile devices from Blackberry, Windows Mobile, and Symbian (Nokia) to the Apple iPhone and iPad. Reports can be consumed through the device or via alerts created to inform users of key information needing immediate attention. The BI Mobile tool provides powerful functionality to answer the call for on-device analytics for today's increasingly mobile workplace.

22.1   Understanding BI Mobile

The BI Mobile application is a separate tool available from SAP BusinessObjects for integration with your Web Intelligence and Crystal Reports content on mobile devices. Knowledge of the architecture of the tool provides increased understanding of the complexities occurring behind the scenes to support the mobile deployment.

22.1.1   Architecture

Under the recommended deployment, the BI Mobile server sits on a separate server from the SAP BusinessObjects enterprise environment housing your BI platform with your reporting documents. This server does the heavy lifting of ensuring security and adequate resources to handle processing and the sizing of your deployment. More detailed information regarding installation, supported platforms, and administration of the BI Mobile environment can be found in the user guides available at *www.sap.com*.

The client-side application is the component installed locally on your organization's mobile devices. This application is available in different versions depending on your devices. For example, Blackberry devices used with a Blackberry Enterprise Server (BES) have different client-side software than non-Blackberry devices or Blackberry devices not registered on the BES server.

Two different types of business intelligence reports are supported for use with the BI Mobile platform: Web Intelligence and Crystal Reports. For the purposes of this chapter, we will focus on the use of Web Intelligence reporting with this tool. Reporting designed for consumption on mobile devices must adhere to certain requirements to accommodate for the various devices, screen sizes, and memory limitations.

22.1.2 Client-Side Installation

Report designers should verify that the organization's mobile device brands and models are on the supported devices and operating systems. Contact your SAP BusinessObjects administrator or visit *http://service.sap.com/bosap-support* for the latest list. If your device is registered on your corporate Blackberry Enterprise Server, your administrator can push the application to your device, allowing the application to download automatically. You may also download the application for a corporate site. It is best to contact your SAP BusinessObjects administrator to confirm the appropriate method within your organization for your specific device.

Once you've installed the BI Mobile client application on your device, you will see a new APPLICATION icon for BI Mobile. Your login credentials should be the same as used to logon to the BI platform environment. You have the option to select to save your password. In addition, there is the option to *auto-connect* that will start BI Mobile each time your devices is switched on. It is important to note that when auto-connecting, you are establishing a connection to the live server data automatically; this can pose a security risk if your device is lost or stolen.

For the purpose of this book, specific device setup will not be covered. This chapter will focus on the specific functionality of creating and consuming Web Intelligence documents for viewing on your mobile devices with BI Mobile.

22.1.3 BI Mobile Home Page

When you connect to BI Mobile, the initial view contains the home page, including links to view local documents, server documents, mobile-ready documents, most recently viewed documents, and an option to search mobile-ready documents, as shown in Figure 22.1. You can also customize your initial view, including setting up a default folder or document.

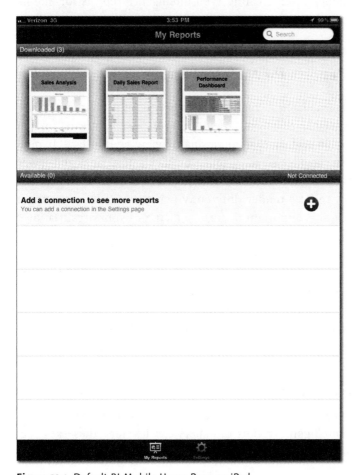

Figure 22.1 Default BI Mobile Home Page on iPad

Local and server documents are available within your BI Mobile application. *Local documents* are stored on your device; they are not accessible by others in the enterprise but *are* viewable even when you are working offline. *Server documents* are stored on the BI platform server and are accessible only when you are in online mode and connected to the server. Local documents can be synchronized with their server counterparts when online to receive any recent document updates.

The key to consumable mobile reporting lies in a report design that takes into account the limitations of the smaller viewing screens of the mobile devices and differences in interactions on mobile devices. There are best practices that report designers should remember when creating Web Intelligence reports for mobile consumption.

22.2   Designing Reports for Mobile Viewing

Although current Web Intelligence reports contained within your enterprise environment are consumable on mobile devices, it is best to create custom reports built for interaction and usability on a smaller viewing interface. In general, mobile devices have smaller screens, touch or click interaction, and fewer pixels. In addition, each device is different in sizing, interaction, and operating system which can make reports render differently per device. When starting a mobile reporting project, it is important to create a matrix of your organization's devices and device operating systems for review. First, this information should be compared with the product compatibility information for BI Mobile as discussed in the previous section. Second, the lowest common denominator should be determined in terms of screen size, device interactions, pixels, etc. so that reports can be designed to interact best with the smallest device. Organizations entering the mobile landscape should consider creating a plan for standardization of mobile devices to help with future support and compatibility concerns.

22.2.1   Supported Web Intelligence Features

A large number of features and functionalities are available within SAP Business-Objects Mobile. Web Intelligence report designers can leverage these key features when building reports for mobile consumption to provide a more relevant user experience:

▸ Setting a default document or folder to open automatically upon logging on

▸ Refreshing reports from the mobile device

▸ Viewing results using keypad shortcuts

▸ Navigating between reports using document linking

▸ Modifying prompt values to view filtered results

▸ Alerting when a specific document is modified, a condition is met, or a schedule is run

▸ Leveraging actions to launch an SMS, phone call, or email

▸ Saving documents locally for offline use mitigates network interruptions and minimizes mobile communication costs

▸ Sending report links by email

▸ Searching for mobile reports in the BI Launch Pad

▸ Drilling on report data for further analysis

▸ Tracking data changes using customizable highlighting

> **Note**
>
> Dynamic or cascading prompts in Web Intelligence documents are not supported for viewing with BI Mobile.

The key to creating a meaningful report for end users is to leverage the most important features available for consumption. There are also a number of report design considerations to accommodate for when building the mobile Web Intelligence document.

22.2.2 Report Design Basics

By utilizing best practices for mobile report design, mobile report developers can create meaningful content that can provide a powerful means of communication regarding the status of the business. Although the type of content used in the report (whether operational, financial, or statistical data) may vary between reports, the key concepts for report writing remain the same.

Use Predefined Mobile Templates

Included with the installation of BI Mobile are images available as templates to provide a sizing guide when creating mobile reports. Images are also available for use in alert icons. To access available skins, open the Report Properties dialog box by selecting FORMAT REPORT from the right-click menu when selected on the report canvas. Figure 22.2 shows the APPEARANCE tab of the Format Report dialog box. You can select default skins are create your own images to the appropriate sizing of your organization's devices by selecting an image saved to a file location, as shown in Figure 22.2.

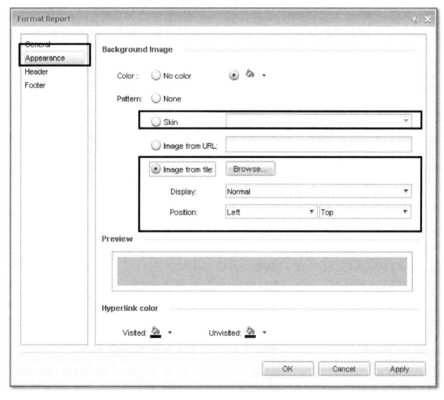

Figure 22.2 Appearance Tab of Format Report Dialog Box

Accommodate for Device Screen Size

When designing for multiple devices types, report designers should adjust the report content to fit the smallest size screen. If making content larger than the screen size, content should consume no more than two times the pixels of the device screen size. Format charts and tables paying close attention to the pixel width and height of each component on the canvas. Position control should be used to gain maximum screen usage. You can achieve maximum real estate by setting the positioning of the content to the upper top left of the page, as seen in Figure 22.3.

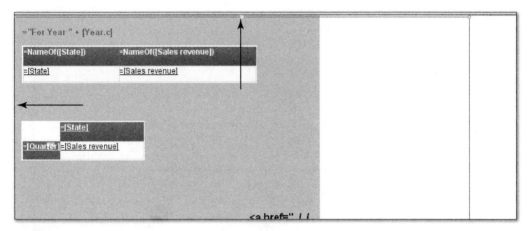

Figure 22.3 Web Intelligence Report Sample with Positioning

To achieve this, set the page header to zero and set the margins to zero for the left and top margins, as shown in Figure 22.4.

Use Mobile Device Simulator

You can see the resulting content as it will be viewed by the end user using a number of device simulators. By visiting the website of your organization's device manufacturers, you can download simulators to use in testing the report display. Your administrator should be able to provide more guidance and assistance in providing this option for your use in report design.

Group Mobile Documents in the BI Launch Pad

The BI Mobile application lets you set a default report or folder for viewing when users navigate to the application on their devices. Organizing mobile documents in a designated folder or category in BI Launch Pad enables the end users to better organize on-device content and quickly navigate to available reports.

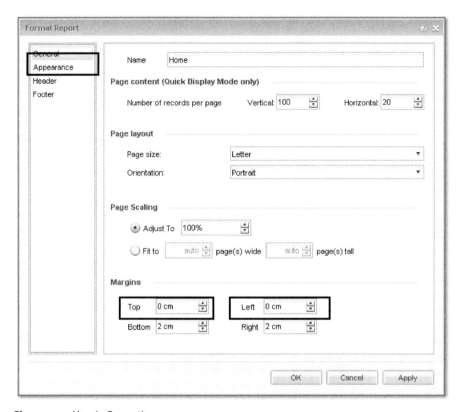

Figure 22.4 Margin Properties

Use Summarized Data

Mobile reporting maintains functionality similar to an executive dashboard. It should be designed in a summarized view with small datasets. Further interaction, such as report linking and drill, can provide added data for the viewer's needs.

Shorten Names and Use Abbreviations

Due to the limited canvas on the devices, it is important to shorten names and labels by using abbreviations (ex: use AZ, not Arizona). Abbreviate numbers with labels. 1K instead of 1,000 can be created by dividing the source data by 1,000 and using number formatting in the report. Font sizes should be limited to three sizes used to differentiate titles, labels, and data.

- Small—Arial 9 pt
- Medium—Arial 12 pt
- Large—Arial 15 pt

Leverage Report Linking

By default, report tabs are converted to a selection list as a home page on a mobile report as seen in Figure 22.5. Report designers should make the tab names short and meaningful for the end user. Names should also be limited to 20 characters or fewer.

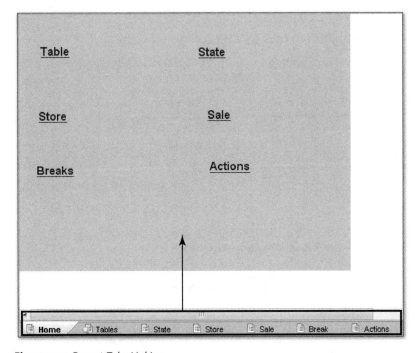

Figure 22.5 Report Tabs Linking

22.2.3 Utilizing Images

Skins provide a model for device screen size of a sampling of mobile devices. By importing skins into your document, you can optimize the viewing experience and ensure the report design maintains appropriate device sizing requirements.

Further discussion of how to import skins appeared earlier in this chapter and was detailed in Figure 22.2.

Images of alerting icons are also available for use in designing your Web Intelligence reports. These provide an easy way to communicate key information that is understandable to the report customer at a glance, enabling him to quickly respond to business needs.

Alerting provides a powerful means of communication to users. Additional alerting features include embedded actions in reports to allow users to communicate quickly to other individuals in the organization and collaborate on business decisions.

22.2.4 Creating Embedded Actions and Document Links

The actions available for embedding in your mobile reports depend on your business needs. These actions provide the end users with a means of quickly and easily collaborating on the report content. Frequently used actions include calling a designated person or sending an email.

Embedded Actions

Table 22.1 defines the available embedded actions in Web Intelligence 4.x along with a description of each action.

Action	Description
Phoneto	Dials a predefined phone number automatically
Smsto	Sends a text message to a predefined recipient
Plookup	Retrieves a number from the device address book to use with the `phoneto` or `smsto` commands
Elookup	Retrieves an email address from the address `bookto` use with the `mailto` command
Mailto	Sends an email message to a predefined recipient

Table 22.1 Embedded Actions

When using actions, there is a defined syntax to enable the functionality in your mobile reports. Table 22.2 details the syntax and supported parameters for each action.

Action	Syntax	Parameters
Phoneto	`laction://phoneto?num='0123456789'$`	num, desc
Smsto	`laction://smsto?num='0123456789'$`	num, desc
Plookup	`laction://phoneto?num=laction://plookup?name='jim brogden'$$`	name, desc
Elookup	`laction://mailto?to=laction://elookup?name='jim brogden'&subject='EBITDA'&body=Why is EBITDA below budget this month?'$$`	name, desc
Mailto	`laction://mailto?to='jim'&subject='EBITDA'&body='Why is EBITDA below budget this month?'$`	to, subject, body, desc

Table 22.2 Action Syntax

Prompts can also be based on actions to create further interaction with the end user consuming the mobile report. There is also a defined syntax to be used with prompts. `@paramName` indicates that the following text designates a prompt value. `Label` is the string that will display on the menu of the mobile device. `Type` is optional but is used to designate the data type that the user is allowed to input in the prompt value. `defaultValue` is also optional, and designates the default prompt value to be used. As with the other actions, `$` indicates the end of the action statement.

This is the format of proper syntax:

```
@paramName='Label|type|defaultValue'$
```

Document Linking

Web Intelligence reports deployed to mobile devices support document linking as defined in Chapter 14. Refer to this chapter for more information on how to create document links. Linking can provide powerful functionality to consolidate data and give access to numerous reports within a single interface providing ease of use for the end user.

22.3   On-Device Viewing, Analyzing, and Interacting

End users can view, analyze, and interact with Web Intelligence and Crystal Reports from their mobile devices. Report designers can create documents for mobile consumption, allowing further analysis and interaction to obtain the greatest value. Mobile reporting goes beyond basic report viewing by including drill, alerts, document linking, and more, as discussed in the previous section. This section provides basic information on how the end user consumes the report content. Consult the product user guide for more detailed information on this functionality and setup.

22.3.1   Viewing

To open a Web Intelligence document on your mobile device after logging on to the application, you must first select the document type: local documents, server documents, mobile-ready documents. You can also access the most recently viewed documents from the home page. Navigate to the document and select the title by either clicking on it or, if you have a touch screen device, tapping on the title. Select OPEN. Use the NEXT or BACK options to move between pages.

22.3.2   Analyzing

Report content can be further analyzed using the drill, document link, data tracking, and prompt options. Report designers set up this functionality to enable further analysis on the mobile device while maintaining maximum screen resolution.

Drilling

When drilling on Web Intelligence reports in BI Launch Pad, a drill up or drill down arrow appears next to a cell, indicating the drill functionality. The same is true when drilling on a cell on a Web Intelligence report on your mobile device. Click on or tap and hold on the arrow to drill on the report.

> **Note**
>
> Web Intelligence documents are available for drill from mobile devices only if the report has been saved in the repository with the drill mode turned on.

Document Links

Document links are available in mobile reports to provide links to additional report content that can provide a more detailed view. Clicking on or tapping and holding on the document link will open up the new document for analysis.

Tracking Data Changes

The track data changes feature discussed in Chapter 17 can provide an added means of data analysis. When this feature is activated on a report, the tracked changes can be viewed as on reports within the BI Launch Pad.

Filtering with Prompts

Using prompts in mobile reports, you can allow the display of data to be streamlined to a more relevant view to provide for more detailed viewing. Mobile report consumers can refresh a prompted report from their devices to filter their results.

22.3.3 Interacting

There are a number of ways to interact with mobile report data, from basic report refresh to complex alerting and actions. These features provide a customizable user experience increasing the value of the resource.

Actions

Embedded SMS, phone, and email commands provide a powerful tool for interaction within your mobile reports. Report cells are set up by the report designer containing actions that allow the end user to perform defined functions. By clicking on an action in your mobile report, you can automatically email a sales manager or call the office or send a text message to an associate. The actions are activated by selecting the cell containing the action then launching the device menu. From the menu, you may select the applicable action: call, email, or SMS.

Refreshing Data

Reports can be prescheduled to refresh to save mobile report consumers time. Large reports can take a long time to refresh and update on a device, so scheduled refreshes avoid this potential issue.

Subscribing to On-Device Alerts

Mobile report consumers can subscribe to alerts on specific Web Intelligence documents that contain alerters. Table 22.3 defines the types of alerters that must exist on a report in order for a user to create a subscription.

Alert Type	When Alert is Activated
Document alert	Document is modified on server.
Scheduled alert	Document schedule is executed on server. Document must have at least one recurrence.
Conditional data alert	Conditional alerter exists on document. User receives an alert each time condition is met.
Scheduled conditional data alert	Document schedule is executed and conditional alerter on document is met.

Table 22.3 Supported Alert Types

In order to subscribe to an alert, you can activate or deactivate alerts on your device for a document. To receive alerts, you must have BI Mobile running on your device with a connection to the server in order for it to receive the alert.

A number of additional options are available for mobile report consumers, including saving reports locally and subscribing to on-device alerts as discussed in other areas of this chapter. Figure 22.6 shows a mobile dashboard on the iPad device.

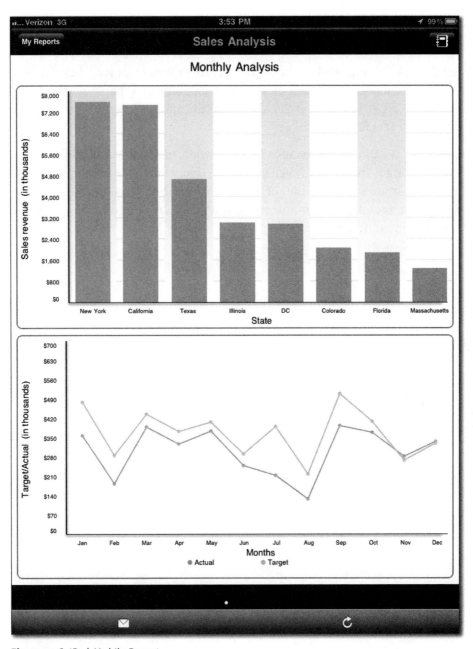

Figure 22.6 iPad Mobile Report

22.4 Summary

The on-device mobile integration capability of Web Intelligence with the BI Mobile application provides a powerful tool for collaboration and analysis. The functionality extends the reach of your Web Intelligence reports to a key audience to the organization providing the means for informed decision-making in a fast-paced, ever-changing market.

Chapter 23 delves into the features of the new Information Design Tool used for universe design. From basic design of the data layer to integration of multidimensional data sources to utilization of multiple database connections, the Information Design Tool provides an integrated source for creation of robust semantic layers for report design.

The SAP BusinessObjects universe plays a key role in solving business problems and creating a successful SAP BusinessObjects business intelligence solution.

23 Universe Basics: The Information Design Tool

Universe design is a topic worthy of its own book because of the wide range of capabilities available when connecting to data sources and designing robust semantic layers for reporting. Consequently, the goal of this chapter is to provide you with an introduction to the basic concepts of universe design and describe the product at the core of an SAP BusinessObjects business intelligence solution.

The SAP BusinessObjects universe is the secure semantic layer that shields business users from the complexities of the database and provides a reliable and consistent data retrieval experience across many of the SAP BusinessObjects tools. The universe is a secure window into the database or data warehouse in your organization.

Universes allow you to graphically visualize selected database tables and views and then create joins to match table relationships in the database schema. You can create objects and categorize them for the fields that business users need to solve business problems. Universes also allow you to incorporate business logic into objects with case statements and other types of calculations.

23.1 Universe Basics

The SAP BusinessObjects universe is the common semantic layer that allows report designers to access the database without having to know any information about the underlying data structure. Being able to query corporate data sources without writing SQL or MDX statements highlights the ease of use of the SAP BusinessObjects suite of business intelligence tools.

<table>
<tr><td>**The Importance of the Universe**</td></tr>
<tr><td>Each universe is a single file that contains a connection to your database and business "objects" aliases to database fields. An unlimited number of Web Intelligence reports are then sourced from a single universe. As the database evolves and structures change, updates flow through seamlessly to reports by making corrections in one place: the universe.</td></tr>
</table>

The success of your business intelligence projects depends heavily on the careful creation of this foundational layer. It's important to note that universes should be created by experienced developers with extensive knowledge of the business and the SQL language. Understanding the structure of the database schema and table relationships is critical in developing a functional universe.

Although the concepts are fairly simple and straightforward, your universes should be carefully designed and tested. Errors in universe design can have profound negative effects on reports, leading to long running queries and, worst of all, inaccurate results.

23.1.1 Introducing the Information Design Tool

In versions prior to SAP BusinessObjects Business Intelligence 4.0, universes were created and maintained using a tool called Designer, which was renamed in the 4.0 platform as the Universe Design Tool. Universes created with this legacy tool have a .UNV file extension. Although originally designed for use with query and analysis tools like Web Intelligence and its now-retired predecessor, Desktop Intelligence, universes constructed with the Universe Design Tool can also power enterprise reports created with Crystal Reports 2011, dashboards created with Dashboard Design (formerly Xcelsius), and Live Office.

SAP BusinessObjects Business Intelligence 4.0 introduces a new universe creation tool called the Information Design Tool. Universes created with the Information Design Tool have a .UNX rather than .UNV extension. In addition to Web Intelligence, universes constructed with the Information Design Tool can also power enterprise reports created with Crystal Reports for Enterprise, dashboards created with Dashboard Design, and Explorer.

> **Converting from Classic UNV Universes to New UNX Universes**
>
> Classic .UNV universes can be loaded from previous versions of the SAP BusinessObjects using the Upgrade Management Tool and continue to be used in Web Intelligence 4.0 without modification. However, to utilize new tools such as Crystal Reports for Enterprise and Explorer or new product features such as the Query Browser in Dashboard Design, classic universes must be converted to the new .UNX format. This procedure will be covered later in the chapter.

Although the Information Design Tool will ultimately replace the Universe Design Tool in an undetermined future version of SAP BusinessObjects Business Intelligence, both are installed with the other client tools such as the Web Intelligence Rich Client, Query as a Web Service (QaaWS) Designer, and Translation Management Tool.

The Information Design Tool supports a wide array of both relational and OLAP data sources, making Web Intelligence ideal for nearly any reporting situation. These platforms are supported by SAP BusinessObjects Business Intelligence 4.0:

▶ Apache Derby and Hadoop

▶ Generic ODBC, JDBC, OLEDB, and text files

▶ Greenplumb

▶ HP Neoview

▶ HyperSQL (HSQLDB)

▶ IBM DB2 and Informix

▶ Ingres

▶ Microsoft Access, Excel, and SQL Server

▶ Netezza

▶ Oracle RDBMS, Hyperion, mySQL, and EBS

▶ PostgreSQL

▶ Progress

▶ SalesForce.com

▶ SAP ERP, MaxDB, NetWeaver BW, and HANA

▶ SAS

▶ Sybase APS, SQL Anywhere, and Sybase IQ

▶ Teradata

You should always consult the Product Availability Matrix, or PAM, to confirm that the vendor and version of the desired data source is supported by the version of the BI platform you are deploying. The Product Availability Matrix is available from the SAP Service Marketplace at *http://service.sap.com/*.

23.1.2 Components of a Universe

The traditional Universe Design Tool has two main panels in its interface, as shown in Figure 23.1. On the right is the schema panel, where the designer defines a data foundation, the tables, and joins in the underlying relational structure. On the left is the universe panel, where the designer creates a business layer of classes and objects that users see when creating Web Intelligence documents. The universe specifies the universe connection, which defines where the data is physically located, but the connection is managed separately.

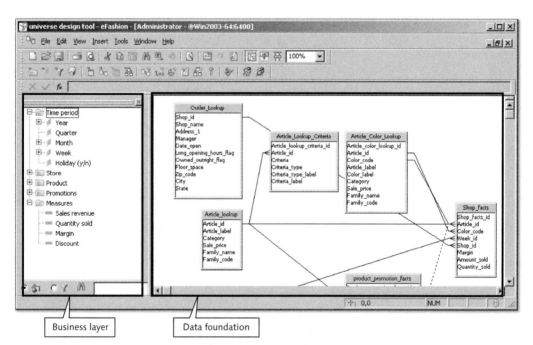

Figure 23.1 Business Layer and Data Foundation of the Classic Universe Design Tool (Formerly Designer)

The Information Design Tool organizes universes into projects. A common relational database universe project will contain three separate files:

- ▶ A connection (.CNX) or connection shortcut (.CNS) that defines the properties of the data source
- ▶ A data foundation (.DLX) that defines the tables and joins
- ▶ A business layer (.BLX) that defines the folders (formerly known as classes) and objects, and a universe connection shortcut that points to a defined universe connection in the repository

These three files are "compiled" by the Information Design Tool to generate a universe file (.UNX) that is stored in the SAP BusinessObjects repository. Figure 23.2 shows a view of the Information Design Tool.

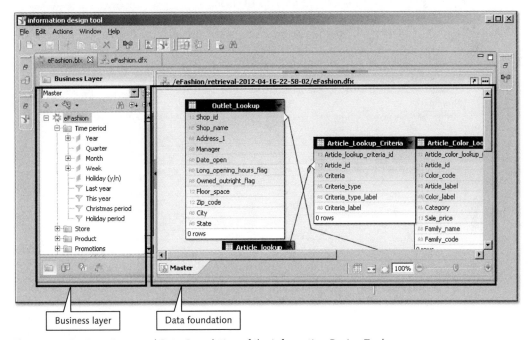

Figure 23.2 Business Layer and Data Foundation of the Information Design Tool

23.2 Creating a New Universe Project

To begin, launch the Information Design Tool from the Microsoft Windows Start menu. Select NEW • PROJECT, as shown in Figure 23.3.

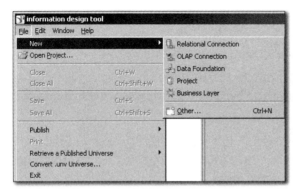

Figure 23.3 Creating a New Project from the File Menu

Next, assign a useful name for your universe project, as shown in Figure 23.4. Note that the project name doesn't need to match the universe name.

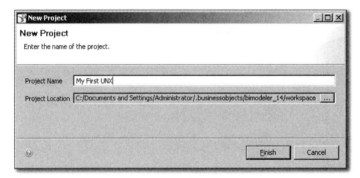

Figure 23.4 Assigning a Name to a New Information Design Tool Project

The project is now ready to accept connection shortcuts, data foundations, and business layers.

23.3 Creating Connections

Two types of connections can be created in the Information Design Tool, local and secured. A local connection can be used when working locally with the Web Intelligence Rich Client. However, a secured connection is required for connections that need to be accessible to users of the BI platform. Secured connections are stored remotely in an SAP BusinessObjects repository. Once created, secured connections can be referenced in universe projects by creating connection short-cuts, which have .CNS file extensions instead of the .CNX extension used for local connections or secured connections stored in the repository.

Both relational and OLAP secure connections are created in the Repository Resources window. You'll need to create a session to the desired SAP Business-Objects system by providing your user credentials. Make sure that the SAP Busi-nessObjects administrator has given you privileges to create and manage connections. SAP BusinessObjects Business Intelligence 4.0 adds a new capability to organize connections into folders. Choose the desired folder and use either the INSERT button at the top of the Repository Resources window or the right-click menu of the folder. From either menu, choose INSERT RELATIONAL CONNECTION, as shown in Figure 23.5. OLAP connections are similarly created by choosing INSERT OLAP CONNECTION (not shown).

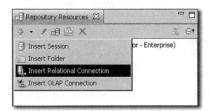

Figure 23.5 Inserting a New Relation Connection into the Repository Resources

Continue to define the connection using the New Relational Connection wizard.

Best Practices for Connections

The following are recommended best practices and settings for connections. These settings are recommended, but they may not be the best solutions for every environment. Each setting should be tested on the developer's own network and database.

▶ **Set the universe connection to disconnect after each transaction.**
This can help to avoid having long run queries bog down the connections.

▶ **Set the Array Fetch Size parameter to the appropriate size for each data-base environment.**
This is the setting that determines how many rows are fetched at a time from the database. A larger fetch size reduces the number of fetches required but has

a direct effect on system memory. There is no magic size, so it may need to be set differently depending on the database platform and its characteristics. Consult with your organization's database administrators to determine the best value.

▶ **Manage connection rights globally in the CMC to simplify the security.**
Except for rare occurrences, it will be sufficient to assign identical rights to all connections regardless of data source because user access is also controlled at the universe level. The typical exception to managing rights globally is when a connection points to sensitive data (such as employee salary) that should not be seen by all universe designers.

▶ **Beginning with SAP BusinessObjects Business Intelligence 4.0, connections can now be organized into folders, just like reports and universes.**
Consider creating a top level folder for each database platform (Microsoft SQL Server, SAP Sybase, SAP HANA, Teradata, etc.) to help document the source of data connections.

▶ **Create useful descriptions for universe connections in the CMC as self-documentation.**
By default, a new connection will have no description, but one can be added later via the CMC. It is also beneficial to document connections and their parameters outside of the business intelligence platform using Microsoft Excel or a wiki.

▶ **Use restraint when creating connections.**
Connections are deliberately separate from the data foundation to encourage reuse. It is not necessary or advisable to create separate connections for each universe, although there are exceptions when certain universes require different access rights to the database than is provided by an existing connection. To avoid redundant connections, it may be desirable to limit the number of users who have the security privileges required to create connections. These rights are managed in the Connections Management area in the CMC.

Now that the connection is created and tested, you can turn your attention to the development of the universe data foundation, which is covered in the next section.

23.4   Creating Data Foundations

A data foundation describes a collection of relational database tables and joins that can be used by one or more business layers. OLAP data sources do not have data foundations because the cube metadata serves as the data foundation. To begin creating a relational data foundation, right-click in the project and choose NEW • DATA FOUNDATION, as shown in Figure 23.6.

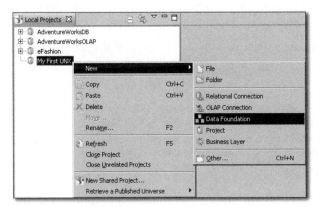

Figure 23.6 Adding a New Data Foundation to a Local Project

23.4.1   Inserting Tables into Data Foundation

You begin creating a data foundation by inserting tables. A list of available tables can be invoked from the Actions menu (shown in Figure 23.7), the INSERT button at the top of the data foundation layer, or from the right-click menu in the Schema window.

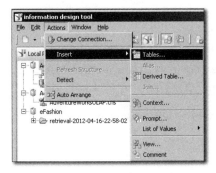

Figure 23.7 Inserting Tables into the Data Foundation

23.4.2 Inserting Joins into Data Foundation

Traditional join types are inner join, outer join, left join, right join, and full outer join. Other joins include the following:

▶ Equi-joins: Two tables are linked when the values in both fields are equal. This type of join is also considered a simple join.

▶ Theta joins: Theta joins are most commonly used in warehouses that don't contain keys and when an equivalent field doesn't exist in both the fact and dimension table. The operator can be anything except equal.

▶ Outer joins: Outer joins occur when one table contains rows that don't exist in the other table. You can select right outer joins, left outer joins, or full outer joins.

Note

It's important that you understand the data before applying these types of joins. Outer joins can have a significant impact on the speed at which a query is returned. This is especially true when views are used.

To create a join, begin by selecting the field in the first table, then dragging the mouse while holding the left button, as shown in Figure 23.8.

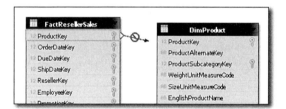

Figure 23.8 Join in Progress

Next, attach the join to the desired field in the second table, as shown in Figure 23.9. The default join is an equi-join. The question marks indicate that cardinality is not set. Join cardinality is an important topic that will be discussed shortly.

Once the initial join is created, double-click on the join to edit its properties, as shown in Figure 23.10.

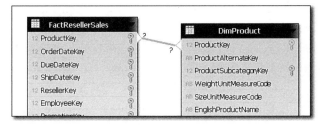

Figure 23.9 Completed Join

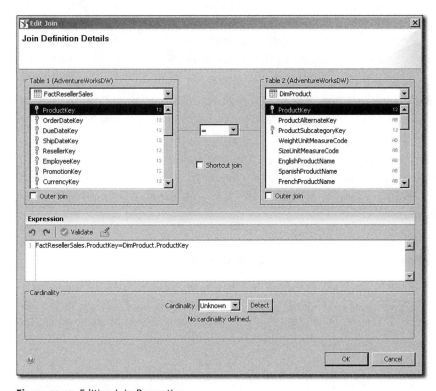

Figure 23.10 Editing Join Properties

Within this window, you can revise a variety of join settings. The following is a list of available join settings that can be edited.

▶ Cardinality: This setting explicitly forces the join to a one-to-one, one-to-many, or many-to-many relationship. By selecting a one-to-many or many-to-many relationship, a crows-foot is added to the join line connecting the two tables.

▶ Detect Cardinality: This setting is used to detect the type of relationship that exists between the two tables.

▶ Set Outer Joins: Two checkboxes labeled OUTER JOIN are located just beneath each table. Check the box just beneath the table that requires all fields to be returned. If both boxes are checked, a full outer join will be created.

▶ Setting Join Conditions: Six default conditions are available in a simple equi-join. These conditions are =, !=, >, <, >=, and <=.

▶ Between Condition: If two fields are selected from one of the tables, then the between condition is set by default. This is very useful when joining to a table that doesn't contain a key or field to join to with an equi-join. An example of this type of join is available in the demo Island Resorts Marketing universe connecting the Customer table to the Age_group table.

▶ Complex Join Condition: If your join requires additional modification to duplicate the business rules in the universe, a complex condition can be used to further customize the join.

▶ Shortcut Join: A shortcut join is an optional path that can be taken depending on which objects a user chooses in his query. Its purpose is to reduce the number of tables required in an SQL statement with the goal of improving query performance.

23.4.3 The Importance of Setting Cardinality

When creating joins in the data foundation, it is important to set cardinality. The cardinality setting has no effect on how SQL is generated. However, it does affect the behavior of the loop detection and resolution tools in the Information Design Tool.

Cardinality can be set automatically in the Information Design Tool but is best set manually after careful consideration of the relationships between tables. Cardinality is based on logic, but cardinality detection is based on data. Whether populated with sample data or production data, the actual data present may be too sparse. In such cases, the automatic cardinality detection may generate an inaccurate result. If the cardinality is inaccurate, the results of the loop detection tools such as Detect Loops, Detect Aliases, and Detect Contexts will be inaccurate also.

23.4.4 Detecting Loops

Loops are inherent in universes because a small number of tables are used to define a large number of potential queries. This creates a problem that rarely exists in a hand-crafted SQL statement: loops. An unresolved loop will result in an inaccurate SQL statement where too few rows of data are returned. Fortunately, the Information Design Tool, just like its Universe Design Tool predecessor, has built-in tools to help the designer resolve loops. Depending on join cardinality of the tables involved, a loop can be resolved with either an alias or a context, both of which are covered in the next section.

23.4.5 Detecting Aliases

Aliases are required when a single table performs multiple roles in the data model. For example, a calendar dimension may be used to represent order date, due date, and ship date. If only a single copy of the dimension table is used, multiple loops are created.

If the loop is unresolved, the universe will generate inappropriate SQL that returns fewer rows than expected, as shown in Figure 23.11. That is because the only rows returned by the query will be those where all three dates have the same value—an unlikely coincidence.

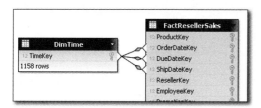

Figure 23.11 Unresolved Loop Requiring Aliases

The solution is to resolve the loop using aliased tables, either inserted manually or by the Detect Aliases feature, which is available from the menu at the top of the Data Foundation window, as shown in Figure 23.12.

The Detect Aliases feature studies the joins in the data foundation and identifies tables that are on the "one" end of multiple one-to-many joins. In our example of three date dimensions, the Detect Aliases feature will insert two new aliased tables and keep the original one in place (see Figure 23.13).

Figure 23.12 Detect Aliases Tool

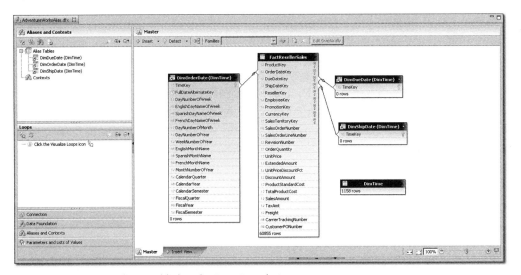

Figure 23.13 Aliases Added to the Data Foundation

Best Practices for Aliases

Once the loop is resolved, take care to ensure that any existing objects in the business layer use the correct aliased version of the table. For example, check that sale date dimension objects use the sale date alias.

One drawback to aliased tables is that the aliases are deleted from the data foundation if the original table is deleted. To prevent this, a best practice is not to create objects on any original tables that have been aliased; instead, use aliased tables exclusively in the data foundation. In the example above, notice that the original DimTime table is never used, only its aliases. Place the original table in an isolated corner of the data foundation canvas. These original tables should be clearly labeled with a comment, warning other universe designers of the consequences of deleting the tables, as shown in Figure 23.14.

Figure 23.14 Warning About Deleting Tables

23.4.6 Detecting Contexts

Contexts are required when a single table retains its meaning in the data model but must be joined to multiple other tables in the data foundation. A common example is a dimension table that must be shared by multiple fact tables. When all of the joins are created, a loop is formed, as shown in Figure 23.15. Without resolution, the SQL generated will result in the desired fact table being joined to other fact tables. The most obvious effect of unresolved loops that require contexts is inflated numerical values in measure objects, as the number of rows returned by the query is higher than it should be.

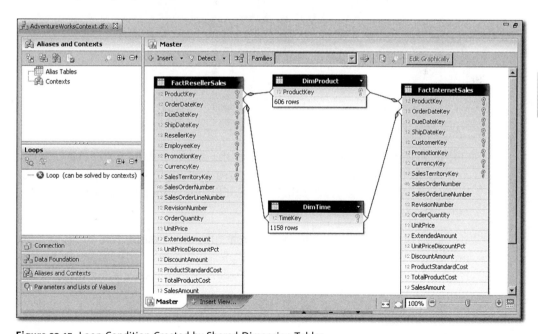

Figure 23.15 Loop Condition Created by Shared Dimension Tables

Like aliases, the loop conditions need to be resolved by the universe designer, either visually or using the built-in Detect Contexts feature, as shown in Figure 23.16.

Figure 23.16 Detect Contexts Button in Aliases and Contexts Area

In our example, two contexts have been identified by the Detect Contexts feature, as shown in Figure 23.17. The default context name is the name of the table containing only the "many" ends of a set of one-to-many joins. These names can be changed, if desired, by clicking on the default name.

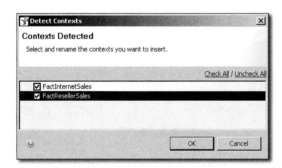

Figure 23.17 Detect Contexts Panel

Unlike aliases, the loop remains present in the data foundation; however, context definitions instruct the SQL generator to create multiple SQL statements, one for each context. Figure 23.18 highlights one of the two contexts that were created in our example.

Using this information will help you create the data foundation layers in your universes. The next step in the universe design process is to create a business layer of business objects organized into folders, which is covered in the next section.

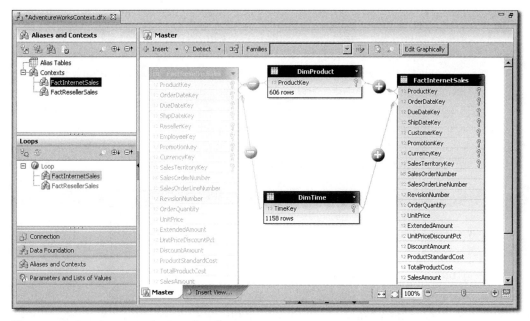

Figure 23.18 One Context in the Data Foundation Layer

23.5 Creating Business Layers

Once the data foundation is established, you can focus on creating the business layer, which is the view of the universe that a user will see in Web Intelligence. The business layer consists of folders, objects, and filters, as shown in Figure 23.19.

Figure 23.19 Unique Shapes for Each Object Type and Filter

Let's look at each separately.

Folders

Folders allow the universe designer to organize related objects into groupings related by the business user. The folder structure of the business layer should be organized according to how a business user visualizes the data model, not how a universe designer or data architect visualizes the data model. For example, customer data might exist in three separate database tables in the data foundation. Resist the temptation to automatically create three folders, one per table. Instead, organize the objects into a folder structure that makes it easy for business users to quickly find what they're looking for.

> **Note**
>
> Folders are known as classes in the Universe Design Tool.

Objects

An object exposes data in the data source to users. In a relational universe, an object can be a single database field, multiple database fields, or database functions. Any SQL that is valid in the database platform's Select clause can be used as the basis for an object.

There are three types of objects in a relational universe: dimension, attribute, and measure. In addition to those three object types, universes based on OLAP data foundations may have the following additional objects types:

▸ Hierarchies
▸ Analysis dimensions
▸ Named member sets
▸ Calculated members

> **Note**
>
> Attributes are known as details in the Universe Design Tool.

Dimension Objects

A dimension, like the one shown in Figure 23.20, is an object that maps to one or more table columns or a function in a database and represents an axis of analysis in a query. For example, Product, Customer, Geography, and Time are common dimensions.

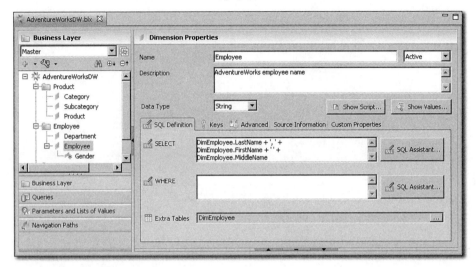

Figure 23.20 Dimension Object

Attribute Objects

An attribute is an object that provides additional information about another object in the universe, as shown in Figure 23.21. Attributes are generally specified when an object does not make sense on its own. For example, an object such as telephone number can be ambiguous but has greater clarity when associated with a parent object such as a customer or employee dimension. Attributes can be defined for dimensions, hierarchies, and levels.

Measure Objects

As their name indicates, measures are objects that measure aggregate data such as revenue, expenses, and quantity, as shown in Figure 23.22. It is important that measure objects specify both a database aggregate function (SUM, COUNT, MIN, MAX, and AVERAGE) as well as a projection function. Omitting the database aggregate may still deliver accurate results if the correct projection aggregate is used. But the resulting SQL statement will not have an appropriate GROUP BY clause. The SQL query will return a much larger result set than necessary, often with a dramatic negative impact to query performance.

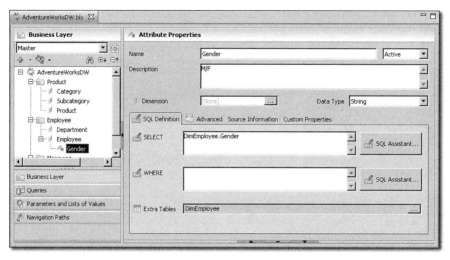

Figure 23.21 Attribute Object

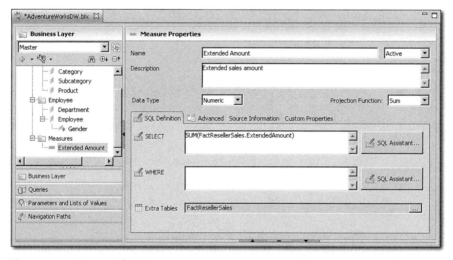

Figure 23.22 Measure Object

Filters

Filters are predefined optional conditions that users can add to queries to restrict the data returned, as shown in Figure 23.23. Users can create their own filters in the Web Intelligence query panel based on other objects. However, universe designers should provide filters for users for commonly used conditions or situations where filter logic is complex. Keeping the filter logic centralized in the universe instead of in multiple Web Intelligence documents makes maintenance easier should the logic for the condition change.

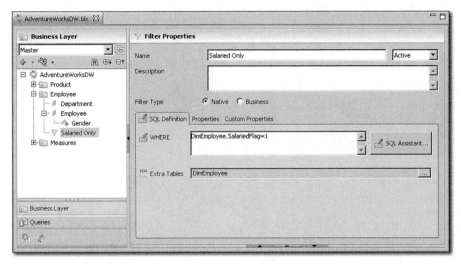

Figure 23.23 Filter Object

Various universe parameters can be set for the business layer:

▶ LIMIT SIZE OF RESULT SET TO *X* ROWS: Limits the amount of data that a query can return to avoid performance penalties

▶ LIMIT EXECUTION TIME TO *X* MINUTES: Limits the amount of time a query may execute to avoid performance penalties

▶ WARN IF COST ESTIMATE EXCEEDS *X* MINUTES: For data sources that provide cost estimates, notifies the user if a query will exceed this threshold

▶ ALLOW USE OF SUBQUERIES: Controls whether a user can create a subquery in the Web Intelligence query panel

▶ ALLOW COMPLEX OPERANDS IN QUERY PANEL: Controls whether a user can use complex operands like Both and Except in the Web Intelligence query panel

▶ ᴀʟʟᴏᴡ ᴜꜱᴇ ᴏꜰ ᴜɴɪᴏɴ, ɪɴᴛᴇʀꜱᴇᴄᴛ, ᴀɴᴅ ᴍɪɴᴜꜱ ᴏᴘᴇʀᴀᴛᴏʀꜱ: Controls whether a user can create a combined query

▶ ᴍᴜʟᴛɪᴘʟᴇ ꜱQʟ ꜱᴛᴀᴛᴇᴍᴇɴᴛꜱ ꜰᴏʀ ᴇᴀᴄʜ ᴍᴇᴀꜱᴜʀᴇ: Generates separate SQL statements for each table that contains measure objects

These parameters are shown in Figure 23.24.

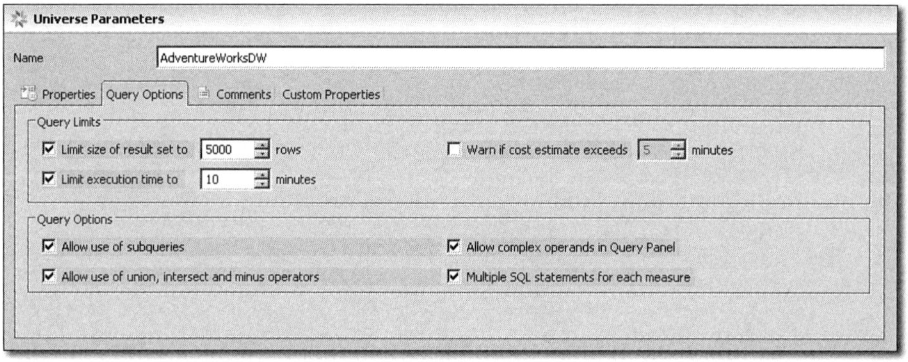

Figure 23.24 Universe Parameters

23.6 Creating Multisource Universes

The ability to create multisource universes is a new capability unique to the Information Design Tool and is not present in the classic Universe Design Tool. Using a subset of SAP Data Federator technology located on the BI platform, you can create universes that combine data from multiple disparate data sources. Data federation, also known as Enterprise Information Integration (EII), allows data to be queried in its original location without the need to use extract, transform, and load (ETL) tools like SAP Data Services to integrate the data in a data store such as a data mart or data warehouse.

To begin, create a universe project in the Information Design Tool that contains multiple connections, as shown in Figure 23.25.

Figure 23.25 Information Design Tool Project with Multiple Connections

Next, add a data foundation to the project, as shown in Figure 23.26.

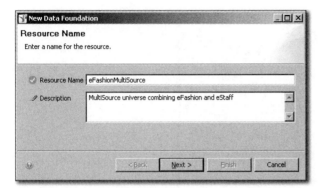

Figure 23.26 New Data Foundation

Assign the data foundation to a local project, as shown in Figure 23.27.

Figure 23.27 Selecting a Local Project

Choose MULTISOURCE-ENABLED as the data foundation type, as shown in Figure 23.28.

You are asked to authenticate to a CMS repository where the secured connections are stored, as shown in Figure 23.29.

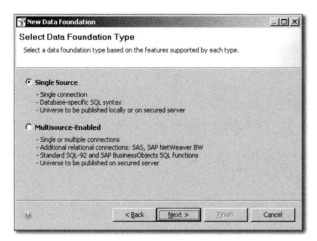

Figure 23.28 Selecting a Data Foundation Type

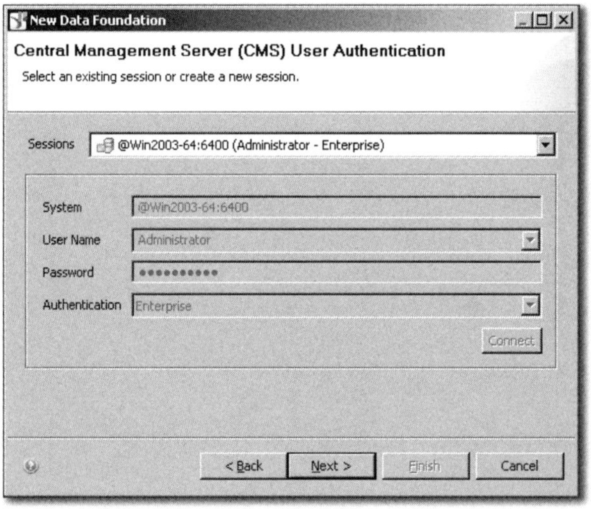

Figure 23.29 Creating a New Session

Choose which connection shortcuts currently in the project will be used for the data foundation, as shown in Figure 23.30.

Define the connection properties for each connection in the data foundation. In our example, we'll give the connection a more human-readable short name and assign a color to its table headers, as shown in Figure 23.31.

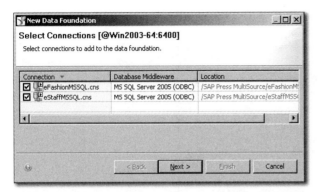

Figure 23.30 Selecting Connections to Add to Data Foundation

Define the connection properties for each connection.

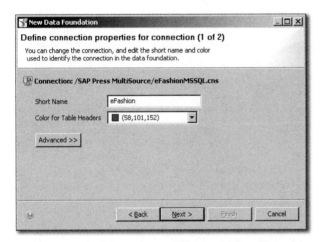

Figure 23.31 Defining Connection Properties for eFashion Connection

Next, define a short name and table header color for the second connection, as shown in Figure 23.32.

Next, add a data foundation on top of the multisource data foundation, as shown in Figure 23.33. Notice that the unique table header colors make it easy to identify the data source used by each table.

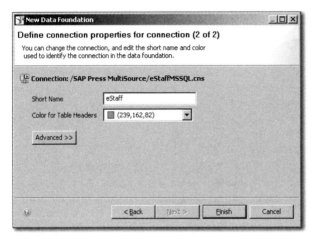

Figure 23.32 Defining Connection Properties for eStaff Connection

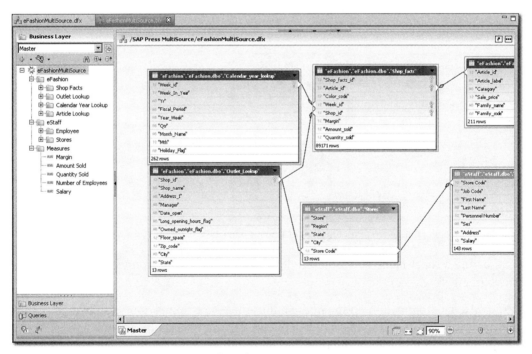

Figure 23.33 eFashion and eStaff Combined in Same Universe

Once the universe is published, confirm that the multisource joins return desired results, as shown in Figure 23.34.

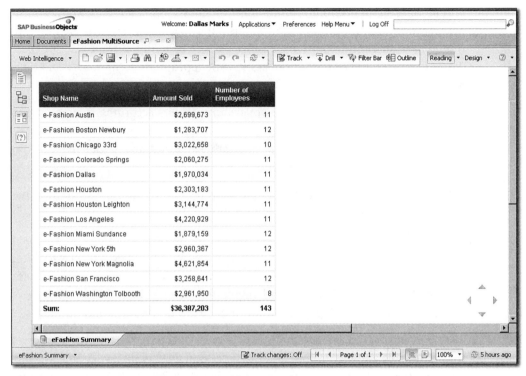

Figure 23.34 eFashion and eStaff Data Retrieved Using Single Universe

This section explored how to create universes that combine data from multiple disparate data sources. We'll cover general best practices for designing universes in the next section.

23.7 Universe Design Best Practices

Although the user interface and workflows for creating universes differ between the Information Design Tool and the classic Universe Design Tool, many of the best practices are identical.

23.7.1 Design with the Business User in Mind

The most important best practice is to design with the business user in mind. Database field names are often quite different from business terms and should always be translated to appropriate object names with commonly known business terminology. In addition to having useful names, each object in the universe should have a clear description. Consider partnering with a subject matter expert (SME) from the user team that can assist with appropriate terminology and definitions.

We recommend that you organize objects into folders according to how an end user might draw the data model on a cocktail napkin, not how it is actually modeled. Use subfolders where appropriate, rather than a single folder that has too many objects to be easily understood.

For multinational organizations, a single universe can be translated into multiple languages using the Translation Management Tool.

Incorporate business logic into universe objects whenever possible to facilitate consistent report development by reducing the need for report-level variables. Business logic such as complex case statements or filter conditions can be centrally maintained in the universe. Changing the business logic in one universe is much easier than adjusting it in dozens or even hundreds of reports.

Keep universes as small and simple as possible by keeping the number of objects to a reasonable amount. The definition of "reasonable" is subjective, but we recommend that you limit your universe to fewer than 200 or 300 objects as a rule of thumb. Let the reporting requirements, rather than the complexity of the data source, determine the appropriate size of the universe. Larger universes are technically feasible but not user-friendly. If users are confronted with a large universe with complex folder structures and thousands of objects, they are likely to send reporting requirements back to the business intelligence team, defeating any corporate self-service reporting strategy. By limiting the universe size, you tend to reduce future maintenance costs and increase end-user productivity.

Because the Information Design Tool separates the data foundation from the business layer, an appropriate solution may be a single expansive data foundation that is shared by multiple business layers, each generating a universe for a logical subset of the data source.

23.7.2 Design for Performance

Universes can be constructed on a wide variety of relational and OLAP database platforms. Although they can be constructed on nearly any data model, creating universes directly on transactional systems is not recommended due to the complex SQL required for analytical reporting. Transforming the data into a star or snowflake schema or OLAP cube will result in better-performing universes.

23.7.3 Design for Maintainability

The requirements for a universe will change over time and therefore require maintenance. Frequently, the universe designer performing the maintenance is not the original universe author, who may no longer be part of the organization. Arrange the tables visually in a logical manner, so the universe is easy to navigate. And take advantage of the new families feature to add color coding to related tables.

Designers should plan for evolution. This includes setting expectations with users for an iterative (which has multiple phases), rather than waterfall (one big deliverable after a long wait), approach to universe design. It may be possible to give users a simple universe that is easy to create and delivered in a short time frame. The first version of the universe may not answer all of the business questions, but it can address a substantial number of them while the business intelligence team refines the second, more extensive, version of the universe.

23.7.4 Design for Governance

Develop your organization's own standards for universe design and development. This is particularly important if universe designers are distributed throughout the organization, outsourced resources, or both. Create governance processes that ensure that corporate standards are followed prior to promoting a universe to the production environment.

23.8 Converting an Existing Universe to a .UNX Universe

Universes created by the classic Universe Design Tool or migrated from earlier versions of the BI platform can be utilized by Web Intelligence 4.0 without modifications. However, Crystal Reports for Enterprise 4.0, Explorer 4.0, and some of the new query capabilities of Dashboard Design 4.0 (formerly Xcelsius) can only be used with the new universe format.

The Information Design Tool can convert classic universes in the .UNV file format to universes in the .UNX format. In this section, we'll cover the steps necessary to convert the sample eFashion.unv universe to eFashion.unx.

The original eFashion universe as seen from the Universe Design Tool is shown in Figure 23.35.

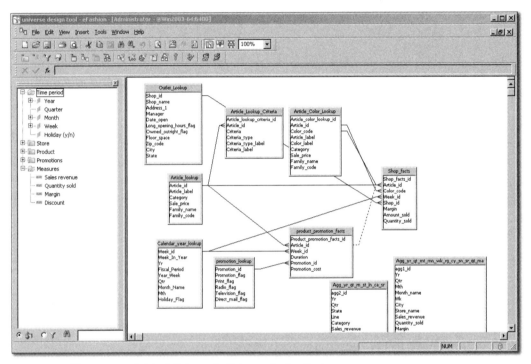

Figure 23.35 Original Universe in Universe Design Tool

To begin, select Convert .unv Universe… from the Information Design Tool File menu shown in Figure 23.36.

Next browse to the location of the original .UNV universe, as shown in Figure 23.37. Notice that this file can be retrieved from either the local file system or from an SAP BusinessObjects repository.

If you choose a universe from the repository, you will be asked to provide valid credentials, as shown in Figure 23.38.

Figure 23.36 Converting UNV Universe

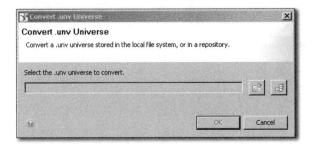

Figure 23.37 Specifying the Original UNV Universe to Convert

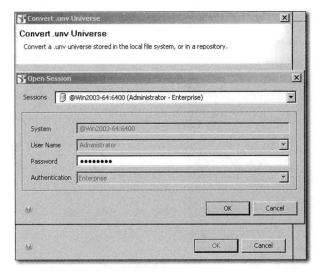

Figure 23.38 Open Session to CMS

Browse through the universe folder structure and identify the desired .UNV universe to convert. In this example, the eFashion.unv is being retrieved from the WEBI UNIVERSES folder, as shown in Figure 23.39.

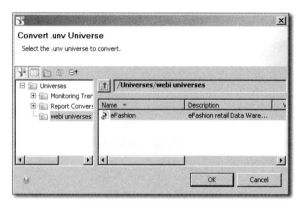

Figure 23.39 Choosing UNV Universe

Next, choose the DESTINATION REPOSITORY FOLDER, which can be identical to the source, shown in Figure 23.40. You can also choose to add the converted .UNX to an existing local project, convert @prompt expressions into universe-named parameters, or save the local project copy for all users, as shown in Figure 23.40.

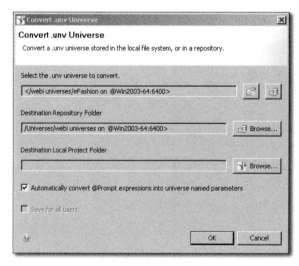

Figure 23.40 Setting Destination Repository Folder and (Optional) Local Project Folder

The Information Design Tool will convert the .UNV, publish the corresponding .UNX, and notify you of its success, as shown in Figure 23.41.

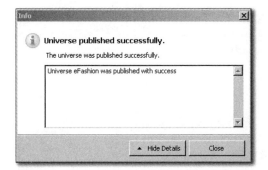

Figure 23.41 Universe Published Successfully

You can confirm that the universe was published to the desired folder by confirming using the CMC, shown in Figure 23.42. Notice the converted universe has an explicit .UNX suffix in its name.

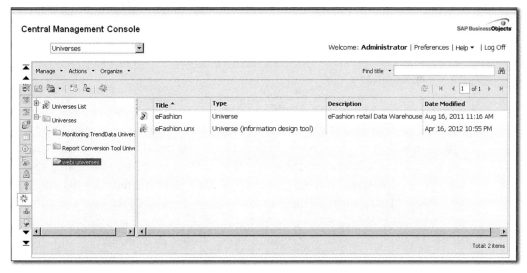

Figure 23.42 Verifying UNX Universe in CMC

The converted universe can now be viewed and modified from the Information Design Tool, shown in Figure 23.43.

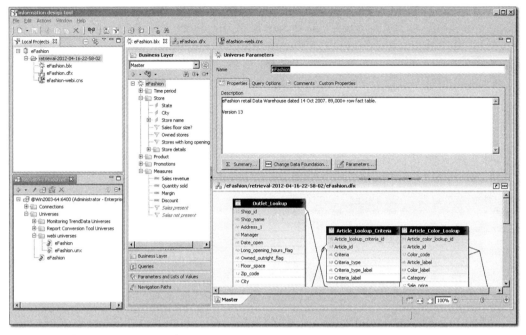

Figure 23.43 Converted Universe in IDT

23.9 Summary

The universe is SAP's patented semantic layer that allows non-technical business users to access and analyze corporate data sources. Universe design is a topic robust enough for its own book. In this chapter, we provided a basic understanding of how the Information Design Tool is used to create universes and how it varies from the classic Universe Design Tool. Universes created with the Information Design Tool consist of three distinct components that are assembled into a universe: the connection, data foundation, and the business layer. More information is available from the Information Design Tool's Help menu, which includes links to online tutorials, as shown in Figure 23.44.

Universes created using the Information Design Tool combine three separate entities: data source connections, data foundations, and business layers. The resulting universe is then published to an SAP BusinessObjects repository with a .UNX file extension.

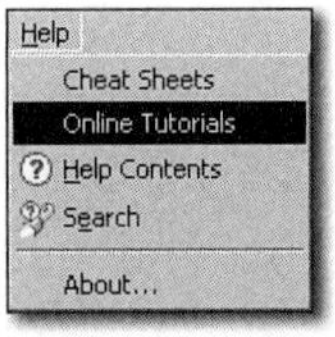

Figure 23.44 Information Design Tool Help Menu

Although universes created by the classic Universe Design Tool can be utilized by Web Intelligence 4.0 without modification, the desire to use other tools in the SAP BusinessObjects BI 4.0 suite may make it necessary or desirable to convert these universes to the new .UNX format using the Information Design Tool.

Feature Pack 3 (Service Pack 4) introduces you to an extensive collection of enhancements to the SAP BusinessObjects Business Intelligence 4.0 platform, including several improvements to Web Intelligence.

24 Feature Pack 3 (Service Pack 4) Enhancements

The enhancements to Web Intelligence 4.0 in Feature Pack 3 (Service Pack 4) increase the functional capabilities for displaying hierarchical data sourced from BEx queries, allow for more consistent and repeatable formatting styles across reports, and improve color assignment capabilities for designing reporting components that more closely fit with client requirements and design conventions. These are just a few of the enhancements introduced in Web Intelligence with Feature Pack 3 (Service Pack 4). The trend of the recent enhancements is to provide users and developers with the new tools for displaying information with improved visual capabilities.

This chapter describes the following latest enhancements of Feature Pack 3 (Service Pack 4) as they relate to Web Intelligence, and will provide a functional overview of each new feature:

▶ Color enhancements
▶ Style sheet modification
▶ Enhanced sorting
▶ Zone formatting
▶ Hierarchical navigation
▶ Waterfall chart

Let's begin by examining color enhancements.

24.1 Color Enhancements

A variety of new color enhancements provides users with more flexibility for customizing the appearance of components. You can assign colors to specific charted elements with as few as two clicks.

Modify columns, lines, and slices in pie charts by selecting the charted element then changing the background color icon found within the FORMAT tab and STYLE subtab. Figure 24.1 shows a new background color being assigned to a slice on a pie chart.

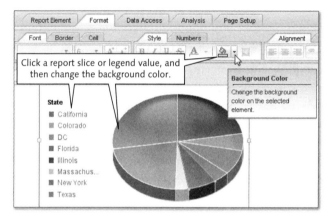

Figure 24.1 Changing the Color of a Pie Chart Element

When you assign colors to element values in charts, the colors remain synchronized throughout the report, including when displayed within a section. Colors in pie charts can be changed by selecting a legend value or pie slice and then changing the background color.

> **Note**
>
> Changes to specific colors override the previous color assignments defined by the selected palette style. After a color has been changed, switching the palette style will override any changes made to background colors of select elements.

Color Changes in Column Charts

You can also change the color of charted dimensional values in column charts can also be done by selecting a column and legend value, and then changing the background color. This method will change all the bars to the new background color selected. To assign a new color to each bar, right-click on the chart and select ASSIGN DATA, then select the same dimensional object in the REGION COLOR section as the object displayed in the CATEGORY AXIS section.

Figure 24.2 shows the Assign Data window and the optional REGION COLOR selection category. By adding the same object to the REGION COLOR, a new color will be assigned when the dimensional value of each bar changes.

Figure 24.2 Adding Region Color to Column Chart

Modifying Chart Style

In addition to changing the palette style of a chart, you can select from the three different chart styles available for quickly changing the appearance of a chart. Figure 24.3 shows the chart styles as they'll appear when a chart has been selected:

- ▶ NORMAL STYLE: Provides classic solid color visualizations
- ▶ FLASHY STYLE: Enhances the appearance of chart elements to gradient 3D-like effects
- ▶ HIGH CONTRAST: Generally assigns black as the background color of the charted values

Figure 24.3 Chart Styles

Tip

Switching the chart style between normal style and flashy style is most effective when the depth setting has been assigned to 2D Look rather than 3D Look.

The depth setting is located in the Format Chart window inside the global property grouping and within the Palette and Style category. Use this setting to set the chart appearance as 2D look or 3D look.

24.2 Style Sheet Modification

Report designers now have the capability to quickly and easily create reports that contain a consistent set of style features as other reporting documents. This new feature allows designers to change the default style of a Web Intelligence 4.0 report by importing a customized style sheet or CSS file.

Users can also export all of the existing formats created in a report to a new, unique style sheet. This is a very powerful feature because it gives report designers the freedom to modify a wide variety of visual settings through the multi-tabbed toolbar, and then save all of those settings into a single CSS file that can be applied to other reports.

To change the default style of a report, click on the PROPERTIES tab while in design mode, and then select the DOCUMENT button shown in Figure 24.4.

Changing the Default Style

Located in the lower left corner of the Document Properties window is a new category listed as DEFAULT STYLE. Within this category is a single button titled CHANGE DEFAULT STYLE. Click on this button to import a new CSS file or export the existing formatting settings to a new CSS file.

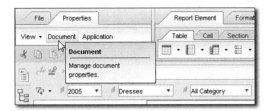

Figure 24.4 Opening the Document Properties

Figure 24.5 shows the bottom portion of the Document Summary window with the CHANGE DEFAULT STYLE option.

Figure 24.5 Changing the Default Style in a Report

After clicking on the CHANGE DEFAULT STYLE button, a new window will be loaded that provides three options. These options are IMPORT STYLE, EXPORT STYLE, and RESET STANDARD DEFAULT STYLE. Figure 24.6 shows the DEFAULT STYLE window with the three options.

Figure 24.6 Importing, Exporting, or Resetting the Default Style

Clicking on IMPORT STYLE allows you to search for a local CSS file to assign to the current Web Intelligence reporting document. Clicking on EXPORT STYLE allows you to save the formatting within the current document to a CSS file. Be sure to choose an appropriate name, folder, and path when saving the CSS file. The file can also be shared with other users or published to a shared directory on a network.

After you've exported a reporting style as a local CSS file, you can begin making edits to the file outside of Web Intelligence and then re-importing into the current report or any other Web Intelligence report in version 4.0 with Feature Pack 3 (Service Pack 4) installed.

Open the CSS file with your preferred file editor, such as Notepad or WordPad. The following is a sample of the settings that can be manually edited in the CSS file:

▶ Font-family

▶ Font-size

▶ Color

▶ Font-weight-bold

▶ H-Spacing

▶ V-Spacing

▶ Page-records-horizontal

▶ Page-records-vertical

▶ Page-format-dimension-width

▶ Page-format-dimension-height

▶ Page-format-margin-top

▶ Page-format-margin-left

▶ Page-format-margin-bottom

▶ Page-format-margin-right

▶ Background-color

▶ Background-fill

▶ Background type

▶ Text-v-align

▶ Text-align

▶ Min-width

▶ Min-height

Formatting is grouped into several functional sections that match the structure of a report. The following is a sample of the formatting groups that contain editable formatting sections:

- General settings
- Report
  - Page body section
  - Page header
  - Page footer
- Cell
- Table

Standardizing on a collection of settings defined in a CSS file provides for a more consistent presentation of reports and a more cohesive overall reporting solution. This feature also saves report developers a significant amount of time compared to working in previous versions and making configuration changes to individual reports.

24.3 Enhanced Sorting

Sorting in charts and data tables is a very common requirement when analyzing data in reports. This analysis feature has been enhanced in Feature Pack 3 (Service Pack 4) to provide users with more flexibility in displaying charted data.

Sorting can become a necessary function when displaying data from two or more measures or dimensional objects. The Region Color feature available when assigning data to charts provides this capability by allowing charts to be created that display two dimensional values for a single measure. Depending on the values being charted, this combination of measures and dimensions can be difficult to interpret. To ease the complexity of displaying and analyzing this type information, the sort feature now allows you to sort by dimension, measure, or by the dimensional value selected in the Region Color section.

Figure 24.7 shows the Sort menu with a column chart selected that contains two dimension objects and a single measure object.

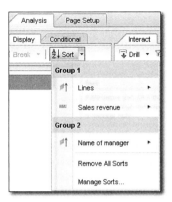

Figure 24.7 Sorting by Group

In Figure 24.7, the [Name of manager] object is being used in the Region Color section while the [Lines] object is the primary Category Axis object. With this feature, you can apply sorts to dimensions in both groups and also to any measure object in the chart. Figure 24.8 shows a chart being sorted by two dimensions from separate groups: [Lines] and [Name of Manager].

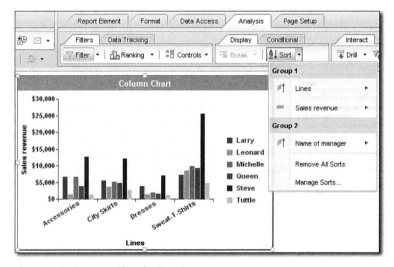

Figure 24.8 Sorting a Chart by Two Dimensions

Multigroup charting displays information in a compound format and is ideal when the number of values in both dimension objects is relatively small.

Custom Sorting

To create a custom sort, click on the small downward arrow to the right of the Sort function and then select the MANAGE SORTS option. This menu provides additional options for customizing sorts on the selected chart. The following options are available in the Manage Sorts window:

▶ Revise the priority of sorts of more than one sort has been added

▶ Modify the direction or order of a chart between ascending or descending

▶ Add a new object to be sorted or remove an existing sort

▶ Define a custom order to sort an object

▶ Reset an existing custom sort object back to ascending or descending

Sorting in a Cross Table (Crosstab)

Compound sorting isn't reserved for charts only. Cross table report elements can also contain multiple sorts applied to the dimension objects in both the columns and rows in the table.

Figure 24.9 shows the sort options that are available when a cross table is selected, the [Category] object is assigned to the Horizontal Axis, and the [Region] object is assigned to the Vertical Axis. You can apply sorting to objects in the COLUMNS and ROWS sections. Use the MANAGE SORTS option to set up custom sorting on either object.

Figure 24.9 Applying Sorts to a Cross Table

24.4   Zone Formatting

Zone formatting gives report designers the capability to modify every aspect of a chart by using the tools provided in the FORMAT tab. The original and more comprehensive method of applying visual changes to charts requires entering the Format Chart window to apply property changes. There, you can make properties and formatting changes to adjust the existing settings within the chart. Properties are categorized into several functional groupings for a complete collection of adjusting settings in one panel.

In addition to the functionality provided in the Format Chart window, zone formatting allows report designers to make changes instantly to a chart zone with only a single click. Make these property adjustments by selecting a chart and then using the various options located in the FORMAT tab.

The following chart zones and properties can be modified using the properties available in the FORMAT tab:

▸ Chart title: Font, border, style, alignment

▸ Chart: Border, background color, size

▸ Value axis: Font, style, numbers

▸ Category axis: Font, style

▸ Axis labels: Font, border, style

▸ Legend: Background color

▸ Legend title: Font, border, style, alignment

You can modify charts quicker than ever by using this new time-saving feature.

24.5   Hierarchical Navigation

Display and interact with hierarchical data retrieved from BEx queries with components ideally suited for viewing multidimensional data. Data tables in Web Intelligence take on a whole new appearance with hierarchical data, and they provide the capability to expand and collapse hierarchy members to view data at more granular levels.

Once you have connected to a BEx query, select members from one or more levels by dragging a hierarchy to the Result Objects pane in the Query Panel. Specific members can also be selected from different levels to create a customized view of the data.

Figure 24.10 shows the Member Selector window displayed when selecting members of a hierarchy in the Result Objects screen in the Query Panel.

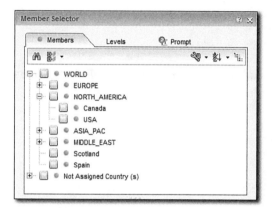

Figure 24.10 Selecting Values from a Hierarchy with the Member Selector

Figure 24.11 shows the LEVELS tab in the Member Selector window, which you can use to access a member through a selected level. Check ENABLE LEVELS to make level-based selections. All member values will be returned through the selected level since levels cannot be skipped using the level-based selection method.

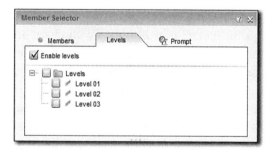

Figure 24.11 Selecting Levels in a Hierarchy

Navigating Hierarchical Data in the Report Panel

Hierarchical data is analyzed in the Report Panel with expandable and collapsible member values. Figure 24.12 shows a hierarchy retrieved from a BEx query and aggregated at the highest level. Click on the plus (+) symbol beside the member to expand and view the children in the second level of the hierarchy.

Country Hier with L	Order Amount	Order Quantity
⊞ WORLD	242,431,244.6	266,818

Figure 24.12 Hierarchical Data Aggregated at the Highest Level

For deeper analysis, continue to expand the child values to view all descendants in a hierarchy. Figure 24.13 shows values from three different levels.

Country Hier with L	Order Amount	Order Quantity
⊟ WORLD	242,431,244.6	266,818
⊞ EUROPE	25,977,635.54	31,009
⊟ NORTH_AMERIC	202,401,620.34	219,944
Canada	17,398,982.36	17,754
USA	185,002,637.98	202,190
⊞ ASIA_PAC	7,656,112.66	9,065
⊞ MIDDLE_EAST	1,540,410.62	2,443
Scotland	250,070.16	408
Spain	4,605,395.28	3,949

Figure 24.13 Expanded Hierarchical Data

Hierarchical Navigation in Charts

You can visually display and interact with hierarchical BEx data with charts in Feature Pack 3 (Service Pack 4). Existing data tables containing hierarchical can be converted to charts by right-clicking on the table and selecting TURN INTO and a chart. You can also create hierarchical charts by selecting a chart from the REPORT ELEMENT tab then choosing a chart to insert onto the report canvas. Once the chart has been added, drop a hierarchy object and measure object from the list of available objects onto the chart. Figure 24.14 shows a hierarchical data set with the top two levels displayed.

You can interact with hierarchical charts by clicking on the member name to drill up or down the hierarchy. You can also right-click on a chart and then mouse over the HIERARCHICAL NAVIGATION option, as pictured in Figure 24.15, to expand.

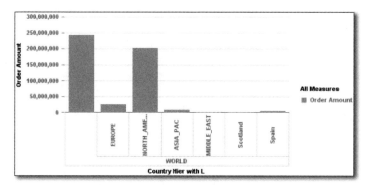

Figure 24.14 Hierarchical Data from a BEx Query in a Column Chart

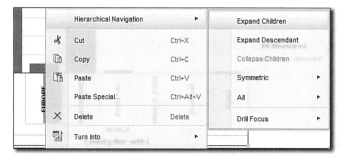

Figure 24.15 Right-Click for Hierarchical Navigation

The Hierarchical Navigation menu provides the capability the current selections to view children, descendants, or all members at lower levels.

24.6 Waterfall Chart

Waterfall charts have historically been used for displaying a running sum of values and the cumulative impact of a measure across a dimensional category. This chart type is new to the Web Intelligence chart repertoire, beginning in Feature Pack 3 (Service Pack 4) of version 4.0.

Figure 24.16 shows a simple waterfall chart created displaying the [Sales revenue] object for three cities (Austin, Dallas, and Houston) in the state of Texas.

It's customary to also include the total values when creating a waterfall chart. This measurement is not included by default in Web Intelligence and requires the report designer to make a configuration change in the Format Chart window.

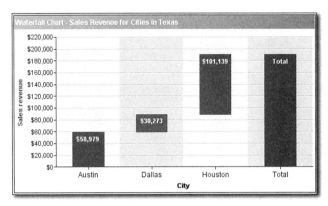

Figure 24.16 Waterfall Chart

After launching the Format Chart window, scroll down the list of modifiable properties in the Global grouping with the General category selected.

To add the totals to the chart, check the box labeled CALCULATE AND SHOW THE TOTAL located in the General section. Figure 24.17 shows the setting used to add the total value to the waterfall chart.

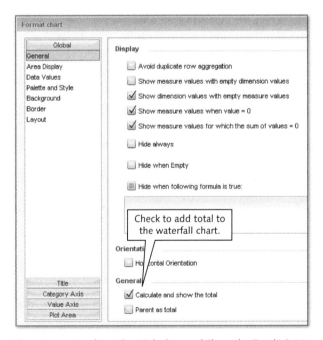

Figure 24.17 Applying the "Calculate and Show the Total" Setting

After checking the box to display the totals, be sure to click on APPLY • OK to accept the changes and return to the Report Panel.

24.7 Summary

Feature Pack 3 (Service Pack 4) delivers several useful enhancements to the SAP BusinessObjects BI 4.0 platform for creating reports with improved visual attributes. Chart colors can be modified on-the-fly with zone formatting, bars and column charts can be revised to display unique colors and the default style of a report can be completely replaced by importing a different CSS style file.

Users and report designers also continue to receive improved functionality in Web Intelligence with the addition of hierarchical navigation with BEx data in the Query Panel and Report Panel and the addition of the waterfall chart component.

Appendices

You can convert Desktop Intelligence reports from SAP BusinessObjects XI 3.x or XI R2 to Web Intelligence to be used in the BI 4.0 release of SAP BusinessObjects. Follow our checklist of best practices for a methodical conversion that produces a highly functioning series of Web Intelligence reports in SAP BusinessObjects BI 4.0 that were once Desktop Intelligence reports.

A   Converting Desktop Intelligence Reports to Web Intelligence Documents

Now that SAP BusinessObjects Desktop Intelligence (commonly known as "Deski") has reached its end-of-life stage with the release of SAP BusinessObjects BI 4.0, the conversion of Deski reports to Web Intelligence is an important topic for customers still using the classic desktop reporting tool. As the product known to many as the original SAP BusinessObjects full-client reporting tool, Desktop Intelligence offered advanced functional capabilities that set it apart from other reporting tools in the market. Many of these were so valuable to business users that many clients opted to continue to use the product.

In fact, even when its successor, Web Intelligence, began to receive an influx of enhancements and improved functionality, many customers found it difficult to trade in the classic desktop client for its zero-client reporting tool successor. Functional differences and the pervasiveness of locally saved documents have continually been cited as leading reasons for continued use of Desktop Intelligence.

By offering a greatly enhanced product that far exceeds the capabilities delivered in Desktop Intelligence, Web Intelligence 4.0 has made a big leap in minimizing the functional differences between the two products. But even with all the enhancements, there are still capabilities in the last version of Desktop Intelligence that are not available in Web Intelligence 4.0, such as Freehand SQL, custom VBA code, and the capability to export a report to HTML. These features and a few others can present challenges in migration and conversion efforts when upgrading from SAP BusinessObjects XI R2 or XI 3.1 to BI 4.0.

A.1   Report Conversion Tool

Except for a few complex scenarios, the Report Conversion Tool in SAP Business-Objects BI 4.0 does an excellent job of fully converting Desktop Intelligence reports into Web Intelligence documents. This appendix focuses on the major steps in performing a successful conversion from Desktop Intelligence to Web Intelligence. The conversion process checklist contains nine key steps for completing an effective report conversion from Desktop Intelligence to Web Intelligence.

> **Conversion Checklist: Desktop Intelligence to Web Intelligence**
>
> ▶ Analyze existing Desktop Intelligence report usage
> ▶ Identify users with Desktop Intelligence installed
> ▶ Publish locally saved Desktop Intelligence reports to the repository
> ▶ Prioritize, consolidate, and eliminate reports that are no longer needed
> ▶ Customize conversion plan and roadmap
> ▶ Perform report conversion
> ▶ Perform post-conversion analysis and validation
> ▶ Manually create unconverted reports
> ▶ Educate users on Web Intelligence 4.0

The steps outlined in the checklist describe general best practices for any Desktop Intelligence to Web Intelligence conversion project. The Report Conversion Tool is used to perform these types of conversions. It's important to know that even though a tool exists specifically for performing conversions, almost every conversion will require some level of manual rework to achieve 100% success.

A.1.1   Analyze Existing Desktop Intelligence Report Usage

Before you create an in-depth conversion plan or rely on a cookie-cutter roadmap to conversion, it's critical to understand what you're dealing with in terms of Desktop Intelligence report existence and usage. We recommend that you perform a comprehensive review of the reporting documents published to the repository in order to begin creating an inventory of Deski reports currently in use.

You can determine actual usage by enabling auditing in the source system to audit the events of the Desktop Intelligence application. Usage statistics are a very powerful indicator of the value of a report. Since Desktop Intelligence is a legacy reporting tool, it's possible that many reports in production have a very small viewership and can be consolidated or eliminated rather than converted. On the other hand, you may discover that a number of published Deski reports are still frequently viewed by business users. The priority to convert these reports to Web Intelligence is high.

The goal of this step is to determine the number of high-value and high-visibility reports to convert to Web Intelligence. It's also to determine which reports can be eliminated. Take this opportunity to perform some clean-up on the production system before attempting to convert every Deski report to Business Intelligence 4.0.

> **Note**
>
> The number of existing Desktop Intelligence reports is an important statistic to the system administrator. It is likely that the number of Web Intelligence Services will need to be increased in order to accommodate the increased number of Web Intelligence reports after conversion.

A.1.2 Identify Users with Desktop Intelligence Installed

Over the course of the last several years, Desktop Intelligence may have been installed on several hundred or even several thousand PCs, depending on the size of the organization. Inevitably, each user will have a number of Deski reports saved locally.

Even though all important reports should exist on the server, to comply with most corporate policies, some reports will exist locally. This is often the case simply because the tool lends itself to working offline and provides the capability of storing .REP files locally.

A.1.3 Publish Locally Saved Desktop Intelligence Reports to the Repository

After you've identified the users and report developers who are still using Desktop Intelligence, ask them to publish all important personal Deski files and locally saved reports to the repository. This step puts potentially valuable reports onto the repository so that the migration team can review, analyze, and then convert them to Web Intelligence.

It's important to get every useful Deski report published to the repository so they can be converted to Web Intelligence and used in the BI 4.0 system after migration.

A.1.4 Prioritize, Consolidate, and Eliminate

Before converting every single Desktop Intelligence document ever created at your organization, take this opportunity to archive or completely eliminate documents that are no longer being used. As companies evolve and data sources change, it's likely that a large number of locally saved Desktop Intelligence reports are no longer needed. You'll recognize the distinction between ad hoc reports and valuable reports that are used by business users.

When you are prioritizing reports, create categories or buckets to differentiate reports based on the frequency of use and the visibility of the data presented in the reports.

A.1.5 Customize Conversion Plan and Roadmap

After completing the first four steps, you'll understand the scope of the project and conversion effort. The volume of reports to be migrated plays a major role in the developing the roadmap and conversion plan. There are two common approaches to conversion:

- Single-pass conversion: The entire repository is converted in one pass.
- Staged conversion: Conversion is segmented by business area or departmental group.

The decision regarding which approach to select depends on the following factors:

- Number of Deski reports to convert
- Complexity of Deski reports
- Amount of rework required to fully convert to Web Intelligence
- Server architecture of the BI 4.0 system
- Combination of any of the first four potential scenarios

When you're preparing the conversion plan, you should also determine report complexity. The difficulty level of conversion can be anticipated after evaluating the Deski reports in the source environment. Any Deski report containing Freehand SQL should be placed into a category of its own.

Detailed analysis of reports containing Freehand SQL can lead to best practices for discontinuing the use of Freehand SQL. The goal is to find patterns in the SQL and common fact tables from the same databases and schemas. These scenarios provide the greatest opportunity to create a small number of new universes that can be used by a much larger number of Deski reports; therefore, these universes should include several objects and predefined filters to increase their usefulness. Changing the data source of Deski reports from Freehand SQL to a universe will simplify the conversion process and increase the likelihood of converting to Web Intelligence.

Depending on the practices of Deski report designers, it's possible that you'll need to manually create some reports in Web Intelligence. These reports should be identified and placed into their own groups. These are the three most common reasons for known conversion problems:

▶ Reports with Freehand SQL
▶ Reports containing VBA
▶ Reports with personal data providers

Reports with any of these three features should be manually revised before converting.

> **Note**
>
> It is possible to convert reports containing Freehand SQL to Web Intelligence but the conversion will generate a new universe containing a derived table for each report. This scenario could produce hundreds or potentially thousands of single-use universes.
>
> Every effort should be made to consolidate the source SQL into a much smaller number of universes that can be used by multiple reports.

After you complete a thorough analysis on the source system and group reports by business area, the likelihood of conversion success, and the need for manual rework, it's time to proceed to conversion.

You can helps stay on track by setting milestones and timelines. Customizing a project timeline will help guide you through the conversion process and ensure that every aspect of the conversion is completed and in the correct order.

Other critical decisions must be made and conveyed to users, such as the following:

▶ Well communicated end date for development of Deski reports in the source system

▶ Documented deadline for refreshing existing Deski reports

▶ Go-live date to begin using reports converted to Web Intelligence in the new system

A.1.6   Perform Report Conversion

Launch the Report Conversion Tool as an administrator and perform the type of conversion described in Section A.1.5:

▶ Single-pass conversion: Convert all reports

▶ Staged conversion: Convert only a portion of reports

As a result, there are two possible conversion paths:

▶ Convert Desktop Intelligence documents to Web Intelligence with the SAP BusinessObjects XI 3.1 Report Conversion Tool

▶ Convert Desktop Intelligence documents to Web Intelligence with the BI 4.0 Report Conversion Tool

Select the appropriate conversion path based on your organization's hardware capabilities in a test environment. Converting Deski documents using the Web Intelligence 4.0 Report Conversion Tool will fully convert a greater number of documents.

After completing a conversion, reports are grouped into three categories:

▶ Fully converted

▶ Partially converted

▶ Not converted

The seventh conversion step leads you to performing a post-conversion analysis. Partially converted reports can be evaluated to determine the reason that it was not fully converted. In many cases, minor manual modifications can be made to fully convert reports. This can be a labor-intensive exercise depending on the volume of partially converted reports.

Reports that are not converted will often need even more manual corrections or will need to be recreated in Web Intelligence rather than converted with the Report Conversion Tool.

A.1.7 Execute Post-Conversion Analysis and Validation

Perform validation on reports that were fully converted. Verify that all data sources, formulas, and report functions continue to work properly in Web Intelligence as they did in Desktop Intelligence.

You need to identify the reason that partially converted documents were not fully completed by reviewing log files. In many cases, these reports can be quickly edited. In other cases, it can be easier to recreate partially converted documents in Web Intelligence rather than making the necessary corrections.

A.1.8 Manually Create Unconverted Reports

As mentioned in the seventh step, it's common that unconverted reports will need to be manually recreated in Web Intelligence if resources permit. Even though Web Intelligence now contains almost all of the function capabilities of Desktop Intelligence, there are still a number of features that will cause Deski reports to not be converted.

You should create a focused strategy for handling reports that remain unconverted even after running them through the Report Conversion Tool. It's possible that the reason reports are not converted can be removed or modified. After making changes, run the Report Conversion Tool again for a second attempt at converting the Deski reports to Web Intelligence.

A.1.9 Educate Users on Web Intelligence 4.0

Invest in user training for all users and report designers who will be using Web Intelligence in a BI 4.0 environment. Training comes in many different forms, including text books, blogs, webinars, e-learning sessions, and official training from SAP and from vendors specializing in providing SAP BusinessObjects training.

We recommend the following resources for learning Web Intelligence 4.0:

- Join ASUG and attend webinars, conferences, and explore online content at *www.ASUG.com*
- Explore content at the SAP Community Network (SCN) at *http://scn.sap.com/ community/businessobjects-web-intelligence*
- Attend official SAP training courses at *www.sap.com/training-and-education/ index.epx*
- Obtain training from private vendors specialized in providing SAP Business-Objects and Web Intelligence training courses.

A.2   Summary

A step-by-step methodical approach to report conversion produces the safest and most effective way to move away from Desktop Intelligence reports in SAP BusinessObjects XI R2 and XI 3.1 and begin using Web Intelligence 4.0 for reporting.

Collaboration between users, designers, and the conversion/migration team is essential to success; in addition, clearly communicating deadlines and the importance of publishing locally saved Deski reports to the repository is an important part in the conversion process. After you analyze all the existing Deski reports in an environment, you need to determine which reports continue to deliver relevant and valuable information to users while also identifying reports that can be retired. Review the last save date and last refresh date of reports to help identify obsolete content rather than converting unneeded reports. You should also look for ways to consolidate redundant reports that may have been repeated many times over.

After a complete analysis, prepare a customized roadmap for converting existing Deski reports. You can perform the conversion in a staged multi-pass approach or single-pass approach depending on the number of documents to convert and level of complexity. Group all reports containing Freehand SQL and evaluate the syntax of the SQL statements in use. Create new robust universes to replace Freehand SQL data sources and produce a semantic layer that can be used by many reports rather than generating a new derived universe for every report containing Freehand SQL.

Third-party tools fill a valuable niche by extending SAP BusinessObjects Business Intelligence 4.0 with very powerful and exciting functionality. With them, you can maximize your return on investment with SAP BusinessObjects 4.0 with very innovative products that offer different functional capabilities.

B Third-Party Vendors

Several third-party vendors on the market offer software products and tools to integrate with Web Intelligence and SAP BusinessObjects Business Intelligence 4.0. These products present many exciting capabilities that extend and complement BI 4.0.

This appendix will alphabetically introduce eight third-party vendors and provide a brief description of their product offerings and key features.

> **Note**
>
> This appendix includes third-party vendors that integrate with the BI 4.0 version of Web Intelligence the authors were aware of at the time of publication. There may be others that were not included. The inclusion or omission of a vendor from this appendix should not be seen as an endorsement or critique of their products and services.

We'll discuss the following third-party vendors:

▶ Antivia—*www.antivia.com*

▶ APOS Systems—*www.apos.com*

▶ Centigon Solutions—*www.centigonsolutions.com*

▶ EBI Experts—*www.ebiexperts.com*

▶ EV Technologies—*www.evtechnologies.com*

▶ GB & Smith—*www.gbandsmith.com*

▶ InfoSol—*www.infosol.com*

▶ LaunchWorks—*www.launchworks.com*

B.1   Antivia

Antivia is an SAP Partner and currently offers three products that seamlessly integrate with SAP BusinessObjects BI 4.0. Their two most notable offerings are the XWIS Enterprise and XWIS Anywhere products.

XWIS is a product that allows you to integrate data from Web Intelligence reports into SAP BusinessObjects Dashboards. It also provides the capability to deliver drillable data grids from universe drill paths. In addition, XWIS provides a fully interactive slice-and-dice panel for selecting dimensions and drilling into detail data.

With BI 4.0, XWIS continues to add value to SAP BusinessObjects Dashboards, slash dashboard development time and total cost of ownership, accelerate adoption and deployment of actionable dashboards, and promote effective decision-making through increased interactivity and greater accessibility. For SAP customers who need to create, maintain, and distribute actionable dashboards, XWIS is the perfect companion to SAP BusinessObjects Dashboards and BI 4.0.

Certified by SAP for its integration with SAP BusinessObjects, the products by Antivia are built to adhere to three fundamental concepts: usability, collaboration, and realization. Let's further explore the Antivia offerings and the advantages they can lend you:

- XWIS Enterprise Platform (comprises XWIS Advantage, XWIS Publish, and XWIS Anywhere)
    - Integrate data from Web Intelligence (including version 4.0) directly into SAP BusinessObjects Dashboards
- XWIS Advantage
    - Connect rapidly and intuitively to corporate data including Web Intelligence, Crystal Reports, SQL databases, and OLAP cubes
    - Merge data from multiple sources to reveal the big picture
    - Create rich, interactive dashboards out-of-the-box, with drilldown, dynamic sorts and filters, synchronized components, and "slice-and-dice"—all built by "point and click"
    - Spend less time and exert less effort maintaining dashboards because dashboards are simplified with fewer queries, and fewer Microsoft Excel formulas optimize performance

▶ XWIS Publish

  ▶ Maximize adoption by pushing fully interactive dashboards to a user's email inbox (or XWIS Anywhere portal), for ease of access

  ▶ Publish personalized dashboards to thousands of users based on profile, so each user sees the right information to help him do his job better

  ▶ Reduce cost of ownership by integrating with SAP BusinessObjects publishing

▶ XWIS Anywhere

  ▶ Organize dashboards for fast and easy access on mobile and tablet devices

  ▶ View and interact with any Xcelsius dashboard, Web Intelligence document, or Crystal Report

  ▶ Enable on-the-go decision-making by creating mobile-friendly versions of dashboards, simply by adding the XWIS MobileView dashboard component

  ▶ View fully interactive dashboards, even when you are offline

B.2 APOS Systems

APOS Systems is an SAP Partner and provides several tools that extend the functionality of existing SAP BusinessObjects Enterprise installations. SAP-certified for integration with SAP BusinessObjects, APOS offers six products that integrate with SAP BusinessObjects.

These tools provide a wide variety of increased functionality and include products for administration, system monitoring, instance management, report bursting, and mapping with location intelligence.

APOS Systems offers the following product offerings:

▶ APOS Administrator: Agile BI Platform Management for SAP BusinessObjects

  ▶ Bulk Report Scheduling

  ▶ Instance Management

  ▶ Object Management

  ▶ Beyond Curative BI

- APOS Insight: SAP BusinessObjects System Introspection
  - Enhanced Audit & Metadata Management
  - Proactive System Monitoring & Alerts
  - Blanket Instance Monitoring
  - Achieving Preventive BI with APOS Insight
- APOS IDAC: Monitor, Manage, and Audit BI Data Connectivity
  - Track queries in real time
  - Receive automatic alerts when established thresholds are exceeded
  - Automatically cancel runaway queries
  - Perform highly detailed audits of BI queries
  - Intervene manually in queries
  - Control access to data for more robust security, compliance, content promotion
- APOS Storage Center: Backup, Archive, Selective Restore
  - Rules-based backup, archive, versioning, selective restore
  - Offline and online archiving
  - Extract and export
  - Intelligent report purging
- APOS Publisher: Complete SAP BusinessObjects Publishing Solution
  - High-volume scheduling interface
  - Robust bursting and document/statement bursting
  - Document consolidation
  - Enhanced distribution using document metadata
  - CMS integration with content management workflows
  - Output/Process Management and assured delivery to printers and email servers
- APOS Enterprise Location Intelligence
  - Location intelligence for telecommunications
  - Location intelligence for insurance
  - Location intelligence for retail

B.3   Centigon Solutions

GMaps Mobile is a mobile app that includes an on-premise connector designed to stream data from Web Intelligence among other on-premise and cloud data sources.

The benefit of using Web Intelligence report parts as a data source is piggybacking on row-level security, report formulas, and formatting. The Web Intelligence design environment becomes a data-staging platform for GMaps Mobile and shields report consumers from data source requirements.

Report designers can utilize skills they already have to merge, calculate, and concatenate objects into a tabular data structure that can be easily consumed with GMaps Mobile. GMaps Mobile uses a single vertical table report part to render geographic data within a map layer. These layers become reusable assets that can be viewed and shared with other GMaps Mobile users. A resulting map view can utilize multiple reports, from multiple data sources, and even multiple repositories to "mash up" geo-spatial data.

GMaps Mobile provides specific requirements for formatting data that can be easily achieved by Web Intelligence report developers of any skill level.

GMaps Mobile views containing Web Intelligence data will render as points within a Google map that can be analyzed not only using measures, but also using an end user's proximity to the locations. For example, if a Web Intelligence report contains a list of hospitals with sales figures, a business person can view those hospitals and sort by sales data or based on the distance from the user's current location. This is a powerful proposition for mobile workers who are in the field selling, repairing, installing, or delivering products to clients.

B.4   EBI Experts

EBI Experts is a software solution provider that strives to help organizations gain better insight into their business intelligence applications by improving agility, productivity, and return on investments.

Two products are currently offered by EBI Experts that are intended to increase user satisfaction and help manage and measure SAP BusinessObjects deployments:

- Enterprise Manager: Advanced SAP BusinessObjects Report Audit Solution
  - Manage and measure the metrics of your SAP BusinessObjects deployment
  - Combine with the auditing features in Web Intelligence to trace activity
  - Use to deliver detailed graphic performance analysis
  - Monitor user activity
- Version Manager: Smart Version Control Software Solution
  - Comprehensive version control tool
  - Manage, compare, and control multiple versions of universes and reports
  - Designed for Web Intelligence and Crystal Reports
  - Simple check-in/check-out features
  - Compare content and structure of versions
  - Web services-based architecture
  - Low entry cost
  - View extended details of universes and reports

B.5 EV Technologies

Since 2008, EV Technologies has become a high-value SAP Software Solutions Partner for SAP BusinessObjects customers by providing support with small to very complex SAP BusinessObjects deployments. Its Sherlock 2.0 product line has received the SAP Certified Integration with SAP BusinessObjects by the SAP Integration and Certification Center (SAP ICC).

Leveraging the strengths of the available SDKs, Sherlock 2.0 is a comprehensive metadata management tool drawing detailed system usage facts and user information from the major components of the SAP BusinessObjects architecture. The Sherlock 2.0 product line is a robust enterprise-level application designed to facilitate ROI tracking, report cost management, and ongoing system growth and stability monitoring for SAP BusinessObjects environments. It allows administrators and developers to improve operational efficiencies and enables business intelligence leaders to make the most effective use of their SAP BusinessObjects investments.

Sherlock 2.0 is made up of the following products that come together to provide a complete view of all areas of SAP BusinessObjects Enterprise usage:

▶ Sherlock CMS Inspector: Provides deep insights and complete system make up by reports type and size, users, groups and security

▶ Sherlock Universe Inspector: Provides detailed universe structure information as well as metadata mapping for data lineage and impact analysis

▶ Sherlock Report Inspector: Provides a complete breakdown of the structure of every report and creates the bridge between the Sherlock CMS Inspector and Sherlock Universe Inspector

Sherlock 2.0 also includes two additional tools for inspecting SAP Crystal Reports and SAP Crystal Reports Server environments:

▶ Sherlock CR Inspector: Provides metadata for detailed analysis of the Crystal Reports content within the platform

▶ Sherlock CS Edition: Based on the proven capabilities of the Sherlock Inspector Suite and adapted specifically for SAP Crystal Server environments, Sherlock CS Edition provides Crystal Server customers the same deep, actionable information.

Sherlock 2.0 includes an optimized universe that allows you to leverage the report and dashboard capabilities of the SAP BusinessObjects tools you already own.

B.6   GB & Smith

GB & Smith currently offers five tools to implement, manage, and document the security rights in your SAP BusinessObjects Enterprise BI 4.0 deployments. These tools provide easy-to-use interfaces for managing complex SAP BusinessObjects deployments and enable you to see the entire 360-degree view of the security configuration.

GB & Smith has the following product offerings:

▶ 360View: BOE Security Solution
  ▶ Implement and manage your groups, users, folders, objects, universes, categories, and servers within a hierarchical perspective

▸ Audit and document your deployed security by exporting to Excel

▸ Add additional custom fields to users and objects

▸ Obtain complete visualization of the security applied on sensitive data or within SOX or BASEL environments for administrators and key users

▸ Track how much space users consume within SAP BusinessObjects

▸ Count your deployed licenses in a click to stay in license compliance

▸ 360Cast: Report Bursting Solution

▸ Visualize your tasks and all generated SAP BusinessObjects instances displayed according to their scheduling status

▸ Check your last scheduling actions on the ergonomic 360Cast Tasks Viewer main page

▸ Display all tasks properties and linked BusinessObjects instances or export them to Excel

▸ 360Plus: SAP BusinessObjects Backup Solution

▸ Connect to several environments with the simple home page connection form

▸ Compare CMS: compare security and actors and every type of content (folders, reports, categories, etc.) by ID, name, and date of last modification

▸ Integrity: License Compliance Solution

▸ Works on any SAP BusinessObjects deployment

▸ Makes you a mouse click away from compliance

▸ Lets you aggregate all your SAP BusinessObjects deployed licenses

▸ 360Eyes: Impact Analysis Solution

▸ Export your entire BOE metadata to an RDBMS

▸ Perform querying, reporting, and analysis of your SAP BOE metadata

▸ Run impact analysis

▸ Follow the evolution of your metadata

B.7   InfoSol

InfoSol has been a SAP BusinessObjects partner for over twelve years and provides a comprehensive range of information systems solutions, including consulting, education, and technical support.

InfoSol is a visionary provider of information systems solutions delivering quality, compelling, and effective business intelligence and custom applications.

InfoSol has the following product offerings:

▶ InfoBurst Enterprise: A state-of-the-art Business Intelligence publishing system that can refresh, burst, and deliver reports and dashboards to your users, customers, and partners

  ▶ InfoBurst Report Bursting: Offers a variety of options for conducting and controlling business intelligence report bursting with a unique drag-and-drop workflow that makes building and managing bursts easy

  ▶ InfoBurst Publishing: Publishes business intelligence reports in a variety of formats for delivery

  ▶ InfoBurst Delivery: Delivers report content and dashboards to a variety of destinations

  ▶ InfoBurst Dashboard Delivery: Delivers an SWF file published from Xcelsius to a variety of destinations in both connected and disconnected modes

  ▶ InfoBurst Actions & Alerts: Offers a variety of actions and alerts that can be executed based on the status of a job (start, completion, or failure), including report bursting/delivery, XDC refresh, and dashboard delivery

  ▶ InfoBurst Scheduling: Includes a robust scheduler for scheduling reporting bursting/delivery, cache refreshes, and dashboard deliveries

▶ 360Suite:

  ▶ 360View: Offers simplified and flexible management, implementation, and documentation of SAP BusinessObjects XI Security

  ▶ 360Plus: Provides simple and logical backup and recovery of your SAP BusinessObjects content

  ▶ 360Eyes: Facilitates auditing and impact analysis of your SAP BusinessObjects environment

▶ MyBI Mobile: A mobile virtualization solution to view and interact with your SAP BusinessObjects content on the iPad, iPhone, and Android without any changes to existing content

▶ Supports Dashboards (Xcelsius), Web Intelligence, Crystal Reports, and Desktop Intelligence

▶ Allows leveraging of existing BI report and dashboard investments on mobile devices immediately and seamlessly

▶ Version Manager: A version control solution specifically designed for SAP BusinessObjects that provides version management, lineage, and data comparison for universes, Web Intelligence, Crystal Reports, Desktop Intelligence, and Word documents

▶ Offers easy viewing of all versions of documents and universes and the environments where published

▶ Offers easy rollback by publishing previous version from Version Manager to BusinessObjects

▶ Provides a history of all publications

▶ Provides an audit trail of all actions performed

▶ Uses color coding to highlight differences when comparing versions of a universe or document (print or export results to XML or CSV)

▶ Features built-in metadata reporting for quick impact analysis

B.8 LaunchWorks

LaunchWorks provides enterprises with commercial-grade on-premise and hosted solutions for sharing business intelligence. LaunchWorks integrates its proven report bursting, exporting, sharing, tracking, and auditing software on high-performance servers that are optimized for minimum response times. Its products have received the distinction of SAP Certified Integration with Business-Objects.

LaunchWorks has the following product offerings:

▶ LaunchWorks LaunchPortal for SAP BusinessObjects: A turnkey secure external reporting portal

▶ Leverages existing SAP BusinessObjects authentication so there is no need for separate security

- ▶ Provides stock and customizable screens for report presentation so you don't have to do develop

- ▶ Provides a highly optimized report processor so you can offload the workload from your systems

- ▶ Contains both a web portal and an API so you can choose how you want to serve your reports

- ▶ Integrates with Crystal Reports, Web Intelligence, Microsoft SharePoint, and Salesforce

- ▶ Enables access controls on user, group, or global level

- ▶ Enables automated scheduling and delivery of reports to your applications

▶ Mobile Launch: Access all of your desktop reports from any Apple IOS or Android device

- ▶ Provides complete drill-down capabilities on all of your graphs and charts, providing further analysis of your data

- ▶ Integrates natively with LaunchWorks LaunchPortal (requires no additional configuration)

- ▶ Offers industry-leading multi-tenancy, bursting, access, and authorization controls

▶ Report Launch: The core of the LaunchPortal software platform

- ▶ Integrate reports: Integrate reports from your SAP BusinessObjects system straight into applications like SalesForce, Microsoft SharePoint, or any SaaS application within days

- ▶ Embed reports: Use Report Launch to proxy reports between SAP BusinessObjects and your web portals, CRM/ERP systems, touchscreen kiosks, and mobile apps

- ▶ Refresh reports: Make both report format and parameter changes on your BusinessObjects backend

- ▶ Simply reports: Get direct access to your SQL database using enhanced dynamic and cascading parameters

- ▶ Integrate reports: Integrate with SAP BusinessObjects, Microsoft SharePoint, SalesForce, InfoView, Web Intelligence, Crystal Reports, and Dashboards

▸ Dashboard Launch: Export Dashboard Intelligence

  ▸ Share Dashboards: Display SAP Dashboards and Web Intelligence Reports via the LaunchPortal framework

  ▸ Embed Dashboards: Embed your dashboards in any of your own portals, SaaS applications, CRM/ERP systems, touchscreen kiosks, and mobile apps

  ▸ Transpose Web Intelligence Dashboards: Translate SAP BusinessObjects Web Intelligence dashboards to Xcelsius dashboards

B.9   Summary

Many third-party vendors such as those listed in this appendix exist in the market today to help users extend the functionality of their SAP BusinessObjects BI 4.0 deployments. The purpose of this appendix was to introduce and briefly describe the product offerings of the known third-party vendors that integrate with SAP BusinessObjects. Using these third-party vendors, you can increase your return on investment with SAP BusinessObjects and provide new functionality that extends a standard deployment.

C   The Authors

Jim Brogden is an award-winning technical author and dashboard designer working as a senior consultant for Daugherty Business Solutions in Atlanta, Georgia. He combines a master's degree in information technology with over a decade of experience delivering world-class business intelligence solutions to a number of Fortune 200 clients. He's the lead author of the first official textbook dedicated to Web Intelligence, a blogger at *http://myXcelsius.com*, an ASUG volunteer, and a contributing author at *http://BusinessObjectsExpert.wispubs.com*. Jim is a graduate of the University of South Alabama.

Heather Callebaut Sinkwitz gained her expertise while working as a Business Intelligence consultant specializing in SAP BusinessObjects training and reporting solutions. She is actively involved in the BI community, serves on the board of the local Arizona BusinessObjects Crystal User Group, contributes to the ASUG Education Influence Special Interest Group and Web Intelligence Influence Council, and speaks at local and national events. She brings her passion for business intelligence and analytics to her current role as the manager of enterprise reporting for Rural/Metro Corporation, where she leads the development of innovative end-to-end reporting and dashboarding solutions. Heather enjoys presenting data in new and unique ways to help businesses make informed decisions at a fast pace to remain competitive in today's market and to clearly differentiate the company for the future. Photo by Lindsay Hallam Photography.

Mac Holden currently works for Inovista Components, a software house specializing in the conversion of dashboards built using SAP's Xcelsius product into apps that function natively on devices like the iPad. Mac has over 15 years of software development and design experience, working primarily with web-based technologies. He has 10 years of experience using various SDKs to create Web Intelligence applications for customers in many different locations and industries. He has also co-authored a number of books on Java Enterprise Development in addition to supplying articles for publications such as *Java Pro*. Mac is currently based in southern Spain and can be contacted at *cmholden@inovista.com*.

Dallas Marks is a principal technical architect for EV Technologies and an SAP Certified Application Associate and authorized trainer for SAP BusinessObjects Web Intelligence and the Business Intelligence platform. Dallas has worked with SAP BusinessObjects business intelligence tools since 2003 and has implemented solutions for a number of industries, including retail, energy, health care, and manufacturing. He is a frequent speaker at local ASUG chapters, national ASUG and SAPinsider conferences, and independent SAP BusinessObjects user groups. Dallas holds a master's degree in computer engineering from the University of Cincinnati. Dallas blogs about various business intelligence topics at *http://www.dallasmarks.org/*. You can follow him on Twitter at *@dallasmarks*. Photo by Morgan Noble.

Gabriel Orthous is a senior development manager for the Business Intelligence group at McKesson Revenue Management Solutions. With more than 14 years in IT managerial and architectural roles, he has experience in object-oriented systems design, development, implementation, post-implementation support, and production procedures. In addition, thanks to a number of large and complex consulting engagements with major companies in the United States and abroad, he has specific expertise in BI, financial reporting, and decision analytics. He is well versed in all phases of the system development lifecycle and agile development methodologies for SAP BusinessObjects, and holds the position of Chair for the Dashboarding and Visualization Special Interest Group for the Americas' SAP User Group. Gabriel has been a global speaker at conferences in Australia, South Africa, and the United States. Most recently he was a speaker at SAPinsider's BI 2012 conference in Milan. Gabriel is an avid cigar aficionado and roller and currently lives in Atlanta, Georgia.

Index

Interested in reading more?

Please visit our website for all new
book and e-book releases from SAP PRESS.

www.sap-press.com